Teaching Thinking Skills

SOURCE BOOKS ON EDUCATION
(VOL. 28)

GARLAND REFERENCE LIBRARY
OF SOCIAL SCIENCE
(VOL. 511)

Source Books on Education

Teaching Thinking Skills
Theory and Practice

Joyce N. French
Carol Rhoder

GARLAND PUBLISHING, INC. • NEW YORK & LONDON
1992

Library of Congress Cataloging-in-Publication Data

French, Joyce N., 1929–
　　Teaching thinking skills : theory and practice / Joyce N. French,
Carol Rhoder.
　　　　p. cm. — (Garland reference library of social science ; vol.
511. Source books on education ; vol. 28)
　　Includes bibliographical references (p.) and index.
　　ISBN 0-8240-4843-1 (alk. paper)
　　1. Thought and thinking—Study and teaching. 2. Thought and
thinking—Study and teaching—Bibliography. I. Rhoder, Carol,
1943– . II. Title. III. Series: Garland reference library of
social science. Source books on education ; vol. 28.
LB1590.3.F74 1992
370.15′2—dc20　　　　　　　　　　　　　　　　91-17257
　　　　　　　　　　　　　　　　　　　　　　　　　CIP

Printed on acid-free, 250-year-life paper
Manufactured in the United States of America

With love to three men who
inspired and encouraged us to be independent
thinkers

In memory:
Donald F. French
and
Thomas L. Norton

To:
John F. Rhoder

Contents

Assessment
Thoughts on Creative Thinking

Preface

The fascination with thinking, how and why people think, how we can teach thinking, has been evident for centuries. This focus is not a fad, but is one which has surfaced again with a current renewed interest in and research on thinking. The proliferation of programs designed to teach thinking and the professional concerns expressed in journals and books highlight the issues in the application of theory. Unfortunately, as we point out in this book, there is evidence that the issues are still unresolved, that teachers are still not focusing effectively on developing thinking skills and strategies, and that students are not acquiring, developing, and using a full range of thinking abilities. We, in the process of clarifying our own thinking on this topic, began to look at it from a number of different perspectives, identifying issues, problems, and possible solutions. It is from this focus that this book has been written.

We have divided the book into three major sections, sections which work separately or together. Part A deals with the theory and research supporting educational programs in teaching thinking. Part B focuses on the educational aspects of teaching thinking. Finally, Part C is an annotated bibliography. Each section stands on its own and can be used alone. However, because of the nature of the content, the sections work best if they are used together. We feel strongly that the best practice is informed by theory and research. The bibliography will provide an overview of important relevant sources and, we hope, will inspire the reader to go to the original source for essential and interesting details and explanations.

First we examine the theoretical foundations of thinking: the skills, strategies, content and products which constitute the components of thinking. A definition of thinking emerges as we explore the definitions of others and examine each of these components. The definition is not complete, however, until we complete our examination of thinking in the context of schools.

Next we examine current practice. We provide guidance in planning for thinking instruction by presenting and exploring a variety of questions. We discuss options for teachers in planning programs. There are many different approaches available to teachers who want to develop their own program. We cite many examples of these kinds of approaches, techniques, and programs. In addition, we use the commercial programs available as examples of different approaches to instruction and relate them to the theories presented. Ultimately, it is up to the reader to determine what is the best approach to use in a particular setting with a particular group of students and teachers. These decisions, however, must be made within the context of theory and research. Finally, after examining instruction we rethink our definition as it relates theory to practice and propose a final definition.

The third section is an annotated bibliography, a compilation of all of our sources. It is presented in alphabetical order, because of the difficulty encountered in categorizing entries into narrow specific categories. To identify relevant articles, chapters, books and monographs we did a computer search of all publications in the field from 1975 to the present date. We did a manual search of leading scientific journals in the areas of cognitive development and educational psychology related to theory, research and applications to instruction. Most of the works cited were published in or after 1985; however, we also included several earlier landmark articles in educational psychology that established direction in the field.

The audience for this book is first, teachers, teachers of children of all ages, classroom teachers as well as specialists, teachers who are interested in promoting thinking through more effective classroom instruction and teachers who are interested in developing programs. We hope this book is useful not only to practicing teachers but also to adults and young adults preparing to be teachers who are in teacher education programs and are concerned with child development and cognitive psychology.

The front line in any process of change must be made up of teachers. However, teachers are not effective without the support of knowledgeable administrators including but certainly not limited to building principals and curriculum coordinators. Thus, an equally important audience is the administration in school districts from the superintendent on down.

There is an additional layer here of those professionals concerned with the role of thinking in schools but who are not directly involved in instruction. This third group includes, but is not limited to, a range of people from test developers to local, state, and national policy makers. All in this group guide instruction and curriculum, test developers by determining what will be evaluated and policy makers by issuing policy statements and funding programs. This third group, while not as immediately obvious, is just as important. We hope that they too will consider the evidence and issues examined in this book.

Joyce N. French
Carol Rhoder

PART A
Theories of Thinking

I

Thinking: An Overview

Introduction

Thinking is something we do every day, often without being consciously aware of what we're doing. Yet something will happen to make us stop and become alert to the fact that we are thinking or that we need to think. We are faced with a problem and we need to make a decision; we read an editorial and wonder if the writer is giving us all the facts; we decide to write a paper (or a book!) and realize that we must organize and evaluate a body of information and concepts and must reach some conclusions. Glatthorn and Baron identify this as "conscious" (152, p. 49) thinking and assert that, "only conscious thinking can be influenced directly by pedagogical interventions" (p. 49). Conscious thinking is our concern.

What is conscious thinking? It is a term that is difficult to define and one that is, as we will see, defined differently by various people. We will explore these definitions and come up with our own definition which will evolve as we examine the issues. To begin, by conscious thinking we mean that thinking which is self-directed, in which the learner plays an active role. Conscious thought enables the comprehension of others' ideas and the generation of new ideas. Let us keep this definition in mind while we examine the current status of thinking in schools, current definitions of thinking, and the components that should be considered in developing our own definition.

Teachers have generally assumed that students would think if they could and, therefore, concentrated instruction on developing skills and strategies in the basic skill areas of reading, writing and arithmetic as well as on disseminating knowledge in the content areas. In fact, this back to basics movement may have been a direct cause, according to Benderson (27), of the plunge in critical thinking ability of the past decade. While there has certainly been some interest on the part of some teachers and school systems on incorporating thinking into school curriculum, this has usually not been an overall focus and the emphasis has been limited in scope (183). Beyer asserts that "the primary explanation for poor achievement [in thinking skills] is that most teachers do not teach these skills" (30, p. 485).

The situation is beginning to change, however. There is now a growing recognition that education consists of much more than teaching basic facts and skills. There is a concern that we need to teach thinking skills and strategies and we are doing very little in that area (78, 263, 398). There is also a concern that much of what we are doing may be counterproductive. Staab, for example, suggests that "perhaps the very process of schooling is inhibiting students' need to think creatively and to reason, and as students progress through the system this condition becomes more pronounced" (363, p. 293). Even though curriculum guides and manuals include the teaching of thinking, it is not being done "consistently in classrooms" (363, p. 293). Cuban suggests that secondary school structures are to blame; they are "anchored in earlier demands for efficiency rather than as responses to theories of learning to reason" (104, p. 672). These structures "bridle reasoning powers by chopping up content into courses, assigning equal chunks of time to each subject, expecting teachers to cover certain topics for final tests" (104, p. 672).

There are a number of reasons for this. Teachers perceive other priorities, such as preparing for tests, establishing routines, finishing the book and the curriculum as being more important (363). The need for order and control and the focus on grades do not foster thoughtfulness (346). Instruction in classrooms may be dominated by the teacher and teacher talk, instruction and practice may consist of worksheets (377). Even more distressing is a finding by Benderson (27) of a widespread view among educators that students are, in fact, unable to think abstractly, unable to make sound judgments, unable to reason and unwilling to challenge authority. Unfortunately, this distressing view of schooling is widespread (186, 249).

Current Status of Thinking Instruction

Over the past few years there has been an increasing interest in incorporating thinking instruction into elementary and secondary curriculum, largely for three reasons. There is a growing awareness, first, that we have many students who are not thinking effectively; second, there is a widespread conviction that effective thinking is a non-negotiable item in today's world; and, third, we are accumulating a growing body of knowledge and research in this area which can be put to use in our schools.

First, and of primary significance, is the concern that a substantial number of students are not effective thinkers. Declining test scores (183, 221, 353), particularly the results of the National Assessment of Educational Progress (NAEP) (27, 159, 183, 234, 253) have been cited as evidence that students can perform well in dealing with rote tasks but not with those demanding thinking.

For example, Chipman and Segal (78) suggest that the NAEP results demonstrate that the problems in student writing lie in the thinking areas not the mechanics, the problems in reading in comprehension not decoding, and the problems in mathematics in solving problems not computing. According to Benderson (27), NAEP results report that students function cognitively at the lowest, most concrete levels, i.e. general knowledge and understanding, and that they have failed to master higher, more abstract levels such as analysis, synthesis and evaluation. The study indicates that while basic skills in reading, writing, math and science have improved, students' ability to interpret, evaluate, make judgments and form supportive arguments has declined. "Students can memorize and recall, but they can't interpret, infer, judge or persuade" (27, p. 6). Nickerson (263) concludes that it is, in fact, possible for a student to finish 12 or 13 years of education without becoming a competent thinker.

The disappointing national test scores have given rise to a cry for reform and rigor in education. Jones suggests that "the demand for rigor has been extended to include an emphasis on higher-order thinking" (183, p. 6). The impact of this trend in declining test scores has been heightened by a "shift from social concerns (How good do our students feel?) to a cognitive perspective (How well do our students think?)" (353, p. 18).

This concern for intellectual rigor has led to the observation that "most teachers do not regularly employ methods that encourage and develop thinking in their students" (234, p. 5). As Nickerson, Perkins and Smith point out, "relatively little attention has been given to the teaching of thinking skills—or at least to the teaching of the skills involved in . . . higher-order activities" (264, p. 48). This lack of emphasis provides us with a unique opportunity. According to Chipman and Segal, "because explicit instruction in thinking and learning skills has received little attention in the schools, it is likely that large improvements are possible" (78, p. 3).

Second, there is a growing awareness of the need for citizens who are clear, effective thinkers. There is a consensus among educators that American education has been successful at teaching factual knowledge but is not providing students with the thinking skills essential to becoming autonomous self-reliant citizens. According to Kinney "it does not require much documentation to establish that critical thinking is an important commodity in a highly sophisticated technical society" (193, p. 1–2). We are not providing instruction and experience in thinking abstractly, in using reason and judgment. He cites the "distressing results" (p. 2) of studies such as the NAEP at a variety of ages and particularly in college-age students. He refers to the need for college students and supervisors, managers, scientists and other professionals to be able to think critically.

This concern is echoed repeatedly in the literature. McTighe and Schollenberger (234) identify the increasingly complex demands of the information age we live in and the need for future generations to organize information and benefit from it. Halpern (159) cites the significant decisions that students will need to make for themselves, their local, state and national governments, and the world. It is this world perspective, particularly the "rapidly changing world economy" (263, p. 8) which Nickerson believes makes the current situation "urgent."

Third, there is a growing body of research in the field which is building on prior research (314) but is also taking new directions and using new methodology. New concepts of intelligence are being developed which have direct implications for both instruction and curriculum in the teaching of thinking. For example, Sternberg (368) states that traditional IQ scores do not necessarily reflect a person's ability to cope with the real world; measures of intelligence should consider a person's awareness of the external world and his ability to adapt to it. Lipman (212) believes language is the basis for developing thinking. Perkins (297) looks at creativity and original thinking as a reflection of intelligence. Thinking processes are being examined with precision and detail. At the same time, ways of teaching the novice how to improve existing skills and strategies, acquire new ones, and transfer them to new situations (78) are being explored. In fact, it may be these promising research directions and results that may make our current efforts successful (263).

The result of these developments is a surging professional interest in incorporating thinking processes into instruction (221, 340). This interest has been expressed by professional organizations associated with the various academic disciplines such as: the National Council of Teachers of Mathematics, the

National Council of Teachers of English, and the National Council for the Social Studies (234). It has also been voiced by organizations with a broad perspective, such as the College Board and the National Commission on Excellence in Education (221). In fact, a meeting on critical thinking at the Harvard Graduate School of Education (1984) promoted the adoption of critical thinking as a basic skill, along with reading, writing and math (242).

Today, a growing number of states are incorporating the teaching of thinking skills into the overall curriculum (184) as well as establishing requirements for completion of school (27) and developing tests to determine if students have, in fact, acquired these thinking skills (333, 391). It is particularly interesting to note that these concerns are echoed and expanded in the popular press (78).

The pressure is on!

Issue: Is it useful to teach thinking skills and strategies?

Considering the uncertainties about how thinking abilities develop, we must address the question of whether we can teach thinking. A question of central concern to educators is the extent to which we can instruct students in the process of thinking. Consider these views:

- Baer cautions that since "we have yet to reach consensus on how we think, how our brains are organized, or how we acquire competence as thinkers" (11, p. 67) we need to proceed carefully in instructing students. We may, in fact, be handicapping our best thinkers by forcing them into "correct" procedures that do not work for them.

- Halpern cites a growing body of research that supports "the idea that the ability to think critically can be improved" (159, p. 9) cautioning that "although it may not be possible to teach someone how to think, it is possible to *improve* the way someone thinks" (p. 6).

- Perkins (294) cautions that there is more evidence that there are gains in intellectual competence from instruction for learners who are performing at a below-normal level. He speculates that in order to see success in normal or above normal performers perhaps we need to instruct more in the specific requirements of specific domains of learning.

- Perkins adds another layer to this concept. While thinking may possibly be as natural as walking, good thinking is performed in the context of "words, images, notes, sketches, outlines, diagrams, and whatnot" (36, p. xii). "Good thinking is full of artifice.... The teaching and learning of thinking must be taken seriously, approached strategically, pursued diligently" (p. xiii).

- Nickerson et al. "view thinking ability as, in part, a matter of good strategy" (264, p. 44). This, they conclude can be taught. They compare this notion of thinking with intelligence which "relates more to the 'raw power' of one's mental equipment, and here, as in other contexts, raw power is one thing and the skilled use of it something else" (264, p. 44).

- Costa (91) suggests that it is possible to enhance intellectual capacity, compensating for handicaps within the person or the culture.

- Chipman and Segal in examining the concept of intelligence propose that "it may be that the critical differences in intellectual functioning rest on the organization and management of our basic learning ability.... We are not the first to suggest that there might be a need for systematic training to improve learning and thinking skills" (78, p. 4).

- Marzano echoes this with his statement that "we might well say that what we call intelligence is largely a function of the

number of organizational structures one can recognize"
(221, p. 34).

- Presseisen asserts that intelligence is not fixed and can be
broadly developed. She cites "the role that parents, schools
and culture play in influencing cognitive development"
(316, p. 2).

These issues related to the development of thinking abilities
and the effectiveness of instruction have enormous impact on
the instruction and education of children.

Definitions of Thinking

The first question we need to address is: "What is thinking?"
This is a deceptively simple question. Unfortunately, as Sigel
points out, "thinking is a term we often use but rarely define
precisely" (353, p. 18). The lack of consensus on a precise
definition of thinking, on the one hand, may mean that "we
cannot even begin to address the extensive problems associated
with the development of students' higher cognitive
performance" (314, p. 48). This lack of precision and agreement
has led to questionable educational practices and has been an
obstacle to research and dialogue within the academic
profession (30). On the other hand, we must consider whether
the lack of a precise definition of thinking may have, in fact,
contributed to a broader, more creative look at the operation of
this fundamental human activity and at our role as teachers in
promoting it and even allowing it to happen.

There are different approaches to defining thinking,
according to Sigel, ranging from "reflection, mediation, and
cogitation (suggesting passive reception) to mental actions
such as conceptualization and problem solving (implying an
active approach)" (353, p. 18). Let's consider some examples of
current definitions and descriptions:

- Costa: "Thinking is the receiving of external stimuli through the senses followed by internal processing" (94, p. 62).

- Sigel: "Thinking is regarded as an active process involving a number of denotable mental operations" (353, p. 18).

- Presseisen: "Thinking is generally assumed to be a cognitive process, a mental act by which knowledge is acquired" (314, p. 43). In a later work she defines thinking as "the mental manipulation of sensory input to formulate thoughts, reason about, or judge" (316, p. 98).

- Ruggerio: "Thinking . . . embraces only purposeful mental activity over which a person exercises some control" (337, p. 1).

- Halpern: "Most people would agree that thinking is complex and that it guides our behavior. In addition, thinking is dynamic; it's something we do. Thinking involves 'going beyond the information given' (Bruner, 1957). We take new information, combine it with information stored in memory and end up with something more than and different from what we started with. It's also private, in that no one else can know about our thoughts unless we choose to communicate them. Furthermore, thinking is so private that no one has direct conscious awareness of her or his own thinking processes" (159, p. 6).

- Nickerson: "Even within the articles and books that are focused on the teaching of thinking, one can find numerous definitions and characterizations of thinking, or, more commonly, of specific types of thinking. . . . If there is one point on which most investigators agree, it is that thinking is complex and many faceted and, in spite of considerable productive research, not yet very well understood" (263, p. 9).

Halpern further suggests that offering a good definition for the term "thinking" is a difficult task. However, "the problem of adequately defining 'thinking' shouldn't prevent us from finding ways to improve it. After all, as Munson (1976, p. 3) astutely observed, 'The truth is that not a whole heck of a lot about a complicated subject can be learned from a definition of it'" (159, p. 6).

We are left with some sense of uncertainty about the definition of thinking but also with a need to continue our investigation.

Characteristics of Thinking

Consider the characteristics of thinking suggested in the literature: thinking is a natural, active process; it occurs within both a physical and personal context; it is influenced by society, requires prior knowledge and the ability to represent knowledge, and is recursive. Let's examine each of these characteristics in detail.

Thinking: A Natural Process

Lowery, for example, holds that all humans engage in thinking without instruction (218, 353). Halpern believes that thinking "comes as naturally as breathing" (159, p. 6). Baer reviews research here and concludes "the evidence that much thinking is defined not via cultural transmission but is instead built into the architecture of the brain, is growing rapidly and cannot be dismissed lightly" (11, p. 67). Costa, however, raises a question here. "Brain researchers are attempting to discover whether thinking is a natural bodily function similar to the heart pumping blood or whether it is the result of intense effort, strict discipline, and careful programming of instructional outcomes" (94, p. 62). These questions certainly must make us reconsider whether we should spend time instructing in thinking skills. If it is a natural process, perhaps there is nothing we can or should do to teach thinking. In spite of his concern Baer suggests that we "challenge and teach" (11, p. 69) students whose thinking is not satisfactory. Even those such as Halpern who believe it is a natural process suggest that it can be improved.

Thinking: An Active Process

Although the variety of definitions of thinking suggests a continuum from passive to active, the current view of the thinking process as active is widely supported (36, 184, 314). Halpern, for example, states that "thinking is not a spectator sport" (158, p. 73). We cannot sit by, passively, and engage in thinking. We must participate. Presseisen refers to the student as a "hypothesis generator [and] constructor of knowledge" (316, p. 5). Remember our previous definitions of thinking? They all involve some form of activity on the part of the thinker. In no instance was there even a hint that the thinker was solely the passive recipient of thoughts. Rather, the thinker was actively engaged in the process of developing thoughts.

Thinking in a Context

The thinking process occurs within both a physical context and a personal context. Lowery (218) identifies the physical context of the brain and the body; Sigel (353) identifies the personal context of the individual's likes, dislikes, and fears. Costa (95, 98) adds to the personal context by including the individual's inclination and willingness to take risks and commitment to engage in thinking. Ennis and Beyer (36) refer to these attitudes as the dispositions which constitute a personal context for thinking.

Influence of Society

There is agreement that the thinking process is influenced by the society and culture in which the individual exists. Exactly how that influence is expressed differs according to various experts in the field. The disagreement centers on the use of the thinking skills and the content and use of thinking itself. Sigel supports the notion that "although it is true that humans, by their very biological similarity, can employ a wide array of thinking skills, the use of these skills will vary as a function of cultural milieu" (353, p. 20). Helu (165) makes a somewhat similar distinction but concludes that the nature of thinking and the skills used are not influenced by society. However, the scope or content of the thinking process is influenced by society and can be different for different groups within that society. Adams (1) sees both the use of thinking and the content of thinking as "shaped" by the culture. While we find a lack of consensus on exactly how society and culture influence thinking, there is certainly general agreement that there is an influence.

Thinking and Knowledge

The thinking process requires prior knowledge, the memory of it, and the use of that prior knowledge (159, 184). Thinking can, in fact, be limited by lack of experience and knowledge (353). Nickerson asserts that "clearly one's ability to think effectively within a specific domain will be severely limited if one knows little about that domain" (260, p. 24). He suggests that "Nobel laureates who are not well informed in their fields are rare" (p. 24). Prior knowledge is not sufficient, however. Thinking requires the ability to "find" that prior knowledge in memory when it is useful and integrate it with new information (50, 159, 317).

Representation of Thought

The thinking process requires language to formulate and express thoughts (159) as well as the ability to develop representations of knowledge and concepts. These, according to Sigel (353), are generally visual or verbal representations but may also take the form of music or gestures (353, 354).

Thinking: A Recursive Process

Engaging in thinking is a recursive not a linear task (184). The thinker prepares to think, thinks, rethinks, checks, rechecks, and concludes at least at that point in time. With new information or in a new situation the process may begin again.

Emerging Thoughts

The definitions of thinking provide us with a background to use in our exploration of the topic of teaching thinking. The characteristics give us a framework for building a model of thinking and instructing in thinking. Notice that we make the assumption that you as readers and we as writers will take active parts in the process of building a model.

II

Components of Thinking:
Skills and Strategies

The variety of definitions of thinking has given rise to differing views of what is needed for thinking to occur effectively. However, there are some common components that are included in most discussions of thinking. The skills and strategies used, the focus or content, and the outcome or product are frequently cited as components of thinking (159, 165, 316). It is critical, though, to stress at this point that these components do not operate in isolation but are interrelated and connected. It seems simpler and more direct to discuss them separately but that does not reflect reality. Nickerson, citing others with this same viewpoint, expresses our concern directly. "While it has been convenient to discuss separately each of several aspects of thinking on which efforts to develop training methods have focused, it must be apparent that these aspects are interdependent in many ways" (263, p. 27).

Skills

The first component, thinking skills, is basic to the concept of thinking because it includes what the thinker needs to do in order to accomplish the task. Jones, Palinscar, Ogle, and Carr define a skill as "a mental activity that can be applied to specific tasks" (184, p. 14). Differences among the theorists center on what the skills are and on how they are organized and related. In fact, various theorists might be categorized according to the perspective they adopt in viewing skills. They may view skills in various ways: the thinker and what he does; the demands made on the thinker by the information processing requirements of the thinking task; or the complexity of the thinking task itself.

First, consider identifying thinking skills according to the approach taken by the thinker. For example, Nickerson et al. identify "two types of thinking, one characterized by such descriptors as analytic, deductive, rigorous, constrained, convergent, formal, and critical, and the other by synthetic, inductive, expansive, unconstrained, divergent, informal, diffuse, and creative" (264, p. 62). They distinguish between two types of thinking skills, "rigorous logical reasoning and exploratory experimental groping for insights" (p. 50). The first is "hypothesis testing" (p. 50) and the second is "hypothesis generation" (p. 50). "An implication of this distinction is that efforts to teach thinking skills should take cognizance of both types" (p. 62). Both are important and both are needed for a balanced approach to thinking.

Sigel also views thinking skills from the perspective of the thinker, identifying "denotable mental operations such as induction, deduction, reasoning, sequencing, classification, and definition of relationships. Each of these processes can function separately or in combination to meet environmental demands such as problem finding and problem solving" (353, p. 18).

A second approach considers the information processing demands generated by the information and how the information is organized and represented. Marzano (221), for example, has identified thinking skills according to how information is organized, processed, understood, and remembered. He includes, as skills, recognition of concepts, relationships, and patterns; reconstruction, evaluation, and extrapolation of information; problem solving; and knowledge of basic input/output processes, content-specific tasks, and of the self as learner.

Costa, after comparing several models of thinking, takes a somewhat similar tack, building on an information processing model and grouping skills into basic "thought clusters: (l) input of data through the senses and from memory; (2) processing those data into meaningful relationships; (3) output or application of those relationships into new or novel situations; and (4) metacognition" (94, p. 62).

Consider a third, quite common approach. Some theorists identify and categorize thinking skills according to their levels of complexity. Early taxonomies such as Bloom's Taxonomy of Educational Objectives (knowledge, comprehension, application, analysis, synthesis, and evaluation) and Guilford's Structure of Intellect are well known and widely cited (221, 314). More recently, Beyer identifies basic, discrete skills and the more complex, multiple process strategies such as conceptualizing, reflective thinking, problem solving and decision making. These complex processes utilize the basic skills in various ways for different purposes. For example, Beyer describes critical thinking as a "combination of operations involving analysis and evaluation" (31, p. 557).

Presseisen (313, 314, 316) in addition to basic (or essential) and complex, adds a third level, metacognitive, and a fourth level, epistemological. Costa (95) not only groups skills according to how the information is processed but also according to levels of complexity. Let's examine what is often included in these various levels.

- Basic level: These basic or micro-level (223) skills are closely related to those identified by Bloom and Guilford. In fact, Beyer suggests that Bloom's list is "the best available inventory of the micro-thinking skills we should be teaching, in our classrooms" (31, p. 556) The terms microlevel or micrological are frequently applied to these basic or core level skills (1, 223, 285).

  Presseisen (316) refers to these as "essential thinking skills" and includes causation, transformations, relationships, classification, qualifications and their component subskills. They form the basis for the complex skills. Costa uses the term "discrete mental skills" (95, p. 67) and includes many of these same basic skills in his list. These discrete mental skills are "prerequisite to more complex thought and are found in the areas of the input of data, processing it, and output of the products" (p. 67). Paul (285) and Adams (l) in addition to classification, include observation and sequencing.

- Complex level: These are the higher order macrolevel or macrological (1, 223) processes which deal with more complex information. Presseisen includes in this category problem solving, decision making, critical thinking, and creative thinking. Costa (94) includes Presseisen's first three complex skills and adds strategic reasoning and logic. Costa adds an additional level of complex skills, creative thinking. Paul (285) also includes creativity and the ability to process complex information and adds the ability to consider more than one point of view in describing macrological skills.

- Metacognitive level: Metacognitive thinking is planful thinking. It is thought about thought. It involves abstracting the basic and complex skills and knowing when to use them. Presseisen includes in metacognitive thinking skills monitoring task performance and selecting and understanding the appropriate strategy. This level provides a way of understanding and regulating the basic and complex skills. Costa does not use this terminology but recognizes the general concept of metacognition by including many of the notions related to it in his final level of "the cognitive spirit" (95, p. 68). Beyer (31) also includes the general notion of metacognition, identifying the need for knowing the rules that govern the choice and use of discrete operations as well as understanding and employing the criteria for effective performance.

- Epistemological level: Presseisen suggests that there is a level of thinking that is required to understand the limits of what can be thought about and understood within a specific discipline. On an epistemological level, students need to understand the dimensions of a content area sufficiently to be able to use and manipulate knowledge. What are the dimensions? They are the nature of knowledge, its limits and validity.

Finally, in considering the skills of thinking, we need to keep in mind the statement made by Sternberg. "The problem, of course, is not that there are close to 1000 personality traits or thinking skills (at least that we know about), but that there are many different names for the same thing, with each investigator having his or her own preferred set of names" (371, p. 252).

Issue: *Are thinking skills hierarchical or non-hierarchical and how are the various levels related?*

The question of whether thinking skills are hierarchical or not is one that has been addressed frequently and in some depth by many of the professionals concerned with the topic of thinking. Ultimately, as we will see later in this discussion, your answer to this question has enormous implications for how you organize instruction. But, here let's look at the theory.

First, are the skills hierarchical? There are those who consider the skills as hierarchical. Costa, in proposing an information processing approach to thinking skills including input, processing, and output, clearly suggests "that these levels of thinking are cumulative" (91, p. 216); a student cannot process without adequate input and cannot produce an outcome without experience in processing. He views all students as engaging in all of these thought clusters, with adjustments made in "the level and complexity of the cognitive task to one more appropriate to the student's current level of intellectual functioning and remain at that level until enough data are gathered or the data are processed sufficiently before moving to higher levels productively" (pp. 216–217).

Others, supporting a levels approach based on micro and macrolevel skills, also may view the skills as hierarchical (31, 95, 218, 235, 316) with more complex skills building on, in some fashion, the basic, essential or simpler skills. Presseisen asserts that skills are hierarchical and that "a solid foundation of all the microskills appears to be a prerequisite of higher-order performance" (316, p. 11).

The support for a nonhierarchical view of thinking skills comes from a variety of sources. While viewing thinking in terms of the activities of the thinker, both Nickerson et al. (264) and Sigel (353) reject the notion of the skills related in a hierarchy, but rather see them used in combination as needed by the thinker and as required by the demands of the situation. Marzano, in reviewing the information processing thinking skills demanded by tasks, emphasizes that these thinking skills "are not presented in a hierarchy" (221, p. 6). The "skills or processes interact in such a highly complex way as to be indefinable in a linear fashion" (p. 7).

There may be a third position here. Jones et al. (184) relate content areas to thinking skills and suggest that the particular content area may influence whether thinking skills are hierarchical and should be so taught. For example, mathematics is an area where concepts and skills are hierarchical while in reading "holistic understanding is desirable" (p. 17). Thus, there may not be some predetermined and unchangeable relationship between micro and macrolevel skills, but rather a relationship determined by the demands of the specific content area.

Second, how are the levels related? There are also, as you have probably figured out by now, differing views on how microlevel and macrolevel skills are related. Presseisen states that "these complex processes obviously draw on and elaborate on the underlying essential skills. Certain of the essential skills may be more significant to one complex process than others, but current research has not clarified a discrete understanding of such relationships" (314, p. 45). For example, the use of comparison and contrast is a microskill often used in decision making and problem solving.

Costa, however, relates the discrete skills to complex by calling the complex skills strategies people use in "situations to which the resolution or answers are not immediately known" (95, p. 68) Adams suggests the distinction between micro and macrological processes is meaningless in terms of the goals for teaching thinking, since "the development of macrological processes presumes operational knowledge of the micrological processes; conversely, the very reason for teaching micrological processes is to build a sound, analytic base for macrological growth" (1, p. 29). However as we will see, she suggests there may be critical differences in effectiveness of the approaches to teaching the two levels.

These complex and metacognitive levels may also be viewed from another perspective, not as skills per se but rather as "dimensions of thinking" according to Jones et al. (184). Marzano et al. (223) also use the term dimensions, defining dimensions as the elements in a "framework" of thinking and as components for understanding thinking. However, while metacognition and critical and creative thinking are viewed as two of five dimensions, problem solving and decision making are seen as "more or less macro-level operations" (223, p. 4), which are part of a third dimension, thinking processes.

The issue of how to view thinking skills is certainly complex and unsettled. The answer to the question raised in the issue of whether skills are hierarchical or not could be "yes, no or maybe!"

Issue: *Is there a developmental sequence in children's acquisition and use of thinking skills?*

The issue here centers on whether there is a developmental sequence in thinking skill acquisition and use or whether children have all the skills they need right from the beginning and develop depth and breadth in them. Clearly this issue is closely related to the issue of whether skills are hierarchical. If you believe that they are hierarchical, you probably also believe that children will follow some kind of developmental sequence as they mature as thinkers. However, you certainly will not be surprised to learn that the literature on thinking reveals a lack of consensus on how thinking abilities develop. You, in fact, are using your thinking skills here.

One view of the development of thinking skills seems to find a difference in the kind and level of thinking which is generally related to maturation. Another view considers that all the skills develop at once and the difference is in the quality and depth of thinking. A third view, which is beginning to be explored, considers that there are differences in both kind and quality, relating the differences to the appropriateness of the thinking task. Let's look at these three points of view.

The maturational view of the development of thinking has been widely supported. Sigel cites Piaget's theory that "thinking competence evolves through stages and suggests that certain competencies and skills emerge at each stage" (353, p. 19). For Sigel this represents a hierarchical view of skills and skill development, with new skills developing from existing skills. For example, Flavell and Wellman (125) suggest that metamemory, a complex metacognitive thinking skill defined as the ability to remember intentionally, to know about one's own memory, develops with age and experience. Lowery describes a hierarchy of thinking capabilities and skills that develop sequentially from birth to early adulthood, are based on a "biological foundation" (218, p. 71) and "are programmed to appear at intervals and spaced well enough apart to let the current capability establish itself" (p. 72).

A second view of how skills are related and develop is suggested by Sigel's discussion of Werner's orthogenetic principle, in which development moves from the global to the more detailed and specific. "Development, then, involves such processes as differentiation, integration, reintegration and de-differentiation of experience, moving horizontally and vertically in a complex organization of patterns. . . . The development of thinking, then, employs both horizontal processes (differentiating groups) and vertical ones (structuring hierarchies)" (353, p. 19). He relates this to the development of thinking skills through an example illustrating the differentiation and re-integration that appears in the development of classification abilities. Sigel concludes that, in fact, "Piaget's notions of stages and Werner's orthogenetic principle complement each other" (p. 19) with different abilities occurring at different stages and with increasing differentiation occurring within and between stages.

Finally, a third view needs to be explored. The question here may be one that is more complex than whether development of thinking is maturational or orthogenetic. It might be a question of whether the thinking occurs in the course of a developmentally appropriate task. Gelman, for example, showed that it was possible for children to demonstrate cognitive competence in ways considered developmentally advanced for them, if the tasks were especially designed for the children. She concludes that "young children's competencies are more like older children's than once assumed" (142, p. 538). She discounts the notion of fundamental differences due to development, and instead, focuses on the suitability of the task. She suggests that "some may be surprised with the finding that young children monitor their own learning and rehearse spontaneously; for, we have heard from some quarters that these are late developing strategies" (p. 543). She concludes that "research over the last decade has revealed some remarkable abilities in young children" (p. 543).

There is a growing body of research which is beginning to document that young children can perform cognitive tasks that have often been considered too advanced for them. We know, for example, that young children have the capacity to think on a metacognitive level, even though they may not do so spontaneously. Markman (219) found that young children, first and third graders, weren't aware when they didn't understand certain information, and they didn't realize they were given incomplete information to complete a task. However, when they were warned that there would be problems in the text they were listening to and given examples of problems, even the youngest children were able to detect the problems and monitor their comprehension failure.

Another variable here may be related to the possession of domain-specific knowledge. Carey, in reviewing research on how children's thinking differed from that of adults, found that "by far the most important source of variance is in domain-specific knowledge" (68, p. 514). In addition, Chi (75) suggests that the capacity of young children to perform at higher cognitive levels in a given domain is related to the amount and structure of their knowledge in that domain. So we see that more than maturation is implicated in the development of thinking. There is also content knowledge and awareness of and suitability of the task.

As an illustration, let's consider an example of thinking from real life. One of the authors was driving on a two lane road through a desert in the American Southwest. As the car approached a crossroad where there was a small group of stores her six year old grandson spotted a sign that said "NO PASSING." He read it aloud. "NO PEOPLE." Before anyone could correct him, he commented "No, that's not right. There aren't any people on the road except there are some at the stores. It must be 'No passing.' The road's too narrow."

In thinking about the message he was using prior knowledge, was engaged in a task appropriate for his age and had appropriate strategies to monitor his comprehension of the sign. He knew that road signs signaled some condition related to the road. The task was appropriate because the message was short. He probably couldn't (and certainly wouldn't) have engaged in the task if the message had been long. He had appropriate information. He knew the word "no" and knew that an effective strategy would be to apply knowledge of initial consonants. If he had known most consonants but not 'p' he would have had inappropriate information. So far, so good. He got a message and immediately realized that it did not apply to this particular situation.

His knowledge of the situation allowed him to make and reject one hypothesis and generate and confirm another. His knowledge that road signs generally signal some condition of the road made him aware of his task: to find out the condition of the road. And finally the length of the message made the task suitable for his level of maturation. His performance concurs with both Markman and Chi: maturation, content knowledge, awareness and suitability of the task were all implicated.

Summary

To summarize so far, in our exploration of the concept of thinking we have looked at the skills of thinking from the perspective of the thinker, the information processing requirements of the task, and the level of complexity of the task. In each case, we have seen how some theorists may view the skills as being arranged in a hierarchical fashion, with one skill developing from and building on other skills while others view skills as arranged in a non-hierarchical fashion, with the skills interacting, combining and recombining according to the demands of the situation and the needs of the thinker. Theorists also differ on how skills are related and how they develop in thinkers. The discussion here certainly illustrates the recursive, nonlinear characteristic of thinking. The development of our ideas can only occur as we examine and reexamine information and issues in new juxtapositions. These different views as we wilt see all have implications for curriculum and instruction.

Questions

At this point there are a number of questions about thinking skills that impact on instruction.

- Do we emphasize microskills, macroskills, or both?
- Do we establish a hierarchy and sequence for teaching individual thinking skills?
- Do we start with the complex skills and teach basic skills as needed using a holistic approach or do we teach predetermined skills in isolation combining them into complex skills?

These questions have direct implications for instruction. In fact, as we will see they form the basis for the development of the various thinking programs.

Strategies

The next component to consider in our definition of thinking is that of the processes or the strategies the thinker uses. To make students good strategy users and "lifelong learners" we need to teach them how to be in charge of their thinking (43). We can't possibly teach students all they need to know to even function and survive in the world today. "The view that everything of importance can be thoughtfully learned by the 12th grade... is a delusion" (411, p. 44). There is too much information in the student's world to know it all directly. Therefore we must concentrate our efforts on the process in addition to the content of thinking to give students the freedom to learn on their own. To do this, students need strategies.

Educators and researchers describe strategies in different ways. For example:

- Jones et al.: The distinction between skill and strategy made by Jones et al. may be useful here. "A skill is a mental activity that can be applied to specific learning tasks. . . .

Strategies are specific procedures or ways of executing a specific skill" (184, pp. 14–15).

- Nickerson: Strategies are likened to "informal principles and tools of thought" (263, p. 17).

- Levin: "Learning strategies" consist of cognitive and metacognitive processes (204). Levin suggests that educators need to design strategy instruction which coordinates both.

- Dansereau: A learning strategy is "a set of processes or steps that can facilitate the acquisition, storage, and/or utilization of information" (105, p. 210).

- Weinstein and Underwood: Strategies are the "how" of learning (405).

In summary, the definitions and descriptions vary but the essential quality which serves to link them is the stress on strategies as a "tool," as the "how," of thinking and as a means of facilitating learning.

Alexander and Judy (2) discuss the relationship between strategy use and domain knowledge and the effect of both on academic performance. They suggest that knowledge of strategies is vital to the acquisition and use of domain knowledge, that increased amounts of domain knowledge facilitate more sophisticated strategy use, and both domain knowledge and good strategy use are critical to academic performance. In fact, incorrect use of strategies may actually impede acquisition of domain knowledge. Thus, we see that not only are the components related, but the relationships among and between components are complex.

In looking at the process of strategy acquisition, research is beginning to tell us that a number of factors are involved (263). We not only need to teach students the strategies themselves but also how to select appropriate strategies for a particular task and when and how to use them during the task. In addition, the question of transfer of strategy use to another task is critical if students are to become effective lifelong thinkers. Finally, we need to examine conditions under which strategy training is effective.

In all of this, students need to be metacognitively aware and in charge of monitoring and managing their strategy use. In examining this component of thinking we need to look at what the categories of strategies are, how thinkers learn to select and use strategies, how they transfer the strategy to other domains, and finally, what conditions are needed for effective strategy training.

Categories of Strategies

First, what are the strategies? There are a number of ways to classify strategies. One way is to break them into two categories as Dansereau (105) does: primary and support strategies. Primary strategies are used to operate on the text material directly, such as comprehension and memory strategies; these may have a direct impact on the target information. Support strategies, on the other hand, are those used to maintain a mental state amenable to learning, for example concentration strategies; these may have an indirect impact by improving overall level of the learner's cognitive functioning. Another way is to divide strategies into Levin's two categories of cognitive and metacognitive.

Weinstein and Underwood (405) combine these two approaches and divide strategies into four categories: cognitive information-processing strategies, active study strategies, support strategies, and metacognitive strategies. Let's consider each of these.

Cognitive Strategies

Organization and reorganization of information and ideas is a critical cognitive strategy for thinking (317). Adams suggests that "the essential characteristic of strategies is that they help guide the search for organization of information" (1, p. 53). This includes organizing prior knowledge, new knowledge and integrating the two (269, 312). The use of organizational strategies such as graphic organizers helps thinkers identify and clarify relationships among information and ideas, including linking new information to prior knowledge and new information to new information.

Teaching students ways to use and develop these graphic organizers when they learn and study has been found to be particularly effective. "Concrete representations can crystallize or give form to concepts and procedures" (312, p. 8). Jones et al. refer to the use of graphic organizers as "spatial learning strategies" (184, p. 14), and advocate the use of frames and graphic outlines to locate and represent information, to select important data and concepts, to relate information from different sources, to link new knowledge to prior knowledge and to restructure prior knowledge. Jones et al. review research in this area and conclude that successful use of graphic organizers requires explicit instruction in identifying key structural elements, using appropriate organizers, and working in groups using cooperative learning. These authors conclude that "skilled readers and writers appear to be able to use frames and graphic outlines effectively to learn from text and to write" (p. 14).

Different cognitive strategies may serve different cognitive purposes. Levin (204) suggests that strategies must match the learner's characteristics, i.e. must account for difference in domain knowledge, level of development, and learning disabilities and differences. They must also suit the type of text to be learned as welt as learning outcomes anticipated. For example, organization strategies in the field of reading in which graphic organizers could be used include knowledge and use of the structure of a text, recognition and use of cue words, and selection of main idea (184, 222, 223, 238).

One way of determining which cognitive strategies are useful to teach is to identify strategies that experts use and use them as a basis for teaching novices (156, 217). This conclusion may help explain the proliferation of suggestions for incorporating these strategies into instruction which are currently appearing in the professional literature. The suggestions often reflect what researchers identify as strategies used by experts.

Active Study Strategies

We will examine two active study strategies that seem useful in developing thinking: self-questioning and summarizing. One strategy that students use to become active learners is to ask themselves questions, making them actively involved in the learning process (217, 340, 419). Wong (419) reviewed 27 relevant studies in this area and found that self-questioning could have three major purposes. It enables students to become active participants, to engage in metacognitive processes, and to activate prior knowledge and relate new information to it. This strategy fosters a spirit of problem finding which is essential to developing thinking skills (152) and when done with peers enables students "to generate cognitive demands on their fellow students" (353, p. 21).

Another active study strategy that is effective in developing thinking is summarizing information. In addition to being able to organize and reorganize information, and ask questions about it, a student must be able to manage information in some useable way. One way to manage information is to summarize it, so that just the information needed to suit the student's purpose is available. Like self-questioning, summarizing may also enable students to become active, metacognitive participants in learning by helping them to understand text and to recognize when meaning is unclear. It may also help students to remember main ideas through having to identify them (5). Students certainly need a considerable amount of instruction and practice in summary writing if the strategy is to be used and used effectively (4, 217).

One area where the impact of active study has been researched extensively is that of reading. Weinstein and

Underwood (405) discuss the importance of active study strategies in successful reading comprehension. They identify a number of ways in which good readers employ active study strategies. For example, good readers are more proficient at note taking and other test preparation, strategies which transform information to be studied into more manageable units which are easier to understand and remember. Good readers make more effort to use their schemas, or prior knowledge about a topic, to help them understand new information.

Good readers also choose the study strategy that is appropriate for the task which will be used to measure how well they learned and remembered. In other words, the study strategy chosen, whether it be highlighting, notetaking, summarizing or any other of the many common strategies students use to study, must be one which requires the same kind of processing that is required in the criterion task. For example, summarizing is a good choice for a study strategy only if the cognitive tasks required to produce a summary are similar to the cognitive tasks required to study for the test. We know that cognitive tasks required to produce a good summary are locating, organizing and recording main ideas. The emphasis here is on the main idea, not information of low structural importance. Summarizing, then, is an effective study strategy only if the criterion task, the test used to measure whether or not the student learned and remembered the information, gives students a chance to report what they learned and remembered about the main ideas only. Therefore in this case the test must allow for free recall, where students can report the main ideas which they would have learned by summarizing. An objective test may tap knowledge of less important information and students who concentrated on main ideas by summarizing may not do so well. Anderson and Armbruster (4) refer to this ability to select the study strategy appropriate for the criterion task as "transfer appropriateness." In addition, they suggest that students need a considerable amount of instruction and practice in summary writing if it is to be effective.

Support Strategies

Fostering a positive attitude and strong motivation to higher-level thinking is an important part of the teaching of thinking. Thinking is hard work. It is much easier to sit back and soak up someone else's answers and opinions than to think, judge, evaluate and formulate one's own. A disposition toward thinking is frequently cited as a characteristic of a good thinker (263, 285, 337). One list that details what this disposition might include is provided by Nickerson (263). This list includes: fair-mindedness, openness to evidence on any issue, respect for opinions that differ from one's own, inquisitiveness and a desire to be informed, and a tendency to reflect before acting. In addition, according to Halpern (158), the desire and motivation to make a greater effort to learn difficult material is a major indicator of a higher-order thinking attitude.

If these are dispositions, what are the affective strategies that support them? According to Jones et al. affective strategies are those which "focus attention, minimize anxiety, and maintain motivation" (184, p. 41). Marzano and Arrendondo (222) refer to affective strategies as those which enable refocusing for a new task and awareness toward the class, the task, and one's own ability. To encourage a positive deeper-level thinking attitude, Halpern (158) suggests that teachers must make students aware that, in addition to knowing facts about a subject, they must also know how to apply them, when to question them and how to relate them to other subjects. They must also be encouraged to view difficult material as a challenge and not a frustration in order to develop the attitude of a deeper level thinker. Covington (100) suggests that the most effective way of developing dispositions for thinking is to link cognitive and affective variables, i.e., teach students effective ways to think.

In thinking about thinking, Ruggiero's comment concerning motivation is well taken.

All the understanding of creative and critical thinking and all the skill in applying that understanding to problems and issues will profit students little if they lack the motivation to think well. (337, p.68)

Metacognitive Strategies

The emphasis on teaching students how to monitor their success or failure in a task, to take steps to insure that problems are overcome and to transfer the newly acquired strategy to different content domains is found almost universally in the current literature. Costa (93) categorizes this as teaching about thinking. Sternberg refers to metacognitive strategies as "executive" strategies. He identifies executive processes as those concerned with "planning, monitoring, and revising strategies for task performance" (367, p. 9). In addition, he suggests that we "provide explicit training in both executive and nonexecutive information processing, as well as interactions between the two kinds of information processing" (p. 9).

The current emphasis on instruction in metacognitive strategies reflects a major refocusing of research efforts and a resultant redirection in our thinking in this area. In the 1970s and early 80s, research investigated whether or not specific learning and studying strategies could be trained. Training programs were attempted which gave explicit instruction in the strategies themselves. In the early 1980s a switch took place in strategy training research. Studies began to focus on metacognitive aspects of strategy use such as strategy awareness, self-regulation, awareness of usefulness, and metamemory. The importance of direct instruction in metacognitive strategies became clear, as did the importance of facilitation of transfer, provision of constant assessment and diagnosis, instruction in context, the teaching of explicit rules and the use of prior knowledge (59, 125, 134, 145, 216, 245, 281, 327).

Strategy Selection and Use

Strategy selection and use appear to be related to two variables. The thinker needs to know what the strategy is and how well it works before he will select and use it. First, research generally agrees that students need to know what specific strategies are. In fact, a student's own metacognitive knowledge about strategies has been shown to affect his/her strategy selection and use (144, 319). Further, students trained to he more knowledgeable, aware of and in control of their own strategies use those strategies more effectively to learn in general (12). Research also demonstrates a relationship between reading ability and strategy use: poor readers are unaware of the need to apply particular strategies to read for meaning (387).

Second, research has shown that when students are aware of the efficacy of a strategy, i.e., how a particular strategy can help them learn, the more likely they are to use that strategy on their own (145). In fact, it has been shown that children, more so than adults, need instruction in strategy usefulness to maintain strategies and increase their use (143). Weed, Ryan and Day (401) also found that when children are aware of the influence of their strategy use on their success, they maintain and continue to use that strategy. Borkowski, Carr, Rellinger, and Pressley specifically link strategy knowledge and use with motivation and affective variables, concluding that when we teach strategies directly we teach students "to believe in themselves" (44, p. 84).

In examining the use of cognitive, active, support and metacognitive strategies we begin to have indications that they are all closely related. An example will illustrate this. Thomas and Rohwer (386) suggest that to be effective in studying, cognitive strategies selected must be specific, that is, there must be a match between the strategies selected, the content under study and the characteristics of the studier. Cognitive strategies must be generative, i.e., the more the strategies elaborate on content the more effective they will be. Strategies must be monitored by the studier; he must combine cognitive and metacognitive strategies; the studier must be in charge, must planfully select, use and evaluate the strategy in use. The strategy selected must also lead to an attitude of personal efficacy, that is, the studier must believe he or she is in charge of use of the strategy.

Strategy Transfer

The next area that must be examined concerns transfer of the newly acquired learning strategy to different content domains. Students must be taught to transfer strategies and be motivated to do so (26, 294, 367). Ghatala (143) suggests that by teaching children that they can control their academic performance and by teaching them how to evaluate, select and monitor appropriate strategies on their own, they develop a sense of confidence in themselves as learners, and they develop a metacognitive understanding of the strategies which is transferable to other strategies. Similarly, O'Sullivan and Pressley (274) demonstrated that training in strategy-utility information, as well as in when and how to use the strategy, enhanced strategy transfer. So, we have support for the notion that students can learn to transfer strategies if taught to do so. However, research on the effectiveness of programs concurs that transfer is not easy and certainly not automatic (147, 263).

Effectiveness of Strategy Training

Finally, we must examine the effectiveness of strategy training. There have been a number of relevant studies in this area that have demonstrated that students can learn strategies and can use them effectively. Pressley (318) reviewed the research on strategy training and use and proposed the Good Strategy User (GSU) model. GSUs know strategies, know about strategies, know content information and know how to coordinate all three. Pressley suggested five principles of effective strategy training: l) teach strategies, 2) teach knowledge about when, where, and how to use strategies, 3) teach general knowledge about factors that promote strategy functioning, 4) teach relevant non-strategic knowledge, and 5) have students practice components of good strategy use and the coordination of components.

Consider only a few examples of work that have influenced this line of thought. Palincsar and Brown (277) conducted a series of studies on Reciprocal Teaching which trained self-regulation of strategies, provided a great deal of student teacher interaction, and used modeling and feedback. Comprehension was increased and students were able to transfer the strategies to new contents successfully. Brown and Day (59) successfully taught summarizing rules explicitly; Lodico, Ghatala, Levin, Pressley, and Bell (216) conducted a study which provided general procedures for gaining knowledge of strategies rather than information about the strategies themselves. Pressley, Borkowski, and O'Sullivan (319) used immediate feedback techniques to train strategy efficacy, i.e., students were taught how a strategy could be useful to them when they studied. Lodico et al. (216) were able to train subjects to monitor their strategies as well as to be aware of the usefulness of strategies.

Strategy training should also link the different categories of strategies. Nickerson (263), in a review of the literature on the effectiveness of strategy instruction, makes some relevant points, cautioning that students are more likely to select and use strategies effectively if they receive specific and detailed instruction and if they have opportunities to recognize and understand how the strategy can be helpful. He stresses that cognitive strategies are "more likely to be effective when they are coupled with the acquisition of metacognitive knowledge and skills than when they are not" (p. 30).

In examining the issue of effectiveness we need to consider that much of the research that has been done in the field of metacognition has been in the area of reading and/or studying. Therefore, it is relevant to note the applicability of general findings to this specific area. Haller, Child and Walberg (157) analyzed the results of an accumulation of research relating reading and metacognition to see if metacognitive training was effective and which strategies were the most easily trained. They found that inconsistency awareness and self-questioning were most successfully trained and the largest effects were found for 7th and 8th graders. These two areas in metacognitive training also relate to cognitive strategy training in organization of information and self-questioning.

We can see that to teach strategies effectively we must teach the strategies themselves as well as how to select appropriate strategies, monitor their successful use, transfer them to other contents, and recognize their usefulness in thinking and learning.

Research Problems

Although a great deal of progress has been made in strategy training research, there are a number of problems and issues which need to be investigated in depth. In spite of the numerous studies that have been reported in this area, Alexander and Judy (2) point to problems in research on the effectiveness of strategy use: young subjects (below 7th grade) are rarely studied, inconsistent criteria are used to define experts vs. novices in amounts of domain knowledge, strategies under study are not consistent or clearly specified, and conflicting definitions and interpretations of domain specific and strategic knowledge are used.

Weinstein and Underwood (405) suggest seven basic issues that need to be addressed as well. They suggest that we identify the types of strategies used by successful learners, investigate the nature and critical attributes of those strategies, decide on the most important strategies to teach, develop methods to assess learner deficits, develop instructional methods and curriculum materials to teach learning strategies, create appropriate instruments to assess training programs, and investigate ways to promote generalization of strategy use across different content areas. Despite these research concerns, Levin (204) suggests that the efficacy of learning strategies needs to continue to be studied empirically since success is often judged by intuition alone.

Summary

In our investigation of the second component of our definition of thinking, strategies, we have looked at four categories. Cognitive strategies, the first category, enable us to organize and reorganize information and ideas in order to clarify relationships among ideas and link new information to prior knowledge and other new information. Active strategies, the second category, utilize self-questioning and summarizing to make students active participants in the learning process. Third, support strategies foster an attitude or disposition towards independent, higher-level thinking. Finally, metacognitive strategies enable the thinker to monitor and control all of these learning strategies.

The research which we have investigated leads us to conclude that we need to train students to know exactly what the strategies are that are available to them, to select the most appropriate one for the task, and to identify how a particular strategy can help them learn. Moreover we must provide explicit training in how to transfer strategies across content areas and in how to monitor success or failure in strategy use.

This focus on strategy instruction is critical if we are to give students the tools they need to be lifelong learners. Our efforts as educators must converge on the continuation of research and the development of instruction, materials and evaluative techniques.

Questions

We have identified a number of questions about strategies to add to our list of questions about skills which also impact on instruction.

- How do we identify which strategies are appropriate for particular thinking tasks and students?
- How do we teach students to select and use strategies appropriately?
- How do we teach students to transfer strategies from one domain to another?
- How do we measure the effectiveness of strategy instruction?

III

Components of Thinking: Content and Outcomes

Content

A cover of the *Journal of Reading* (February 1987) featured a quote from Jules Renard: "To think is not enough; you must think of something." This notion of the importance of content in thinking is widely supported. Nickerson et al., for example, state that "thinking involves thinking about something; thinking about nothing is an exceedingly difficult thing to do" (264, p. 48). Helu (165) refers to content as the focus or scope of thinking.

Content and Thinking

What is the content of thinking? Helu goes on to say that it is "the range of subjects, areas, topics, ideas, etc., which thinking actually covers" (165, p. 47) and is influenced by society. Content will vary from individual to individual, from society to society, and for a particular individual will vary at different times and in different situations and will vary over the span of his life.

Content may be the focus of thinking, but Nickerson et al. suggest it plays a larger role than merely forming the scope of our thinking. They indicate that "on the one hand, thinking is essential to the acquisition of knowledge, and, on the other hand, knowledge is essential to thinking" (264, p. 48). This interdependence of thinking and knowledge suggests a number of things. We must analyze the knowledge needed in particular instances, identify concepts and content relevant to the particular age level of the students, and provide specific instruction in it (221). In addition, we need to help students construct "bridges" between prior knowledge of content and new knowledge (45, 338). The particular structure of a body of knowledge may influence how the content can be studied and the kind of strategies that can be used (317). Remember Jones' suggestion that in some content areas skills may be hierarchical and in others holistic.

There may be another link between knowledge of content and thinking. Chi suggests that perhaps children are capable of using thinking strategies in ways not anticipated by the developmental, maturation approach. Children's capability may depend on their prior knowledge of the content or the subject under consideration. She proposes:

> that strategy usage is not a simple matter of whether a given cognitive strategy is or is not available to and usable by the child depending on his stage of maturation. Instead, the use of a given cognitive strategy, it appears, has a complex interaction with the amount and structure of the content knowledge to which the strategy is to be applied. (75, p. 457)

This brings us to still another aspect of the content/strategy interaction. The use of a given cognitive strategy may depend not only on the amount and structure of the content knowledge but also on how well the thinker is able to retrieve that knowledge from memory when needed (74). Students may have the content knowledge needed to trigger thinking strategies in the sense that Chi (75) describes but may not be able to retrieve it spontaneously when it would help them to understand new information, i.e., the content knowledge may have been available in the thinker's memory but not accessible to interact with thinking strategies.

Thus, a thinker's content knowledge in a given domain will affect his/her ability to think and learn in that domain, but that knowledge must be available and be able to be activated or accessed. However, having knowledge in a domain does not guarantee that it will be accessed when needed (50, 51). In fact, a student may not recall content knowledge which would help him to think and learn in that domain. In discussing this problem of access, Bransford, Sherwood, Vye, and Reiser (50) refer to Alfred North Whitehead's (The Aims of Education, 1929) original description of this "inert knowledge" which may be accessed only in a limited, restricted set of conditions even though it is applicable to many more.

In fact, research has shown that both content knowledge and procedural knowledge within a domain, such as problem solving in math, often remain inert, even though they may aid learning of new information. Gick and Holyoak (147) have shown that transfer of knowledge of how to solve a particular problem to aid in the solution of a second, analogous problem is not always automatic. In addition, Brown, Campione and Day (58) have found that knowledge of particular learning strategies themselves, such as categorization and rehearsal, may often be inert. Finally, Perfetto, Bransford and Franks (291) found that subjects do not even use obvious cues to access information to solve problems that are closely related to each other.

We think of this as "transfer paralysis." The reason for this, according to Adams (1), is that knowledge of a particular procedure, i.e., problem solving, when taught within a specific domain, i.e., math, results in the generation of a specific domain-related schema for solving those problems. We have no reason to expect this schema to be spontaneously transferable to a new domain. We might consider this domain-specific schema as a kind of inert schema, not easily accessible in the Whitehead sense. Content is certainly needed for thinking to occur; it is the "medium of instruction" (1, p. 34). The difficulty is that "if the goal of the course is to teach thinking and, therefore, to maximize transfer, the materials or content through which the course is developed should reflect as diverse and broadly useful a set of problem domains as is possible" (p. 34).

There is still another dimension to the component of content and that is epistemic cognition, or "the skills associated with understanding the limits of knowing, as in particular subject matter, and the problems that thinkers can address" (314, pp. 47–48). Chambers refers to "the epistemological contexts in which all thinking occurs: the contexts provided by each form of knowledge and its disciplines" (71, p. 5). This implies that each content area has its own dimensions, rules, models and skills for thinking. We think it also implies, and Chambers concurs, that "we require . . . teachers . . . who understand the structure of their particular discipline and how it is different from that of other disciplines and who can pass on such awareness to their students" (pp. 5–6). Math instruction is a good example of this problem. Elementary teachers may not understand the discipline well enough to teach students to think in it. Poetry is another good example of this problem. Again, in a slightly different way, we see interrelations between content and thinking.

Issue: Are thinking skills and strategies generic and/or content-specific?

This state of interdependence between content and the skills and strategies of thinking raises a significant issue. Nickerson et al. suggest that "perhaps the single most controversial question regarding skilled thinking is this: To what extent is there such a thing as generally skilled thinking versus thinking that is skilled in various specific contexts?" (264, p. 57). The issue can be phrased several ways. Is there a body of thinking skills that is applicable to every content area or does each content area generate its own set of thinking skills? Other possibilities must be considered; perhaps it is not an either/or issue. Are there both a set of generic skills that apply to all content situations and a set of content particular skills for each area? Is there one set of generic skills with particular skills emphasized or useful in particular content areas? If content is influenced by society and culture, are skills also influenced by them, or are they distinct from the influence of society? These issues are of considerable importance to the theorist. In addition, as we will see, they are also of importance to the teacher charged with providing instruction in thinking. Let's consider some different views on this basic and critical issue.

Lowery, basing his scheme of thinking skills firmly on a biological foundation, concludes that there is a "sequence common to all cultures" (218, p. 77) and there are "content-free thinking capabilities (which overlay earlier capabilities containing content)" (p. 77). Helu bases his scheme on a philosophical foundation but arrives at a similar conclusion. "Thinking itself (in its essential character as a process) does not differ in any situation whatsoever" (165, p. 47). These are strong words which must, of necessity, stress generic thinking skills and capabilities that transcend content and culture. The implication here certainly is that we should offer instruction in thinking skills as a separate subject. In fact, in reviewing a number of the separate programs, Bransford, Arbitman-Smith, Stein and Vye conclude that "despite a lack of hard data, we feel that there are general skills that may be applicable to a wide variety of contexts" (49, p. 203). They caution, however, that programs must make provision for transfer of these general skills and strategies.

Not everyone agrees. Chipman and Segal consider the idea of generic skills as an "attractive one" (78, p. 14). However, they also point out that it is "an unproven idea. . . . A more likely hypothesis is that general skills must be built on the foundation of skills that have developed to an advanced state in at least one and probably more than one specific domain" (p. 14). Nickerson et al. also link skills to content, making a "distinction between general and specific skills" (264, p. 45), the general skills useful for "approaching cognitive tasks" (p. 45) and the specific skills useful in "particular types of problems" (p. 45). "The accumulating evidence that skilled thinking is often more context-bound than one might suppose cannot be ignored"

(p. 58). They recognize the existence of general thinking abilities but are pessimistic. "People can easily deceive themselves about the generality of skills exercised by instruction" (p. 58).

The same question regarding whether skills can be generalized has been raised about thinking strategies. Perkins, for example, cites some general cognitive strategies, such as "asking 'why not?'" (294, p. 354), problem finding, and evaluating and revising a product, that may be general strategies. However, their usefulness and effectiveness are so connected to the thinker's knowledge of content that "often novices do not have the resources in a particular domain to gain much from a very general strategy" (p. 355).

In a later article, Perkins and Salomon (301) discuss the context-free vs. context-bound issue. They make the distinction clear. Consider the wise leader of a small country under siege by a larger, much more powerful one. The leader realizes that his country needs to out-think rather than overpower the enemy. He has only one resource—the reigning world chess master. The leader thinks that if he uses this man's intellect, which is so sharp in chess, and teaches him politics and military theory, they might be able to outmaneuver the enemy.

This example, according to Perkins and Salomon, demonstrates the roles of general knowledge vs. context-bound knowledge in the thinking process. The domain-specific, context-bound believers would say the chess master only knows the moves of the chess game; why should we think that "chess strategy" will carry over into politics and the military? Those who believe some skills may be transferable to domains other than those in which they were learned might say that there are some analogies between chess strategies and those used in politics and war, control of the center, for example. Therefore, given enough political and military training, the chess master may be able to transfer some of his chess expertise to help his country. Those who view thinking skills as generic and context-free would say of course, the chess master has certain general problem solving abilities; he can plan ahead, explore alternatives, assess strategic options, as a politician or military leader would. He should do well in outmaneuvering the enemy.

Perkins and Salomon say none of the above is completely right. How well the chess master can transfer his chess skills, or more specifically, how bound to the game of chess his strategies are depends on several things. "Does he already have some general principles ('control the center-any center') rather than entirely contextualized principles ('control the middle squares of the chess board')?" (p. 24). Can he intentionally, metacognitively, abstract chess principles? Or is he a gifted seat-of-the-pants, intuitive chess player with little reflective, introspective ability?

These authors seem to suggest that general cognitive skills and domain-specific knowledge are interdependent. General skills are flexible and operate differently in each domain; they do not replace domain-specific knowledge. A certain amount of knowledge in a new domain is necessary to be able to apply a generic skill. The chess player can use his generic "cover the center" strategy, but first he needs to accumulate knowledge of politics and the military. They conclude that "the case for generalizable, context-independent skills and strategies that can be trained in one context and transferred to other domains has proven to be more a matter of wishful thinking than hard empirical evidence" (p. 19). However, they concede that "there are general cognitive skills; but they always function in contextualized ways" (p. 19).

Presseisen also links skills and content, in somewhat the same ways as Perkins and Salomon. She suggests, however, that "some complex thinking processes may be more relevant to certain subject areas than to other" (314, p. 45), linking, for example, problem solving in mathematics and science, and decision making in social studies. This distinction is important. She appears to hold that the skills are generic, simply more appropriate for one area than another. She adds to this idea in a later work. "The several thinking skills can then be developed in depth in the various contents, and subject interrelationships can be sought" (316, p. 41).

Transfer and Content

There is another aspect to this topic which we should consider. We have discussed the possibility that two of the components of thinking, the skills and strategies, may be specific to the content, and tied to the context in which they were learned. For example, a given thinker may understand how to solve problems in math, because he learned this thinking skill in math. But he may not spontaneously transfer this skill to solving social studies problems. Consider now the possibility that another one of our components, the content itself, may also be tied to the context in which it was learned. We all know the child who got one hundred on every spelling test but in real life can't spell those same words.

Brown, Collins and Duguid take this perspective on the way in which content knowledge is specific to a particular context and not spontaneously transferable to a new context. The authors focus on the nature of the content knowledge itself within a particular domain. They suggest that the thinker's prior content knowledge itself may be context-bound. They suggest further that school activities and content knowledge learned in school are confined to within the culture or context of the school itself and are limited to use within the "self-confirming" culture of the school. Consequently, the authors suggest "contrary to the aim of schooling, success within this culture often has little bearing on performance elsewhere" (61, p. 34). They have taken Adams' idea that the skills and strategies are content-bound and gone a step further.

In this same work, Brown et al. offer the example of learning vocabulary through dictionary exercises. Dictionaries are self-contained cultures, in and of themselves, and their definitions are irrelevant and impossible to understand without real world context. Instead of negotiating meaning, reasoning intuitively and resolving issues through everyday activity, students use dictionaries to acquire new concepts through precise, well-defined problems, formal definitions and symbolic manipulations of normal school activity. People who have acquired a knowledge base from real world experience approach comprehension and problem solving in a pragmatic, relevant, resourceful way that they could not do with a generic, abstract, "school-learned," domain-rigid sort of schema. Problem solving, the authors suggest, needs to be carried out in conjunction with the environment. This is distinct from the generic type of thinking which Adams suggests should precede thinking within a context. Rather the problem solver should use his or her environment, envision a physical situation, when possible.

Further, Sternberg and Martin (374), in a discussion of why certain approaches to thinking skills instruction may not work, also believe that this school-learned, generic knowledge may be inert. Students have knowledge of problem solving procedures, for example; they have been taught such, but their problem solving knowledge is inert, and inaccessible when needed because of the kinds of problems used to teach. They do not sufficiently resemble real-world everyday problems. They often are too well-structured, too simple, have one right answer. Thus, little or no transfer from the classroom to the real world is likely.

In fact, Brown et al. (61) suggest that schooling actually disregards and even discourages problem solving heuristics that students bring with them to the classroom from the real world. We think Whitehead would concur. He argued that the traditional education of the times—which some would say has changed little fundamentally through the last six decades—fostered that entrenched, inert, narrowly focused knowledge. That knowledge, according to Chi (75), is needed to interact with cognitive strategies to produce a good thinker.

Thus, if knowledge is "indexed" or marked by the situation in which it arises and is used and this contributes to the performance of subsequent tasks (61), it would follow that, rather than teach generic, context-free concepts, it is important to situate them in a real-world environment. Content knowledge, such as the learning of new words, needs to be embedded and implicit in the situation and culture in which it is likely to be used.

What can we do to facilitate access to content knowledge acquired in one domain and useful in another, for example, words learned through dictionary definitions which are useful in writing a story? Bransford et al. (50), in a review of studies on the facilitation of access, suggest that students need "conditional knowledge" about the content and procedures they are acquiring. That is they need to understand how their new content knowledge can help them acquire new content and procedures in the future. This kind of conditional knowledge, when learned along with new content, should result in a knowledge base in a particular domain that is organized in a way that is more easily generated in a variety of relevant conditions. Theorists (150, 356) have indicated that this conditional knowledge facilitates access by inducing relevant schema, and empirical studies have supported this notion (see 50).

Summary

There certainly is no definitive agreement on whether thinking skills and strategies are generic or whether certain ones are more important for particular content or whether in fact particular content requires particular skills. However, if we believe that spontaneous transfer of specific, generic thinking skills and strategies from domain to domain is the ultimate goal of thinking skills instruction, we need to evaluate the different approaches to instruction in terms of this goal.

Questions

Add the following questions to your list:

- Do we identify and instruct in generic thinking skills and strategies and/or in skills and strategies that are appropriate for each content area?
- Do we instruct in thinking skills in isolation or within content areas?
- How do we ensure transfer to all content areas and to real life situations?
- How do we teach content in such a way as to make it situation-free and transferable?
- How do we balance instruction in content and in thinking?

The Outcomes of Thinking

There is no firm and final consensus on exactly what the outcome or product of thinking is. However, as Baer points out, no matter how the product is defined, it's the product, not the process used, that ultimately provides "proof of good thinking" (11, p. 69). Let's consider the general kinds of products that are possible.

One important product of thinking is often identified as knowledge. However, the definition and scope of knowledge can vary widely. The product may be new knowledge for individuals (314) but it might also be knowledge that "is integrated with previous experience, forming an ever-increasing knowledge base" (353, p. 20). In addition, the knowledge that is the product of thinking may be "something more than and different from what we started with" (159, p. 6). Halpern, in outlining this view of knowledge, quotes Bruner's phrase concerning "going beyond the information given" (159, p. 6). Knowledge thus becomes not only the accumulation of other people's knowledge but also the development of new, unique, different thoughts, ideas, concepts and their representations. The representations can take an infinite number of forms from a written product, an invention, an advertising campaign, a lifestyle.

There is another view of the product of thinking. This view does not stress the identifiable outcome such as the accumulation of knowledge or the generation of an idea or a concept. Rather, this view of the product of thinking examines the traits of the thinking individual and suggests that the purpose or outcome of thinking is, as Sternberg states, to "enable us to acquire knowledge and to reason with it, regardless of the time or place of the kinds of knowledge to which [the skills are] applied" (322, p. 53). This notion of the development of an independent, competent, purposeful thinker able to function effectively in future, unknown situations is emerging as a powerful purpose for instruction in thinking. Thinking is viewed as a way of guiding human behavior. This product has enormous long range implications.

What, then, are the qualities of good thinkers? Costa (95, pp. 66–68) identifies the behaviors of intelligence and categorizes them according to their function in taking in information, deriving meaning from information, communicating, applying and evaluating meaning and monitoring behavior. What emerges from these behaviors is the description of an individual, competent in basic and complex thinking skills, who is independent, goal-oriented, self-regulating and self-monitoring, as well as flexible.

Glatthorn and Baron take a different approach but end up with a similar view of the good thinker. They group behavior according to three thinking processes: "the search for goals, the search for possibilities, and the search for evidence" (152, p. 50). The good thinker is conscious of his acts, critical and reflective in his approach and confident that thinking is a productive activity. Although the categories of thinking skills differ, the end result is remarkably similar. These qualities of independence, competence, and self-regulation appear repeatedly in the literature (78) as qualities of good thinkers. However, in addition, there may be more involved here—a sense of curiosity, a belief that it is important to learn, a sense of pride in learning (260). Many of the qualities of a good thinker come under the category of dispositions, a willingness to think, to risk, to incorporate criticism.

One major educational implication leaps out at us from these descriptions of the product of thinking as both the development of knowledge in its broadest definition and as the development of independent thinkers. We must design instructional strategies and curriculum that enable the student to assume responsibility for his learning and development. Different writers in the field express it differently, but this theme appears repeatedly. To use a familiar educational term, the locus of control must pass from the teacher to the student.

A second, equally important, educational implication is that the student must not only think but must learn to regulate and monitor his thinking. We must emphasize the skills, content and strategies of thinking as a major focus of the educational process. In addition, the current views of the product of thinking reinforce the notion of metacognition as a thinking skill and strongly suggest that the student become aware of the process of thinking and strategies for monitoring success and coping with breakdowns.

An Emerging Definition

At this point what do we think thinking is? We would describe it as the orchestration of skills, strategies and content knowledge, in a planful way, to enable the thinker to generate his own new product.

This book is concerned with all these aspects of thinking as well as with how we can design instructional programs to enable thinking and to encourage its development.

PART B
Thinking in Schools

IV

The "Thinking" Classroom

Our concern with promoting the goal of thinking must be firmly anchored in educational settings. First, we will consider the characteristics of a "thinking" classroom and then examine a series of decisions that need to be made.

The "Thinking" Classroom: A Description

A classroom that promotes thinking must reflect the characteristics and components of thinking. Clearly, they are all interrelated. Now, let's examine the characteristics of a "thinking" classroom.

Thinking: The Goal of Learning

Students must realize that the goal of learning is thinking (91, 363). If the materials used are read, memorized and given back to the teacher, the student gets the message that this process is the focus and end result of education. Unfortunately, this message has been given to countless students. One of the critical questions in developing a program for teaching thinking skills that must be addressed is "Are intelligent behaviors valued as a goal of education?" (91, p. 211).

This implies there will be an emphasis on such activities as the development of materials, on the training of teachers, on the valuing of thinking rather than covering materials and passing tests. Without a commitment of time, effort and funds the message received by students and by the community is that while we may say that we want students to be critical, creative thinkers we really want them to finish the workpages (neatly and with no spelling errors!). As a critical element of this total commitment, students must see adults engaging in the process of thinking, modeling intelligent behavior, and acting on it (91, 363).

Students Actively Involved

Probably one of the most widely cited characteristics of the "thinking" classroom is the active involvement of the student in the process of learning and of thinking. Teachers "can help, but we cannot do it all" (354, p. 55). The learner must construct learning and meaning, not be the recipient of the learning (183, 221, 340).

This may be evident in a variety of ways. The classroom ambiance will foster inquiry, encourage other interpretations, and emphasize asking questions not just answering them. Unfortunately, this is not always the case. Frequently "seatwork is the principal activity" (377, p. 75) and instruction is often dominated by teacher talk, not student talk (152, 353).

Risk Taking Encouraged

The social climate of the classroom is one where risk taking rather than conformity is encouraged (90, 340, 377). To phrase it slightly differently, the "teacher's role is to help keep conditions safe from testing" (354, p. 61). Failure can be accepted. The environment encourages uncertainty. It may be uncertainty for the student as he explores and, certainly of equal importance, uncertainty for the teacher. Joyce points out that the student may "develop solutions we have not thought of. We have to expect this and learn to love the uncertainty it creates for us" (186, p. 7).

Thinking: A Group and Individual Process

The thinking classroom views learning as a group experience with commonly accepted goals. Respect for the opinions of others is essential as is an attitude of curiosity. Within this setting, however, students also need personal attention from the teacher and opportunities to develop an individual sense of competence and to feel pride in their thinking (260, 340).

The "Thinking" Classroom: Why Not?

If these are characteristics of a thinking classroom why don't we see this kind of environment in every classroom? Raths, Wassermann, Jonas, and Rothstein (325) offer some possibilities. Teachers haven't been trained to think effectively themselves. Testing in schools encourages recall of information not thinking about information. Thinking on the part of students may encourage them to raise questions about schools, suggest alternatives, and, in fact, question the authority of those in charge. In addition, teachers haven't been trained to teach thinking skills and strategies. In 1989 there were only ten states that mandated instruction in thinking; only six of those states required training for the teachers (154). Finally, Nickerson points to "the practical reality of today's classrooms and the noneducation responsibilities imposed on teachers as factors that militate against classroom environments that are conducive to the promotion of either thinking or thoughtfulness among students" (263, p. 40).

The "Thinking" Classroom: The Decision Making Process

> The choice of how best to teach thinking faces the educational community and the public. Nothing is more basic or deserving of prompt attention and resolution. (353, p. 21)

In discussing preschool programming to develop thinking, Sigel and Saunders suggest that "five types of decisions . . . have to be made in creating or selecting a conceptual model" (354, p. 41). The decisions relate to the familiar questions: what, where, when, how, and who. The question Why teach thinking? has already been explored. We will examine the remaining questions now. The basic questions posed by Sigel and Saunders are very useful for focusing and organizing our thoughts, but we will elaborate on them in order to examine all aspects of the problem for a wider population.

Curriculum

- What should be the focus of the thinking curriculum?
- Where in the overall school curriculum should instruction in thinking take place?

Instructional Goals

- What should we teach in order to foster effective thinking?

Instructional Methodology

- How should we teach in order to promote and develop thinking effectively?

Materials

- What materials should we use in instruction?

Timing and Duration of Instruction

- When and for how long should instruction in thinking take place?

Evaluation

- How should we evaluate students in order to promote and facilitate thinking?
- How should we evaluate programs for effectiveness?

Participants

- Who should be involved in instruction and what is the instructor's role in a thinking program?
- How will teachers be trained for program implementation?
- Who else should be involved in thinking programs?
- Who should receive instruction in thinking?

During our investigation of those areas requiring decisions, we have found and will discuss many specific examples of ways that the questions have been addressed and implemented in practice. The variety here is impressive. There are, of course, numerous examples of prepackaged programs that stand alone or are incorporated into the school curriculum. There are programs that have been instituted as part of content area classrooms, such as social studies, science and mathematics, areas we have traditionally considered ripe for thinking skills. In addition, there are many examples available from the fields of reading and writing instruction, areas traditionally considered "basic skills."

There is a substantial and growing view that while these two areas of instruction, reading and writing, certainly include basic skills, they also include the development and use of thinking (267, 416). As early as 1917, Thorndike noted the strong link between reading comprehension and thinking, in his famous article "Reading as Reasoning." As recently as 1990, Cole concluded that "reading itself has come to be viewed as a higher order skill involving use of personal knowledge to construct meaning from text, use of monitoring and self-correcting strategies, and use of schema or patterns to guide reading" (81, p. 4). Pearson and Raphael (289), also in 1990, link reading comprehension and thinking, citing many examples of overlapping skills and strategies. Levin (204) spells it out for us. Cognitive strategies for reading comprehension such as activating prior knowledge through advanced organizers or analogies, skimming, asking questions, mapping and networking, paraphrasing, imaging, notetaking, reviewing, and summarizing enable a thinker to identify and relate information and ideas and are powerful tools to develop and promote high level thinking.

In a similar fashion, writing is viewed as a thinking process and as a process requiring thinking (42, 170, 173, 223). We find the same prethinking, using prior knowledge, constructing meaning, monitoring and self-correcting, using schema to guide the process and the product. We can apply many of the same words to writing as we can to thinking: recursive, active, strategy driven, generic and content-specific skills. Applebee (7) suggests several connections between the process of writing and thinking. For example, planning to write can be the generation of new ideas, the formulation of new connections with old ideas and prior knowledge. Reviewing and revising may involve attention to the consistency of an argument and even change its meaning. The active nature of the writing process itself compels the thinker to be aware of the quality of his/her understanding, to detect deficiencies or inconsistencies in that understanding and to attempt to clarify them. "As a process of thinking, writing is unparalleled. It leads us through the maze of our thoughts, helps us to organize our knowledge, and proclaims our feelings" (244, p. 37). For these reasons, much of the research and many of the applications of thinking theory can be found in the areas of reading and writing.

In considering how to deal with the components of thinking and make instruction effective in schools, two thoughts become obvious fairly quickly: first, the components are interrelated and decisions cannot be made regarding one component independent of decisions on others; and second, the decisions made will reflect a particular view of thinking.

Let's examine each area requiring a decision. We will consider curriculum and instructional goals as components in choosing a program, leaving instruction, materials, timing, evaluation, and personnel for consideration under implementing a program. First, we will examine some guidelines for choosing a program in order to provide a framework for reviewing these components.

Guidelines for Choosing a Program

Let's consider the guidelines that some researchers have proposed. Sternberg (367) suggests that a program chosen should:

- be theory based
- be socioculturally relevant
- provide training in both executive (monitoring) and nonexecutive (skills needed to get the task done) skills
- be responsive to the motivational and intellectual needs of students
- allow for individual differences in students
- link training and real world situations
- include an evaluation component
- only make modest claims for future success.

Glade and Citron (149) suggest that a program chosen should:

- be taught to teachers relatively quickly
- have materials easily available
- balance content and processes
- be integrated into current courses
- have demonstrated evidence of effectiveness

Chance (72) suggests that schools look at any program to be adopted in terms of: assumptions, goals, methods, materials, audience, teacher qualifications, benefits, problems, and evaluation available on the program.

These three lists are representative of the areas of concern, cautions and guidelines expressed by those in the field even though not everyone agrees on the content of the areas. The lists are useful because they all address a number of similar areas, areas which we have also highlighted in our review. One area needs to be particularly emphasized here. If a school is to adopt an existing program, the effectiveness of the program must be examined. Unfortunately, this is also an area in which we have a great deal to learn. As Brainin asserts, we are faced with "an embarrassment of riches in choices of materials and methodology, but only the beginnings of research concerning them" (45, p. 140). This problem is compounded when a school elects to develop its own program. There may well be no research base available.

Finally, in choosing and implementing a program, Nickerson et al. remind us that:

> On balance, the results of research most directly related to thinking . . . are supportive of the view that the teaching of thinking is a legitimate and reasonable educational objective. The literature does not provide clear and incontrovertible prescriptions regarding how the teaching should be done. (264, p. 142)

―――――――――――――― **V** ――――――――――――――
Choosing a Program:
The Curriculum

The question of "what" to include in curriculum generally and what instructional goals we should have in particular is certainly basic to the development and adoption of any program. Let's examine a series of questions.

The Focus of the Curriculum

What should be the focus of the thinking curriculum?

The literature suggests that there can be three approaches to the development of a thinking curriculum. We can teach for thinking, of thinking, and about thinking (48, 93, 231). Let's look at each of these approaches and at some examples of them.

Teaching for Thinking

Teaching for thinking provides opportunities to develop language and cognition using teacher directed instructional strategies such as questions, discussion and cooperative learning (93, 231). These are teaching strategies that teachers who value thinking have been using for years. The aim in this approach is to engage students in thinking about content. The thinking is a tool for interacting with content.

There are a number of concerns about relying solely on this approach to teach thinking. One potential problem with this approach is that students may not realize that they are engaged in thinking, that the goal of learning is thinking, and that they will eventually be able to do this without the presence and the aid of the teacher. Further, a difficulty with this approach is that teachers tend to equate teacher questioning with student thinking. Depending on the questions and on the classroom atmosphere, that may or may not be true. This approach does not teach the process of thinking (231); it allows for the practice of thinking. We certainly need to encourage practice but only if students have been taught what to practice.

Teaching of Thinking

Teaching of thinking provides this kind of instructional situation. Those who advocate teaching of thinking generally advocate the teaching of particular thinking skills and processes. This can be done by direct instruction or it can be done by the inquiry method (231), but in either case the student concludes the instruction by learning that there are skills and strategies that will help him be a more efficient and effective thinker.

Examples of teaching of thinking abound. We could certainly include a wide range of programs here.

- Instrumental Enrichment teaches individual microlevel skills in isolation using content-free materials. (167, 208, 220, 226, 343, 393)

- CoRT aims at enabling individuals to make better use of their innate intelligence through direct instruction in critical thinking tools which can be applied in various content areas as well as real life. (106, 107, 108, 109, 115, 226, 237)

- Beyer advocates including both micro and macrolevel skills using direct teaching of thinking. Students are told what skill they are going to learn; they learn it; they practice it; they master it; they apply it. He also suggests using indirect instruction when the students are able and the task is appropriate. (36, 38)

- Philosophy For Children uses an inquiry approach and stresses critical thinking. While discussing novels specifically designed around philosophical issues, students examine issues and develop reasoning abilities. Lipman stresses that "whether or not the children who do these things know the names of the skills they employ is relatively unimportant; what matters is that thinking becomes something they enjoy doing and do well" (212, p. 213). (67, 111, 180, 211, 212, 213, 226, 328, 393)

In these programs the materials used and the teaching strategies employed differ, but the aim in all of them is to teach students thinking skills and strategies.

Teaching about Thinking

Teaching about thinking involves teaching students to be aware of their own thinking processes, to select and use appropriate skills and strategies, and to monitor success and failure in academic and real life situations. Teaching about thinking can include both metacognition and epistemic cognition (93, p. 21). Programs including metacognitive components are more common than those dealing with epistemic cognition.

The variety of programs stressing metacognition in one way or another is wide, ranging from Talents Unlimited (16, 343, 345) and Tactics in Thinking (9, 192, 222) to CoRT. The way the curriculum is developed varies considerably. Consider two different approaches. The program may introduce the subject of metacognition directly and teach procedures directly. Strategic Reasoning (149) focuses on six fundamental (basic or micro) level skills in both academic areas and real life. Students use specifically developed materials to explore and practice the skills. In all areas "the teacher outlines metacognitive strategies needed to use the skills effectively" (149, p. 198). In another approach, Analytic Reasoning (339, 406) uses a strategy to develop metacognitive awareness also advocated by McTighe

(231). The think-aloud procedure enables pairs of students to examine and support the thinking process being used to solve a problem. Here we see two approaches, one where the teacher outlines the metacognitive procedure, the other where the students work it through themselves. Both aim at developing metacognitive strategies.

Epistemic cognition, while not as common, is sometimes included. Tactics, for example, includes instruction in content area thinking skills along with learning-to-learn and reasoning skills (9). Philosophy for Children encourages the comparison of the processes and thinking strategies used by artists, scholars and scientists (93). Again, different approaches have similar aims.

In summary, we can see that in practice there is little consensus here. However, in making decisions about whether to teach for, of, or about thinking, we need to keep in mind the emerging conclusions about the effectiveness of strategy instruction: the importance of recognizing and understanding how the strategy can be helpful (263); and the significance of a student's metacognitive knowledge about his own use of strategies (12, 144, 319). Findings such as these must make us examine further before settling for teaching for thinking.

The Placement of Thinking Instruction

Where in the overall school curriculum should instruction in thinking take place?

It will come as no surprise to find that theorists and educators draw on their theoretical background to develop educational plans concerning where to place thinking instruction. Should we provide separate instruction in thinking and then deal with the question of transfer to content areas? Should we provide instruction within the content areas with the aim of insuring transfer and application? In addition to being one of the major, immediate issues facing schools, Grice and

Jones (154) suggest that this issue provides us with a useful way to categorize programs.

Let's consider common approaches to this issue.

Separate Instruction on Friday Afternoon

Bereiter (28) identifies two approaches that are widely used and which he says are not effective. One of these is to offer instruction as an enrichment activity on Friday afternoon to everyone or only to students identified as gifted or talented. Although this has certainly been widely used in the past, few professionals seriously propose this approach now in light of other effective alternatives.

Separate Instruction on a Sustained Basis

A second approach which Bereiter, for one, also considers ineffective is to offer instruction as a separate subject matter apart from content and to stress only thinking skills. This is a common approach with schools often "importing various thinking skills programs from the commercial market, usually as self-contained adjunct courses" (183, p. 6).

However, not all agree that this second approach has to be ineffective. One important advantage to this approach is that separate courses allow for instruction by the most "adept" (11, p. 70) teachers. Transfer will be accomplished by "infusion" into content areas by regular classroom teachers. This approach may also be useful for particular populations. For example, Jones et al. modify a strong support for integration of thinking instruction into content instruction and "support adjunct skills instruction with a strong content emphasis and much effort to make application to the content areas, but only for younger and low-achieving students" (184, p. 17).

The critical issue with separate instruction, of course, is transfer to other situations. Adams (1) reviews self-contained macrolevel programs which have demonstrated varying degrees of success at transferability. She suggests that, to maximize transfer, a thinking skills course should result in a single, well-integrated schema, centered on the thinking skills which it was intended to develop, and then be richly elaborated on with real world content. For example, she notes that CoRT and Productive Thinking show little evidence of transfer, while Philosophy for Children has demonstrated significant gains in reading comprehension and logical thinking, because, according to Adams, it fosters a single, contextually rich, well-integrated "thinking" schema. The concerns about the transfer of skills and strategies acquired and polished in separate programs is echoed by many in the field. Resnick (329) reviewed programs and concluded that there was a serious lack of transfer in many of them. However, Delclos, Bransford and Haywood (110), in reviewing the separate program Instrumental Enrichment, conclude that if the program is combined and integrated with content curriculum, it should transfer. In fact, they highlight the problem of transfer. Separate programs need to allow for the resolution of this issue.

Self-contained separate programs have taken a variety of forms and have focused on a variety of thinking skills. However, one element that many of them have in common is that the basic instruction and materials are developed by others and provided to the teacher. In addition, many of them have tried, in some fashion, to cope with the problem of transfer to content classrooms or real life situations.

Let's look at some examples.

- Philosophy for Children (211, 212, 213) teaches critical thinking through a series of especially developed novels dealing with philosophical issues.

- *Building Thinking Skills*, a series of books, also teaches critical thinking but through practice in related microskills using hierarchical paper and pencil tasks (13). After completion of the tasks, class discussion facilitates transfer.

- Future Problem Solving (101, 102) also uses a series of books, but these books present a practice problem about a world issue which teams of students solve. Transfer of skills and strategies is developed through solving real community problems.

• *Think About* (60) uses a series of television programs which present real life problems drawn from various content areas and provides direct instruction in problem solving. Follow up classroom strategies are suggested in order to help students make the transfer to other situations.

Any program which focuses on thinking as the central topic is undoubtedly making clear to the students that thinking is the goal of instruction. Students are very aware that the reason they are in a program designed to teach thinking is to engage in thinking. However, the program must also make explicit the need to transfer the thinking skills to all learning.

Instruction Integrated into the Content Areas

A third approach that is widely accepted, in theory at least, is the integration of thinking skills into the total curriculum and the various content areas. According to its advocates, this approach addresses two major concerns: thinking skills are content-specific and thinking skills may in fact be context-bound. There is certainly a body of opinion that suggests the total integration approach is the most effective way to insure competence and spontaneous transfer. The integration approach is needed since transfer across domains is not automatic (99, 163) and thinking skills will not be maintained without the sustained practice available in the content areas (337).

Let's look at what some of the experts in the field say.

• McTighe and Cutlip: "Thinking is fundamental to all subjects and therefore should be addressed as part of every subject" (232, p. 186).

• Glatthorn and Baron: We should "teach thinking in all subjects, wherever appropriate. Evidence suggests that such multidisciplinary approaches are more effective than single courses in thinking" (152, p. 52). They recognize that there may be differences in application in different content areas, but a multidisciplinary approach allows for both the development of a general model of generic skills (Adams' single thinking schema) and specific applications.

- Bereiter: Bereiter agrees with this notion and goes even further saying that "the promotion of thinking skills should be deeply embedded in the whole fabric of an instructional program" (28, p. 77). He holds that thinking skills should "permeate the instructional program" (p. 75) and must be integrated into already accepted educational objectives, "making already recognized instructional objectives contingent on activities that also promote thinking skills" (p. 76).

- Joyce: Joyce cites Bereiter and concurs, adding that "to teach the basic subjects without teaching thinking simultaneously not only neglects thinking, but is inefficient. Students learn more traditional substance when mastery is generated by models that also produce intellectual growth" (186, p. 6).

- Beyer: Beyer reviews the research and suggests that "skills taught in isolation from subject matter are not likely to transfer easily to other situations where they can be used productively" (31, p. 559). Thus, he advocates teaching skills across all appropriate content areas. Appropriate, for Beyer, means appropriate to the level of cognitive development of the child and to the demands of the subject areas in each grade level.

What does this mean in practice? It certainly suggests the need for broad curriculum revisions as well as inservice and preservice teacher training programs to integrate thinking into the curriculum (377). Curriculum revisions require that teachers be able to identify and teach the content-specific skills needed for their discipline. In fact, they may be the best ones to do this. It is not surprising to note that programs developed by school personnel frequently take this form. The Irvine Thinking Project (383) and the Inclusion Process (422) are two examples of programs developed by school personnel who have identified what needs to be included, revised curriculum to include it, and then taught the program within the regular classrooms using academic materials. The Inclusion Process uses two kinds of lessons: focus lessons for introducing, defining, and demonstrating each skill; application lessons in which the skill is applied in a content area (424).

If thinking instruction is to be integrated into the classroom it suggests that teachers need to be thoroughly trained. For example, Talents Unlimited (16, 343, 345) is designed to develop critical and creative thinking in elementary and secondary students. Over 20,000 teachers in 1,500 schools in 49 states have been trained to use this program which requires thorough staff development to integrate the target talents into the regular academic areas. The need for thorough training in integrated programs is consistently cited, whether it is for training in teaching strategies such as asking questions (Irvine Thinking Project) or in potential problem areas such as how to transfer skills to academic content (Tactics for Thinking).

In addition to integrating thinking into academic content areas, Sternberg (367) also integrates thinking and content by linking training in thinking to "real-world behavior." He cites the difficulty of transfer of these skills, going beyond linking the teaching of thinking to content areas and suggesting linking thinking to the demands of real-world tasks and to the behaviors expected in real-life situations. He provides the example of using newspapers, historical texts, scientific texts as the teaching materials. Sigel and Saunders (354), in discussing preschool education, make a similar suggestion. They advocate using a thinking approach in all aspects of the preschool program, not limiting it to the cognitive areas but also including social and physical areas.

A number of the programs that have been developed have taken the issue of transfer seriously and have been concerned with insuring transfer to real life situations. Some programs, such as Think About, use real life problems as the content of the program. Future Problem Solving uses world problems as the content and includes follow up with student-identified real problems. Both academic and real life materials and problems are used in the Inclusion Process and Connections (243) to promote this link.

Finally, in considering this form of program implementation, consider Chambers' comment that "we need good teachers who can make children think in the *particular discipline the teacher is teaching*" (71, p. 6). The highlighting is Chambers'. We would also highlight the phrase "good teachers."

Separate and Integrated Instruction

The problem may not be as simple as these three alternatives suggest, however. Consider the position taken by Adams (1). She advocates generic, content-free instruction, followed by concrete, context-full application, at least for microlevel skills. Basing her argument in schema theory, she suggests that we shouldn't teach thinking skills within a content area, because we can't abstract a single integrated thinking schema. Schemas which are not interrelated in experience, like skills taught in context, will not be interrelated in memory. Teaching thinking skills within a particular context inhibits their transfer from one schema to another. Thinking skills taught in a particular content, such as math or science, can only be accessible in the content. Students will develop a thinking skill accessible within a certain topic, rather than a general thinking schema. However, Adams suggests, a course which develops a schema about thinking with one "thinking schema" as a result, with explicit teaching and use of analogies, will enable students to access generic skills which were taught in another domain.

Adams cites the first part of the Odyssey program, which she helped to develop, as well as other microlevel programs. These are abstract, generic, content-free programs, using dot matrices, figures, lines and the like for content. Since this approach teaches thinking skills in the abstract, content is conceptually neutral and therefore should be transferable from domain to domain. However, Adams notes that skills taught generically don't always transfer readily, and so she suggests including practice using materials in diverse domains. Students need concrete experiences to abstract from.

Adams discusses two microprograms which have varying success at transfer. Intuitive Math and Think, developed for remedial grades 4 and up, are generic microprograms which include materials in various content areas for practice and transfer. Adams notes the impressive results which these programs have produced. Instrumental Enrichment (IE) is supposed to be a generic, content-free program. However, in order to train for transfer, after each generic exercise students practice using "bridging" examples from content areas. Adams suggests that, since the students must rely on their own life experiences for bridging examples, the "transfer training" aspects of the IE program may not be as systematic or comprehensive as they should be. She notes the poor results in transfer to general school achievement for the program.

It may be that in order for transfer to occur students need direct instruction and application. Perkins and Salomon take a "synthesis position" between generic skills and domain-specific knowledge. They advocate a separate course, mixing direct instruction in general thinking skills and in content knowledge. They note that "most efforts to cultivate general cognitive skills have not focused on bringing together context-specific knowledge with general strategic knowledge. Rather, they have taken the form of courses or minicourses segregated from the conventional subject matters and make little effort to link up to subject matter or to nonacademic applications" (301, p. 23). They suggest that this "intermingling of generality and context-specificity in instruction" (p. 24) is the most promising approach. "It gets beyond educating memories to educating minds, which is what education should be about" (p. 24).

There are variations on this theme.

- The Higher Order Thinking Skills program (306, 307, 308, 309) develops thinking through teacher questioning and discussion of simple problems presented on computers, in team competitions or through drama. Students work through and discuss the problems. Then, application is made in content area classrooms.

- Ruggiero (337) suggests that, at least for college students, the most desirable situation is to have separate courses in thinking with specific thinking objectives in the various content areas.

- A program developed by secondary school teachers in a district in Arkansas (39) provides separate instruction in thinking with trained content area teachers providing applications in their classrooms.

- Still another variation is offered by Learning to Learn (163). High school students can take the program as a separate year-long credit course. As part of the course requirements, the students are required to adapt the skills and strategies to content courses being taken concurrently. Here, the emphasis is on integration but on integration performed by the student not the content teacher. Interestingly, this program also offers as an alternative incorporating the Learning To Learn skills directly into the content classroom by the content area teacher.

The question of where instruction will be provided is closely linked to all the other issues we will consider. A decision cannot be made here without considering implications for instructional goals, instructional methodology, evaluation, and personnel.

Choosing a Program:
Instructional Goals

*What should we teach in order to foster the develop-
ment of independent, motivated, effective thinkers?*

This is certainly a matter of vital concern. The general
framework offered by Sternberg (371) should be useful here. We
need to make the same caveat offered by Sternberg that, while
theorists and researchers differ in the list and names of
processes discussed, they are frequently talking about similar
concepts. This lack of consensus is widespread in the field but
seems particularly difficult here.

Sternberg suggests that we conceptualize thinking in terms
of three processes: nonexecutive performance, nonexecutive
learning processes and executive processes.

- *Nonexecutive performance processes* include the skills of
  thinking.

- *Nonexecutive learning processes* are defined by Sternberg as
  learning strategies and are similar to the cognitive strategies
  of organizing and elaborating information identified by
  Weinstein and Underwood (405).

- *Executive processes* are the metacognitive processes of
  monitoring and directing attention which Weinstein and
  Underwood (405) include as metacognitive strategies in
  their list of strategies.

In addition, we will begin with an area which some feel is
basic, that of content knowledge.

Content Knowledge

The notion that we need to think about something is widely accepted. Therefore, it follows that we need to teach content. For example, in order to develop and analyze concepts in social studies, students need to have a background of facts and events. This notion is cited for all areas and for all ages (222, 260). The concern here is that gaining knowledge of content is not necessarily teaching thinking but may, in fact, be practicing thinking (231). There is, of course, even the possibility that teachers will teach content knowledge in such a way as to encourage rote learning and discourage thinking.

In addition, students need to know how the information in a specific area is organized and how it is processed (316, 317). In order to insure that this kind of learning takes place, teachers need to analyze the curricular requirements and the way material is presented in text and other sources (71, 377) as well as understand and teach how information is organized within a particular field. Perhaps even more critical, teachers need to decide what is important for students to learn in the content areas (357).

In order to learn and think about content, appropriate prior knowledge is critical. "A major difference between experts and novices is in both the amount and the organization of prior knowledge" (403, p. 591). We will discuss the organization of knowledge later. These comments address the issue of having appropriate prior knowledge, but as we have already discussed, availability is one thing, accessibility is another. The fact that a learner has knowledge doesn't mean that he can access it or use and apply it in a wider context. In fact, accessing may depend on the representation and quality of organization of knowledge (147, 291).

One of the critical areas teachers need to address is helping students access their prior knowledge with teacher help and with increasing independence. There are some specific techniques that have been developed to meet this need.

- *K-W-L or What I Know, What do I Want to Learn, What I did Learn.* This technique was developed as a three step process which could be used independently to access prior knowledge, identify areas of concern and interest and organize and relate new information to prior knowledge (69, 174, 268). As part of the group process of initial brainstorming, students also identify possible categories of information. The teacher models the active thinking required when reading for information, encouraging students to take a more active approach to reading and learning. Through practice and the use of graphic organizers students become independent in their use of this strategy.

- *PReP or Pre-Reading Plan.* This technique was developed and researched by Langer as a diagnostic/instructional activity for teachers (200). The three step procedure includes: brainstorming by students to identify initial associations with a concept, reflecting on those associations, and, based on the discussion, reformulating and adding to the initial responses.

It appears that the key is not just to teach content but also to link thinking and content. Consider the alternatives provided by programs aimed at thinking instruction. A few programs,, such as Tactics, advocate linking thinking and content information by direct instruction in content area thinking skills. Others, such as Analytic Reasoning or CoRT, link thinking and content by using academic content as the material for instruction in a separate thinking program. The Odyssey Program (l) also links content and thinking using another alternative. This approach provides direct instruction in thinking skills, using content materials and includes "domain-specific challenges" and extensions. Finally, programs such as Talents Unlimited or Guided Design (254) teach thinking skills in the content classroom, thus promoting the link between thinking and content. Talents Unlimited, for example, has been

implemented on the elementary level (16) and on the secondary
level (345).

In addition, many of the writers in this field provide
examples of lessons and units which link thinking and content
in all grade levels (36, 184, 191, 269, 337). This is the kind of
approach that teachers who are well grounded in their field are
likely to adopt. It is a potential advantage for instructing in
thinking shills within the content classroom. The link can be
made strong.

Skills: Nonexecutive Performance Processes

Sternberg's performance skills encompass the micro and
macrolevel skills identified by Presseisen and others. Teaching
micro and macrolevel skills, according to McTighe and
Schollenberger (234), is the teaching of thinking. It is also one
way to categorize thinking programs, according to Adams (1).
The problem for us is not whether to teach these; the problem
centers on whether we should teach both levels and whether
they are hierarchical or nonhierarchical (183, 222, 260, 367).

Issue: *What is the impact on instruction and
curriculum development of teaching micro
and/or macrolevel skills and of a hierarchical
or nonhierarchical view of thinking skills?*

Two aspects of this issue are closely related: should we
teach micro and/or macro level skills and should we teach them
in a hierarchical or holistic fashion?

The notion that skills are hierarchical in nature, as we have
seen, is certainly supported by theorists in the field. This view
suggests the need for discrete, sequential skill instruction. One
example demonstrating the link between theorist and
practitioner will illustrate this approach. Beyer (30, 31, 34, 36)
advocates separate skill instruction beginning with the basic
skills. Complex skills should not "be introduced in detail before

subordinate skills have been mastered" (31, p. 559). His suggestions are quite specific. A limited number of skills need to be introduced sequentially at each grade level. Teachers should begin with basic, discrete skills in the early grades and add simplified versions of analysis, synthesis and problem solving in intermediate grades. Additional analytic skills and simple decision making can be introduced in middle and junior high school with metacognitive training and critical thinking in grades 8 through high school. Presseisen's level of epistemology would only be possible for teachers like us! Jackson illustrates, with a detailed description and lesson plan, a practical application of Beyer's views. She suggests that teachers "select a skill, identify its main attributes, introduce it at a time in the curriculum when the skill is needed and therefore meaningful, develop guided and independent practice lessons, and intersperse these practices throughout the year" (176, p. 33).

Costa generally concurs, stating that since "levels of thinking are cumulative" (91, p. 216) students must have adequate preparation at the input and data accumulation level before moving into higher levels of thinking. Presseisen also asserts (316) that skills are hierarchical and we must teach discrete skills. This approach yields a curriculum in which, at each grade level, the student engages in activities at one level of complexity, extending his capabilities but not requiring or, in some cases, even encouraging him to move to a higher level of thinking.

Those who view the development and acquisition of thinking from a maturational perspective suggest similar education implications. We must teach different skills and different skill groupings as children develop cognitively and linguistically. At each stage, Lowery proposes the need for "a horizontal curriculum... in which students are challenged to use a particular stage of thinking with different materials at various levels of abstraction without the progressive requirement of having to be at a more and more advanced developmental stage" (218, p. 77). Presseisen stresses students' need to "develop competence in the essential skills" (314, p. 45) in the elementary years and then receive instruction in the more complex thinking processes.

In practice we find some programs which advocate instruction essentially in microlevel skills such as Instrumental Enrichment. In addition, Adams (l) cites several "micro-programs" which generally use abstract, content-free materials, such as dot matrices or geometric figures, and focus on such generic, isolated skills as observation, classification, and sequencing. Microprograms which she reviews include Instrumental Enrichment, Intuitive Math and Think. Nickerson has also reviewed similar programs focusing on micro or, as he labels them, basic skills. He found some evidence that these programs could "improve one's performance on certain IQ tests" (263, p. 12), but cautions us strongly that "increased scores, by themselves, do not justify the conclusion that whatever improvements have been realized are not limited to test-taking performance but will generalize to other contexts" (p. 13).

There are other approaches which have been taken using micro skills as the focus for a program. BASICS (264, 349) provides teachers with model lessons in 18 basic thinking/learning strategies which are to be incorporated into content area lessons. This program, with its emphasis on transfer to content areas, recognizes the difficulty found in other microprograms. However, Nickerson et al. (264) found little research evidence to support or refute its effectiveness in making this transfer.

Another way of developing a hierarchical curriculum which includes both micro and macro level skills is illustrated by the Odyssey program (1, 425). Using a series of lessons, students move from foundations of reasoning and understanding language to verbal reasoning, problem solving, decision making and inventive thinking. The Strategic Reasoning Program also includes micro and macro level skills, with students beginning with fundamental thinking skills, using nonacademic material, moving to using the "fundamental thinking skills as a tool for communication, learning, reasoning, and problem solving" (149, p. 199) with academic materials. Next, students learn to transfer and apply all skills to academic areas and finally to real life situations. In this last example, the hierarchy involves not only the skills but also the tasks and materials.

Consider, in contrast, Marzano's view that "any hierarchy or list of thinking skills is by definition invalid" (221, pp. 6–7). Others (264, 353) agree, suggesting that the skills are not hierarchical and can be used independently or together, depending on the thinker and on the situation. However, some skills, such as reasoning, creative thinking and problem solving, are more complex than other skills.

This nonhierarchical view of thinking skills can be translated into practice as suggested by Sadler and Whimbey. They propose that "trying to break thinking skills into discrete units may be helpful for diagnostic purposes, but it does not seem to be the right way to move in the teaching of such skills" (340, p. 200). They advocate using a holistic approach. Jones (183) concurs, warning us against skill-driven learning in which skills are isolated and are ends in themselves.

A number of programs have been developed that view thinking skills instruction holistically. Analytic Reasoning, developed by Whimbey and Lochhead (410) for high school and college students, is certainly one. Philosophy for Children for elementary and secondary students is another program that takes the same perspective. In both of these, skills and strategies are not taught through direct instruction but rather through student inquiry, using questioning and discussion.

Macrolevel programs may have as their major focus one or more of the macro level skills, with many combinations possible. Future Problem Solving certainly focuses on problem solving but also includes critical and creative thinking. Creative Problem Solving (283) emphasizes both creative thinking and problem solving, while including critical thinking. Talents Unlimited emphasizes both critical and creative thinking.

Tactics for Thinking includes reasoning, content and learning-to-learn skills. Guided Design focuses on decision making but considers critical and creative thinking as integral parts of the process.

Remember the notion advanced by Jones et al. (184) that whether skills are hierarchical or not may be related to the specific content areas? In mathematics discrete skills are taught in a sequential manner. In reading instruction, skills may be taught holistically but the content changes in terms of its complexity and the variety of topics included. The implication here is that we must examine the content area specifically and then determine whether skills will be taught sequentially or holistically.

The question of the organization and relation of thinking skills is raised by those concerned with an overall view of thinking but is certainly not definitively answered. Commonly, we find programs that include instruction in both micro and macrolevel skills. An immediate concern for those planning the scope and sequence of a school curriculum including both micro and macrolevel skills is whether skills should be presented in a hierarchical manner, with one following sequentially from the last beginning with the microlevel and moving to the macrolevel, or whether the approach should be a holistic one, with the more complex skills introduced from the beginning and with the basic or microlevel skills taught as needed. Schools need to make some very basic decisions about what to teach at the various grade levels.

Strategies: Nonexecutive Learning Processes

These are the learning strategies identified by Sternberg and are certainly related to the four levels of strategies identified by Weinstein and Underwood: cognitive, active, support and metacognitive. We will include the first three here, saving metacognitive for Sternberg's executive processes. First, let's examine instruction in the cognitive strategy of organizing information, the active strategies of self-questioning and summarizing, and the support strategies of valuing and reflecting during thinking. Then we will examine the most effective ways to teach strategies so that, after training in the strategy is finished, thinkers may use the strategies automatically, appropriately, and independently as well as know how to transfer the strategies to new information (260, 294).

Cognitive Strategies: Organizing Information

Visual representations of information and concepts enable the thinker to organize information in such a way as to relate new information to new information, relate prior information to new, and reorganize both into a new framework. Teaching students ways to use and develop these visual representations, or graphic organizers, when they learn and study has been found to be particularly effective.

For example, graphic organizers may be used at the beginning of, during, and/or at the end of the act of thinking. They can give a thinker an "advanced organizer," or focus, a means of organizing, integrating and summarizing information and ideas (184). Graphic organizers may be developed from the structure of the text and from information and concepts within the text. The critical element here is linking concepts within and between sources and new information to prior knowledge. Kinds of graphic organizers usually used include semantic webs, maps, chains, charts, and semantic feature grids (179, 184, 223, 239, 312). "These are powerful pedagogical tools because they allow students to visualize concepts and the hierarchical relationships between them" (312, p. 11).

Numerous specific examples can be found illustrating this strategy. For example:

- *Organizing information for decision making.* McTighe and Lyman (233) propose the use of a decision-making model with boxes and spaces for identifying the problem, goal(s), alternatives, pros and cons, decision(s) and reasons.

- *Problem solving in social studies.* Jones et al. (184) provide specifics on transferring a problem solving, graphic organizer to the problems of Jackson's presidency.

   Organizing information for a mathematics concept. Gallo (137) reinforces the importance of graphic organizers and provides several examples in thinking about the metric system in mathematics.

- *Thinking about literature.* Yeager (426) uses Sanders' Taxonomy of Critical Thinking as the basis for developing organizers in the field of literature. She provides many specific examples.

- *Constructing a graphic tower to visual inductive thinking.* Clark, Raths, and Gilbert (79) demonstrate how the process of constructing a graphic tower, moving from the concrete to the theoretical, enables students to view their own thinking and manipulate and reorganize information to reach generalizations.

- *Organizing for critical thinking and problem solving in home economics.* Watts (399) uses a grid to help students identify characteristics of fabric and categorize fabric samples in order to determine fabric construction.

- *Organizing for problem solving and writing.* Olsen (271) views the writing process as a way to develop thinking skills across content areas. She suggests that writing develops thinking by providing enough guided practice so that students "internalize a workable problem-solving process" (p. 107). She offers several lessons which illustrate the stages of composition, moving the students through all levels of thinking. The stages include prewriting, precomposing, writing, sharing, revising, editing, evaluation, and extension activities.

- *Organizing information in terms of story grammar.* McTighe and Lyman (233) advocate developing a flow chart to construct a story map.

- *Organizing information for further study.* Carr and Ogle have taken K-W-L one step further and added Plus. The plus is a mapping activity after the three parts of the organizer have been filled in. The map requires the student to "organize and relate text information for further study" (69, p. 628).

- *Organizing in content areas.* Organizing information is a critical part of content area thinking programs. For example, Learning to Learn provides direct instruction in organizing in general and in organizing subject-specific information (163). Content area teachers can be trained in this approach and/or use content-specific manuals to help students make the transfer from the general to the specific.

How do we teach students to construct these graphic organizers? Not surprisingly, the act of construction requires organizing and thinking about information. In reading, construction is frequently connected to what students already know about the topic and the text structure which is used in any reading or would be used by the student in writing (185, 238, 239). The structure is, in fact, determined by the nature of the information (179). For example, in learning about different kinds of animal homes, a comparison and contrast chart springs to mind. In the process of constructing the organizer, students look for relationships, missing information, categories of information, etc. All of this takes time. The process is not learned quickly or applied quickly.

The unifying theme in all these sources is that the teacher must be adept at understanding the particular content and providing either instruction, general guidance or explicit examples of appropriate organizers.

Active Study Strategies: Self-Questioning and Summarizing

> If teachers really wanted to teach students how to engage in
> thinking, rather than ask questions of the students, they
> would teach students how to ask their own questions. (36, p.
> 154)

We know that it is critical for students to ask their own
questions. The problem is how do teachers enable and
encourage students to do this? Wong's (419) review of research
in student generated questions found that students could be
trained to ask questions for three purposes. She also established
two constraints that made the development of self-generated
questions difficult. All purposes were effective if certain
conditions were met. First, think about the purposes, then the
constraints, and finally the conditions.

The three purposes for questions relate to strategy areas of
concern to us. Student generated questions can help relate new
information to prior knowledge. Wong suggests the use of
questions relating to text structure as a way of invoking this
purpose. Second, to develop active processing of text and of
information, students can be taught to ask "questions that
shape, focus, and guide their thinking" (p. 228). These are
generally higher-order questions. Third, students can be taught
to generate questions that develop metacognitive awareness
and control. To develop these, students learn to generate
questions that direct their attention to particular parts of the
problem or the text. For example, in problem solving, the
questions might include: Have we identified the problem? What
are three possible alternative solutions? Other questions will be
discussed under the topic of problem solving. In reading
comprehension, a question might be: What is the main idea of
this paragraph? To monitor their effectiveness, students can ask
such questions as "Is there anything in this paragraph I don't
understand" (p. 231). We can see that these purposes for self-
generated questions relate to several of the strategies we have

discussed and highlight the characteristics of the thinking individual.

In addition to the purposes for self-generated questions, Wong also investigated the constraints which would hinder the development of self-questioning strategies. The two constraints identified by Wong's review of the research literature certainly make sense. First, she examines the effect of the lack of prior knowledge of content on student-generated questions and concludes "that to ask a question, you must have an optimal amount of prior knowledge for the particular subject at hand" (p. 240). This seems to strengthen the notion that content knowledge or domain-specific knowledge is critical for thinking and provides another rationale for insuring some kind of link between content instruction and thinking. Second, Wong establishes that with [...] metacognitive "awareness of the functional importa[nce of the questions ... and] of task demands" (p. 240) stu[dents will genera]te and use their own questions. This const[raint seems to suggest that stu]dents need opportunities to see [for themselves how questions] will help them and they need to [know why they are engaged in] a thinking task and what is inv[olved. This second finding i]s certainly supported by research [on effectiveness of strategy trai]ning.

Finally, Wong identifies the three conditions critical to effective self-questioning instruction no matter what the theoretical perspective of the researcher or the purpose for generating questions. Students needed sufficient training to achieve a criterion level; they needed to receive direct instruction on the part of the teacher or explicit written instruction in how to generate questions; and they needed sufficient time in order to process the information and generate relevant questions.

Bean (23) reviewed a number of studies in this area and cautions that if instruction is to be effective, students need substantial and direct teacher guidance, particularly in the area of transferring self-questioning strategies.

Approaches taken in teaching students to generate questions range from highly structured to seemingly unstructured. A continuum of approaches includes:

- *PAAR.* This highly structured strategy requires that students develop) questions through planning, answering, assessing and reviewing (36). Detailed guidance is provided in learning to work through these steps. Students engage in group brainstorming, using graphic organizers as part of the question-generating activity.

- *Relating verbs to levels of questions.* Hoezel (168) suggests using Bloom's Taxonomy of Educational Objectives as a basis for another approach. She provides a list of specific verbs related to the different levels of the taxonomy to use to generate questions.

- *The Thinking Matrix.* McTighe and Lyman illustrate the use of a Thinking Matrix in which the vertical axis contains types of thinking and the horizontal axis contains "points of departure for inquiry, which vary according to the subject area" (233, p. 19). They provide the example in language arts where using the intersection of character and cause/effect might suggest to the student the relevance of a question on the cause and effect of the hero's death.

- *Using questions that access cognitive and support strategies.* The Cognitive Learning Strategies Project (404) includes student questions relating to such strategies as organizing information (How could I represent this in a diagram?) and activating prior knowledge (What does this remind me of?).

- *Modeling the use of questions in reading and writing.* Hudson-Ross (172) advocates teacher modeling of questions while reading a passage, followed by student application, first in reading and then in writing text.

- *Story grammar and text structure questions.* Another approach is to develop questions based on story grammar

(358) and/or based on the structure of knowledge in a particular content area (252). Questions can build connections within the text and between the text and the student's prior knowledge.

- *Dialogue prompted questions.* Others rely more on the development of student-generated questions in the course of dialogue between teacher and students and among students. K-W-L and Reciprocal Teaching both provide opportunities for student-generated questions. K-W-L gives the student three specific generic areas in which to identify information and ask questions. Reciprocal Teaching, which will be discussed in detail later in this book, explicitly teaches questioning, as part of developing metacognitive strategies. "The teacher's response to students' questions can reinforce for students the value of their questions and can be used to turn questions into dialogue (354). Students may be motivated to develop their own questions if they know they will be directing them toward other students, not just toward the teacher (337).

There are a number of programs that include student-generated questions as a part of the curriculum. Sadler developed a program very similar to Analytic Reasoning in which he emphasized the importance of student-generated questions because "the questioning process is basic to intelligent understanding" (339, p. 185). The goal in this program is to develop analytic and problem solving abilities and apply them to content areas. In fact, the questions formed a critical feature of the program. Heiman (163) in developing the Learning to Learn Program identified self-generated questions as one of the hallmarks of effective thinkers. Students are specifically taught to predict questions and answers.

Finally, we have to take seriously the comment by Hudson-Ross (172) that student-generated questions empower students. This certainly gets to the heart of the matter.

Another study strategy that makes students active thinkers is summarizing. This strategy enables students to focus attention on the main ideas and to select the important information in a text. By reorganizing information and writing about it, students process the information in a greatly elaborated way, helping them to actively construct meaning from text. Anderson and Hidi (5) suggest that two types of thinking are needed to summarize a piece of text. Students must select information which should be included or rejected in a summary. The student must then reduce ideas by substituting general ones for more detailed, lower level ones. Several factors influence this selection/reduction process. The length, complexity and type of text is important. Shorter, simpler narrative text appears to be easiest to summarize. In addition, the presence of the text while summarizing eliminates the possibility that some information is omitted because it was forgotten rather than because it was judged to be unimportant. Finally, whether the summarizer is writing for himself, to understand the text better, or for the benefit of another reader, affects the length, content and form of the summary.

Researchers have also explored how summarizing can be taught. Anderson and Hidi (5) make some recommendations regarding summarization instruction: 1) choose a short, easy text with familiar concepts to begin summary writing instruction; 2) let students see the text while summarizing, to make the task easier; 3) teach students to look for clues to help them identify information of importance to the author; 4) teach students to write summaries for their own study purposes first, as a first step to writing more formal summaries for other readers; and finally, 5) teach students to write finished, polished summaries for other readers, emphasizing appropriateness of length, knowledge of material, mechanics and consideration of audience.

In addition, these authors suggest that the strategies involved in writing a good summary develop with age. They also indicate that there are three trends in instruction in summarizing: teaching a set of summarizing rules to be applied to texts, using summarization to monitor and ensure comprehension, and teaching content with summarization techniques to ensure that content is understood. Let's look at examples of each.

- *Teaching summarization rules.* It may be possible to identify what strategies an expert uses to generate a good summary and then teach these strategies directly (53). For example, Brown and Day (59) developed a list of summarization rules based on the theoretical work of Kintsch and van Dijk (1978) and were able to predict the order of difficulty experienced by students using these rules. The rules, in order of difficulty, are: a) delete trivia; b) delete redundancies; c) substitute a superordinate for a list of actions; d) select a topic sentence if one is available; and e) invent a topic sentence if none is available.

  Hare and Borchardt (160) took Brown and Day's summarization rules and added their own summarization rule, combine or eliminate paragraphs, and a rewrite, or "polish the summary," rule. They were able to teach high school students to use these rules, to remember them over time and to transfer them to closely related summarization tasks.

  In addition, Winograd (415) investigated the rules students thought they were supposed to use to summarize a piece of text and found that most students knew that they had to find the most important ideas in the text. He also found that good readers were more sensitive to important information in the text than poor readers and that they were able to convey more ideas without using more words.

  GRASP (Guided Reading And Summarizing Procedure) is an instructional procedure developed by Hayes (161) which provides a step by step demonstration of summarizing. The teacher leads students through the steps of summary writing and then demonstrates how to use the strategy independently. The teacher first explains the reasons for learning how to summarize, then guides students as they read to remember specific information, identify major topics and reorganize the information in a useable way, and finally, the teacher demonstrates how to convert the reorganized information into a summary. Hayes suggests that the procedure is an effective one because it makes the summarization process clear and facilitates independent use as well as sharpening recall, self-correction and organizational skills.

We know what steps a student needs to go through to generate a good summary. We know that direct instruction in the use of these rules may be an effective way to teach students to generate good summaries (332). While research may support these results they have not always found their way into schools. Garner (138) investigated twelve K–12 teachers and found that little direct instruction in rules for summarization is actually given.

• *Using Summaries to Monitor and Ensure Comprehension.* Summarizing is one of the four strategies used in Reciprocal Teaching (277) an instructional strategy which fosters interaction between teacher and student, and among students. In addition to summarizing, Reciprocal Teaching uses self-questioning, clarifying and predicting strategies to facilitate comprehension as well as comprehension monitoring.

Annis (6) also found that having students generate their own summaries at the end of each paragraph read aided their basic understanding of the text. It helped the students to focus attention and to encode the material in a personally meaningful way by using their own words.

• *Teaching content with summarizing techniques to ensure that content is understood.* Graphic organizers, charts and matrices serve as summaries of text content which may aid comprehension. In addition, Roller (334) suggests teaching students to be aware of and to use the structure of a passage to guide construction of summaries to aid comprehension. She asks questions such as: does a text use a general or specific organization, or does it compare and contrast? Are there text aids that identify its structure, such as headings, objectives, text-provided summaries, or, we would add, key words? Students can use these features of the text to develop summaries, and thus improve comprehension.

Support Strategies

The attitude a student has toward thinking and his approach toward the task is becoming an increasingly important and recognized aspect of instruction in thinking (262), one in which the teacher as model is critical. Teachers can promote this by fostering such qualities as curiosity, pride, respect for the opinion of others (38, 66, 260). "The teacher who finds the world an incredibly interesting place is far more likely to produce inquisitive, information-seeking students than one who does not" (260, p. 24). These suggestions, while certainly admirable and difficult to quarrel with, seem somewhat fuzzy. Here the teacher as model is a positive but somewhat general figure.

However, the teacher as model can also be more specific. Some researchers have attempted to identify specific educational methods for developing support strategies using the teacher as a model. For example, the development of a reflective approach, rather than an impulsive approach toward thinking tasks has been cited as a positive goal for teaching (263). Verbal self-instruction in how to be deliberate and reflective in particular tasks has been found to be effective in increasing time spent in solving problems and increasing "accuracy of performance" (263, p. 23). This positive self-talk may also aid in promoting positive attitudes toward thinking and appropriate attentiveness to the task. This self-instruction technique is developed through "the use of cognitive models and scaffolding for teaching self-instruction, in which a teacher initially demonstrates the process by using self-instruction to direct his own performance and then uses similar instruction to guide the child's performance, and gradually the child takes over the teacher's role and instructs himself" (263, p. 23). Reciprocal Teaching is a good example of cognitive modeling, scaffolding and learning to self-instruct.

The concern for including support strategies in thinking programs is evident in a number of the published programs. Odyssey (1) specifically focuses on instilling and reinforcing attitudes of learning and thinking. Analytic Reasoning (406) does not teach one process for solving problems; rather it stresses attitudes, such as persistence in analyzing and remaining accurately involved, patience, and avoidance of wild guessing. The Institute for Curriculum and Instruction (ICI) has developed a model which focuses on the desired behavioral characteristics students may display when they take "intelligent, ethical action" (349, p. 7) when they complete their schooling and uses these characteristics as the focus for the curriculum. The content of the various academic disciplines is the vehicle for helping students achieve these goals.

Metacognitive Strategies: Executive Processes

By its very nature metacognition must be linked to something. Metacognitive strategies have been taught as part of thinking programs, as part of a content area or as part of skill instruction. Let's look at some of the links teachers have used.

Metacognitive and Specific Thinking Tasks

One way to teach metacognition is to link the strategies to particular thinking tasks such as comprehension. For example, Bondy (43) links metacognition and comprehension by having children keep daily logs to direct their attention to their own learning processes. Teachers also model thinking and learning tasks. In addition, Bondy advocates facilitating comprehension through adequate feedback instruction in self-questioning, summarizing, and rating of comprehension. Notice how while she is linking metacognition and comprehension, certainly a logical link, she is using cognitive strategies to accomplish it.

Metacognition and Macroskills

Problem solving includes a range of processes such as problem identification, solution monitoring, the use of feedback, and the translation of information into action. They are those "skills used in actually carrying out task performance" (367, p. 9). These same skills can also be built into a metacognitive strategy. They can form the basis for a heuristic that can be used to monitor success or failure in the process of problem solving.

The Inclusion Process (422) links metacognition to problem solving and critical and creative thinking as well as instruction in content area thinking. Here the link is complex and forms a network for the thinker in a number of areas of thinking.

Metacognition and Cognitive Strategies

Still another approach links metacognitive strategies with cognitive strategies (197). Remember Haller, Child and Walberg (157)? Remember Nickerson (262)? They cite the effectiveness of linking instruction in metacognitive strategies to cognitive strategies. Reciprocal Teaching (277), Informed Strategies for Learning (ISL) (280), and K-W-L (69, 268) teach students how cognitive and metacognitive strategies work. While linking cognitive and metacognitive strategies they also focus on comprehension. The task to be accomplished is a critical part of metacognition. You are doing something, using some set of cognitive strategies and monitoring success, failure or breakdowns.

Teachers of Reciprocal Teaching explicitly teach nonexecutive and executive strategies such as questioning, predicting, summarizing (active study strategies) and clarifying (a support strategy). They also teach where, when and why to use the strategies (metacognitive, executive strategies). For example, they teach students how prior knowledge can help them to understand new information, how to activate prior knowledge when learning something new as well as when and why they should do so as they read and learn. Teachers also motivate students to activate the strategies, to use them when appropriate and to be aware of their effectiveness.

A closer examination of one of these procedures may help clarify how the link can be promoted. Reciprocal Teaching consists of a dialogue between teacher and students and among students, with the teacher participating as both a leader and a group member. It involves direct instruction by the teacher with gradual transfer to the learner. Initially the teacher does most of the work, modeling all the strategies, while the students respond and elaborate on the teacher's questions, clarifications, summaries and predictions. Gradually the students are given the opportunity to assume more and more responsibility for learning. The teacher first serves as model, encouraging students to reflect on the process. Eventually, as the students take over, the teacher serves as a coach and facilitator, and the students regulate their own comprehension.

The program is a heuristic in the sense that it provides a specific set of steps to take which are generalizable over a variety of content areas. Through modeling and immediate feedback, it also provides training in executive, control strategies and allows students to reflect on their strategies. Reciprocal Teaching has proven to be durable over a period of time and transferable to a variety of learning contexts (277, 278, 329). It also promotes independence by systematic and gradual transfer of responsibility for learning from the teacher to the student.

Informed Strategies for Learning (ISL) (280) also encourages students to take an active role in their learning by a series of lessons and dialogues, using metaphors, to inform students about strategies: which ones they are using, how and when to use them, and why they are useful for learning. Knowledge of strategies and motivation to use them provide a combination of knowledge, skills and attitudes to encourage thinking and learning.

Other programs have also been designed to link metacognitive and cognitive strategies. K-W-L is one example. Another, somewhat similar approach is "What I Know" which also combines text comprehension and cognitive and metacognitive strategies (164). Using a graphic organizer similar to K-W-L, students and teacher together fill in two columns which are headed What I know and What I now know. The third column is headed What I don't know and is completed by identifying facts and concepts that are confusing or where knowledge is incomplete. The initial role of the teacher is to model the process, with students gradually assuming more responsibility. The form and the procedure provide a metacognitive framework for students to organize information, identify and activate prior knowledge and monitor difficulties in comprehension.

Metacognition, Academic Tasks, and Cognitive Strategies

These areas are all closely connected. In reviewing good programs to promote strategy awareness and use in reading, Brown, Armbruster and Baker (56) discuss programs which have been proven in the classroom as well as in the lab. These authors suggest that the best programs enable students to coordinate, and ultimately control four variables: 1) the text, i.e., sensitivity to text difficulty, important information, contextual constraints and text structure; 2) the tasks and purposes of reading, i. e., to understand, to skim or to study;

3) the strategies they must use, i. e., compensatory strategies, study strategies; and 4) their own characteristics as learners, i.e., ability, motivation and other affective states that influence learning. Good strategy training programs should include training in the strategies themselves, information about the significance of the strategies and training in monitoring and regulating the strategies. They should be reliable, durable, enable transfer across settings and tasks, be instructionally feasible, demonstrate a clear improvement on the target task and show independent evidence of a process change which can be attributed directly to the specific effects of training, rather than to other reasons, such as increased motivation. Two successful training programs that meet all criteria are Reciprocal Teaching (277), a laboratory to classroom process, and ISL (280), a curricular development approach.

An interesting example of an approach which combines academic tasks, cognitive strategies and metacognition is provided by Wade and Reynolds (394). They give students a Strategy Definition Sheet, listing strategies used when studying, expository text. Students use the sheet to identify the strategies they use, as well as when and how they are used. A record sheet listing the same strategies provides students with a way of monitoring actual use.

Programs designed to develop metacognition have demonstrated success with middle school children (268, 277) and with children as young as third grade (280). This fact leads us to conclude that we need to rethink Beyer's suggestion to wait until high school to train higher level thinking skills such as metacognition.

Issue: *How do we train the strategies and promote transfer?*

We have two concerns with teaching strategies: how to help students learn a strategy and how to promote transfer of the strategy. First, a number of approaches have been developed to teach students strategies including providing instruction in a series of steps to be taken, reasons for using the strategy, and specific circumstances for use as well as providing detailed explanations, modeling, and feedback for effective strategy use. Let's look at each of these and then examine strategy transfer.

Traditionally much emphasis in strategy instruction has been placed on teaching students algorithms or heuristics. An algorithm is a set of specific procedures or steps that are suitable for one particular situation. Unfortunately, they are of limited usefulness because of the narrow approach taken (403). An algorithm only applies to one situation. An additional difficulty is that the student has to match the algorithm to the appropriate situation.

A heuristic is a general approach that is designed to fit more situations. A strategy heuristic is developed from an analysis of the thinking task which breaks the task into general steps that the learner can perform readily. Instruction focuses on teaching what particular steps to take and when to take them. One of the earliest and most popular heuristics is "How to Solve It" developed by Polya in 1957 for problem solving (264). Other heuristics, or general purpose strategies (263, 264), have been developed since then which aim to give students specific, generic steps to thinking and solving problems in a variety of content areas, including for example, Patterns of Problem Solving, a college level mathematics course (264).

The difficulty with heuristics is that they may not be perfect for all tasks since in order to be generalizable they must be vague enough and broad enough to cover all situations. Thus, they are sometimes labeled "weak methods" (263, p. 18). However, they are valuable as they remind the thinker of possible steps to take and may be particularly helpful for complex tasks which require a lot of structure and therefore lend themselves to a heuristic analysis. Many programs to teach heuristics have been found to be effective in the performance of the heuristic itself and several have successfully been transferred to other contexts (264). The key here seems to be that if a heuristic is to be effective, students must have experience with it in a variety of contexts. Again, we see the link between thinking and content.

In addition to providing students with some kind of script or list of questions that will guide them through the strategy, Levin suggests that effective strategy instruction should specify how and why a given strategy works in terms of cognitive processing principles. Levin provides two examples here. "Concrete organizers facilitate students' comprehension of unfamiliar complex concepts through connections made with familiar ones" (204, p. 11). "Mnemonic techniques facilitate students' memory for specific information through the provision of both encoding elaborations and direct retrieval paths" (p. 11).

It also appears useful to teach students the circumstances in which they would use particular strategies. There have been a number of theorists and researchers, for example, who have developed sets of cognitive strategies that are useful for reading. Levin (204) will provide us with one example. The cognitive strategies of activating prior knowledge through advance organizers or analogies, skimming, asking questions, mapping and networking, paraphrasing, imaging, note taking, reviewing, and summarizing enable a thinker to identify and relate information and ideas and are powerful tools to develop and promote high level thinking.

Finally, in order to insure effective strategy training, teachers, according to Nickerson, must provide "detailed explanations of the strategies and of the conditions under which they should be used, modeling of the strategies, and feedback to students about their own use of them appear to produce more lasting effects than more perfunctory explanations of the strategies" (263, p. 18). Information about the effectiveness of strategies and specific feedback in concrete situations also have positive effects on strategy acquisition and use.

Not only must students be taught to think, but they must also be able and motivated to use their competencies and strategies in new situations. Two examples will illustrate this. The Productive Thinking Program is a self-instructional program using a series of student workbooks which "provides heuristics for generating and evaluating ideas and for embedding them in an overall organized approach.... the program concerns itself not only with producing ideas but with assessing them as well" (264, p. 210). The lessons provide examples of, experience with, and strategies for effective problem solving. Nickerson et al. reviewed the history of research on the effectiveness of this program. and concluded that while performance on problems similar to the training problems might be enhanced, "for problems and tasks of a markedly different character, there is no compelling evidence that the Productive Thinking Program helps" (264, p. 212). The findings on the effectiveness of the CoRT Program are similar. A series of heuristics in the form of questions are taught to students in a series of isolated lessons. These authors concluded that evaluation studies tended to support the finding that students performed well in similar situations, but not in dissimilar ones.

This problem of transfer of strategies to new situations, according to Adams, is the most vexing of all problems associated with thinking instruction. She too found little evidence of transfer to different thinking tasks as a result of the Productive Thinking, or CoRT programs. She did, however, find evidence of transfer for students completing Philosophy for Children. The transfer came on standardized achievement tests, particularly reading comprehension. She suggests that one possible reason for this might be that the reading materials used produce "a single, contextually rich, but thematically integrated and logically well-articulated schema" (1, p. 37). In other words, the materials provide a context in which, through a variety of situations and concrete experiences, students call abstract processes and strategies and practice transferring them to new situations.

Various programs have addressed the issue of transfer in a variety of ways. Connections advocates teaching a skill or strategy directly and then applying it to a particular situation or piece of text in order to make the connection between thinking and academic and real life situations. Other programs, such as Tactics, address the issue of transfer to content areas by including this issue in the teacher training program. More examples of how different programs address the problem of transfer will be discussed when we consider where to place these programs in the overall school curriculum. That question just by its very nature include consideration of transfer.

Issue: What do we emphasize in instruction?

> Perhaps no one will be so indiscriminate as to call thinking skills instruction a frill, but it is often treated as one, just one more burden on an already heavily loaded curriculum, one more competitor with the things teachers are held accountable for. Consequently, no matter how readily teachers agree that more should be done to promote thinking skills, it is reasonable to predict that thinking skills instruction will tend to be passed over by more standard activities directed toward the three R's and subject-matter instruction. (28, p. 75)

Is this the reality of instruction in thinking? The array of items to include in instruction certainly raises a difficult question for teachers, principals, and curriculum developers. Where do we put the emphasis? Teachers are concerned with "covering" the curriculum. This often suggests a specified number of workbooks, stories, problems over a specified period of time (221). This issue is addressed by many in the field. For example:

- Bellanca: Teachers must spend more time helping students apply new skills and less time covering material (26).

- Staab: We can't judge teachers on the basis of how much material they have covered (363).

The way the problem is solved reflects the underlying theory of thinking advocated by the theorist. For example, de Bono (108) advocates separate thinking instruction but acknowledges that because of time constraint it might be necessary to include the program as part of a curriculum area, while Joyce (186) stresses that we cannot teach thinking separate from content. But no one who is seriously concerned with the issue of thinking will settle for "covering" content without teaching thinking skills and strategies in some fashion (45).

> We know that people do not necessarily become good thinkers as a consequence of completing conventional subject matter courses. (263, p. 43)

This is not negotiable.

VII

Implementing a Program:
Instruction, Materials, and Duration

Instructional Methodology

How should we teach to promote and develop thinking effectively?

In examining instructional procedures there are two levels which teachers must consider. We will only examine the second level in depth. On one level we find the basic management requirements needed to keep the classroom an environment in which learning can occur and in which the teacher demonstrates an understanding of planning, learning theory, and leadership abilities (26, 184). Marzano et al. after citing the importance of these managerial or executive skills conclude that "certainly these roles are vital, but we need to go beyond them to explore what teachers do to help students learn" (223, p. 134).

On another level, we find the teacher focusing on ways to make thinking happen in the class. Our concern here is with this level, the instructional strategies the teacher can use to directly enable and encourage thinking.

It would be convenient and certainly reassuring if we could provide one model for instruction, one way for teachers to go about insuring that students will learn to think or at least improve and use the thinking abilities they already have. We can't. In fact, the existence of more than one strategy may be an advantage. The various strategies may be used in combination, "not only to pyramid their effects but to address the different kinds of objectives and thinking that we want to engender" (183, p. 6). This notion is echoed by Strong, Silver and Hanson (378) who also tie the choice of the teaching strategy to particular learning objectives. For example, they suggest that command and demonstration are useful for the mastery of basic skills, while inquiry promotes concept formulation and critical thinking. We will examine two basic instructional models and a number of teaching strategies.

Instructional Models

Direct Instruction

Direct instruction of thinking skills and strategies has received considerable support (11, 31, 34, 36, 37, 44, 73, 150, 152, 183, 184, 231, 281, 316, 424). Beyer is adamant on this topic, stating that for students "the most crucial ingredient is direct instruction in the nature of specific thinking skills and how to use them" (29, p. 44). This view may follow from Beyer's notion of thinking skills as hierarchical with each requiring individual instruction. However, consider the view of someone with a different theoretical perspective. Jones et al. also advocate using direct instruction while at the same time stating that isolating and teaching skills hierarchically may "fractionate learning in instances where holistic understanding is desirable" (184, p. 17). Direct instruction can be done within a context, providing modeling and coaching for students with an increasing role tor the student. Whether you view thinking skills as hierarchical or nonhierarchical, you can advocate the use of direct instruction.

Direct instruction includes explicit instruction in the skill or strategy emphasizing why, when, where and how to use it. The model generally used includes an introduction, explanation, demonstration, application, guided and independent practice, reflection and transfer. Modeling by the teacher is a critical element in this form of instruction (31, 34, 36, 37, 176, 221, 222) particularly with novices (159, 184). The direct instruction model, by making students "consciously aware of *what* they are doing, and of *how* they do it" (31, p. 558) insures that all students will be reached and that learning about thinking and thinking itself will occur in all content classrooms.

Numerous examples can be found of direct instruction of thinking skills and strategies (36, 37, 73, 176, 184, 316). It also forms the basis of instruction for a substantial number of programs ranging from instruction in microskills in the Instrumental Enrichment program to instruction in the macroskills of problem solving and critical thinking in the Connections program.

Indirect Instruction/Inquiry Learning

The other end of this instructional continuum is the indirect model of instruction using inquiry learning. This approach requires that the students identify "procedures, rules, or criteria" (36, p. 89). They are not presented to the students. Ruggiero (337) provides a description of the inquiry method in which examples are presented first and students discover the conclusions or principles. This is in contrast to direct instruction in which students are given the conclusions or principles and a series of examples which document what they are to learn. Teachers who may have tried both models will not be surprised to find Bellanca (26) stating that good inquiry teaching is more difficult than direct instruction. The teacher not only fosters a sense of uncertainty (152) but must also be able to tolerate uncertainty. The student becomes the constructor of knowledge through active involvement and interaction with other students (353). Teachers with a preplanned agenda know how unnerving it can be to let students loose! Who's in charge anyway?

What is required on the part of student and teacher for inquiry learning to happen? Nessel, Jones and Dixon (255) cite four features of inquiry learning. First, students must select a topic for study. The topic may be completely generated by the student or may be from a list suggested by the teacher. Second, students need to pose questions relevant to the topic. Here we see an important role for student generated questions. Then students look for the answers to their own questions, either from text or from a variety of sources. Here, we can see the relevance of organizing information. Finally, students need to share their answers and conclusions. Before they can share, they need to monitor their performance. Strategies for thinking become an integral part of inquiry learning.

Perhaps one of the keys to inquiry learning, is the role of the teacher.

> Facilitating students' discovery of mathematical concepts requires far more than a laissez-faire approach in which the teacher does little other than stay out of the way. Rather, this difficult and demanding form of teaching requires teachers to examine the cognitive structure of the concepts to be taught and then to create series of experiences that will offer students the opportunity to explore the domain and discover these concepts. (357, p. 41)

Here we see the teacher as one who is competent in the content of instruction, is aware of the structure of the discipline and is familiar with the materials and experiences useful to the student. Here is another facet to the link between thinking and content. It is particularly interesting to note the importance of this epistemological level of cognition to teachers as well as to students.

Again, specific suggestions abound in the literature, from a very detailed analysis of a thinking lesson for middle school students using content area material (36) to extended projects for early elementary age children (191). Problems presented in the form of dialogues or situations as well as case studies are particularly conducive to this kind of instruction (337). Graphic organizers have been suggested as a way of helping students manipulate and reorganize information during the process of inquiry learning (79). Mathematics and science instruction can also lend itself to this kind of learning (82). According to Simon (357) students need opportunities to discover mathematical concepts. Thinking programs have been developed based on an inquiry approach to instruction, such as Philosophy for Children and HOTS (Higher Order Thinking Skills).

An Alternative

It may not be a question of whether to use direct instruction or an inquiry approach. It may be useful to use both. Beyer, who is certainly a strong advocate of direct instruction, also sees the value in using an inductive strategy when the task is "relatively uncomplicated" (36, p. 89) and with average or above-average students, those with a substantial relevant background knowledge, and those who have shown they can think. He also advocates combining, the two approaches in one strategy, called a developmental strategy (p. 115) by beginning with inquiry learning, students build their own models and representations, create their own cognitive dissonance, and develop their own motivation. The inquiry learning is followed by direct instruction which "provides information and guided practice for helping, them resolve the discrepancy on a need to know basis" (p. 116). Beyer asserts that this model is applicable to a wide variety of students and situations.

Marzano et al. also envision the possibility of using more than one instructional model. In discussing core thinking skills, such as classifying, they suggest that "to encourage younger and low-achieving students to use classifying, it may be necessary to provide them with explicit instruction, extended practice, and feedback" (223, p. 84). In discussing scientific problem solving and decision making, they advocate and describe in detail an inquiry approach. They conclude "that no single pedagogical model fits all types of knowledge equally well" (p. 137).

Teaching Strategies

For either one of these teaching models, direct instruction or inquiry learning, we can apply a variety of teaching strategies:

The Teacher as Mediator

> It is in mediating the relationship between context and content that teachers make their greatest contribution. (317, p. 8)

The teacher is seen as a mediator, interacting with students as they move through the process of thinking (91, 123, 183, 222, 316). This role views the teacher as the link between skills, strategies, and content when students are engaged in the process of thinking. The teacher as mediator makes statements that explain or engage the child in the task, asks questions that will provide answers useful for assessment, and provides additional information as needed (114).

The teacher as mediator, for example, is a critical feature of Instrumental Enrichment. Feuerstein views the mediator is intentionally imposing " himself or herself between a child and some external stimulus" (123, p. 46), changing in some way the child's perception of the stimulus, insuring that the experience "transcends" the immediate and works toward a long-range goal. Finally, Feuerstein stresses the role of the mediator in providing objects and experiences that are meaningful.

> To help teachers verbally mediate students' understandings of conceptual learning is more difficult leadership role than to ensure adequate task engagement or adherence to certain lesson plan formats. It is, however, a role that gets at the heart of effective instruction. (114, p. 27)

The Teacher as Model

Modeling, or demonstrating, discussing and detailing the thinking processes involved in tasks, provides students with a way of getting "inside the head" of an expert thinker. One of the problems with teaching thinking is that while procedures can be demonstrated and products produced, it is very difficult for novices to be part of the process, part of what the thinker is thinking while thinking. Modeling enables the novice to become part of the process. In addition, modeling by the teacher demonstrates to students the importance of the thinking process and the relevance of the process for them (337). While modeling teachers are also models of the qualities of effective thinkers (92), engaging in "displaying curiosity, open-mindedness, and reflection, qualities they seek to cultivate in their students" (232, p. 189).

How can a teacher model the process for students? The key here is to model all parts of the process: the uncertain approaches, the questions asked, the false starts, the errors, the recursive efforts as well as the successes, the promises fulfilled and the solutions achieved. In fact, Nickerson et al. found that this approach "staying closer as it does to the learner's actual circumstances, yields superior gains" (264, p. 267). The students can imitate the inner speech the teacher displays, gradually reducing the amount of thinking aloud and increasing the difficulty of the task.

The Teacher as Coach

According to Ruggiero (337) this is one of the most useful teaching strategies available. A coach encourages and allows students to become increasingly active and independent, provides situations and problems conducive to student thinking, allows students to struggle and work through the problem without always giving them the right answers.

In order to learn how to think well, students need practice. They need to become active participants in the learning process. For the teacher, this means change . No longer can the teacher dominate, lecture, pontificate. He or she must relinquish the role of "font of all wisdom," step to the sidelines and observe and coach the learning process.

Jones et al. (184) describe this process as "scaffolding" and offer some specifics including: gradually increasing the demands of the task, fading the amount of support, involving students in determining when a strategy is useful, providing visual prompts for completing the task and gradually removing them.

Ruggiero (337) offers some suggestions for becoming good coaches:

- motivate students to be more self-directive in their thinking and to lean on you less and less;

- create and maintain an atmosphere where independent thinking is prized, where the process by which students think critically is more important than their answers, where they are encouraged to express their thoughts, accept criticism in a positive way and learn from their mistakes;

- provide ample opportunity to challenge their thinking abilities;

- allow them enough "struggling time" with a problem to enable them to generate strategies for coping with confusion and frustration but not too much so as to lose them; give them enough encouragement to keep going;

- encourage students to apply what they learned about good thinking to a new, independent situation and reward them for doing so.

Ruggiero suggests that teachers are good coaches when they can apply "controlled impatience" when students are struggling to avoid discouraging them.

The Teacher as Questioner

There has been a long-standing and universal concern with the role of teacher-generated questions in the classroom, probably because this is such a widely used instructional strategy. Let's consider some of the conclusions that have been drawn in the area, keeping in mind that questions can be used to clarify thinking as well as to encourage and develop thinking (126). As you will see, not everyone is in total agreement here on instructional procedures.

- *Use questions, not statements.* Questions place a cognitive demand on the student and thus are more effective than statements (333).

- *Word questions carefully.* Questions should be carefully worded to engage students in thinking and should be on higher levels in order to require higher-level thinking (26, 90, 91, 135). Open-ended questions using probes such as "tell me about...," "why...," "what if...," require that the child think about his response (354) and extend it in the same area or into new dimensions (26, 377).

- *Sequence questions.* Asking high level questions may not be enough to engage students in high level thinking. Teachers assume that if they ask a high level question students will be encouraged to think on a similar high level in order to answer the question. Beyer suggests that "research on questioning provides little convincing support for this claim" (36, p. 152). In order to insure that the desired result occurs, he suggests asking questions in a sequence beginning with literal recall and progressing to higher levels of information processing, and finally ending with questions requiring application of new learning. He refers to Taba's earlier work which also suggests the usefulness of sequencing questions. He cautions that this sequencing of questions alone is not enough.

- *Use questions that relate to the source of information.* In comprehending text this may refer to: text explicit, text implicit, and experiential questions. Bean proposes this framework because the questioner here is "on reasonably solid ground" (23, p. 339) compared to the somewhat subjective categorization of questions into levels of thinking. Questions may also relate to how the information is organized in terms of meaning relationships(252). For example, questions about written text might relate to text structure. In problem solving, questions might relate to cause and effect.

- *Teach students how to answer questions (30, 135).* Beyer warns us that asking questions does not teach students the process of thinking and, in fact, may be testing rather than teaching. In order to teacher the process, we must provide "direct instruction on how to answer such questions" (30, p. 488). Programs, such as QAR (Question, Answer, Relationship) (324), have been developed in order to teach students how to answer reading comprehension questions by examining the text, their own prior knowledge, or both sources.

- *Respond to student answers effectively.* In order to give students time to think through the question and relate it to what they know from all sources, teachers need to allow sufficient wait time (36, 187, 233, 337). They may paraphrase answers in order to encourage rethinking and elaboration (97). In fact, teachers need to develop a variety of responses, such as withholding judgment, playing the devil's advocate and encouraging descriptions of how the student arrived at the answer (233, 337).

- *Encourage students to work in groups in responding to questions.* Think-Pair-Share (233) is a teaching strategy in which the teacher asks a question, students think, then discuss their responses in pairs, and finally share responses with the larger group.

- *Create a supportive, inquiring atmosphere.* An atmosphere of risk-taking where opinions and ideas are encouraged is required for effective questioning (113).

Not only do students need time over the course of years to develop thinking skills, but Beyer as well as Glatthorn and Baron suggest they need "wait time" during each experience "to deliberate—to reflect about alternate possibilities, to weigh the evidence, and to come to a tentative conclusion" (152, p. 52). The implication is clear. Teachers must refrain from stepping in with the right answer, from switching from the student who is thinking to the student who is waving a hand, ready with "the answer."

These conclusions about questions are reminiscent of the characteristics of the thinking classroom in which students are actively involved, risk-taking is encouraged and thinking is the goal. In fact, McTighe and Cutlip view questions as one of the hallmarks of a "thinking" classroom (232, p. 188). One school district with a Thinking Project has attributed the positive results obtained to the effective questioning strategies used by teachers, not to the use of direct instruction in thinking (382). Some programs, such as Philosophy for Children, the Irvine Thinking Project, and HOTS, rely heavily on the effectiveness of teacher questioning in order to engage students in thinking.

The Teacher as Discussion Leader

Group or total class discussion can play a critical role in the development of thinking abilities. In fact, discussion is the foundation for effective teacher behavior (97, 99) to develop student thinking. Discussion can be used during direct instruction; talking about thinking "begets thinking" (91, p. 219). Discussion is critical during inquiry in order to develop thinking skills and strategies (152, 353). During a discussion the teacher can model the thinking process and build a scaffold which allows the student to assume the teacher's strategies (364). In addition to discussing the procedures and rules related to the skills, students should also follow the application of the skill with a discussion on "how best to use" (31, p. 559) it. Discussion for Beyer (31, 36) is a thread running throughout instruction.

How common is discussion in classrooms? Staab reviewed the literature on classroom discussions and found that "little time is provided for constructive talk, especially in the upper grades, and the talk that does exist is largely for the purpose of establishing routines and eliciting and reciting facts" (363, p. 294). Not only does this state of affairs preclude the benefits to be derived from the discussion of ideas, but Staab suggests that it also conveys a message to the students. They may come to view thinking as less important than memorizing and understanding material as less important than finishing it. Palincsar (276) concurs with these discouraging findings but suggests that we can change the situation.

What does a discussion involve? It requires that students talk to each other, not just to the teacher. They must feel free to talk. The goal is not necessarily to arrive at one final answer but rather to explore possibilities. Discussions can be free with the teacher providing little guidance, semi-controlled by the teacher or tightly controlled with the teacher providing rules and guidelines for both procedures and content.

How can we encourage discussion in the classroom?

- Allow for risk taking (113).

- Start with questions. The questions can direct thinking and can become the beginning of a dialog as students examine and defend positions (23, 337, 354).

- Encourage student brainstorming, questioning and elaboration (113, 184).

- Use statements that require a reaction (113, 255).

- Encourage discussion, debate and defense of different points of view (174).

- Discuss the process and procedures and rules used in thinking (31).

- Switch roles, having the student assume the role of teacher in a dialog (183).

- Allow for wait time (113, 186, 187, 255, 337).

In the process of becoming comfortable with leading and enabling discussions, it may be useful for a discussion leader to examine excerpts from discussions with explanations showing the role of the teacher and the students as well as the kinds of thinking being used. Palincsar (276) and Bean (23) provide a variety of examples.

Numerous thinking programs include discussion as a critical ingredient. This is obviously so in programs such as Philosophy for Children and HOTS which are based on inquire learning. However, discussion also plays a role in Instrumental Enrichment in which the transfer to content areas is made through class discussion.

So far, the emphasis has been on teacher-led discussion. There are, however, other alternatives in which the teacher hands over responsibility for the discussion to students. Remember Reciprocal Teaching? Students have a major role in conducting and participating in discussion, along with the teacher. Another alternative is cooperative learning. This approach has been developed as means of involving students as primary agents in the discussion in order to further the goal of learning, and thinking. Cooperative learning is based on a heterogeneous group of students working toward accomplishing a common goal. The responsibility for achieving the goal is shared by members of the group but each member has individual responsibility (177). The teacher's role is that of facilitator, monitor, observer. The groups can be set up in a structured way, in order to insure that each student participates (189) . By assigning numbers, roles, responsibilities to each student, they all contribute to the group discussion. In whole-class group discussion frequently only the high achieving students enter into the dialogue. In cooperative learning, during small group discussion, everyone has a role and a reason for participating. During large group sharing, by using a predetermined structure for participating, all members join in. There are a number of different ways to group students insuring that all will participate in different ways (188, 420).

The results of using cooperative learning have been cited as being positive. Slavin found in reviewing 60 current studies that "there is wide agreement among reviewers of the cooperative learning literature that cooperative methods can and usually do have a positive effect on student achievement" (359, p. 52), provided the group is working on group goals and there is individual accountability. Joyce, Showers, and Rolheiser-Bennett found that when cooperative learning approaches were used "the more complex the outcomes (higher-order thinking, problem solving, social skills and attitude), the greater the effects" (187, p. 17).

What might be some explanations for these positive results? Simon, in looking at mathematical problem solving, explored reasons why inquiry learning, using cooperative learning groups, was successful. He suggested that "first, students are exposed to diverse thinking and problem-solving approaches. Second, they develop metacognitive skills" (357, p. 42). It is the group interaction and discussion about what strategies to use, what information is needed, when to drop an ineffective strategy, what strategy to try next, and how to evaluate a solution that empowers the student in developing "the metacognitive aspects of problem solving" (p. 42).

It is becoming very clear that to teach thinking, the teacher does not simply open up the teacher's manual and start talking! The students' needs and background knowledge, the requirements of the task, and the skills and strategies to be used must all be matched to the instructional procedures.. In addition, of course, we must be concerned with the materials used to implement and facilitate instruction.

Materials

What materials should we use in instruction?

The materials used in instruction reflect the view held of thinking and of its importance in the curriculum. The decision as to whether to use materials designed specifically to teach thinking skills or whether to use content materials obviously depends on your decision on whether to teach thinking as a separate course or as part of content courses or both. However, in addition to this basic decision there are considerations in choosing materials wherever thinking instruction takes place. Bereiter emphasizes that every page of a textbook must answer the question: "How is your approach to teaching thinking represented on this page?" (28, p. 77). Consider the arrangement of the materials. Can connections between materials be made by students using a number of items (354)? In addition, materials must focus on thinking, over time, not just on one page of the workbook and in the various content areas. They must reflect a total approach to thinking.

Let's examine some of the various materials used. The materials can be categorized in variety of ways, a problem which compounds the difficulty of analyzing them.

We might look at whether the content is presented in verbal, figural, or spatial form. A few programs such as Instrumental Enrichment and Odyssey or the workbook series Building Thinking Skills use these three kinds of content, while the majority of the programs focus on verbal content. The use of figural and spatial content implies that microskills are probably a significant or at least introductory part of the program. In describing the Odyssey program, Adams states that:

> Each of our targeted thinking skills in [sic] introduced through the sorts of abstract teaching materials typical of micrological approaches. Then, throughout the balance of the course, these same thinking skills are used, and thereby refined, elaborated, and contextualized, over and over again, as the

means of developing the various macrological and domain-specific challenges of each or the other Lesson Series. (1, p. 51)

These lessons include "as many diverse, content-specific, and intellectually complex extensions as we could squeeze in" (p. 52). Thus, Odyssey provides us with a rationale for including a variety of forms.

Next, we categorize materials according to their content. The materials in many programs present a problem to be solved. In these cases, the materials are specifically developed for a particular thinking program. Both the purpose for using the materials and the kinds of materials developed may vary. The constant element here is that the materials present a problem. Specifically developed problems using using content materials are presented to the students in the program Analytic Reasoning with the aim of developing problem solving abilities. Although the content is academic, the focus is on the process not on the acquisition of content. While this approach has been widely used, there have also been questions raised about it. For example, Sternberg (368) suggests that the problems used should not be limited to academic ones but must include real life problems if transfer is to be made by the students. This caution has been taken seriously by a number of programs. Think About presents a series of television programs dealing with real life problems in a variety of areas. The purpose is to engage in problem solving in a way that can transfer to real life. Connections presents both academic and real life problems in an attempt to deal with both elements.

Most of the problems presented are fairly short and contained. However, Perkins, who is also concerned about the issue of transfer to real life, questions whether these short problems will accomplish that. In later life, nonstudents undoubtedly be faced with long-term projects they need to complete, such as starting a business or writing a book. "Complex, ongoing, often indefinite in their requirements, and open to diverse approaches, projects confront those involved in them with difficulties not represented in the microcosm of the isolated problem" (294, p. 347). (Authors' note: We can certainly relate to this statement!)

Others have taken this notion and developed it into total programs for children. For example, Katz and Chard present a project approach for preschoolers, kindergartners and elementary school children based on the belief that "the project approach . . . provides a context in which all aspects of children's minds can be engaged, challenged, and enriched" (191, p. xi). Future Problem Solving, while not using a project approach, presents complex, real life problems. Students can enter state and national competitions as they solve serious problems they may encounter in the future. In both of these examples, the materials used involved substantial and sustained involvement on the part of the students.

The regular content materials used in the classrooms may become the source of materials for instruction. The emphasis in this approach is not on developing materials but on training teachers to utilize existing materials. These programs range from teacher and school developed ones, frequently focusing on teaching for thinking, such as a program developed in Irvine, California (382), to programs developed by outsiders which focus on teaching of and about thinking, such as Tactics for Thinking. In some programs, even though there may be some lessons specifically designed for direct instruction in thinking, practice, and follow-up use content materials, as in a program developed in Arkansas (321).

We can also categorize materials according to how the content is presented. In Philosophy for Children, specially written novels encourage the discussion of perennial questions in order to develop critical thinking. Adams suggests that one reason for the success of this program in reading comprehension and/or logical thinking is the materials. The novels provide "a single, contextually rich, but thematically integrated and logically well-articulated schema (1, p. 37). The stories enable the reader to participate with the characters in an evolving, memorable series of events requiring and encouraging, thinking and the processes of thinking. The Program for the Fostering of Reading and Thinking includes a series of literary texts which "require the reader to enter into the world described" (203, p. 545) as part of the thinking process. A program in North Carolina also uses literature, but quality literature "raising timeless questions" (8, p. 48). Here, the literature becomes a vehicle for encouraging thinking in students. Ruggiero suggests that "perhaps the best source of exercise material . . . is media reports of current events" (337, p. 123).

Non-book materials can be used. Maxwell (225) suggests using games as a natural, enjoyable, motivating way of teaching thinking skills. Ruggiero (337) advocates cartoons and thought provoking quotations as well as current events. The HOTS program presents simple problems using computers, drama and team competition. We have already mentioned the use of television as a medium.

The conclusion that emerges from these categories and descriptions is probably no surprise to teachers and administrators. The materials can certainly be varied but must relate to your definition of thinking and to your conclusion as to where in the overall school curriculum instruction should take place. One example will demonstrate how one school district met this problem.

A large urban district identified the need to provide instruction in thinking skills. The administration decided that including it in the content areas was "ideal" but not practical because of the size of the district. They decided to use materials that isolated thinking skills instruction" (412, p. 51). These materials could be used for both staff development and student instruction. Commercial materials were chosen from readily available sources and were used as the starting point for district developed "interdisciplinary modules."

By now you are certainly wondering how long all this is going to take. There are a lot of things to include in instruction, a lot of ways to deliver instruction, and a variety of materials that can be used. This doesn't sound like a project for alternate Friday afternoons. It sounds like it 's going to require more than that .

Duration of Instruction

When and for how long should instruction in thinking take place?

Beyer addresses this issue directly, stating that "research suggests that massed practice of skills is not as effective in promoting learning as intermittent practice and reinforcement over a long period of time" (31, p. 559). Instruction should be provided on a regular basis (186) and the teacher must allow sufficient time for students to become comfortable and proficient (91). Allowing sufficient time for thinking and thinking instruction also gives students the message that thinking is important because time has been allocated to it in the school day. The implication is clear (36). In order to insure this sufficiency of experience, we need a commitment to teach thinking skills throughout the child's school experience, not just in those particular classes and grade levels taught by a committed teacher.

We can't assume that instruction will be effective overnight or quickly. There is no "quick fix" (232, p. 186) for improving thinking abilities. Lowery (218) would say that because the development of thinking skills is closely related to biological development it is imperative that we allow ample time for the development to take place and that we do not assume an even, constant development but rather allow for the uneven continuum of growth. Halpern warns us that "there are no quick and easy crash programs that will make you a competent thinker overnight" (159, p. 10). It is interesting to note that designers of a variety of programs and approaches support this view. Instrumental Enrichment, for example, is based on "3 to 5

1-hour lessons per week for 2 to 3 years" (264, p. 154). The Odyssey program (l) provides 100 1-hour lessons. HOTS advocates 35 minutes of instruction a day for four days a week for two years (308).

If we provide all this instruction, how will we know that it has been effective? How can we determine if students have acquired and are using the skills and strategies we have decided are needed? How should we assess students' individual abilities and evaluate thinking skills programs?

VIII

Assessment and Evaluation

Student Assessment

How can we assess students in order to promote and facilitate thinking?

The question of assessment is particularly important in school settings, because, as Marzano points out, "students tend to take seriously only those tasks for which they are held accountable" (221, p. 2). If we don't test for thinking, students may not view thinking as important. If we test for literal recall, students will assume that literal recall certainly must be important. Beyer suggests that testing thinking skills directly as "an integral part of each major subject matter classroom test where thinking is being taught calls student attention to the importance of thinking as a legitimate learning and teaching objective" (36, p. 244). We will thereby "give value" to instruction in thinking as well as receiving important information about students.

In addition, teachers tend to teach tasks for which students are held accountable. In fact, both researchers (263) and practitioners (320) confirm that testing procedures have the potential of directing instruction, particularly for "new . . . underprepared . . . insecure or embattled teachers" (63, p. 31). These teachers may "teach to the test." This is certainly not a surprise to those of us who have worked in schools. According to Cole "informal and formal reports abound of teachers paying increased attention to sets of objectives and the tests designed to measure student mastery of them" (81, p. 3). The real challenge may be to make the tests so useful at identifying what we actually want students to do as part of the process of thinking that teaching to the test is a positive experience (263, 411).

This concern for measuring and assessing competency in thinking skills is evident on the state level as well as on the individual school level. Some states such as Connecticut (19, 372), California (194, 402), New Jersey and Illinois (184, 391) have developed and are developing statewide tests designed to measure thinking abilities. One reason these have been put in place is to encourage and even insure that instruction in thinking will take place (263, 333). However, not all states have taken this approach. For example, Maryland has not developed a statewide test for assessment of thinking skills because of the real danger of local programs being driven and directed by the test (232).

The difficulty is that we are only beginning to deal with the issues of how to measure thinking abilities on a widespread scale. Chipman and Segal identify this as a problem area, stating that "current emphasis on measuring competencies and training for the competencies measured may be creating a still more unfavorable environment for the development of these more complex competencies that we do not yet know how to measure" (78, p.2). Our lack of skill in measuring thinking skills is widely noted (30, 31, 91, 263).

First, let's examine the problems and future directions in assessing thinking skills and then look at what is being done now. One major problem in the assessment of thinking skills is that of assessing noncognitive and nonverbal aspects and individual differences in style. Snow (361), for example, identifies as one affective component the confidence a student has in using a particular thinking strategy. This is viewed as a significant variable in the effective use of that strategy in combination with relevant skills and content knowledge. But how do you measure confidence? Other traits such as motivation for continued learning and self-efficacy are equally elusive. Snow reviews some alternatives based on computer programs using task response with distractors and free-response to personality inventories.

Another problem is that assessment techniques need to identify the processes which underlie performance in a given strategy in order to develop appropriate instruction (133, 351). The difficulty with assessment of process is that, since different people will use different strategies in the same situation and one person may have a variety of strategies available (351, 361), one test at a given point in time may not be sufficient. For example, Siegler (351) cites problems with chronometric measures in attempting to identify cognitive processes used in a given situation. Chronometric measures assume that we can identify what process a student used to think about and solve a problem by how long it took to do so. Siegler, however, points out that students at different cognitive levels may use a variety of strategies, all taking different amounts of time due to their differing abilities. Thus, all these variables may confound the time measure. The strategy students use may not be readily identifiable by chronometric measure alone.

What are some other possibilities? Snow (361) reviews a variety of approaches all designed to assess strategy acquisition, development and use on a daily, weekly or monthly basis. The techniques include, for example, computerized tutoring with immediate assessment and student teaching of the material/task learned. Siegler (351) suggests video taping a student engaged in a cognitive task as well as verbal reports immediately after completion of a task.

We have identified the difficulty of assessing the variety of strategies available to the thinker. There is another side to this problem: the difficulty of assessing performance in tasks that are unstructured. There is a problem in developing a structured, easily administered and scored test to assess product and process in tasks that may be unstructured and may have more than one answer (263). The solution to this problem may be the development of tests that require performance on extended tasks and which require considerable judgment on the part of the examiner (131). We may need to combine multiple choice answers with think-aloud reports or probes on the part of the examiners (266).

But, these ideas are in the works. What is being done now? Suggestions for assessing thinking abilities range from developing standardized, norm-referenced tests (19) to the use of a non-quantitative approach (19, 222, 411). In the development of standardized tests which measure thinking, Baron and Kallick, reporting on tests developed in Connecticut, stress the need to specifically include thinking skills in content area tests as well as to "isolate, separate from subject matter, significant and instructable thinking skills that are developmentally appropriate" (19, p. 285).

While useful information may be obtained from standardized tests, we need to move into the classroom and examine ongoing, qualitative data in our efforts to assess thinking. Costa cautions that "while *competency* may be demonstrated in a single test, *effectiveness* is demonstrated by sustained performance in a variety of situations that demand selective and spontaneous use of different problem-solving strategies rather than singular, isolated behaviors" (98, p. 288).

Let's examine some quantitative as well as qualitative indicators of growth in the acquisition and use of thinking competencies.

Quantitative:

- Comparison of the performance of a student on low and high level thinking questions on standardized tests (323).

- Performance on a standardized test designed to measure thinking, such as the Cornell Critical Thinking Test, the Watson-Glaser, the New Jersey Test of Reasoning Skills. While Ruggiero (337) provides an annotated list of some of the major tests available, he cautions that tests may not be highly refined and probably are not testing thinking in real life situations.

Qualitative:

- Teacher observations. Teacher logs can include student behavior and response to questions (19, 194, 323), perseverance, decreased impulsiveness, flexible thinking, awareness and monitoring of thinking, review of completed work, problem posing and solving, questioning, use of prior knowledge and experiences, transfer to new situations including real life and content areas, use of precise language and enjoyment of problem solving (98).

- Think-aloud protocols or self-report on thought processes (98). Student journals or logs can be used to reflect on thinking (19). Essay questions can be developed in which the student describes not just his answer but also the process he used to solve the problem (221).

- Student activities. Peer interviews about thinking strategies (19) and student construction of tests including both the questions and the answers (63) are two examples of sources of information available when students are actually engaging in thinking.

- Responses to teacher-made tests. Beyer (36) offers some guidelines for developing tests which measure specific thinking skills within content areas. He suggests that initially the teacher cluster together all questions which assess performance on the particular skill or strategy that has been taught in one section of a content area test to underscore the importance of that skill or strategy. Questions assessing performance on a newly introduced skill should require students to: define the skill, identify an example of the skill in use, execute the skill several times and explain to others how to execute the skill. Eventually, once the skill or strategy has been used enough, scatter those test items throughout the test and cluster questions on a new skill. Test items should also be developed which assess proficiency in several thinking skills at once. Later, only after students have had an opportunity to practice the skill in a variety of content areas, tests can assess proficiency at transfer.

The content material used in tests should be carefully chosen. Beyer suggests that in order to assess students' thinking skill proficiency, content material of the test items should be well within the student's level of understanding, should use one set of data for several questions to focus on the skill rather than the content and should be similar but not the same as the content in which the student learned the skill. Beyer gives several good examples of specific skills assessment in various content areas.

Teacher-made tests should require students to think over a sustained period of time, to integrate information across a series of items, to transfer in a variety of settings including other school related content areas, personal and real life situations and novel contexts (36, 320).

- Responses to homework assignments. Ruggiero provides specific guidelines for evaluating student homework, including two basic forms which may be adapted to a variety of content areas. His caution that "performance patterns are more discernible when several samples of work are examined than when a single sample is" (337, p. 185) is well taken.

- Portfolios of student work. A portfolio of student work can document development and change in thinking process and in product (19, 63, 418). Seeing change and development or the lack of it gives students a chance to examine critically their own progress as learners, as well as giving teachers a chance to see their own accomplishments. Making students responsible for choosing what will go into the portfolio is itself an exercise in critical thinking. The act of putting together a portfolio is a reflective one. The student explores critically: "What am I learning? How have I changed?"

- Exhibitions and performances. Wiggins (411) advocates the use of "authentic" tests in which students demonstrate what is taught and learned through exhibitions and performances of their work.

- Student self-assessment. Wade and Reynolds (394) provide students with a self-assessment sheet which they complete and score to monitor the success of their use of cognitive strategies.

The question of how to assess students is not settled and is certainly not going to go away.

> Unless teachers assess explicitly, continuously and consistently the thinking skills they teach, the direct teaching of thinking is not likely to lead to the kinds of student proficiencies in thinking deemed most desirable today. (36, p. 244)

Program Evaluation

How should we evaluate programs for effectiveness?

The issue of program evaluation is one that is certainly foremost in the minds of those concerned with and/or in charge of programs. In fact, Bereiter poses a critical question. "What evidence is there that your program does improve thinking skills?" (28, p. 77). We cannot take success for granted. Unfortunately "strange as it may seem, it has been the rare exception rather than the rule for programs training intellectual skills to receive anything even approaching adequate evaluation" (367, p. 11).

In conducting program evaluation, Rankin (323) suggests the use of: context evaluation (a needs assessment), input evaluation (review of promising practices with a resulting program decision), process evaluation (formative evaluation to make ongoing revisions), and product evaluation (summative evaluation designed to continue, stop or revise the program).

He holds that summative evaluation needs to be more rigorous and scientific than formative.

In designing and carrying out formative and summative program evaluation, we can look for evidence of:

- Increased teacher knowledge of thinking skills and strategies (26).

- Increased teacher ability to use questioning techniques to probe and extend thinking (323).

- Increased student participation (26).

- Reduction of student impulsivity and lack of organization (47, 98).

- High level thought and organization reflected in writing samples and in student descriptions of the thought processes used (323).

- Durability and transfer of training (47).

- Greater value and emphasis placed on thinking within the school curriculum (26).

In program evaluation, Rankin cautions that we must develop approaches that measure what we are trying to teach. He provides useful examples. Don't evaluate creative thinking by asking students to solve subtraction problems. Instead, ask "The number four is the answer to what questions?" (323, p. 274).

The use of these observational, perhaps somewhat informal measures, as instruments in summative evaluation is not fully settled. On the one hand, Costa considers this approach capable of providing "convincing evidence" (47, p. 11) that thinking instruction is effective. On the other hand, Rankin asserts that "objectives must be stated and measured as precisely as possible. Controls are needed for reliability, validity, objectivity, and comparison; and side effects and costs must be examined" (323, p. 273).

The inclusion of quantitative data from test scores is certainly relevant in program evaluation. However, Bellanca warns that we cannot expect improvement rapidly. Beginning with observational data first, "you could predict meaningful achievement increases in two or three years" (26, p. 15).

What kinds of quantitative data can we obtain?

- Tests specifically designed to measure thinking. For example, in the field of critical thinking commonly used tests include the Cornell Critical Thinking Test, the Watson-Glaser, or the New Jersey Test of Reasoning Skills (323).

- Tests developed by individual states to measure thinking. A number of states including California, Connecticut, and New Jersey have developed their own tests of thinking (323).

- Item analysis of tests administered for other purposes. Programs have compared the performance of groups of students on questions measuring high-level thinking as compared to performance on questions measuring memory, basic skills, and low-level thinking (323).

- Academic improvement. Since a number of the academic areas, such as reading and mathematics, involve high-level thinking, improvement in these areas may reflect improvement in the use of thinking skills (412).

In determining how to develop program evaluation, consider Costa's (47) finding that there is little statistical research to document that instruction in thinking skills has been effective. There has been widespread concern expressed about the effectiveness of thinking programs and about how we evaluate them (262, 342). For example, Sternberg and Bhana reviewed evidence of effectiveness for five programs. They identified a number of issues dealing with how the evaluations of program effectiveness were conducted and found that "available evidence [was] so scant as to preclude any firm decisions" (373, p. 62). Nickerson also found evaluation data "sparse" (262, p. 40) and concluded that "what should be taken as evidence of the success or failure of an approach is a matter of debate" (p. 41). We need to continue to use quantitative data but also need to examine qualitative indicators to find evidence of initial effectiveness and of the durability and the transferability of training particularly to real life.

Finally, Adams, in discussing evidence of success of thinking programs, concludes that

> True thinking unquestionably promotes learning, understanding, and more thinking. It thus follows that there is one best measure of the success of such a course. That measure would assess whether impact of the course increases with time and whether students who received the course continue to outlearn, outperform, and 'outadjust' their peers who did not. On this question, there is unfortunately very little data. (1, p. 38)

IX

Participants

The cast of characters that must be considered in any successful program certainly includes teachers. However, it must include more than teachers. It must include administrators, state and local agencies, parents, and students.

Instructors

Who should be involved in instruction and what is the instructor's role in a thinking program?

The question of which teachers to involve in instruction obviously depends on where instruction is going to be based and how and where skills and strategies will be applied. A total, comprehensive program based on a district-wide commitment requires total involvement of all teachers; a separate, self-contained program might be managed and instructed by one or two teachers in a building. In fact, depending on your perspective, this might be seen as an advantage for separate programs. For example, Lipman, the developer of Philosophy for Children, states very clearly that "not every teacher is cut out to teach Philosophy for Children" (212, p. 213). The best trained and most competent, enthusiastic teachers can be the instructors. However, since the transfer of skills and strategies to all academic areas and to real life seems important, the ultimate involvement of all teachers in some fashion seems inevitable no matter what the program design (397).

The interdependence of all decision-making areas is certainly apparent here. You may choose a program based on your acceptance of a particular theory and its supporting research. This will determine how many and which teachers you involve. On the other hand, the availability and willingness of particular teachers may be one of the deciding factors in the final choice of a program.

In determining which teachers should be included we need to view the teacher as more than an instructor, as a decision maker as well as an instructional leader. The teacher as decision maker has become a popular phrase. In this role the teacher specifies the content to be learned, the cognitive strategies the student needs, and the appropriate instructional strategies (122, 184). Consider these examples:

- Teachers in one school district, after being trained in three different programs, made individual decisions based on student needs and teacher interest regarding which approach to implement in their classes (304). This is certainly viewing the teacher as a decision maker!

- Teachers in another district were trained in CoRT and were allowed to "make their own decisions regarding if, when, and how they will apply CoRT" (237, p. 33).

- Strahan (377) in describing the role of the teacher specifies that the teacher assesses the student's level of thinking, analyzes curricular requirements, observes interactions within the classroom and extends thinking through planned experiences. Strahan labels this as guided inquiry. It is that. It is also decision making.

These views all suggest that the teacher functions on a sophisticated level; the teacher is not merely reading from a manual. In fact, the teacher is clearly viewed as a thinker!

The role of the professional as instructor is always assumed and often explicitly stated. However, there are other possible roles for the teacher. The professional might be involved in developing long and short range goals, exploring resources and developing budgets (26). The teachers in one small secondary school decided to include problem solving and student independence in answering questions in the overall school curriculum (39). These teachers developed four long range goals and explored resources in the community in order to develop real life problems for their students. "Thinking of themselves as a community of learners" (52, p. 62), teachers in another district developed a k-12 program linking thinking and writing in all content areas. This involvement in all aspects of program development seems particularly useful as a means of encouraging "ownership" of a new and sometimes demanding program. The teacher in this role is an instructional leader.

In looking at the various facets of professional involvement in thinking programs, we cannot deny the fact that teachers need to be thinkers themselves. If the focus for students is on thinking, it is equally important for teachers (17).

> To fail to require that teachers be competent in thinking skills strategies can only undermine the outcomes of these programs for teachers. (154, pp. 340–341)

Few teachers have been trained in thinking and there are very few certification requirements along these lines (154). Most of the training in thinking and in teaching thinking is on-the-job training.

How will teachers be trained for program implementation?

> Most teachers use a very narrow range of practices; they expand that repertoire only when they are provided substantial and carefully designed training. (187, p. 42)

> A well-designed curriculum should not require large amounts of inservice training. A heavy inservice requirement is inconsiderate of teachers' time and school budgets. And worse, it is a symptom that the success of the curriculum depends not on the guidance and materials it provides, but on the individual efforts of teachers to interpret and go beyond what it provides. (1, p. 45)

These two statements, both by highly respected members of the educational community, certainly reflect different views, views that we must examine in making the critical decisions needed for program implementation.

Once the teachers to be involved have been selected, many consider that the decision to provide inservice training seems non-negotiable (45, 337, 378). The need for staff development is seen as critical because teachers are often accustomed to teaching in a manner that does not encourage thinking and frequently even discourages thinking (154, 186). However, Schlichter reports that "nearly all teachers can be successful in learning new teaching strategies" (343, p. 119).

Not everyone agrees that staff development is essential. Adams (1), for example, strongly asserts that programs should stand on their own with a minimum of teacher training. The question seems to be whether the materials and the curriculum will bear the brunt of the success or failure of the program or whether the teachers will. If it is the teachers, then they need to be comfortable and knowledgeable about what is being asked of them. Thus, we find in many programs the heavy emphasis on inservice training.

There is another set of concerns expressed about programs requiring extensive inservice training (349). Extensive training requires committed, available teachers. Each district will need to determine for itself if an acceptable cadre of teachers is available. There also need to be provisions made for training teachers who enter the program after the initial training has been given. This problem is not, of course, insurmountable. One district, after implementing a program which required extensive training, developed a group of teachers and administrators who assumed the responsibility for planning future inservice and for training new teachers (9). Another program, one providing extensive manuals, lessons and training filmstrips for teachers, also provided for the training of district/site coordinators and regional trainers to train future teachers (414).

Think about the findings on the effectiveness of strategy training and on strategy transfer and apply it to teachers' learning new teaching strategies. We know that in order to learn and transfer new strategies the learner needs specific, detailed instruction and opportunities to understand how the strategy can be helpful. The learner must be in charge of the strategy, understanding it, recognizing its usefulness, and being motivated to use it as appropriate for the task and the participants. No matter how thorough the teacher's manual for any program is, it seems essential for teachers to receive training that will answer their initial and ongoing questions and will provide them with a peer support group in which they can share successes and failures.

Staff development can't be a "one-shot" (26, p. 17) effort; it must be on-going and part of a continuous approach to inservice education. Joyce stresses that we cannot "make educational changes without the pain of sufficient investment" (186, p. 5). This means that teachers need repeated opportunities to become familiar with the instructional approach and will benefit from "coaching" (186, 343) in the classroom. Staff development is so important that it has been suggested that one of the responsibilities of state departments of education should be to encourage staff development within schools and provide training for the trainers (232).

How do the programs stack up on the question of inservice training? Not surprisingly, programs like Philosophy for Children (1, 180, 211), Tactics for Thinking (9, 192, 222), and Talents Unlimited (16, 343, 345) in which teachers play a critical role in questioning, leading discussions and transferring to other areas require extensive staff development. Programs like Odyssey (1) and Strategic Reasoning (149, 431) which provide detailed plans, manuals and materials rely much less on inservice training.

The professional literature suggests that programs for staff development in teaching thinking may consider some of the following aspects. The programs may:

- provide the staff with a thorough grounding in relevant theory. This insures that the professionals have a foundation for understanding the development of thinking skills and strategies and can plan and implement instruction accordingly (54, 343).

- involve the staff in the development of curriculum as part of the training process (343).

- provide demonstration and modeling of teaching and learning strategies (54, 304, 343).

- allow opportunities to try suggestion with students (54, 192, 304).

- provide for coaching in the classroom by trainers and/or peers and discussion of suggestions by participants (9, 54, 192, 304, 343, 382).

In addition to direct staff training Ruggiero (337) suggests other support services such as developing a professional library, establishing a network including other teachers and schools, sending teachers to conferences and obtaining or developing audio-visual and computer programs on thinking.

The implementation and impact of a staff development program can differ and need to be considered in planning the program. For example, Arredonodo and Marzano (9) describe an approach to staff development which includes many of the elements listed above. At the end of the training process teachers chose the thinking strategies they wanted included in the program. Curriculum development, instead of completely preceding staff development, also grew out of it. Brooks found that as a result of a similar staff development experience some teachers changed "the sequence of curriculum introduction and presentation" (54, p. 25); others changed their way of using questioning techniques; while others modified or adapted lessons.

Is a staff development program worth the time and effort? Nickerson is adamant in his affirmation that it is.

My own view is that the quality of teaching has been the single most important factor determining the success or failure of most efforts to teach thinking of which I am aware. If this perception is correct, it represents a problem with respect to the evaluation of programs, but perhaps more importantly, it points up the great importance of adequate teacher training. (262, pp. 42–43)

Administrators and Parents

Who else should be involved in thinking programs?

The Principal

The role of the principal in this, as in all curricular and instructional areas, is critical (377). The principal may, in fact, be "the key person" (249, p. 16) by making thinking skills a "building priority" (p. 16), developing evaluation procedures for staff that will reward the teaching of thinking skills, providing inservice for teachers, and encouraging and allowing for adjustments in existing curriculum. Principals might even become involved with students in thinking programs. For example, one principal conducts a session once a week in which real life problems are presented to teams of students (39). Costa (47) puts the responsibility for modeling effective thinking squarely on the shoulders of school administrators. Ruggiero sums up the role of school administrators by stating that "the most helpful roles an administrator can fill are ENABLER and ADVOCATE" (337, p. 207).

State and County Agencies

These boards also have a responsibility (232) and a unique opportunity to promote thinking in schools. They have the ability and the facilities to develop awareness, provide assistance and financial aid in the development of pilot projects, disseminate information, train trainers, and establish a network of users as well as develop a county or statewide instructional framework. A few examples will illustrate directions some boards have taken. The San Diego County Office of Education has provided 15-hour training each month in Tactics for Thinking (192). The Arkansas Department Of Education, in collaboration with two other agencies, provided funding and expertise to a local school district in developing a program which focuses on critical thinking and multicultural awareness (321). The Maryland Department of Education provided three grants to a local school to incorporate the Inclusion Process into the content areas (422).

Parents

Since we know that thinking doesn't stop at the end of the school day, we must recognize the important contribution parents can and do make in affecting the level of thinking abilities of their children. Daily life experiences, intellectual exchanges and the kinds of activities that children are encouraged to do clearly impact on their thinking skills. Unfortunately, we see little recognition of parents' influence on children's thinking in the literature. However, there are some signs that parents are recognized as part of the process. One school district, in developing a series of Socratic seminars to develop critical thinking, included parents in the initial training (8). Parents were invited to attend the seminars and encouraged to continue the experience at home. Parents in some schools have been so supportive of the critical thinking and multicultural project mentioned above (321) that the project has undergone voluntary expansion. Parental involvement in a Cognitive Instruction project in a large urban district received high priority (412). The aim was to educate parents and increase their involvement at home. Parents attended workshops, completed lessons at home with their children and visited school.

Students

Who should receive instruction in thinking?

Students who have been identified as gifted and talented have traditionally been the focus for instruction in thinking skills. However, questions have been raised about teaching students who are already able to think how to think. In fact, Baer (11) cautions that because there are so many unknown variables in our understanding of thinking and how to teach it that we may actually handicap able thinkers. Perkins (298), in responding to Baer, reassures us that even able thinkers may not be able in all arenas and might benefit from learning new strategies, which they can drop if they do not prove useful.

Recently, educators have been examining the effects of instruction on other groups. New definitions and descriptions of intelligence have been generated over the past few years, which suggest that even the most handicapped students can benefit from thinking skills instruction. For example, Sternberg (366) refers to intelligence as a set of thinking and learning skills applied in school and everyday life problem solving; these, according to Sternberg, can be identified and taught. Whimbey and Lochhead (410) define thinking as a complex set of skills which can be learned through practice. Feuerstein, Jensen, Hoffman, and Tand (123) reject the idea that intelligence is an inborn, unchangeable set of abilities and instead, emphasize the processes involved in intelligence which can be self-regulated and modified. In fact, Instrumental Enrichment was developed for the "at risk" adolescent.

These new notions of intelligence suggest that all students at any level can continue to develop intelligence and increase their ability to think at higher levels. These ideas hold special promise for students at even the lowest levels of academic performance. Ruggiero asserts that "students in regular and even remedial programs not only need instruction in thinking; they need it more than students in honors classes" (337, p. 13). In fact, as a result of the disturbing data on the need to improve student thinking, McTighe and Cutlip (232) see the need to include all students in programs. Costa (99) agrees, including all children from the gifted to those with Down's Syndrome. Thinking skills instruction need not be reserved for the "gifted and talented" who probably think pretty well already. Low IQ students need not be doomed to remedial drill and practice forever.

With appropriate intervention, we can affect almost any student's ability to think. Jones (183, 184) concluded that low achieving students as well as younger students appear to benefit from instruction in thinking. Chipman and Segal suggest that teaching thinking skills to lower socio-economic students may "hold promise for ameliorating the persistent problem of unequal school success for the diverse social and ethnic groups that make up our society" (78, p. 3). Resnick concludes that there is "a new challenge to develop educational programs that assume that all individuals, not just an elite, can become competent thinkers" (329, p. 7).

In practice, in fact, a wide range of students are included. A few examples will suffice. Programs include students in: elementary, middle (Odyssey), middle and secondary (Project IMPACT, Instrumental Enrichment, Learning to Learn), or all levels (CoRT, Philosophy for Children, Talents Unlimited). Some programs identify a particular kind of student as a target audience. For example, Creative Problem Solving suggests including gifted middle school students and all students on the secondary level (283). Instrumental Enrichment is designed specifically for low-functioning, at risk adolescents (123). HOTS, a computer-based program, was developed as a compensatory program for Chapter 1 students in grades 3–6 (306, 308). A large urban school district with a very high minority population developed a Cognitive Instruction project designed to meet the particular needs of their students (412).

In matching students to programs or in developing programs within school districts, we need to examine the programs carefully to insure suitability for students. For example, Philosophy for Children was developed for all children from kindergarten through high school (212). However, concern has been expressed about the appropriateness of the material for all children. Adams reviewed this program and concluded that the especially written novels used constituted one of its major strengths but also seemed to limit the program to "scholastically solid, culturally mainstream classrooms" (1, p. 37).

In view of the range of students who may be included in programs, it is important to note that there is widespread agreement that the needs of the students, whether developmental or educational, must be identified and incorporated into the planning of programs. For example, Sigel and Saunders cite the need for appropriateness of "activities, irrespective of the developmental model" (354, p. 46) as well as for appropriate "timing" of the activities. Sternberg suggests that programs must allow for and encourage individual differences as well as "be socioculturally relevant to the individuals who are exposed to the training program" (367, p. 7). This is certainly one of the major reasons why seven school districts and a state education department developed McRAT (Multicultural Reading and Thinking Project) which is designed to increase cultural awareness, develop critical thinking and teach explicit generic thinking skills and strategies (321).

Summary

It is apparent that no one can work alone on a thinking project. In the best of all programs, well trained, committed teachers who are good thinkers themselves and who have the support and involvement of administrators and parents engage all students in thinking.

X

Problem Solving and Decision Making

You might say that we have left the best until last. When you think about thinking, the first thing that comes to mind for most of us is problem solving, critical thinking and creative thinking. These are the buzz words. These are the words emphasized by the various programs. These are the categories school boards and administrators include when they want to reassure taxpayers and parents that they are current and doing a great job. We have deliberately left these until the end because without a theoretical understanding of thinking and without knowledge of how to teach thinking it is difficult to consider these specific areas and what is being done in terms of instruction.

The "dimensions of thinking," according to Jones et al., include areas such as "comprehending and composing, problem solving and decision making, critical and creative thinking, and metacognition" (184, p. ix). Perkins (294) offers a similar list including: reasoning, problem solving, inventing, learning, planning and decision making, communicating and understanding. We have already had a great deal to say about metacognition. We will examine that area further as part of these other dimensions. We have elected to isolate the popular areas of the problem solving and decision making, critical thinking and creative thinking but to examine each also in relation to reading and writing as well as to content area instruction.

The relationships between problem solving, critical thinking and creative thinking are complex, at best. Let's look at only a few examples. Stonewater views critical thinking as the umbrella and sees problem solving as "an important aspect of critical thinking" (376, p. 34). On the other hand, Nickerson et al. see problem solving, "enhanced by a number of metacognitive skills" (264, p. 110), as the umbrella and include creative thinking under it. Ruggiero (337) includes both critical and creative thinking as parts of the problem solving process.

If we add decision making to the mix, we further complicate the relationships. Yinger (427) views problem solving and decision making as the umbrellas with critical and creative thinking as essential elements. Beyer (36) concurs; problem solving and decision making are both complex strategies requiring critical and creative thinking, which are not strategies. Finally, Nardi and Wales suggest that decision making is the heart of any educational program. It includes problem solving and creative and critical thinking. For example, in the process of decision making, they stress that students "learn how to think critically" (254, p. 223). Critical thinking and problem solving represent "the enabling skills" (395, p. 41) required for decision making.

To compound the matter, Beck, after examining all these areas, concludes that "the terms higher order thinking, critical thinking, problem solving, and reasoning are virtually synonymous. So while we can't define the abstraction precisely, we know it when we see it, and it is highly valued and important for learning and living" (25, p. 676). On that note, let's look at each of these categories of thinking.

Definitions and Descriptions

First, we need some sense of how the various thinkers define and describe problem solving and decision making.

- Polya: "Solving a problem means finding a way out of a difficulty, a way around an obstacle, attaining an aim that was not immediately understandable" (in 159, p. 350).

- Flower: "A problem, however, is simply any situation in which you are at point A and need to find some way to get to your goal, point B. Problem-solving is the act of getting there, of achieving goals" (127, p. 43).

- Resnick and Ford: A problem is "a situation in which a person wants something and does not immediately know how to get it" (330, p. 23). Whether a situation is a problem depends on the person.

- Presseisen: In problem solving the task is to resolve a known difficulty. The end result is a solution. In decision making the task is to choose a best alternative and the end result is a response to the problem (313).

- Halpern: Decision making is similar to problem solving. In both cases there is the recognition that a problem exists and there are options to be considered. Many decisions are made in solving the problem. Decision making differs from problem solving in that there may be a number of possible solutions (159).

- Beyer: Decision making involves choosing from a number of alternative solutions. Problem solving is coming up with one solution. If that doesn't work, you come up with another one (36).

Descriptions of problem solving and decision making in the literature range from following steps in a heuristic, or specific discrete strategies for solving clear cut, well-defined problems (as in math or logic), to a more global view of a problem as any information to be understood and learned, by either reading or listening, including the ill-defined, amorphous problems of real life. In this description the problem is conceptualized as the act of thinking itself.

In the past, we as teachers assumed that students knew how to think and solve problems automatically, whether in math or everyday life problems. We concentrated on developing content area knowledge. However, in the past decade or so an interest in research and teaching of thinking and problem solving has evolved.

Problem Solving Components

For effective problem solving the problem solver needs a number of abilities: generic skills and strategies, content specific skills and strategies, knowledge of the content of the problem to be solved as well as metacognitive awareness of himself as a problem solver. Do these components of problem solving sound familiar?

Generic Skills and Strategies

There are two approaches that have been taken in explaining how thinkers solve problems. One is to look at the steps or stages in problem solving and the other is to explore the anatomy of a problem. Both require the use of skills and strategies but are viewed from different perspectives.

Theorists and researchers have proposed sets of steps, ranging from the simple to the fairly complex. Generic skills and strategies in problem solving are the procedures which the problem solver actually goes through when solving a problem, whether the problem is a simple, well-defined, well-structured one or more global, social one.

- Polya: The list of "stages" (in 264, p. 75) developed by Polya in 1957 included: understand the problem, devise a plan, carry out the plan, look back, and check results. Polya's list was originally proposed for mathematics but has since been adapted for other areas.

- Beyer: This list of five "strategies" (36) includes: recognize the problem, represent the problem, devise/choose a solution plan, execute the plan, and evaluate the solution. In adding the strategy "represent the problem," he is highlighting one of the heuristics Polya included as part of "understanding the problem."

- Sternberg: This list is expanded to include: problem identification, process selection, representation selection, strategy selection, processing allocation, solution monitoring, sensitivity to feedback, translation of feedback into an action plan, and implementation of the plan (366).

- Stonewater: This list includes: identify the problem, state the problem objective, list the constraints, assumptions and facts, generate possible solutions, determine the most likely of these, analyze, synthesize and evaluate the solutions, and report, implement and check results (376).

- Bransford et al.: Generic problem solving skills include encoding and organizing information in an easily accessible format, understanding the significance of information, testing and revising hypotheses throughout the procedure, knowing when there is insufficient or inconsistent information to solve a problem, adjusting to the demands of a specific task, being aware of one's failure to comprehend, and using appropriate compensatory strategies (50).

These lists of "stages," "skills," or "strategies" all suggest some common elements: the problem solver needs to identify the problem, figure out how to solve it, and decide if he did a good job. This general approach has been widely implemented in programs designed to teach problem solving. For example, in the television program Think About and the classroom program Connections students receive direct instruction in a sequence of steps and strategies to take in the process of solving problems moving from identifying the problem to evaluating the solution.

Within this framework there seem to be some crucial areas in which strategies need to be applied effectively. Nickerson et al. identify the limiting factors in thinking as encoding the matter to be thought about (identifying the problem), "operating on the encoded representation" (264, p. 51) (figuring out how to solve the problem), and moving effectively toward an identified goal (deciding if the task is well done). Of these stages or strategies there are two that appear particularly critical according to Gick (146). These are the generation of a representation of the problem and the solution process. The strategies used for each of these may differ depending on the knowledge of the problem solver and the problem itself. Gick also found that "some recent studies suggest a positive relationship between conscious use of strategies and problem solving" (p. 113). The specifics that might be included under each item may differ according to the content domain of the problem, the difficulty of the problem itself, and the competency and content knowledge of the thinker.

The same general sequence is often suggested for decision making, with the recognition that more than one possible decision can be made. Here, too, the steps can be translated into programs. For example, the program Guided Design provides explicit instruction in the steps of decision making. Beyer (36) includes the following steps: define the goal, identify alternatives, analyze and rank alternatives, judge highest-ranked alternatives, and choose the "best" alternative.

Nardi and Wales (254) have recognized that the process may differ according to the thinker and the problem. They identify four operations for simple problems for young children: state the goal, consider the options, prepare a plan, take actions. For more complex problems and more mature students, these four operations can serve three different processes: find the cause of the problem, solve the problem, and anticipate potential problems.

Another way to look at problem solving is to explore the anatomy of the problem. Newell and Simon (in 146, 159) suggest we look at the basic parts, or structures, which constitute all problems, and reduce each problem to its anatomical parts in order to understand and solve them, rather than following a series of stages or steps to solve problems. Newell and Simon identified a set of procedures problem solvers use generically across all domains and kinds of problems. They refer to this approach as means-end analysis. According to Newell and Simon, the problem solver goes through certain steps when solving any problem. The problem solver:

- assesses his or her present state, determines what his/her problem is;
- assesses his or her goal state, what kind of solution is required;
- identifies simpler subgoals which are directed toward the final goal;
- develops a series of actions to arrive at a subgoal solution, reducing differences between present state and goal state.

This approach may be used differently by different problem solvers. According to Newell and Simon, experts, those who have a great deal of knowledge in the content of the problem, work forward from present state to goal state (from the problem to the solution) in a serial manner while novices, those who have little content knowledge, work backward from goal state. They assess the goal state and determine the unknown. Unknowns then become subgoals and means-end analysis is repeated backwards to find the problem state, as in a maze (in 275). Once again, we see that content knowledge is critical to expert thinking.

Owen and Sweller (275) state that use of means-end analysis by novices is ineffective because it requires great cognitive effort, and therefore interferes with ability to acquire knowledge and schemas necessary to become an expert, to be able to solve problems more efficiently. According to Owen and Sweller, means-end strategy causes heavy cognitive load because the problem solver must perform a variety of activities simultaneously. He or she must: consider the problem goal, the current problem state and the relation of the current state to the goal state, all at the time. Therefore, novices use many cognitive resources, which might otherwise be used to learn new content knowledge. Owen and Sweller conclude that means-end analysis may be the least efficient problem solving procedure.

This means-end analysis approach to problem solving has been characterized by Polson and Jeffries (310) as an information processing approach. There has been relatively little done to translate it into programs that could be adopted for school settings.

No matter what approach is taken to problem solving, one strategy that seems important is the ability to monitor success or failure at a task. Metacognition is routinely identified as significant in the process (264). It is this important strategy of metacognition that makes instruction in problem solving particularly difficult because students see the product of problem solving, not the process. The process is not obvious. The student seldom sees the recursive nature of problem solving. In fact, it is this difficulty which provides much of the impetus for teacher modeling, using a think-aloud procedure, for demonstrating the hidden, metacognitive nature of problem solving (326). In addition, research suggests that we need to train metacognitive skills in combination with domain specific knowledge as is done in Reciprocal Teaching, for example.

There clearly is no consensus as to exactly how thinkers engage in problem solving. It is relevant, however, to note the frequency with which the act of problem solving is linked in some way to the content of the problem. In addition, we can consider the act acquiring information itself as a form of problem solving. For example, Bransford et al. (50) see the entire task of acquiring any new knowledge, both content information and metacognitive skills, as a kind of problem solving.

They suggest the "IDEAL" model for problem solving: Identify, Define, Explore, Act, and Look and Learn.

Content Specific Skills and Strategies

In addition to generic skills, the problem solver needs to have content specific skills and strategies. We have already explored this subject in relation to general thinking skills. These are often identified as knowledge of the particular skills and strategies useful in solving problems in a particular content area such as math or economics. There are indications that domain specific skills (competencies within a domain) develop together with general thinking and problem solving skills (50)

We will examine this more closely when we look at problem solving in the content areas.

Content Knowledge

We have already identified the importance of content knowledge in problem solving. Effective problem solving depends strongly on the nature, quality and organization of the content knowledge available to individuals (50, 355). Therefore, acquisition of knowledge in a content area promotes development of problem solving skills in that area as well as strategy use and problem solving ability in general (57).

Content knowledge influences problem solving ability because knowledge in a particular content area or domain helps the solver to generalize and store procedures for solving a problem in that domain in larger, well organized "sets," or "chunks," in memory (77). An expert in mechanics, for example, represents a "set" of formulas for solving a mechanics problem by a single concept or chunk (77). This efficient way to remember how to solve a problem in a particular content area lets the expert solve problems in his content area more automatically, giving him a chance to use more of his cognitive energy on nonautomatic problems. For example, a skilled reader, reading about a topic that he knows very well, can decode and retrieve information, establish relationships with prior knowledge and read and understand automatically, leaving more cognitive energy to learn new information on the topic. Thus, we can see that the amount of knowledge a problem solver has in a particular content influences how well a problem in that content can be solved. It is not, however, solely a question of amount of knowledge. We can also see that misconceptions may also cause difficulties and must be addressed by teachers (153).

Clearly, content knowledge has an important role in the development of problem solving as well as all thinking skills.

Sources of Difficulty

In examining the components of the problem solving process, we can identify a number of places where the process itself can present difficulties to the thinker. We know the difficulties of solving problems in unfamiliar domains and we recognize the difficulties of transferring problem solving skills and strategies to new, unique and different situations. In addition, we find, in the literature, specific areas where difficulties can arise. Green, McCloskey, and Caramazza (153), in looking at problem solving in physics, identify the problems generated by inaccurate and incomplete prior knowledge in the content area. We have already identified the importance of this and we recognize the difficulty of solving problems in unfamiliar domains.

Difficulties may also arise in representing the problem, both graphically and in memory (146,264). Representation of the problem involves the cognitive and active study strategies already discussed. For example, Halpern (159), in representing problems, advocates: writing it down, drawing a graph or diagram, making a hierarchical tree, making a matrix, and manipulating models. These are certainly the construction of graphic organizers already identified as a powerful cognitive strategy.

There appear to be a number of areas that can cause difficulty in representing the problem. Larkin (202) found that novice problem solvers in physics constructed naive representations of the problem because they lacked knowledge of the scientific (content) framework of the problem as well as procedural and epistemic content knowledge. The expert solver in a particular domain, however, can represent a problem accurately and completely in terms of a schema containing both factual and procedural knowledge for solutions (159). The same problems may be represented at different levels of complexity according to the expertise of the solver (76). Siegler (351) advances the notion that the problem solver must be able to encode the problem, i.e., represent the problem in memory. When this is done inaccurately, incompletely, or at too low a level for the particular problem, it results in ineffective problem solving. Greeno (in 310) found that representations must be coherent, accurately describe the task, and relate to the solver's prior knowledge. These three criteria need to be met if the thinker is to solve the problem effectively and efficiently.

In addition, there are indications that the problem itself can affect the act of problem solving. Problems can differ along a number of dimensions: the difficulty and complexity of the problem to be solved, the nature of skills required, and the ease of identifying the appropriate strategy to be used (264). Problems also differ in the relevance of their content to the problem solver (400).

Programs designed to teach and develop problem solving will need to recognize these potential difficulties.

Problem Solving and The At-Risk Student

If the task of solving problems can present difficulties to thinkers, and if particular problems themselves present difficulties, we need to consider the additional difficulties that at-risk students may encounter. Due to the cumulative effects of their lack of achievement they frequently have less content knowledge in general. Less content knowledge means fewer opportunities to group sets of procedures for solving problems and, of course, fewer instances in which problem solving will be automatic. Problem solving procedures which are not automatic take lots of cognitive energy and leave little energy to learn something new. Development in thinking and learning becomes a downward spiral. This fact reinforces the importance of teaching thinking skills to low achieving students and to linking content and thinking.

Learning disabled problem solvers may not have the same problem solving abilities, strategy use, or procedural knowledge as the nondisabled. Research indicates that they are likely to have a limited understanding of their own cognitive activities, how procedures such as means-end analysis contribute to their own learning (141), or how to utilize a problem solving strategy (87, 246, 384). There are indications that at least for middle school students, there may be approximately a two year lag in problem solving strategy development (21).

These difficulties may be compounded by affective and situational constraints experienced by the handicapped as well. Learning disabled children may "attribute success to external factors and failure to effort" (44, p. 67) which results in a poor self-image and ineffective use of metacognitive strategies (360). In addition, problem solving requires risk-taking. This, according to Cook and Slife (86), can be a problem with handicapped students because of their common attitude of "learned helplessness." The teaching situation itself may add to the difficulties. Because of time constraints within the school day, it is often more efficient for the teacher to provide solutions rather than spend time having students reach those solutions themselves.

Instruction

The instructional models and teaching strategies already discussed are also relevant in the teaching of problem solving. The strategies (cognitive, active, support and metacognitive) underlie discussions about teaching problem solving. We will only highlight one of the major ones and mention some that appear repeatedly in the literature.

Heuristics and Problem Solving

One instructional strategy that has been both popular and enduring has been teaching students to use heuristics in problem solving and decision making. We have already pointed out in Chapter 6 the advantages and disadvantages of this approach. Now, we need to examine more specifically how this approach has been adapted to problem solving and decision making, commonly using questions and/or lists.

One of the earliest and most commonly used and adapted heuristics was developed by Polya (in 264), based on his model of problem solving and designed to be used in the field of mathematics problem solving. In general, emphasis is placed on verifying the unknown and the known facts and the conditions, relating the solution of a particular problem to the solution of other known problems, graphically and visually representing the problem, and simplifying or making the problem more general. Polya provided a list of questions that would guide the solver through the areas to be considered.

This approach has been developed and used to help the thinker work through the process and solve the problem. One heuristic that is aimed at fostering the student's metacognitive knowledge about success in problem solving presents an interesting format based on questions. In a "thinking journal" (18) the student responds on a regular basis to questions about progress in problem solving: What was the problem I had to solve? How did I solve it? (identify thinking strategies, not solutions) Did I solve it? Well? What other kinds of problems (in school and every day) could I solve using these strategies? Where else are the strategies applicable?

Additional issues and questions about other aspects of problem solving are also included in the thinking journal. These include: Identify a problem, dilemma or conflict of interest to you. What questions do you have about this situation? Generate as many as you can over a period of time. How can the strategies learned in class help with this problem? What are you learning about responding to real life situations as a result of recording your thinking processes in this journal? Note the link between academic problems and real life problems. Note also the emphasis not just on solving the problem but also on identifying the strategies used.

Another approach using heuristics is a list of 14 general strategies suggested by Halpern (159). These are presented to the student in some detail with numerous examples from various content areas as well as real life. The strategies may be used alone or in combination, depending on the problem and on the solver. They include such items as representing the problem (this is familiar!), means-ends analysis, simplifying, brainstorming and restating the problem. The key here is that these are general approaches, general strategies that can be used over a wide variety of problems. It is up to the solver to be familiar enough with them and their effectiveness in particular situations so as to choose wisely. This is a broad approach and one which illustrates one of the drawbacks of general heuristics. Not everyone will become expert enough and confident enough to choose wisely. The role of the teacher here is clear.

Discussion

One teaching strategy that appears repeatedly in the literature on problem solving is the need for students to engage in discussion as part of a group process of problem solving (178, 305, 355, 376). Think aloud activities, for example, enable students to help each other identify breakdowns in solving the problem and share ways to solve it (85, 190, 214, 406).

Organizing Information

This is a widespread strategy both for teaching and for helping students solve problems on their own. For teaching, it enables students and teachers to identify misunderstandings and misconceptions as well as original and helpful ways of representing problems (190).

Problem Solving and Academics

It is here that we face the reality of problem solving and decision making in the classroom. This is no longer theoretical. It is a question of "how do I plan a program and what do I do on Monday morning?" As you have undoubtedly figured out by now, we will suggest alternatives. You will make decisions.

Teaching using a problem solving framework may involve more initial work on the part of the teacher and make take more class time than reading the chapter and answering questions or memorizing procedures. However, it may be a trade-off. How much learning and thinking takes place in a traditional approach compared to a thinking, problem solving approach? How much are students motivated to become actively involved if they are presented with a problem, academic or real, and join their peers in solving it? These are the kinds of questions teachers and administrators must consider in developing instruction in problem solving.

Consider again the definitions included at the beginning of this section and their implications for the classroom. The suggestions made by those concerned with educational practice frequently fit into three categories. One group views the task of learning content material as a problem solving task. We might relate this to Polya's definition of problem solving as a "means of finding a way out of a difficulty." We will examine

Sternberg's view of the task of writing as an example of this approach.

A second group suggests that teachers and students can thoughtfully and purposefully choose problem solving or decision making as a way of identifying the problem in a text or a content situation and solving it (62). The solution may lead to a new path or task, improved comprehension of the text or new knowledge. This is reminiscent of Flower's (127) view of problem solving as the act of reaching goals. There are numerous examples of this in the literature dealing with academic problem solving.

Finally, consider the third group, those who say that part of the process of engaging in an academic task is decision making, which involves choosing from a number of alternatives. We will see how the practitioner includes this in instruction. Implied in these last two views of problem solving and decision making is the question of whether instruction will be integrated into the academic area in which it is taught or will be separate with some provision for transfer. Not everyone addresses this issue directly, but it certainly needs to be considered eventually.

In viewing problem solving and content areas, we will look at only a few suggestions in order to provide an overview of some of the possibilities. There is a substantial body of opinion which advocates teaching the process of problem solving and decision making as part of content area instruction. In a review of the research on teaching problem solving, Picus, Sachse, and Smith (305) conclude that instruction in problem solving should be integrated into the content areas and that all content areas are appropriate. Two of the generic programs that have been developed with this premise are Guided Design and Connections. They both include direct instruction in the steps in decision making, relating instruction to content areas.

Problem Solving and Writing

The relationship between problem solving and writing is not a simple straightforward one. Writing itself can be an act of problem solving or problem solving can be a vehicle for engaging in writing. Clearly these two approaches are closely related although not always explicitly recognized.

Writing as an Act of Problem Solving

This approach has been clearly and explicitly detailed by Sternberg (366). He has taken his steps in problem solving and applied them to the task of writing, viewing writing as problem solving. Let's examine this view in some detail. His steps include:

- Problem identification is choosing a topic.

- Process selection is identifying sources of information for the topic.

- Representation selection is the process of representing the information internally (in the writer's head) and externally on paper in the form of notes, note cards or diagrams.

- Strategy selection implies that in writing you don't write the introduction until you have completed the research and gathered the data.

- Processing allocation requires not allotting so much time to doing research that you don't have enough time to write.

- Solution monitoring requires that the writer keeps track of what has been written, what is currently being written and what needs to be done.

- Sensitivity to feedback involves both the writer's own view of how well the writing is going as well as getting feedback from others.

- Translation of feedback into action means that once the feedback is received, from whatever source, the writer refocuses and reorganizes the writing.

- Implementation of an action plan suggests that the writer will outline and focus on the next writing task.

Sternberg has certainly made these links clear and to these two writers, actively engaged in the act of writing, the argument is persuasive.

Problems as a Vehicle for Engaging in Writing

In one writing program problems are the vehicle for beginning the task. Students are presented with a "specific problem and a body of detailed and proscribed data" (112, p. 168). Together with the teacher they explore ways the problem can be solved, examine an explanation of how authors have solved similar problems, and analyze a sample essay and develop a plan. Students then write their own essays. Next, in a group without the teacher, they attempt the same process. Here, problems and the problem solving process become a vehicle for organizing, understanding and engaging in the writing process.

Writing Using a Problem Solving Process

Authors have focused on a particular aspect of the problem solving process. Using Sternberg's framework, consider this possibility: Meeks suggests the use of peer response groups in order to allow students an opportunity to talk aloud about their writing. This enables the writer as a talker to "listen to the internal voice that is the core of all learning" (236, p. 119). The writer/listener also hears the voices of others giving feedback on the writing. Here is an example of Sternberg's sensitivity to feedback. The next part of the process, the translation of feedback into action, occurs as an integral part of the response group. Meeks asserts that this is metacognition about writing.

Writing as Problem Solving Using Heuristics

Flower suggests that "writing is a thinking process. To be more specific, it is a problem-solving process" (127, p. 3) and Flower and Hayes (128) suggest it is a process of decision making. It has much in common with problem solving in other areas. For example, the writer needs to use prior knowledge and problem solving strategies. Flower suggests that "heuristics—that is, efficient strategies or discovery procedures—are the heart of problem-solving" (127, p. 44) and have a good chance of succeeding. She provides nine steps in writing, beginning with exploring a problem, using creative thinking to "seek out ideas without trying to edit or tidy them up"(p. 71) and organizing ideas, which helps turn them into "clearly stated ideas" (p. 82) with a logical argument. This sounds like critical thinking. In using a heuristic approach for engaging in writing, Flower suggests using a hierarchical tree as a way of organizing the ideas and information. Shades of graphic organizers! Note also that Flower places creative thinking and critical thinking under the umbrella of problem solving using cognitive strategies. In addition, Brostoff (55) suggests providing students with detailed questions and checklists to use while writing, to identify and state problems and to evaluate hypotheses.

Problem Solving and Reading

Again, we have a dual approach in which reading may be viewed as a problem solving act and in which problem solving becomes a useful strategy for the reader. We can see these strategies used separately or together.

Comprehending Narrative Text Using a Problem Solving Framework

Beck (25) advocates that the teacher direct students to identify problems as they appear in the text and to answer specific text-related questions in the course of the reading which will focus attention on possible solutions as they become evident in the text. Students may also focus on creative solutions they generate. In all cases, the teacher is asking the questions, questions relating to the details of the particular story.

Comprehending a History Text Using a Problem Solving Heuristic

The use of a problem-solving frame, illustrated by Jones (182), enables the student reading a history text to identify who had the problem, what was the problem, what caused the problem, what were the negative effects, what actions were taken to solve the problem, and what were the results of these actions. Here a problem solving approach is used as a heuristic to aid comprehension of a social studies text.

A Decision Making Framework for Expository Text

Shenkman (350) teaches comprehension fostering and monitoring and critical thinking using a procedure called LETME: Link new information to prior knowledge, Extract information and ideas, Transform by organizing and reorganizing through summarizing and mapping, Monitor progress, and Extend through critical thinking. Students make decisions in each one of these areas as they progress through the text, completing a LETME study plan.

Comprehending and Decision Making in Cooperative Learning Groups

Decision making can aid in comprehension while at the same time reading and analyzing narrative text can introduce students to decision making strategies, according to Kuhrt and Farris (196). They suggest a specific procedure. Students read the text to a certain point and discuss as a group in order to identify the problem. Then, before proceeding, in cooperative groups, they search for alternatives. In the search for alternatives, Kuhrt and Farris use a decision-making chart with alternatives down the left side and criteria for judging them across the top. The group discusses pros and cons and assigns points to each alternative. The reading of the text is completed and the author's alternative is evaluated and compared to the one chosen by the group. This approach, according to the authors, empowers both teacher and students.

Critical Reading Through Cooperative Problem Solving

Here we find cooperative problem solving suggested as the vehicle for engaging students in critical thinking as they read. Flynn (129) uses Bransford et al.'s (50) IDEAL approach, which consists of Identifying, Defining, Exploring, Acting and Looking. Problem solving strategies are suggested for the various steps. For example, diagrams are useful for representing the problem in Defining. Flynn emphasizes the recursive nature of problem solving and points out that students may need to work through the cycle of steps more than once. The problem solving procedure aids in understanding the text, the cooperative learning aids in developing "critical thinking through discussion, negotiation, clarification of ideas, and evaluation of other's ideas" (p. 666).

Some Thoughts on Problem Solving and Reading

Consider the elements included in these suggestions and how they vary. In the first alternative, the teacher asks specific oral questions based on a problem solving framework, not general problem solving questions. In this approach the teacher is using problem solving to guide the students. The students respond in a group. We must be concerned here with whether the students, as well as the teacher, understand the problem solving framework. Remember Gick's finding that students need to use the strategies consciously.

In the second alternative, the students respond individually to general problem solving questions in the form of a heuristic that might be used with any text. Both the questions and answers are written. Here they have a graphic organizer using a problem solving heuristic. In the third alternative, students also use a heuristic to make decisions as they comprehend, engage in critical thinking, and use problem solving strategies. In using these strategies teachers need to consider the importance of discussion in the process. Do students discuss the process and the product with their peers and with the teacher?

In the fourth alternative, students are in cooperative learning groups with assigned responsibilities. No questions are asked by the teacher, rather the students generate the alternatives, issues and criteria they think are relevant. They use a grid to organize the information. They are using a specific decision making process in order to comprehend and interact with the text.

In the final example, we see problem solving explicitly linked to critical thinking, using cooperative learning groups. In this alternative, two areas of thinking have been linked and made clear to the students. They are using and applying specific strategies, including cognitive, active study and metacognitive ones. The emphasis is on learning through inquiry and discussion, with the teacher providing a scaffold.

Consider how these differences in approaches relate to what we suspect is useful for instructing in the knowledge and the conscious use of the cognitive, active study and metacognitive strategies effective thinkers use. Consider also the use of the instructional strategies of discussion and cooperative learning. In making the critical decisions on what to include in thinking instruction, and how to include it, we need to examine alternatives from every perspective.

Problem Solving and Mathematics

In considering problem solving in math, we need to be concerned both with strategies used and with prior knowledge, since so much of the knowledge in mathematics, in terms of skills and content, is sequential. It has been found that older children outperform younger children in solving math word problems (247, 331). While such differences may reflect more complete conceptual knowledge of the problem domain, or more sophisticated problem solving procedures, Riley, Greeno, and Heller (331) hypothesize that the greater problem solving ability of older children is the result of an increase in the complexity of their conceptual knowledge. They cite studies that indicate that problems with the same arithmetic structure, i.e., those requiring the same operations but different conceptual structures, i.e., semantics, differ substantially in their level of difficulty for children. Further, problems that are difficult in their wording are made easier by changing the wording in appropriate ways. Riley et al. point out that this emphasis on the importance of conceptual knowledge is not to say that knowledge of formal arithmetic is any less important. On the contrary, the authors state that "an important possibility is that acquisition of certain conceptual structures depends upon the knowledge of formal arithmetic that children acquire through school instruction" (p. 155).

Here, one again, we see confirmation of the complex links between content knowledge and thinking, in this case problem solving in mathematics. One of the difficulties in this field has been the emphasis on direct instruction in content and the second place given to problem solving. In 1980, the National Council of Teachers of Mathematics took a firm position. "Problem solving must be the focus of school mathematics in the 1980's" (207). It is useful to note that in 1989 that same group still identified as one of five broad goals for students the need to learn to solve problems (365). However, progress has definitely been noted. According to Hyde and Bizar in 1989 "a very heartening situation in the state of mathematics education today is the shift toward problem solving" (174, p. 95).

How can students learn to engage in problem solving in mathematics? Let's look at only three suggestions out of many possible ones. These examples illustrate that what is being suggested for problem solving in other academic areas as well as for thinking in general is also appropriate for mathematics.

Mathematics Problem Solving and Active Learning

Consider Steen's (365) recommendations for instruction which include the suggestions that we: actively engage students, encourage teamwork,stimulate creativity, require writing, and encourage discussion. We must move from such instructional techniques as telling students and encouraging rote memorization to these techniques which will promote inquiry and problem solving.

Cooperative Learning and Problem Solving in Mathematics

Simon suggest using cooperative learning, an instructional strategy which has not traditionally been included in mathematics classrooms. He particularly links problem solving and metacognition with this instructional procedure. "A student who is working alone is less likely to become aware of managerial or metacognitive processes in problem solving" (357, p. 42).

Using Problems and Problem Solving Heuristics to Initiate Learning about Mathematatics

Hyde and Bizar (174) use problems that are meaningful, real and engaging to students in order to begin the cyclical process of problem solving and learning mathematical content, concepts and procedures. Problem solving should not be saved for the end. Students use Polya's four phases of problem solving and actively choose strategies and monitor their use. A series of questions is suggested as a heuristic for self-monitoring throughout the problem solving process.

Computers and Problem Solving

The hope has certainly been that by engaging students in learning programming and also by engaging them in computer programs which teach thinking, they would become effective problem solvers and would transfer these abilities to other domains. The outcomes here have been disappointing (210). Some suggestions to overcome this difficulty of learning and of transferring have been made (224). Black, Swan and Schwartz (40) found that structured opportunities to engage in problem solving were effective in learning the problem solving process. They suggest that in order to insure transfer we need to provide instruction in strategies using a forced approach, to model metacognitive processes and to require that students detail the procedures they are using. Linn (210) makes generally similar suggestions, including the need for structured, explicit instruction, attention to areas of difficulty, and the need for organization of information and procedures. The critical role of the teacher is cited by both sources as essential if students are to transfer skills and strategies from the computer to academics or real life.

Problem Solving and Science

Problem solving in science has been loosely equated with using the scientific method. However, here again, we find the emphasis on strategy selection, flexibility in the use of strategies (96) and the critical importance of monitoring and controlling the strategies chosen and used (215). The same concerns, cautions and components are evident in problem solving in science as are evident in all areas.

Problem Representation in Science

"The central difference between expert and novice solvers in a scientific domain is that novice solvers have much less ability to construct or use scientific representations" (202, p. 150). This certainly sounds familiar by now. It is a common concern. Larkin (202) suggests that we teach students to construct graphic representations of the problem or to invent notions. The graphic representation is certainly familiar. The point here is that there are many ways to represent the problem. The critical element is to make this a major focus of instruction, emphasizing, as does Lochhead (214), the matter of selecting among possible representations.

Content Knowledge and Problem Solving in Science

The need for appropriate prior knowledge in order to think about a scientific problem is a matter of common concern (153, 174, 202). The problem of popular misconceptions in science is particularly troublesome. Both Green et al. (153) and Hyde and Bizar (174) stress the need to directly confront the misconception and actively engage the students in examining it and restructuring knowledge to accommodate the new, accurate knowledge.

Problem Solving and Social Studies

A problem solving approach to social studies allows students to enter into the process of solving community, institutional and historical problems. Let's look at only three examples.

Understanding Social Studies by Solving Problems

Guysneir recommends presenting problems to be solved, not questions to be answered, in order to involve and motivate students. He suggests that teachers use "a well-defined, controversial problem" (155, p. 19).

Using Computers for Problem Solving in History

Copeland (88) describes the use of computers as a data base and as a model of the inquiry process in solving historical problems.

Problem Solving, Critical Thinking and Graphic Organizers in History

Bean, Sorter, Singer, and Frazee (24) report on a program in which students were taught to construct graphic organizers in order to evaluate possible options of how historical problems might have been solved. They actively and critically engaged in decision making in small groups.

Problem Solving across Curriculum Areas

The notion of "anchored" instruction is advanced by Bransford, Vye, Kinzer, and Risko (51) in which students are provided with extended problem solving situations, often on a videodisc, in which they are actively engaged in finding the problem, solving it, reasoning, and learning relevant content material. The critical element in this approach is that students view the situation from multiple perspectives and extend the strategies into various content areas. Bransford et al. describe The Young Sherlock Project in which students use a heuristic (an organizing framework) to guide their viewing of a mystery, analyze other mysteries, and write their own. The approach "generated a wealth of information" (p. 407) which was acquired and used by the students in different content areas.

Social Problem Solving

Problems in Social Problem Solving

There is a genuine concern that solving academic problems is not sufficient. Sternberg (368, 371) repeatedly emphasizes the importance of transferring all thinking skills developed in the classroom to everyday life. He suggests that if we want students to be able to use the problem solving skills we teach them in everyday life, we need to give them practice with these skills in everyday life problems. Unfortunately, he points out, most of the problem-solving skills taught in the classroom are clear-cut, neatly formulated, well defined and well structured. Information required for academic solutions is available in the problem itself or from what the student is presumed to know. Academic problems require definite, predictable strategies generating definite, predictable alternatives and solutions. Answers are straightforward and right or wrong. Problems "go away" when they are solved.

Life, as we well know, is not like that, however. Everyday problems are seldom simple; choices and possible solutions are not always readily apparent. Problems can be complicated, messy and stubbornly persistent. Often we must first recognize that a problem exists and understand exactly what the problem is. In addition, everyday problems may have more than one right solution, and solutions may have important, personal consequences. Simon (356) refers to these everyday social problems as ill-structured problems, which often require prior experience and external sources of information to be solved. Their solutions are more complex, not always clear cut, and, unlike school problems, all information required for solution may not be contained in the problem, or even readily available. Therefore, problem solving as taught in school may not be readily generalizable to the real world.

Social problem solving is a cognitive skill critical to coping in the real world, in both the social as well as educational sense (290). Nezu defines it as "the process by which people identify or discover effective means of coping with problematic situations encountered in real life" (258, p. 42). Problems pervade all areas of students' lives. There is, of course, no need to point out the difficulties in coping with school and life problems in the 1990s. Clearly we are not preparing our youth with skills necessary to face these problems. Increases in aggressive behavior, substance abuse, suicides, juvenile delinquency and juvenile crimes are rampant. An urgent need to take some steps to begin to remedy the situation is obvious. Teaching children to use problem solving skills learned in the classroom to solve real life social problems is one sensible direction for educators to take.

In fact, research indicates that there is a high correlation between being an effective problem solver and the ability to cope with stress (259), that teachers and peers view children who produce the least consistent quality of problem solutions as also the least socially competent members of their class (168), and that depressed college students rate themselves as poor problem solvers (258).

Solutions for Social Problem Solving

Since problem solving ability appears to be related to social competence, direct training in problem solving in the classroom and in transfer of those skills to the real world makes sense. Since we can't be sure that the skills we are training in the classroom will transfer from those simple school problems to everyday life, it is important to identify effective methods for solving all kinds of problems, in a variety of situations, to enable transfer and generalization to real life situations as well. There are a number of approaches that are advocated. Sternberg and Martin (374) suggest that training programs include a variety of content domains and teach transfer of the skills to problems in our everyday lives, reflecting everyday problem solving and decision making, in an effort to teach students how to solve real life, social problems. Training in skills such as identifying problems, generating alternatives, and evaluating alternatives and consequences, using real life problems, should help students cope with their own real life problems.

Simon (356), however, takes a somewhat different tack. He advocates teaching generic problem solving, since the amount and kind of content knowledge required to solve an ill-structured, everyday life problem changes constantly. In fact, according to Simon, even the conception of an ill-structured problem changes during the process of solving, depending on the solver's prior knowledge and the availability of outside sources of information. Further, he suggests ill-structured problems might be divided into smaller, well-structured ones to ease solution.

Not everyone concurs completely with either of these views, however. According to Nickerson et al., problems in the laboratory or in an academic setting require the same skills and strategies as are required by real world problems. "We do assume that such problems have some properties in common with those encountered outside the laboratory, and that approaches that work well in one context are likely also to have some utility in the other" (264, pp. 65-66). They suggest instruction in generic problem solving.

The approaches to including real life problems in the instructional program vary, particularly in regard to whether both real life as well as academic problems are included.

One approach is to present students with real life problems followed by the identification and solution of real life problems of concern to the students. It is interesting here to note that although the focus is on real life problems, it is possible to include curriculum content in these problems. Examples of this approach include:

- Future Problem Solving in which students study real life problems, then generate and solve their own real life problems;

- the television program Think About, which presents students with real life problems which are used for direct instruction in problem solving. Students then apply and practice strategies to their own real life problems. In addition, however, skills and content from the various academic areas have been included in the program;

- INTERFACE, a total immersion program, which was developed in a middle school. In this program students solve a real life problem that is of importance to them (70). All curriculum areas are included in the problem.

Another approach is illustrated by Strategic Reasoning (149), which introduces thinking skills, develops nonacademic thinking skills, transfers thinking skills to academic situations, and finally applies the thinking skills to real life problem solving.

In still another approach, students in Guided Design begin with decision making using real life problems. Once they are comfortable with the process they are introduced to academic problems. This bears some similarity to the approach already mentioned in mathematics taken by Hyde and Bizar in which they use math problems that "are posed in rich, meaningful contexts" (174, p. 95), problems which are real life problems for their students, such as how to break the class of 28 students into groups of three or four. Then, academic math problems are introduced.

How do students engage in real life problem solving and decision making? The suggestions here include many of the ones that are used in academic problem solving, with the recognition that the problem is a fuzzy one and may need to be broken down into smaller, manageable parts in order to organize relevant information and relate concepts. In both academic and real life problem solving, data and information must be gathered in order to understand the problem and generate solutions. One difference is that in real life problem solving we often find the students moving outside the school and into the real community (39, 70).

We find that some of the strategies are used in both academic and social problem solving. For example, the same decision making chart that was used to identify and rank possible outcomes in reading narrative text, suggested by Kuhrt and Farris (196), is also suggested by Halpern (159) as an effective device for decision making in real life. The chart or matrix enables, almost forces, the thinker to identify alternatives, break the problem down into manageable units, and organize the problem in the same way it enabled comprehension of text.

The same emphasis on group learning and discussing is found in solving real life problems as in solving academic problems. When a secondary school (39) wanted to involve students in solving problems in the community, the school was organized into teams, with the teams working together to develop and critique plans for solving the problems solicited from the community. The solutions and the names of the team members were sent to the organizations presenting the problem. In addition, students working in groups solve real problems that involve academic skills and content.

Summary

We can see that the focus on problem solving is a current concern. It is clear that instruction in both academic and social problem solving is needed and can be effective. In fact, research shows that both generic and content based training is effective. The onus is on us as researchers and educators to continue to develop this aspect of thinking instruction. We may not completely understand or agree on the relationship between problem solving and critical thinking but we know that critical thinking is an essential aspect of thinking. That should be our next concern.

XI

Critical Thinking

Teaching children to think critically has been perhaps the most popular, fastest growing part of the thinking skills movement. Why is this? The interest probably comes from two major sources: a combination of a growing conviction that we must have adults who are critical thinkers and a dawning awareness that we are not achieving this result.

On the one hand, there is a widely accepted viewpoint, almost a truism, that we need critical thinkers. In our complex political and economic global environment, critical thinking is essential. It is also morally justifiable because "being able to think critically is necessary condition for being educated" (265, p. 40). Kinney, in addition, states that "it does not require much documentation to establish that critical thinking is an important commodity in a highly sophisticated technical society" (193, pp. 1–2). He cites the need for college students and professionals such as supervisors, managers and scientists to be able to think critically.

Unfortunately, as we have already pointed out, educators are concerned about how well we're doing in this area, based on observations, school based studies and standard test scores. Norris (265) cites evidence from critical thinking tests, such as the Cornell Critical Thinking Test and from psychological research which indicates that high school and college students do not perform well on tasks that demonstrate critical thinking competence. The problem is compounded, according to Kinney, because college students may not be convinced that it is important to think critically. They see industry hiring people without examining their knowledge of and training in critical thinking.

In response to these disturbing concerns, education is now looking at critical thinking in a new light. We have traditionally focused on critical reading as a major skill students need to acquire. This has provided educators with a natural and comfortable transition into examining the larger, related issue of critical thinking. We see indications that critical thinking is becoming an accepted part of school programs, ranging from state mandates for elementary and secondary students (27) to courses for college students (118).

Definitions and Descriptions

Attempts to define critical thinking have differed along several dimensions. It has been defined both by its form and by its function, including the skills and strategies it encompasses as well as the levels of complexity involved. If you are uncertain about a definition after reviewing the ones we include, consider two comments. Beyer calls critical thinking "one of the most abused terms in our thinking skills vocabulary. Generally, it means whatever its users stipulate it to mean" (36, p. 32). Moreover, in looking at other definitions and developing their own, Walsh and Paul conclude that "defining critical thinking can seem as challenging as defining love" (396, p. 13).

There are certain elements that may or may not be included in a definition. One element is concerned with whether critical thinking is convergent or divergent. Another describes what the critical thinker does. A third element focuses on the attitude or disposition of the thinker. You don't usually find all three elements in every definition.

Critical thinking may be viewed as either a narrowing or expanding process, i.e., as either convergent or divergent thinking. Beyer states unequivocally that "critical thinking is convergent" (36, p. 35), contrasting it to creative thinking which is divergent. Kinney, in relating critical thinking to problem solving, concludes that "critical thinking is better considered an expanding, exploratory process than the progressive narrowing process of problem solving" (193, p. 5). The lines are drawn.

Another element often considered is what the critical thinker does. There are a number of perspectives on this. One task that is frequently included is that of evaluation. According to Beyer, "specialists today appear to agree that critical thinking is the assessing of the authenticity, accuracy and/or worth of knowledge claims and arguments" (33, p. 271). We find this assessment aspect of critical thinking included in many of the definitions. Nickerson et al. refer to this as a "filtering" (264, p. 88) process but one that also helps establish a direction. Ruggiero states that "critical thinking evaluates" (337, p. 28) ideas.

Beyer (36), for example, elaborates on this notion of analysis of knowledge and evaluation of worth. He goes on to describe a number of specific mental operations used by the thinker which constitute critical thinking, and which, when combined, analyze and evaluate a given argument or bit of knowledge. Beyer's opinion is that critical thinking is not a catch-all phrase to describe all thinking skills, as it is often used, such as comparing, predicting, judging, classifying, generalizing and questioning. He states that the term "critical thinking" has erroneously been equated with Bloom's Taxonomy, logical reasoning and problem solving.

Let's consider two more examples of definitions focusing on what the thinker does. According to Svinicki and Kraemer "the critical thinker. . .is an independent thinker capable of seeing clearly, thinking objectively, and acting wisely on his or her own behalf" (379, p. 62). Now, we have added "taking action" to the list of tasks. Norris (265) also describes critical thinking in these terms. In order to think critically one must assess one's own and others' views, be able to produce alternate views and actions, make reasonable hypotheses and inferences, and be "disposed" to think critically. This list of tasks bears some similarities to Beyer's, for example, but also includes some of the tasks Beyer criticizes. In addition, Norris highlights the third element, that of disposition.

This internal, affective element, a kind of "propensity" or inclination to think critically is increasingly included in definitions. It connotes the ability to think more deeply, control one's own thoughts and be motivated to think. Norris (265) describes it as a "disposition" and Beyer as a "frame of mind" (36, p. 35), inclined to consider all sides and search for truth. Hudgins and Edelman describe critical thinking as "the disposition to provide evidence in support of one's conclusions and to request evidence from others before accepting their conclusions" (171, p. 333). Yinger suggests that attitudes and dispositions influence thinking, including a disposition to search for evidence, make mistakes, take risks, and exhibit an attitude of "constructive discontent" (427, p. 26). The common element here is the emphasis on the affective. Skills and cognitive strategies aren't sufficient in critical thinking.

Paul, in considering the dispositions of the thinker, makes a useful distinction. He views critical thinking in two ways.

> In a *weak sense*, critical thinking skills are understood as a set of discrete micrological skills ultimately extrinsic to the character of the person; skills that can be tacked onto other learning. In the *strong sense*, critical thinking skills are understood as a set of integrated macro-logical skills ultimately intrinsic to the character of the person and to insight into one's own cognitive and affective processes. (285, p. 5)

Paul, in a later work, suggests that "philosophical thinking is very close to . . . strong sense critical thinking" (288, p. 473). Here, he clearly adds another dimension, that of philosophy in contrast to psychology.

Finally, let's consider Walsh and Paul's view of critical thinking which includes "interpreting, analyzing or evaluating information, arguments or experiences with a set of reflective attitudes and skills and abilities to guide our thoughts, beliefs, and actions" (396, p. 13). They add an important dimension, that of the result of critical thinking. It is not simply an exercise. There needs to be a purpose and an outcome.

In examining critical thinking we also need to explore how it is related to other kinds of complex thinking. We have already indicated that the relationship is certainly not settled. Depending on whose description you read, you can find critical thinking cited as an element of problem solving and decision making (427). You can find it discussed as a corollary to creative thinking (337, 427). You can find it identified as the umbrella, the focus under which problem solving is located (376). For example, critical thinking is defined by the National Council of Teachers of English as "a process which stresses an attitude of suspended judgment, incorporates logical inquiry and problem solving, and leads to an evaluative decision or action" (383, p. 64).

In describing critical thinking, theorists and researchers identify and describe its components, components with which we are already familiar.

Generic Skills and Strategies

In discussing problem solving we reviewed the stages or steps that are frequently included in solving a problem and discussed the skills and strategies it appears that problem solvers use. While there may be different opinions about the various steps and procedures, one point that seems to be universal is that problem solvers do, in fact, engage in a series of steps, possibly in a recursive manner, often beginning with defining the problem and ending with solving it. One of the differences cited between critical thinking and problem solving is that critical thinking does not seem to involve a series of sequential steps. In critical thinking, the skills and strategies are not seen as part of a sequence but rather as a group of skills and strategies chosen and used as needed by the particular thinking task (35). They can be used alone or in any combination.

Since there is no one set pattern, procedure or heuristic that can be learned and called up for every situation, there are more demands placed on the critical thinker. In problem solving the thinker can use a heuristic, possibly a piece of paper with a list of steps to follow or a set of questions to answer, while working through a problem. The thinker has guidance in making important decisions. However, in critical thinking, the thinker has no list of steps to take but must determine what is required by the task, retrieve and review the various skills and strategies, and apply the appropriate one or combination. This uncertainty undoubtedly puts additional responsibility on the critical thinker, but also on the teacher. The teacher must be cognizant of the attributes of each skill, the conditions under which it is useful, the criteria for choosing and using it, and the rules applicable for applying and monitoring it (36).

In looking at the generic skills and strategies of critical thinking, we find the same categories here as in thinking in general and as in problem solving. Let's examine them.

One set of generic skills which is frequently included in a list of generic critical thinking skills is that of reasoning (27, 67, 159, 261, 264). The question of what is involved in reasoning has intrigued philosophers and psychologists for years. Nickerson, for example, takes a broad view of reasoning and suggests that it involves "the production and evaluation of arguments, the making of inferences and the drawing of conclusions, the generation and testing of hypotheses. It requires both deduction and induction, both analysis and synthesis, and both criticality and creativity" (261, pp. 1–2). He identifies language, logic, inventiveness, knowledge, and truth as concepts closely related to reasoning.

Paul suggests that we need to ensure that "students receive a substantial amount of practice in reasoning dialogically or dialectically so that they become comfortable with and skilled in weighing, reconciling, and assessing contradictory points of view through rational dialogue, discussion, and debate" (285, p 13). This viewpoint is consistent with the rationale for having reasoning form the basis for a number of the prepackaged thinking skills programs such as Philosophy for Children, Analytic Reasoning, and Strategic Reasoning. It has also been included as an important element in programs such as Odyssey and Tactics. Reasoning has also found its way into assessment. The California Assessment Program, focusing on what the thinker does, adopted as its definition of critical thinking "the skills involved in (reasonably) deciding what to believe and do" (402, p. 1). Beyer in examining reasoning suggests that it is "the lubricant" (36, p. 30) in many of the critical thinking skills.

Closely allied to reasoning is the role of logic in critical thinking. Whether logic is considered part of critical thinking directly (27) or a component of reasoning (159, 261) the skills associated with logical thinking are frequently included in generic lists of skills. Halpern (159), for example, provides us with detailed accounts and descriptions of the various rules of logical thinking.

But this is theoretical. Practically, what options can critical thinkers choose from? Beyer (36) gives us 10 mental operations that will aid critical thinking. The list includes: determining the reliability of a source, the factual accuracy of a statement and the strength of an argument, distinguishing between verifiable facts and value claims, and between relevant and irrelevant information, and detecting bias, unstated assumptions, ambiguous arguments and logical fallacies and inconsistencies in a line of reasoning.

Lists like this can be found in many sources, although they might have different labels (117, 396). For example, Halpern (159) includes distinguishing fact from opinion instead of distinguishing verifiable fact from value claim. Also, instead of listing this along with other skills, she ties it directly to language and critical thinking. The label is different but the intention is the same. Does all this sound familiar? Have you seen these items in curriculum guides, in lists of skills, possibly reading skills? In fact, as Beck (25) points out, critical thinking has been a traditional focus of reading instruction. These kinds of generic skills have been part of reading instruction for some time.

While many approaches to critical thinking stress reasoning and/or a set of specific critical thinking skills, there is a growing recognition that we have to go beyond that. We are beginning to see new emphasis placed on the use of strategies in critical thinking, strategies that show a strong resemblance to those suggested earlier: cognitive, active, support and metacognitive strategies.

First, consider the cognitive strategy of organizing and reorganizing information. In order to engage in critical thinking, Yinger (427) suggests that the thinker must be able to organize and manipulate information. There is certainly intuitive appeal in this idea. If you are attempting to distinguish between fact and opinion while reading a newspaper article, for example, you certainly will need to organize the information into those categories if the writer has not done it for you. If the writer has used these categories you may want to reorganize the information in a way that is most useful to you and that takes into account your prior knowledge.

The active study strategy of student-generated questions is repeatedly cited for promoting critical thinking. Perkins, Allen and Hafner contrast the critical thinking skills of a skilled reasoner with a "make-sense" approach in which the thinker, in order to reduce cognitive load, determines that an argument appears to "make sense." A skilled reasoner, on the other hand, asks questions, refusing "to accept at face value what seems to be an adequate account" (300, p. 188). The authors conclude that this process can be taught. Yinger (427) concurs and suggests, in addition, that the questions asked are related to how thought is organized. This stresses a useful relationship between these two strategies.

Support strategies have been identified previously as significant in thinking, but they are particularly stressed in relation to critical thinking (116, 117, 260, 427). One important reason why dispositions and positive attitudes toward critical thinking are important is advanced by Swartz (380). She suggests that a major problem in instruction is that of transfer of critical thinking skills and strategies to various academic tasks as well as to real life problems. This transfer will not occur without critical attitudes in students.

If we are concerned with such dispositions as the willingness to take risks, confidence, attention to detail, open-mindedness, flexibility, persistence (to name only a few) what can we do to promote these in the classroom? We can attend to the physical environment, give instructions that will permit students to think, and demonstrate an encouragement of critical thinking and of the products of critical thinking (427). We can also use an inventory as the basis for an interview to determine critical thinking dispositions and as the basis for instruction (380).

Above all, researchers and educators have shown that the critical thinker uses his or her metacognitive knowledge and applies metacognitive strategies in a planful, purposeful way throughout the critical thinking process. Beyer (36), for example, divides critical thinking into four skills: distinguishing relevance from irrelevance and fact from value judgements, detecting bias, and determining the credibility of a written source. He then gives a specific list of criteria the critical thinker must consider for each skill and a series of steps to go through to execute the skill. For example, if a thinker has "decided" to determine the credibility of a written source, he or she must consider the following list of criteria: the author's reputation for accuracy and expertise in the field, the absence of conflict of interest or risk to the author's reputation, and agreement with other sources. After considering this criteria the thinker must then go through a series of steps, for example, identify goals, clues to look for, and patterns among clues as well as match evidence found to criteria. Clearly, to follow Beyer's procedure one must be metacognitive, planful and purposeful.

Glade and Citron (149) also focus on the importance of metacognitive strategy use in critical thinking. They have developed a Strategic Reasoning program based on the premise that training in the verbalization of thinking processes—a metacognitive strategy—enables students to be better learners, reasoners and problem solvers, and to transfer these skills to academic and real life situations.

Finally, Gallo (137) uses metacognitive strategies to develop critical thinking. She suggests that improved critical thinking requires developing the processes of observation, analysis, inference and evaluation, and among her recommendations for practice she includes the development of executive processes and metacognition. Her program, Think Metric, demonstrates the value of using metacognitive strategies in critical thinking.

Content Specific Skills and Strategies

There is substantial support for the notion that critical thinking skills may be generic. There is also, however, the view that holds that how the thinker engages in critical thinking is content specific (27). This implies that how you think critically may be related to the specific material under consideration. Related to this may be Beyer's belief that critical thinking is not an intact process in the way that problem solving and decision making are. Rather, the thinker chooses from among the skills the one or ones appropriate for the task. For example, in sorting through scientific data, there may be little need to distinguish between fact and opinion but a great need to distinguish between relevant and irrelevant data. Thus, there may be some skills that are more appropriate for a particular content area than for others. This is reminiscent of our discussion of the ways skills and content may be linked.

Content Knowledge

The need for appropriate and sufficient content knowledge is cited almost universally in relation to critical thinking (118, 159, 171, 261, 303). Nickerson's definition of reasoning joins two of the areas we are examining. "Reasoning is viewed here as a matter of both attitude and knowledge: one is unlikely to reason well about any subject unless one is deeply desirous of doing so, and one has some knowledge of the subject about which the reasoning is to be done" (261. p. 1).

Critical thinkers need more than a large knowledge repertoire. They also must have the ability to evoke particular knowledge when needed and integrate information from various sources (300). In addition to facts, they also need concepts and principles (427). This, in fact, has been cited as one of the reasons why instruction in critical thinking "must be embedded in every subject and not just a few scattered courses here and there" (27, p. 3).

Instruction

Thinking is natural, but unfortunately critical thinking is not. (396, p. 18)

This statement fairly well sums up a commonly felt rationale behind critical thinking instruction, a rationale which is supported by research. Norris describes the famous Milgrim experiment (1963) in detail to demonstrate evidence that people do not think critically for themselves. The subjects in this experiment let their commitment to obey an order, in this case to administer shock treatments, take over their own judgments and moral principles. Subjects in the Milgrim experiment knew they were acting immorally, yet they continued to follow directions. "The results point to a breakdown between critical thought and action, a link that instruction in critical thinking is intended to forge" (265, p. 42).

Let's consider another aspect:

Individuals who do not think critically, reflectively, effectively are not likely to be able to teach others to do so. (263, p. 39)

If there is a need to instruct, this statement by Nickerson highlights the role of the teacher in instruction. There is certainly a possibility that teachers and administrators are not critical thinkers. In fact, this concern is frequently implied and sometimes stated directly in the literature (282, 285, 288). Teachers may not be critical thinkers themselves because they have not had effective models. Alternatively, they may be thinking critically but may not be aware of how they are doing it (130). In either case, they need to develop their critical thinking skills and an awareness of the skills and strategies they use as well as those they might use. This might be done by learning along with the students, by attending conferences on thinking, by working in tandem with a colleague or university person, and by taking university or inservice courses (27, 35, 121, 130, 285, 396).

Educational institutions have concluded that the teaching of thinking, and critical thinking in particular, is crucial to the success of American education, and provisions for such education must be made a permanent and integral part of our curricula nationwide. The question as to how this monumental task is to be accomplished is by no means resolved.

Instructional Issues: One New, Three Familiar

The instructional issues raised here are, for the most part, the same ones that we have examined for thinking in general and for problem solving. We will review the positions taken specifically by those concerned with critical thinking in regard to three familiar issues: whether to teach isolated skills or provide a holistic experience, whether schools should develop their own programs or use prepackaged ones, and where to place critical thinking instruction in the curriculum. We will begin, however, by looking at a new issue, one closely identified with critical thinking in particular.

Bloom's Taxonomy: A New Issue

This issue, which arises when instruction in critical thinking in particular is examined, is whether to use Bloom's Taxonomy of Educational Objectives as a framework for instruction and also assessment. On the one hand, the Taxonomy appears simple, easy to apply to content areas, and manageable for teachers. However, there are those who take issue with equating the six levels in Bloom's Taxonomy to critical thinking, instead equating the Taxonomy with microlevel skills which may be used in critical thinking but which do not represent critical thinking (27, 36). Paul (286) contends, for example, that the Taxonomy teaches students to think critically by simply asking questions which require analysis, synthesis and evaluation. This is not sufficient. Ennis (117) cites the vagueness of the concepts in the Taxonomy and the lack of criteria for judging success. In addition, according to Paul, the Taxonomy may actually hinder critical thinking because it fosters thinking as a one-way hierarchy, i.e., knowledge can lead to comprehension, but comprehension can never lead to knowledge. The Taxonomy does not allow for the recursive, interdependent nature of the skills of critical thinking.

It is not uncommon in practice though for the levels in the Taxonomy to be used to plan critical thinking programs. Consider only a few examples: a college critical thinking course (379), an elementary and secondary writing program (270), a teacher developed social studies program (15), and teacher developed instructional and assessment procedures (428). These examples from very different levels of both teaching and assessment incorporate Bloom's levels as the framework for guiding the curriculum and related activities. Reliance on the levels in this Taxonomy provides a framework for the microlevel skills but unfortunately does not provide a broader framework for integrating them into the complex task of critical thinking or for incorporating useful strategies into critical thinking.

Isolated or Holistic Instruction

Because we are by now familiar with the following three major issues raised about critical thinking we will not review the basic arguments but will examine them only in relation to critical thinking. First, should we teach isolated skills or provide holistic instruction? The positions taken here resemble those taken in the larger arena of thinking in general. Beyer (36) certainly represents those advocating isolated skill instruction, believing that students need specific instruction in the various thinking skills in order to acquire each and transfer it to new situations. In fact, Beyer (35, 36) offers explicit strategies and guidelines for introducing and teaching critical thinking skills. These include inductive and direct instruction and strategies for guided practice, which concentrate on focusing students' attention continuously on the skill itself as well as on metacognitive aspects of what they are doing. The critical thinking program IMPACT (414) is an example of a program in which the basic level skills needed for critical thinking are taught sequentially and hierarchically. Girle (148), on the other hand, believes that a focus on the small units and the details is negative and impractical because the critical thinker, examining issues in isolation not in context, looks for fallacies and doesn't create concepts. Philosophy for Children represents this point of view in action as does Analytic Reasoning.

Prepackaged or Teacher Developed Programs

Our second issue is whether teachers should use a prepackaged program or develop their own program. There certainly are an abundance of prepackaged programs which have as their main focus critical thinking (CoRT, Philosophy for Children) or at least include it as an important secondary feature (Guided Design, Talents Unlimited, Think About). So, finding a prepackaged program is not a problem. This approach also may have the advantage of requiring less teacher training and involvement, often a consideration for busy teachers. Paul

(285) advocates as an immediate, short-term strategy the training of master teachers in a few excellent programs, such as Philosophy for Children. This use of a prepackaged program and a few excellent teachers would provide the catalyst for instruction in thinking skills.

However, critical thinking is an area where teachers may feel comfortable in developing their own program. Because critical thinking has been an educational concern for longer than most of the other areas, teachers are often more familiar with it and are receptive to including it in a program. Even teachers who are unfamiliar with the various skills and strategies of critical thinking can work along with their students and inductively discover what they are, according to Beyer (35). In addition, Swartz found that "teachers who have taken the time to understand critical thinking based on their own experience and study have turned away from pre-packaged curriculums in favor of infusing critical thinking into the restructured content of their own teaching" (381, p. 43). It may be that the component of teacher training may link these three issues. If a teacher feels comfortable with instructing in critical thinking, then it will be more likely to appear as a natural part of content teaching.

Separate or Integrated Instruction

Our third issue concerns whether critical thinking instruction should be provided separately or integrated into the content areas. This issue, particularly for critical thinking, may be linked to whether teachers feel comfortable developing their own program. We have already explored much of the controversy that exists about this issue and will only look specifically at critical thinking in relation to it. Ennis (119) presents four instructional approaches to teaching critical thinking: 1) critical thinking taught separately—without content, 2) infusion into content subjects—deep, well understood subject instruction in which students are explicitly instructed to think critically, 3) immersion instruction in which students are instructed in a subject and encouraged to think critically in it but thinking skills are not made explicit, or 4) a mixed model—students receive instruction in general principles of critical thinking as well as subject specific critical thinking instruction. He suggests that, since content knowledge is essential for thinking in any domain and sufficient practice within a content area is necessary for transfer of critical thinking abilities to other domains, general thinking programs are not likely to be effective.

The push for teaching critical thinking in content areas is strong. Swartz (381) advocates integrating teaching critical thinking in all content areas and at all grade levels, rather than using a prepackaged program or curriculum. This calls for a restructuring of the content curriculum incorporating skills, strategies and instruction relating to critical thinking into the traditional course content (151, 302). According to Swartz, teachers who are willing to do this, who will take on the enormous task of understanding critical thinking and incorporating it into all their teaching, prefer to bring critical thinking into their own coursework themselves rather than through prepackaged programs. Swartz states that this brings out the best in teachers as well as in students.

There is another dimension to this discussion of separate or integrated instruction. Paul (285), for example, combines content area instruction with instruction in critical thinking in real life. This is a familiar issue, certainly not unique to critical thinking. It is however, reinforced by those who identify the need for critical thinkers to apply skills and strategies in real life and who recognize the need to provide real life situations to facilitate transfer (381)

Up to now, according to Paul (285), schools have been concerned with a technical approach to critical thinking instruction, using carefully controlled problems, not dealing with the real world. He suggests that we need both a short and a long term approach. For the short term approach he believes we should understand and teach micrological, analytic critical thinking skills within content areas. He provides a slightly different link between critical thinking and content knowledge, suggesting that critical thinking is an essential precondition of content knowledge. Knowledge is not something which can be taken or memorized from a book. It is the result of the critical thinking activities of the learner. "Giving" students bits of knowledge without their use of any rational thought is indoctrinating, not educating them, according to Paul. Knowledge must be an achievement, information students have "rationally assented to" (286, p. 38), not memorized.

As for a long term strategy, Paul says instruction must go far beyond teaching a "shopping list of atomic academic skills" (285, p. 10). Critical thinking involves "human and social emancipation," "fair-mindedness" and "a pervasive organizing core of mental habits" (285, p. 10). Over the long term we must teach students nontechnical, dialectical, integrative thinking. Paul states that "when we think dialectically we are guided by principles not procedures" (p. 11). Since life problems are not always logical and straightforward and in fact might be disjointed and confused, many levels of thinking and decision making are often needed. Thus we must know how to develop dialogues, encourage not just opinions but "reasoned judgement" (p. 13) on all sides of issues. It is the philosophical view of critical thinking that provides the framework for Paul (288) to suggest that in teaching critical thinking we need to infuse it in all subject areas and relate it to the ideas students already have. Paul takes a global approach to teaching critical thinking.

The Issues in Action

In practical terms, how have schools addressed these three issues? Schools have explores the implications of isolated vs. holistic instruction, prepackaged vs. teacher developed programs, and separate instruction vs. integrated. They have mixed and matched, making decisions in each area which seem appropriate to their students and their teachers. Certainly they have chosen prepackaged programs and have offered them as separate instruction. These same programs have also been implemented in a variety of ways in the other classrooms. For example, Rembert (328) illustrates how Philosophy for Children can be implemented in a social studies classroom as a supplement to the textbook. Schools have also elected to develop their own critical thinking programs (251). One inner city program includes 18 critical thinking skills identified by the teachers that all teachers incorporate into their lessons (27). In another program (27) developed by a school district, a specialist comes into the classroom and teaches critical thinking as a separate topic but as one related to the particular content area. The specialist uses an inquiry approach, focusing on a major issue, such as good and evil, which will integrate the different content areas. Again, decisions made in one area impact on others, and all decision reflect underlying views of thinking and how to develop and enhance it.

Instructional Strategies

We have examined the major issues associated with instruction in critical thinking. Now we need to examine instructional strategies. Again, we will only highlight some of the suggestions made by those concerned directly with critical thinking since we have already discussed the strategies in some detail.

Direct Instruction/Inquiry

The controversy over whether to use direct instruction or inquiry learning is heard loud and clear in the area of critical thinking. According to Beyer (36) our failure to develop students who are critical thinkers is due to: 1) lack of a clear definition of critical thinking skills, and 2) lack of systematic, direct instruction in this skill. There are certainly programs that have followed Beyer's admonition concerning direct instruction and critical thinking, including, for example, programs developed both by outsiders such as CoRT and those developed by school systems, such as McRAT. On the other hand, the need for student inquiry and discovery of the skills and strategies is also cited and implemented in programs such as Talents Unlimited and in teacher developed programs such as that reported by Common (84) in which conversations are used to enable inquiry and develop critical thinking in history and social studies. Simulations are also suggested as a means of developing critical thinking (205).

Discussion

This is an instructional strategy that appears repeatedly and consistently in all areas of thinking instruction and is certainly reinforced in critical thinking (89, 362, 383). Hudgins and Edelman (171) add an interesting and potentially very useful dimension to our understanding of this strategy. They trained teachers to encourage critical thinking by leading small groups of children in discussions. Results of the study indicate that teachers talked significantly less, children spoke significantly more, and when they did speak, they gave more evidence than unsubstantiated conclusions. The authors reinforce the need for inservice training if teachers are to use this strategy successfully. They suggest that inservice training programs should provide demonstrations of how to lead discussion groups.

Class discussion to promote critical thinking may take a specific form, for example, Reciprocal Teaching (277, 383) or cooperative learning in order to facilitate discussion and insure that all students actively and productively participate (362).

Classroom Atmosphere

The ambiance created in the classroom by the teacher is frequently cited as important in teaching thinking. However, it is probably cited more consistently for critical thinking than any other area. If dispositions toward critical thinking are important then it follows that the classroom needs to encourage this through a risk-free environment, an atmosphere where debate and disagreement as well as sharing become important (427).

Materials

Because critical thinking is so closely linked to content, it is particularly important to consider the materials used in instruction. We should insure that the material used to teach critical thinking has content validity, transfer potential, provides appropriate and sufficient reinforcement (362), and is socially and personally relevant to students, to promote generalization and transfer (195). Questions concerning bias, value claims, relevancy, unstated assumptions, logical inconsistencies and ambiguities about the materials under study may be used to train students to think critically as they read and listen.

Critical Thinking and Academics

Before examining specific suggestions and approaches taken, we need to comment on two aspects of thinking in academics: first, the relationship between critical thinking and reading and writing, and second, the content areas in which critical thinking instruction is generally found. In assembling information for this section we found that many programs to promote thinking link reading and writing. This may be the result of much of the research that is appearing in the current professional journals suggesting that many of the same cognitive processes occur or are reinforced in these two activities. In addition, critical thinking is often cited as a necessary condition for effective reading comprehension and writing.

However, seldom do the articles document the effects of linking reading and writing on critical thinking itself. Tierney, Soter, O'Flahavan, and McGinley report on the results of a "unique" (389, p. 163) study of college students in which they found that "reading and writing in combination are more likely to prompt critical thinking than when reading is separated from writing or when reading is combined with knowledge activation or answering questions" (p. 134). This is only one study conducted using one age group. However, it identifies for us the role of reasoning in both of these activities and points out that "unfortunately, the potential of reading and writing activities to enable thinking and learning often goes unrealized in instructional settings" (p. 136).

The second aspect to consider is the content areas in which critical thinking instruction is generally found. In looking at critical thinking instruction in schools, we found that much of the professional literature deals with critical thinking programs, and critical thinking as part of writing, reading and social studies. Tama, in conducting a search in the ERIC date base, found exactly what we have found. That is good news for us, as authors, because it confirms and strengthens our finding, but bad news for us and for the profession because, as Tama concludes, "it was disheartening to see that the references were limited for the most part to language arts and social studies. As educators we have the intent and we have the means to develop students who can reason and reflect across all content areas" (383, p. 65). We certainly do not have indications that this is happening in all the content areas.

Finally, the examples will illustrate that critical thinking, reading, writing, and the content areas overlap. In reality, we can't separate them. In fact, we as authors have questioned where to place one of the examples we will describe. Should an article by Ericson, Hebler, Bean, Smith, and McKenzie (121) be cited under reading, under English or under social studies? Finally, after discussion, we decide to use it as a bridge between reading and the content areas. It provides us with an example of how instruction needs to deal with all of these elements.

Critical Thinking and Writing

A dual relationship exists between critical thinking and writing, just as it does between problem solving and writing. Critical thinking is certainly needed in order to produce effective text. However, in recent years as more professionals have begun to look at the process of writing and at the task of developing and refining critical thinking, the view that writing can be used to develop critical thinking has emerged (7, 311). Let's consider some examples of these two relationships.

Critical Writing and Reading Through Dissonance Resolution

Dissonance can occur when the expectations of the writer/reader do not match the text. Fitzgerald stresses the impact on critical thinking of resolving these dissonances. Peer discussion and teacher led discussion of both student text and text developed by authors outside the classroom help "students to work through the dissonance-resolution thought process" (124, p. 47).

Writing Across the Curriculum for Critical Thinking

Langer and Applebee describe how to develop a district wide project based on the premise that "writing is one of the major contexts for extended, critical thinking about a particular topic" (199, p. 37). The writing must come from exploration and discovery about complex topics not as a result of rote memory of skills learned. Writing activities may involve teacher "scaffolding" to aid students in organizing information, the manipulation and reorganization of ideas and information, and the development of reasoned arguments.

Developing Critical Thinking by Engaging the Writer

Being engaged in a meaningful way may help a writer to think more abstractly. Students' writing may be more abstract and show higher levels of thinking the more personally meaningful it is (375). Sternglass notes "a writer must be strongly urged to create a meaningful task from a generalized one if increasingly complex cognitive strategies are going to be exercised and fostered" (375, p. 10).

Clarifying Thinking and Making Judgments Through Journal Writing

The internal dialogue prompted by journal writing and learning logs as well as the external dialogue resulting from sharing with teachers or peers promotes critical thinking by helping students to clarify their thinking, make judgments, and explore their own reactions to text (341, 383, 430). The journal can be unstructured or can be reactions to generic questions about text.

Developing Critical Thinking Through Writing

The UCI (University of California, Irvine) Writing Project is based on the premise that writing is a form of problem solving and can be used to develop critical thinking. Bloom's Taxonomy was used to identify the thinking skills to be included in the program. Its authors recognized that "all thinking is critical" (270, p. 33). Composing is viewed as a sequence of steps, a process involving prewriting, precomposing, writing, sharing, revising, editing, and evaluation. In each of these steps writers use creative and critical thinking and in many instances link reading to the writing. Organizing information through maps and grids is a recommended strategy. In this example both of the links between writing and critical thinking are evident: writing using critical thinking and writing to promote critical thinking.

Critical Thinking and Reading

In looking at the relationship between reading and thinking, we are certainly aware of the traditional view of the need for critical thinking in order to insure that reading comprehension takes place. As Beck asserts "there is no reading without reasoning" (25, p. 677). Norris and Phillips (267) go so far as to conclude that critical thinking is, in fact, the process the reader uses to comprehend. However, as in writing, there is another way of viewing the relationship. Reading can be a way of developing critical thinking. "The reading program is a superb vehicle for developing and enhancing reasoning" (25, p. 677). We will examine a few examples of suggested strategies.

Promoting Reasoning Through a Think-Aloud Process

SOAR (Stress on Analytical Reasoning) involves pairs of college students in explaining their thinking and "reconstructing their chain of reasoning" (407, p. 122). Discussion to encourage precise thinking is the key to this approach. The same approach is used with developing and analyzing a student's own writing. It has been particularly recommended for weak students. Analytic Reading was developed for minority high school students and uses many of the same techniques (388).

Conflict and Cognitive Dissonance Resolution Through Reading

Dissonance resolution can refer to the conflict between ideas as exhibited in exploring issues. Critical thinking and critical reading can be developed by engaging students in resolving conflicts, often from the real world but related to content in English or social studies courses. The teacher's role is to find interesting, current conflicts to be resolved, develop students' abilities to reason, through discussion, identification of fact vs. opinion, and substantiation of arguments and conclusions. The teacher, in addition, may model many of the thinking skills involved (130).

Literature for Critical Thinking

Literature, as a reflection of life, is a natural source of material to teach critical thinking and to develop the dispositions of a critical thinker. Commeyras (83) advocates using a grid in an inquiry approach to analyze characters in narrative text. The analysis and class discussion are focused on critical thinking dispositions and abilities, such as seeking evidence and withholding judgment until there is sufficient evidence. She has included a number of our components in this approach: using a graphic organizer to organize information, a heuristic to monitor comprehension, and class discussion to develop support strategies.

Literature, Problem Solving and Critical Thinking

Also using literature but combining problem solving and critical thinking, Roth (335) makes the point that good literature is often based on a problem which can lead to the development of critical thinking skills. She includes skills such as planning, decision making, reflecting and evaluating, involving the reader in a range of thinking activities. She notes a variety of literary selections on all levels from kindergarten through high school and suggests ways in which they might be used to pose problems and promote critical thinking.

Critical Reading, Critical Thinking and Problem Solving

The links between these areas have already been suggested in the discussion on problem solving. We will only reinforce the links here referring the reader back to the discussion of Flynn (129) who clearly sees critical thinking as a part of problem solving and suggests that reading provides the forum for instruction, and to Kuhrt and Farris (196), who also view the relationship in a similar fashion, adding a metacognitive strand.

Critical Reading and Thinking in English and Social Studies

Ericson et al. describe a school and university collaboration which developed strategies for English and social studies teachers to use to promote critical reading, thinking and discussion in these two content areas. Emphasis is placed on "the development and evaluation of arguments" (121, p. 431) through activating prior knowledge, making predictions and testing and evaluating them. The strategies used are the anticipation-reaction guide and text previews. Both of these involve students in organizing and reorganizing information. The students are put into cooperative learning groups to facilitate the process. Thistlewaite (385) also links these areas, adding a metacognitive strand through the use of checklists or heuristics.

Mathematics, Science and Critical Thinking

Math and science are often perceived as presenting problems to the students, problems to be solved by the thinker. In math we may have word problems such as determining how many apples Johnny can buy. In science we may have problems such as determining the kind of crop to be grown in a particular geographic region. These examples are, of necessity, limited. We could have chosen a host of others. They represent, however, the kind of thinking that teachers may highlight in these areas. What is frequently not highlighted in math and science problems is critical thinking, particularly reasoning and evaluation (64, 383). We will include only one example in this area.

Inquiry Learning for Critical Thinking in Math and Science

Collins (82) advocates the use of the inquiry method to teach critical thinking in both math and science. This allows the teacher to model the scientific method and involves the students in the critical thinking process. He provides specific examples of questions and cases that the teacher can use for discussion.

Computers and Critical Thinking

There are examples provided in the literature for using computers to teach critical thinking, particularly focusing on the development of reasoning. This might be done by teaching programming to students (40, 279) or by having students engage in interactive programs designed to teach reasoning (103). However, there are cautions raised about the use of computers here (80). Furlong and Carroll (132), for example, have concluded that we are better off training expert teachers to teach reasoning than we are developing software programs because reasoning is context bound. For example, reasoning in BASIC probably will not transfer to reasoning in French.

Critical Thinking and Social Studies

Unfortunately, while everyone advocates including critical thinking in the social studies curriculum, it frequently is not included in actual lessons (32, 282). This may be partially, at least, due to the fact that teachers don't feel ownership; they're not involved in the planning process of incorporating thinking into social studies (22). Let's consider some of the suggestions that have been made to rectify this situation.

Inquiry Learning, Critical Thinking and Social Studies

Walsh and Paul (396) advocate using inquiry learning to develop critical thinking. Three elements are essential: coaching, group discussion and guided practice. They span the grade levels, using social studies, as well as other content areas, as the vehicle for developing both dispositions and skills.

Explicit Instruction in Evaluation of Social Theory

Blair suggests that we as teachers of history and social science learn the outlines of critical theorizing in these fields ourselves, that we begin to teach precise critical vocabulary at an early age to enable critical judgment, that we teach critical thinking explicitly, and that we show students how to evaluate a theory of history or social science, and give them plenty of practice at it. He uses a case against an Alberta social studies teacher, Keegstra, to demonstrate how and why we should teach students to think critically. Keegstra taught students that there is a Zionist conspiracy to rule the world, that Hitler was justified in his treatment of Jews and that the Holocaust was an exaggeration. Blair used the case to teach students to evaluate Keegstra's views, to question his theory as an historical theory, to identify flaws in his research methodology, and to examine his attitude toward the study and teaching of history. According to Blair, if we do not teach our students to think critically, we "risk miseducation—the sort of thinking about history and the social sciences that allegedly was illustrated and taught by Mr. Keegstra" (41, p. 164).

Direct Instruction in Analysis and Synthesis Using Social Studies

According to McFarland, the social studies curriculum should include the teaching of analysis and synthesis and this should begin early in elementary school. Two teaching strategies are suggested to develop and improve the ability to distinguish relevant from irrelevant material. In the first, students evaluate a list of five words and select the one which is irrelevant to a given social studies topic, combining the remaining words into a sentence about the topic. In the second strategy students develop relevant arguments to support a particular points of view by identifying and defending several point of view on a given topic. McFarland concludes that "using important social studies content to serve as the focus for practice increased retention of that content and also promotes the development of a critical thinking skill that students can apply to any content" (228, p. 278)

A Metacognitive Strategy for Critical Thinking in History

O'Reilly (273) discusses the fact that history is an especially good context for teaching critical thinking since there is often disagreement in reporting on people and events in history. Students must be taught to be skeptical, to counter the "textbook truth" syndrome, and to question what they read. The author does this by convincing the students of something and then pointing out the weaknesses in the argument.

Students are taught to identify and evaluate evidence in their discussion and in their textbooks. O'Reilly suggests a four question guideline called PROP. Is the evidence primary or secondary? Does the author have a reason to distort the evidence? Is there other evidence? Is it public or private? Students are also taught to look for cue words such as "thus" and judgment words such as "good," "bad," "right," "wrong."

Critical Thinking and Decision Making with a Graphic Organizer

We have already discussed the strategy developed by Bean et al. (24) linking decision making, critical thinking and social studies content. We refer to it here to highlight the connections between these areas. Students develop a graphic organizer to organize the historical information, predict events which might happen next, evaluate the options, and read the rest of the text to confirm the prediction.

Using Critical Thinking to Solve Social Problems

Baker and Anderson (14) provide an outline for a course which develops reasoning abilities and critical judgment to solve social problems. Students engage in defining the problem, assessing evidence, determining cause-effect relationships, clarifying value judgments, and assessing logical consistency in solutions. This is still another example of the links between these areas and leads us to the topic of critical thinking and real life.

Critical Thinking in Real Life

As in the literature on problem solving, there is a major concern expressed in the literature on critical thinking that we are not including real life critical thinking as a routine feature of instruction (193, 368, 429). The differences between critical thinking in academic areas and critical thinking in real life suggest that we cannot expect transfer to occur, but we must teach students to recognize and negotiate these differences. Three examples will illustrate some of the concerns here. First, Perkins, Allen and Hafner distinguish formal reasoning from everyday, informal reasoning. In the former, the premises are given and are "sacrosanct" (300, p. 179). In the latter, the premises "must be generated by the reasoner" (p. 179). Second, the rules of logic may be difficult to apply and even inappropriate in real life critical thinking in contrast to academic critical thinking (159). Paul (285) suggests that the everyday problems themselves may not be logical. Third, Yinger (427) adds that issues in real life deal with uncertainties not often found in academic issues. Looked at from this perspective, we begin to understand the concern held by a number of experts in the field that we must specifically include instruction in real life critical thinking.

The issue of critical thinking in real life is linked to problem solving as well. In fact, critical thinking, problem solving, and decision making are intertwined in real life as well as in academia. If we fail to recognize this then, as Sternberg suggests, in teaching critical thinking "we are preparing students to deal with problems that are in many respects unlike those that they will face as adults" (368, p. 194). In order to prepare them, students must apply critical thinking to real life situations. Sternberg (368, 369) developed a program, Intelligence Applied, in which students are taught general intellectual skills, but with a particular focus on critical thinking, using real life problems. Certainly, this approach has been the thrust of some of the prepackaged programs that have been developed. For example, the situations developed for the characters in Philosophy for Children provide student with real life situations in which to apply critical thinking skills.

Assessment

There are two concerns regarding assessment of critical thinking. First, we must determine how a given critical thinking test is, in fact, testing critical thinking. Beyer (33) traces the history of various attempts to assess critical thinking including tests developed by Ennis (1962) and Watson and Glaser (1980). He points out the major difference in these two tests. Ennis' test measures discrete items in order to identify each skill; the Watson-Glaser test measure these skills in a larger context. "Whether or not an individual is proficient in critical thinking clearly depends on whose test or model or inventory of critical thinking is used as a standard of measurement" (p. 274). Second, we must determine the source of errors. Norris (265) suggests that critical thinking tests themselves should be evaluated to insure that correct results are actually the results of thinking critically. Seemingly simple errors may actually be the result of deficiencies in higher levels of cognitive ability and control rather than a lack of critical thinking ability specifically.

Quantitative Assessment

Quantitative assessment of critical thinking certainly appears to be more widespread than assessment of problem solving. Arter and Salmon (10) suggest that assessment for problem solving occurs more in subject area tests, while assessment for critical thinking can be found in separate tests as well as in subject area tests. Possibly this is because critical thinking instruction has been part of the school curriculum for longer than problem solving has and possibly because critical thinking is viewed as a set of separate skills.

One issue with quantitative tests is that often, of necessity, the structure of the test requires only one correct answer (10, 27). However, that one answer may not reflect a student's ability to think critically. Whether your definition of critical thinking focuses on convergent or divergent thinking, there are often a number of possible answers, some perhaps more defendable than others. We need to consider how and why the student arrived at an answer (250, 428). Standard test scores of critical thinking may not be sufficient. One test where this issue is addressed is the Ennis-Weir Critical Thinking Essay Test (27). Students analyze a letter to the editor. "Students are graded according to the cogency of their analyses. If a student provides a brilliant defense for a week paragraph, he or she can still receive a top grade" (p. 17).

An additional concern with quantitative assessment is that tests that look at the individual skills of critical thinking miss the larger picture, the holistic view of the critical thinker. "Reducing critical thinking to a series of skills is like painting by number . . . Unlike jigsaw puzzles and most automobiles, critical thinking cannot be taken apart and reassembled without damage" (250, p. 2). Based on this concern, Moss and Petrosky (250) describe a citywide test in which students respond in a critical essay to a social studies passage. The test includes an analytic scoring guide to insure that the responses are scored on the basis of the student's critical thinking and not on the basis of writing skills.

Quantitative tests to assess critical thinking can be developed by publishers, state agencies and teachers. Commercially available tests range in format from highly structured, multiple choice to open-ended essay tests. They are reviewed in a number of sources (10, 248, 337). Ruggiero in his review concluded that

> The fact that the teaching of thinking has been advocated for almost a century and accepted as an educational imperative by an increasing number of educators for almost a decade might lead one to expect thinking skills testing to be highly refined and numerous commercial tests to be available. Such is not the case . . . . There are as yet 'no fully comprehensive critical thinking tests'. (337, p. 186)

An alternative to specific tests of critical thinking is to assess critical thinking as part of other achievement tests. Whimbey (409) examined the correlations between tests designed to measure reasoning and the New Jersey College Basic Skills Placement Tests (NJCBSPT) and concluded that the reasoning abilities measured by the special tests were also measured by the NJCBSPT. Thus, no special reasoning test is needed. This is particularly interesting because Whimbey included in the special tests his own Whimbey Analytical Skills Inventory. He also suggested that reasoning could effectively be measured by reading comprehension tests.

In addition, the current movement to teach thinking skills has provided an impetus toward statewide testing of thinking and, especially, critical thinking. Current state tests, while few in number, illustrate some significant trends. The Connecticut Statewide Mastery Test (372) was developed by a broadly based group of professionals in the fields of testing and of thinking skills theory and research. Considerable effort was made to base the test on a range of theory and research. The test developed by California (194), one of the first, illustrates a varied approach to the testing through objective questions, student essays, and critical thinking skills vocabulary, using content such as history and social studies. The California Assessment Program (CAP) assesses changes in critical thinking and dispositions in California's teachers and students (402). Included in the list of abilities is mind changing, as the result of better or more evidence; a questioning spirit; dialectical skills, such as the ability to summarize a case succinctly or qualify conclusions when evidence is imperfect; willingness to listen to all sides and to detect weak logic; and finally, a love of reason. Ruggiero, in discussing statewide tests, predicts that "progress will necessarily be slow. Nevertheless, by the end of this century such testing may be the rule, rather than the exception, in American education" (337, p. 196).

Finally, we must consider quantitative tests developed by teachers. Testing of critical thinking by teachers will require considerable training. Beyer (36) suggests developing critical thinking tests within subject content areas. He advocates using some of the existing tests as models, for example using the format of the Cornell Test of Critical Thinking as the basis for developing questions for testing continuous thinking. He also models the evaluation of essay questions on the critical thinking essay developed by Ennis and Weir.

Qualitative Assessment

Other approaches to assessing critical thinking attempt to assess both the product in actual academic situations and the process as students perceive it. The suggestions are varied. For example, teachers can use regular classroom activities such as projects, exercises and homework assignments (428). The assessment may be done informally by the teacher or it may be done using a response format, as suggested by Ruggiero (337). The response format guides the student through a series of questions in the skills of critical thinking and enables the teacher to evaluate the student's reactions quickly. The assignment itself may be written to encourage the student to describe or relate the process and the reasons for a particular response or answer (36).

Another possibility is self-assessment by the student or assessment by student and teacher together (428). In order to provide some structure for this method, an inventory of skills and strategies (396) and/or of dispositions (380) can be used. These same inventories can then also be used as a framework for instruction.

Summary

We have seen that the investigation of critical thinking processes, the integration of critical thinking instruction into the curriculum and the evaluation of students as critical thinkers has become a major focus in education and curriculum change in recent years. The issues related to instruction in critical thinking are closely aligned with the issues of problem solving and thinking skills instruction in general. Should we teach critical thinking in isolation or in a holistic way? We have discussed theorists and educators who offer arguments for each. Should we use prepackaged programs or should teachers develop their own? Here the answer depends, in a large part, on the attitudes, training and critical thinking abilities of the teacher. Should critical thinking instruction be provided separately or integrated into the content areas? This decision must be concerned with the willingness of teachers, the close link between content and critical thinking, the importance of transfer and the need to teach critical thinking in real life.

We have explored a variety of instructional models, strategies and materials which contribute to fostering the critical thinking abilities of students and discussed the integral relationships among critical thinking, reading, writing and content area instruction. Finally, our investigation has led us to conclude that while assessment instruments are better developed and more widely used than those for problem solving, there are some problems inherent in testing such a multifaceted aspect of thinking. Most notable are the concerns about measures which require a single, simple answer, which may not reflect the thinker's mental processes, and those measures which may not actually test what they purport to.

What does all this mean? It means that there are certainly unknowns in the area of critical thinking. However, this does not in any way reduce the importance of it or negate our responsibility for including it in the curriculum.

XII
Creative Thinking

We envision ourselves thinking creatively while sitting in a meadow, drifting in a canoe across languid water, walking slowly down the middle of a crowded, bustling city street. Wonderful, beautiful, creative thoughts come in an inspiring burst of insight. This is great!

Our next task is to examine creative thinking. Everyone certainly endorses creative thinking and no one would say that we should not encourage it in schools. However, our review of the literature we found far fewer references to creative thinking than to critical thinking, problem solving or decision making. Only one example will suffice. A major work in the field of thinking, *Thinking And Learning Skills*, Volume 1, edited by Segal, Chipman and Glaser (1985) contains only three references in the index for a total of four pages for creativity or creative thinking. All three references are part of the discussion of Philosophy for Children, a program in critical thinking. Volume 2 of the same work includes three references for a total of 11 pages on creative thinking. The two volumes together contain a total of 1,154 pages of text.

While Treffinger cites the fact that "creativity has been a topic of considerable interest to educational and psychological researchers for more than three decades" (390, p. 15), the interest has been primarily focused on gifted education and seems to have peaked in the early 1980's. In addition, creative thinking has not been a focus of educational interest for nearly as long as critical thinking has been (337).

Creative thinking almost appears to be a stepchild in the arena of thinking. We were both encouraged and discouraged

when, after writing this sentence in an early draft, we found
Halpern quoting Lowenfeld's statement that creativity is
"education's stepchild" (159, p. 419). We were encouraged
because it is always reinforcing to find someone of substance
agreeing with your conclusions and even using the same
powerful word. We were discouraged to find that the statement
was originally made in 1962; we reached the same conclusion in
1991!

Why is creative thinking a secondary topic in educational
research? We can make some hypotheses. First, educators have
been nourished on Bloom's Taxonomy of Educational
Objectives. "It would be difficult to find a more influential work
in education today" (286, p. 36). However, the major focus of
the taxomony is certainly not on creative thought. In fact, out of
the six levels the only one that has been construed as a
component of creative thought is synthesis.

Further, when we are looking for immediate results, for an
improvement in basic skills, for marketable competencies, we
are probably not looking at teaching creative thinking, except in
very specific areas, such as in advertising or writing. We have
been immersed in the drive toward basic skill development and
there are few who have considered creativity as a basic skill.

In addition to our speculations about the lack of interest in
creative thinking, Perkins (46) suggests that the lack of interest
may be a result of the fact that we don't know as much about
creative thinking as we do about critical thinking. He also cites a
serious shortage of useful research in the area of creative
thinking programs and program effectiveness.

Not only have we not emphasized creativity in instruction,
but we have rarely included it as a priority in assessment. For
example, the influential NAEP measures the critical thinking of
students but not their creative thinking. Rarely do major
nationally standardized assessments measure creative thought.
These are the tests that drive education.

Keeping these concerns in mind, let's look at what the literature does suggest for defining and teaching creative thinking.

Definitions and Descriptions

Views of Creative Thinking

One confusion that appears in the literature has also plagued us. We refer to the interchangeable use of the terms "creative thinking," "creative behavior" and "creativity." Seldom is there a distinction between them, yet to the layman, creativity seems the broadest, referring perhaps to musical and artistic abilities, those areas producing tangible products in addition to ideas and concepts, i.e., both behaviors and concepts. We will also use the terms interchangeably, recognizing that there may be distinctions but instead focusing on the similarities in the terms and on the cognitive aspects of creativity.

Definitions and descriptions of creative thinking often include reference to one of three main questions. Is creative thinking a set of specific abilities or not? Is creative thinking characterized by divergent or convergent thinking? How is the product of creative thinking characterized?

Perkins says that creativity is not a specific set of abilities but more a point on a continuum of thinking. "Creativity is not an ability; it is a way of deploying one's abilities" (46, p. 14). It is not a single, specific ability or talent. Rather it is more a matter of degree. "It can be modest as well as grand. . . . Creative thinking is thinking patterned in a way that tends to lead to creative results" (292, p. 18).

Nickerson et al., however, do see creativity as a specific set of abilities and focus on its product as well. "Creativity is that collection of abilities and dispositions that lead to a person frequently producing creative products" (264, p. 88).

Halpern focuses on the product of creativity. She says a definition of creativity must include two variables: uniqueness and worth. "Creativity must include a sense of originality, uniqueness or unusualness as well as an evaluation of how well the solution solves the problem" (159, p. 406). "Creativity is defined by its products. Creative thinkers are identified when the thinking is completed and their products are judged as worthy or not" (p. 416).

Costa suggests that creative thinking involves "the behaviors of novelty and insight. We use them to create new thought patterns, unique products, and innovative solutions to problems. Because they are so idiosyncratic, they are difficult to define and reproduce" (95, p. 68).

A more comprehensive way to describe creativity is to take into account all aspects of the thinker's environment, both past and present. Woodman and Schoenfeldt (421) suggest that we need to consider elements of personality, cognitive ability and social development when we describe and measure a creative person and to consider the interaction between these aspects of their past experience and the current situation. For example, descriptions of personality often include creative behavior, such as an aesthetic sense, broad interests, attraction to complexity, autonomy, high self-esteem, and traits such as locus of control, masculinity/femininity, and narcissism. Cognitive elements relevant to creative behavior may be field independence, approaches to problem solving, and divergent thinking. Social factors such as organizational environment and characteristics of the work group, family and social background may also need to be considered in descriptions and measures of creativity.

After an extensive review of the literature, Treffinger (390) concludes that there is not, and probably won't be, one single theory of creativity nor one instrument that can identify and measure it.

Relation to Other Thinking Skills

While there are certainly differences among the theorists as to how creative thinking relates to other areas of thinking, one relationship appears repeatedly in the literature. Creative thinking is closely linked to critical thinking (36, 46, 337, 427). This is particularly interesting because a common image of a creative thinker is of a wild haired, colorfully dressed dreamer inventor, poet, etc. We don't generally think of someone who is also critical. Let's look at how these two kinds of thinking can be linked.

Creative thinking and critical thinking are not only closely related, they are inseparable according to Perkins (299). To be creative, the thinker must think critically. "The creative thinker has to be critically aware, because creative thinking, except in the simplest situations, involves the generation and sifting of possibilities and reworking them. That has to be a critical process" (46, p. 15). The two products of thinking, primary products, such as poems and theories, and critical products, such as reviews of poems and theories, both involve critical and creative thought. To generate primary products, one must think critically; critical products may also be creative.

Yinger (427) suggests that critical and creative thinking occur simultaneously and that the interaction of the two are an integral part of complex thought such as problem solving and decision making. According to Yinger, all thinking involves creative, productive aspects, such as generating ideas or possibilities, elaborating on or transforming them, and combining and recombining them. Thinking also involves critical, evaluative aspects, such as testing, verifying and evaluating ideas. Yinger demonstrates that problem solving, decision making, idea production and invention all involve both creative and critical thought.

Nickerson et al. concur with the idea of a close relationship between critical and creative thinking. "It would seem that critical thinking is a necessary, but not sufficient, condition for creativity" (264, p. 88). Both critical and creative thinking are required for creativity. They suggest that both the generating and the critical filtering of ideas may occur in different phases of the processes and that generating ideas is not necessarily equated with creativity and filtering of ideas with critical thinking. "Both are responsible for the ultimate originality and appropriateness of the product" (p. 88). Critical filtering fosters the creativity of the product. "Critical thought can be uncreative. But creative thought cannot be uncritical" (p. 89).

Beyer describes the close link between creative and critical thinking as well. He suggests that "in thinking for virtually any purpose—to resolve a problem or make a decision or conceptualize—one engages in creative as well as critical thinking over and over again. . . . The intermixing of these various kinds of thinking in any specific thinking act merely attests to the complexity of thinking" (36, p. 37). Beyer compares creative and critical thinking.

> Whereas creative thinking is divergent, critical thinking is convergent; whereas creative thinking seeks to generate something new, critical thinking seeks to assess worth or validity in something that exists; whereas creative thinking is carried on often by violating accepted principles, critical thinking is carried on by applying accepted principals. (36, p. 35)

Ruggiero sees critical and creative thinking linked in the "three main thinking activities: making decisions, solving problems, and analyzing issues. . . . All three require imagination, open-mindedness, reflectiveness and resourcefulness in obtaining information" (337, p. 19).

Finally, the link between critical and creative thinking may be seen as complementary rather than as opposite (223). Grice and Jones (154) suggest that we should be teaching both. Because the first is concerned with evaluation of ideas and the second with the production of ideas, we need both.

Creative thinking is also linked in the literature to problem solving. Many people "in fact, consider creative thinking and problem solving to be quite similar. For them, creative thinking is problem solving applied to creative ends" (36, pp. 35–36). Isaksen and Parnes (175) suggest that problem solving has creative aspects and includes creative and critical thinking. Creative thinking produces new outcomes, while problem solving produces new responses in new situations.

Generic Skills

There are several sets of generic skills that are frequently associated with creative thinking. One set includes such cognitive skills as the ability to generate many and different ideas, sometimes referred to as ideational fluency in the literature. Another is the ability to make associations between remotely related items. However, while these generic cognitive skills find their way into programs designed to teach creative thinking and into lists of creative thinking skills, there are questions as to their usefulness and effectiveness.

First, ideational fluency is often associated with creativity. In fact, Halpern suggests that "all of the strategies for creative thinking are designed to increase the 'flow of ideas'" (159, p. 426). However, Nickerson et al. (264) view ideational fluency as an inefficient way to develop creative ideas. Perkins (46) goes so far as to question whether ideational fluency has much to do with creativity at all. He notes that often people who are recognized by their peers as being particularly creative do not necessarily score high on tests which measure ideational fluency. He believes that measuring ideational fluency as a correlate to creativity may actually limit research in this area.

Second, the usefulness of the ability to make remote associations is also questioned. Halpern (159) suggests that creative people may have this ability, the ability to take ideas from different domains and combine them successfully in a new way. She calls this synergy. Nickerson et al., however, rebuke the popular belief that creative thinkers associate items generally remote in concept. They cite difficulties with research findings and with the concept itself and suggest that skill in making close analogies is probably more useful than making remote analogies. They conclude that "in general, the case for specific cognitive abilities underlying creativity is not strong" (264, p. 93).

Another set of skills often associated with creative thinking is comprised of those skills involved in problem solving. Nickerson et al. (264) suggest that problem finding, a first step in problem solving, is essential in thinking creatively. They cite research showing that the ability to explore and examine possibilities in finding problems is more useful than the ability to solve the problems themselves. Defining a problem is a second step in problem solving, and here mobility in defining the problem is an essential skill. A creative thinker may be more mobile, i.e., able to make the problem more general, more specific, more abstract, or more concrete. He may be able to take the problem and reinvent it or change it in some novel way according to Perkins (292). Halpern (159) suggests that every creative act involves a novel way to define a problem and to select information which is relevant to finding a solution. The more a creative person thinks about a problem, the more ways he/she can define it. The nature of the solution will change with every new definition of the problem.

In contrast to critical thinking, logic, it appears, has little to do with creativity (46). In lists of skills, for example, it is not uncommon to find logic associated with critical thinking, not creativity (154). If not logic, then what about insight? Halpern (159) refers to this as serendipity and proposes that highly creative people may make happy, unexpected discoveries. Perkins suggests that insight does have a place in creativity, but it is probably the result of "short conscious chains of thought that happen quite rapidly" (46, p. 14) rather than one unconscious thought. This issue, whether an insight is the result of conscious or unconscious thinking, is certainly open for debate. Marzano et al. advocate that no matter whether insight is conscious or unconscious, it probably helps to put the task aside for a while. "During these breaks in the action, the mind (consciously or unconsciously) often generates insights that can help to complete the task" (223, p. 28).

If these are the skills, what are the strategies for creative thinking?

Strategies for Creative Thinking

Cognitive Strategies

Cognitive strategies are not usually stressed in developing creative thinking. One that does sometimes appear is using a checklist of categories, questions or adjectives in order to organize creative ideas and to aid in generating new ideas. Halpern cites a creative idea checklist by Davis and Roweton (1968), "Aids in Thinking of Physical Changes" (159 p. 423), e.g., add or subtract something, change color, materials, shape, size, design and rearrange parts. Another checklist cited by Halpern is a set of questions by Parnes (1967) which highlights aspects of possible new ideas, such as effects, implications, repercussions and timeliness. Other than checklists, few suggestions appear in the literature concerning the use of cognitive strategies to develop creative thinking. The lack of stress on cognitive strategies is not surprising in view of the limited support for cognitive skills in creative thinking.

Active Study Strategies

Nickerson et al. cite a typical list of active strategies including: brainstorming, effecting imaginative transforma-tions, listing attributes, challenging assumptions, seeking a new entry point, setting a quota for ideas. They note that few of these strategies "have been subjected to empirical validation, and efforts to check whether creative people in fact use such strategies are rare" (264, p. 97). Again, we are faced with uncertainty and with a lack of concrete information in our investigation of creative thinking.

Research on brainstorming, one of the most commonly used active strategies in creative thinking, has mixed results, according to Nickerson et al., partly because it is difficult to conduct and evaluate research on this strategy. "It seems reasonable to conclude that brainstorming works better for creative group problem solving than the hide-bound kinds of meeting it was intended to loosen up, but may well not be the best of several alternate procedures" (264, p. 99). Halpern also questions its value, suggesting that although the quantity of ideas may increase, their quality may not. She takes a realistic view in looking at brainstorming. "At the very least, brainstorming is fun" (159, p. 422).

One active strategy that is also suggested for creative thinking is teaching students to ask questions. This strategy is one that is certainly intuitively appealing and one that is cited in all areas of thinking. Beyer (36) includes questioning as one heuristic for creative thinking. Perkins' (292) set of questions for creative design is another. This list includes: What is the purpose? What is the structure? What are some model cases? What are the arguments for and against the design? To encourage a questioning attitude and thereby foster creativity, Nickerson et al. (264) suggest that we provide good role models, note attributes of well-known creative figures, and reinforce signs of creative attitudes when they occur.

Support Strategies

One similarity between critical thinking and creative thinking is the emphasis on dispositions toward thinking. We find the same kinds of things cited in both areas. Mental attitudes are an important element in creativity (65). "Very strong connections with creativity appear in studies of attitudes: creative people value and seek originality, practice autonomy, tolerate ambiguity, and so on" (264, p. 100). In order to be creative, a thinker must be willing to take risks and experience failure and be self-motivated (292). This element of intrinsic motivation seems particularly important in view of the fact that teachers may not always provide positive reinforcement to students who are generating creative ideas or answers not found in the teachers' manual. In addition, Halpern (159) includes the characteristic of sensitivity as an important disposition which a creative thinker must have. Highly creative people may be more sensitive to the physical world.

Is it possible to teach these dispositions, to insure that students learn support strategies to enable them to think creatively? Nickerson et al. (264) have some suggestions:

- Provide good role models in the classroom. It is difficult to argue with this; good role models are needed in all areas of instruction. However, there is no question that this places a lot of responsibility on the teacher, especially on a teacher who may not value creativity or see him/herself as a particularly creative person.

- Examine attributes of creative people. This may be a way to provide models in addition to (or in place of) the teacher. This notion is the basis of the program started by McCormick (227) on inventors in which children study inventions, inventors and the invention process.

- Provide positive feedback for creative behavior. This means that the teacher needs to tolerate risk and uncertainty. The disposition of the teacher becomes important here.

The fact that we have raised concerns about the suggestions made by Nickerson et al. in no way means that we disagree with them. In order to implement them, however, we need to be aware of the potential problems we mentioned.

Metacognitive Strategies

Traditionally, we have given little consideration to metacognitive strategies and creativity. In fact, as Perkins (299) points out, that when ideas or inventions "'bubble up' from some subterranean combustion" (299, p. 426) there is little thought of metacognition. However, the view of creativity suggested by Perkins and by us "demonstrates ample room for mindfulness and control in creative thinking" (p. 426). Laney's suggestions for instruction (discussed under Creative Thinking and Writing) are examples of practical applications of this view.

Content

The role of content knowledge in creative thinking has rarely been identified specifically. However, it is undoubtedly assumed. Perkins (292), for example, identifies the need for competence in the subject area in which the thinker is engaging in creative thought. However, there is a growing recognition of the importance of content knowledge in creative thinking. Halpern, in revising her book, *Thought And Knowledge*, added the following sentences to the section on creativity. "No one can become a creative scientist or great author or talented artist without factual knowledge and technical skills that are relevant to their chosen field. If you want to promote creativity, there is no substitute for subject matter knowledge" (159, p. 418). It is difficult to imagine thinking creatively about a topic when you know nothing about that topic.

Product

One thing that is unique about creativity is the overriding concern with the creative product. In fact, the product is almost more than a component of creativity. For some it is creativity. Nickerson et al. state that "creative persons are persons who, by virtue of their creativity, frequently make creative products, so 'creative' with reference to products is definitionally primary" (264, p. 87). If it is a component, it is certainly the primary one. Ruggiero concludes that "the creative thinking model focuses primarily on the production of ideas" (337, p. 18). This comment seems to limit creative products to ideas, but they can certainly include graphic and auditory representations, conversations, even lifestyles.

What are the characteristics of a creative product? There is remarkable similarity in descriptions of the basic characteristics. Perkins, who stresses that creativity involves a creative product (46), suggests that the product be original (292). Nickerson et al. agree that the product must be original and add that it must also be appropriate. "Creative products stretch or break boundaries" (264, p. 88). Halpern's (159) example of liver flavored ice cream provides a unique example of the creative product. It is certainly original, unique and unusual. These are all qualities associated with the creative product. Is it creative? Halpern suggests it is not because it would not be considered good or useful, required characteristics of the creative product. We suspect that Perkins and Nickerson et al. as well as many of our readers would not order liver flavored ice cream or consider it a creative product.

Putting It All Together

It is useful to see how one expert in the field combines these components into a view of creative thinking. Perkins measures creativity in terms of output and proposes six components of creative thinking which describe the way a creative person functions and contributes to creative output. First, "creative thinking involves aesthetic as much as practical standards" (292, p. 19). Creative thinkers expect products which are aesthetically "original, fundamental, far-reaching and powerful" (p. 19). Second, creative thinking requires that the thinker pay attention to his purpose as much as to his results, that he examine and reexamine his goals, problems, possible solutions, and approaches to thinking. Perkins' third component is that creative thinkers be mobile more than fluent, i.e., rather than generating lots of different solutions, the creative thinker must be able to make problems more abstract, more concrete, more general or more specific as needed. Fourth, creative thinkers work on the edge of their competence, rather than the center; they take more risks, push themselves, are able to work under stress and to accept failure as part of the process. Fifth, the creative thinker must be objective as well as subjective and must be able to accept criticism and be self-critical. Perkins' final component is that the creative thinker must be more intrinsically than extrinsically motivated, that is motivated by internal rather than external goals.

Instruction

What is the school's role in developing creative thinking? McCormack (227) makes an important point. Children tend to think creatively at an early age. It is society's pressure to conform that represses these creative urges. It may be that schooling may actually be counterproductive to creative thinking. Perkins suggests that the school often contributes to this repressive situation by providing instruction which he says may "work against the creative pattern of thinking" (296, p. 60), since schools generally present knowledge as a given rather than as the product of a creative effort to accomplish something, and give students tasks that do not exercise or allow creative effort. We need to be sure that the school does not contribute to this repression but, in fact, counters it and advances creativity.

The role of the teacher in instruction is always central. This seem particularly true in teaching creative thinking. The single most important influence on the development of creativity may be the teacher (136). In order to exercise this influence fully and appropriately teachers need training. The need for inservice education is cited frequently. It may be helpful for teachers to participate in a network with other teachers to share ideas as well (136, 175, 390). The personal qualities and attributes of the teacher are important in teaching creativity and need to be considered in planning programs. For example, Treffinger (390) suggests that teachers may assume different roles in developing creativity: a teacher of creative thinking skills, a leader in practicing and applying them to complex skills, a facilitator in applying creative thinking to real life.

Can we teach creativity? The answer is a somewhat qualified "yes." Isaksen and Parnes (175) cite a number of studies that show that creativity can be trained because it is innate and consists of skills. Halpern (159) also is cautious, suggesting that it can be cultivated. Costa, referring to the behaviors of novelty and insight, believes "however, that with properly designed instruction, they can be developed"(95, p. 68). Nickerson et al. add to this qualified view. "If we take as the goal of 'teaching creativity' not producing Beethovens and Einsteins on an assembly line, but rather moderate but useful improvement in creative work, that goal seems attainable" (264, p. 100).

Instructional Issues

The issues that must be addressed by educators will come as no surprise. First, should instruction be provided in terms of isolated skills or based on a holistic approach? Second, should we use prepackaged programs or develop our own? Third, should instruction be provided separately or as part of content area instruction?

Isolated or Holistic Instruction

Because we are now certainly familiar with this issue, we will look at only two opposing viewpoints on how to present creative thinking. Consistent with his view of all thinking skills, Beyer suggests that although critical and creative thought are an integral part of all thinking, they can be taught individually and as isolated skills. "These thinking operations can be identified as discrete operations. It is thus possible to attend to them individually, to intervene and to provide instruction in each of them; this will enable the entire process of thinking to work better whenever it engages" (36, p. 37). In the Odyssey program, creative thinking is taught in fifteen lessons, focusing on specific skills and strategies. It is interesting to note that these lessons occur after 85 lessons on individual skills in reasoning, understanding language, verbal reasoning, problem solving and decision making. Inventive thinking is the final unit.

Ruggiero concurs that creative thinking and critical thinking are closely related to each other and to problem solving and decision making. However, rather than advocating the teaching of critical and creative thinking as individual skills as Beyer recommends, Ruggiero proposes that we teach both of these kinds of thinking in an integrated, holistic way. He suggests a five stage process of integrating creative thinking into the whole realm of thinking. The stages include: exploration, expression, investigation, idea production, and evaluation/refinement. In the stage of exploration, for example, a number of possible strategies (including a heuristic, a list of questions to be asked) are provided to stimulate "a state of wonder or discontentment" (337, p. 33) and to develop "greater sensitivity to experience" (p. 35). In this stage of exploration students are finding and exploring problems. Programs have been developed which take a holistic perspective, including Philosophy for Children and Odyssey of the Mind.

There may be a middle ground here. Treffinger proposes a model of creative learning which includes three levels. In the first level, Learning Basic Thinking Tools, students receive instruction in "divergent or 'creative' . . . and convergent or 'critical' thinking tools" (390, p. 16). In the second level, Learning and Practicing Problem Solving Models, students apply these individual skills to more complex situations. Treffinger suggests using programs like Creative Problem Solving, Odyssey of the Mind, or Future Problem Solving. Here the instruction is holistic. Finally, in the third level, Dealing with Real Problems and Challenges, Treffinger acknowledges the need to teach for transfer to real life while also recognizing that "there is very little research evidence regarding students' involvement in Level III, or about the degree to which educators can successfully function as facilitators of creative learning at Level III with their students" (p. 18).

Prepackaged Programs or Teacher Developed Programs

There are a number of programs that include creativity as one of the components. We have already mentioned a representative sample of them at various points in our discussion of thinking. Let's look specifically now at the Creative Problem Solving Model (175). This is a program that can be adapted to various situations. It combines both divergent and convergent thinking and links creative and critical thinking within a context of problem solving. Instruction is offered as a separate course with application and transfer to all content areas. The steps taught include: objective finding, data finding, problem finding, idea finding, solution finding, and acceptance finding. Students are provided with activity books and teachers with teachers' manuals in order to insure instruction in the various skills. Substantial teacher training is included in this program in order to facilitate additional curriculum planning and implementation into all content areas.

Finding a program is not a problem. Finding one that will provide effective results and that will transfer the results to other situations may be a problem however. In his review Perkins (292) found that most prepackaged programs have had poor results or results that have not transferred. Treffinger reached very similar conclusions. "The research evidence also suggests, however, that the effects of 'creativity training programs' (globally described) are not uniform across age or sex groups or over all criterion measures" (390, p. 17). As Treffinger recognizes, there are so many research questions that need to be answered here that it is difficult to determine why there has been such a lack of success from these programs. Does this mean that teachers should develop their own programs? Surely not without careful, thorough training and guidance. The amount of training and materials support in the prepackaged programs suggests that teachers developing their own program would certainly need substantial support. Is there room for a combination of the two approaches? Treffinger's model of creative learning is appealing because of this combination approach.

Talents Unlimited may offer a way for teachers to develop their own program while receiving substantial training, support, and guidance from a prepackaged program. The emphasis is on teaching critical and creative thinking within the regular academic classroom. The program combines training for teachers and students in productive thinking (creative thinking), decision making, planning, forecasting, and communication. Teachers develop their own lessons based on the concepts and assumptions of Talents Unlimited. The lessons are not provided by the program. One interesting reason proposed for allowing and encouraging teachers to develop their own program for thinking in general is that it enables teachers to develop and use their own creativity (174). The approach of Talents Unlimited certainly allows for that.

Separate or Integrated Instruction

This is the same issue with the same concerns which we have already explored. There is certainly widespread support for the notion that creative thinking must be integrated into all content areas (175, 390). Because of the difficulty of transferring skills to new situations, Perkins suggests presenting skills in isolation and sharp focus, then providing opportunities to apply. This approach has been built into the Creative Problem Solving model (284). The problem is that we don't know how well and how often teachers actually provide opportunities or "bridges" (46, p. 17) for transfer. It may be hard to convince and train a lot of teachers. "It's a complex issue that yields no easy solution" (p. 17). It seems particularly difficult for creative thinking, which perhaps helps explain why it is labeled a "stepchild." This discussion also reinforces the need for teacher training.

Instructional Strategies

The question of how to instruct to develop creativity is one that seems to need more investigation before we can feel confident in what we are doing. Halpern (159) reviewed a number of creative thinking programs and found a core of common principles that they shared. Programs designed to teach creativity should teach students to think of different ways to accomplish an objective and then how to select the best one. They should also teach students how to ask relevant questions, how to discover when a problem exists, and how to evaluate the quality of an idea by its consequences. Finally these programs must teach students the value of persistence when they fail. In order to accomplish this, teachers should: provide plenty of examples and exercises to model and practice creative skills; provide unstructured situations; reward original and relevant ideas; let students know that their ideas are valuable; help them enjoy the creative process; and provide students with a tangible plan for finding creative solutions. These findings highlight some of the instructional strategies we have already identified and illustrate how they can be applied to instruction in creative thinking.

In planning instruction schools can evaluate their normal teaching methods which may stifle rather than encourage creativity and promote creative thinking by "focusing on aesthetics, purpose, mobility, objectivity, and intrinsic motivation, and by encouraging students to work at the edge of their competence" (292, p. 18)

Creative Thinking, Academics, and Real Life

Unfortunately, creative thinking is not generally stressed in the academic areas or in real life. Few suggestions appear in the general literature and those that do frequently offer general advice such as using materials that are interesting and relevant (175) or are related to real life (227). There is one area, however, in which there is information available, creative thinking and writing.

Creative Thinking and Writing

If there is one area in the curriculum that we associate with creativity, it is writing. "Writing is one of the most creative tasks we can be asked to do" (159, p. 427). Yet, the instructions to teachers on linking creativity and writing often tend to be general (198). Create a risk free environment. Let children explore ideas. Brainstorm possibilities. It is possible, however, to be more specific.

Creative Problem Solving and Writing

Laney (198) reports on a project in which Parnes' steps in creative problem solving have been applied by Lundsteen to writing. According to Laney, Parnes' stages include: gather the facts, define the nature of the problem, list ideas for solving the problem, evaluate ideas and come up with a solution, and implement the chosen idea and "sell" to the appropriate people.

These stages are adapted for writing, with the bulk of student activity occurring before the actual writing begins. "Gather the facts" is two steps: stimulation of impressions from a variety of sources and recreation from prior experiences or the stimulus itself to determine what this particular writer has to say about the topic. "Problem finding" is a process of creative problem selection in which the creative problem is selected or developed by either the student writer or the teacher. "Idea finding" for writing is oral consultation in which the student confers with other students to brainstorm and clarify additional ideas and completes a planning worksheet. "Solution finding" occurs after the student has written a rough draft. The student consults with himself and others as part of the process of evaluating and revising the writing. "Acceptance finding" involves sharing the written text both orally and in writing and is comparable to finding acceptance for the creative solution to a problem.

Creative Writing and Graphic Organizers

Laney (198) also suggests the use of a creative thinking worksheet listing story elements which students use to brainstorm different kinds of characters, settings, and plots. Another creative thinking worksheet is used to develop character traits for the various characters in the story.

Assessment

If creativity is hard to define, describe and include in instruction, it is also difficult to assess (159, 390). The widely shared concept of the "wild haired inventor" that we described originally is the concept the lay person uses to describe a creative person. No other precise operational definition is needed. To measure creativity as a scientific construct, however, a different standard is necessary. Woodman and Schoenfeldt (421) attest to construct validity issues which frustrate psychologists who attempt to measure creative behavior scientifically. Identifying the specific cognitive processes involved in generating a new and useful idea, for example, is not a simple task. Further, as Halpern suggests, "the relative lack of success at predicting or measuring creativity seems to be inherent in the nature of creativity itself" (159, p. 416). We have few standards for comparing products; we are uncertain about what constitutes creative activities; and "creativity is a multidimensional concept. . . . It is difficult to imagine a single test that could predict success in every possible area" (p. 416).

Lists of a limited body of commercially prepared tests of creative thinking are available (10, 337). Some suggestions for teacher developed tests appear in the literature, but they tend to use the formats we have discussed already: essays, open ended questions, observations, writing samples.

Thoughts on Creative Thinking

It would be wonderful if this discussion of creativity answered all questions, provided definitive direction, and reassured all teachers that they would be able to develop creative thinking in their students by allowing for the moment of creative insight every Thursday afternoon from 2:00 to 2:30. None of these things are possible. We are fairly certain that creative thinking is closely allied with critical thinking. In fact, it is critical thinking that enables us to decide that liver flavored ice cream is not a creative product. We also know that the teacher is a dominant force in the development of creative thinking. The teacher must value it, allow it to happen, and foster its growth. We know that support strategies are critical; the student must be comfortable taking a risk, accepting criticism as part of the process, and being mobile in finding, developing and accepting alternatives. We all value creative thinking but compared to problem solving and critical thinking probably are less certain about how to foster it and may even be more uncomfortable, as teachers, with fostering it. However, just because creative thinking is a "stepchild" we cannot allow it to be forgotten. It is certainly an area to be researched, explored and reviewed.

XIII

Thinking: Resolving Issues

An Emerging Model

We have explored many ideas and examined many issues. The bottom line is that if we are going to teach thinking we need to reach some, at least tentative, conclusions about what we think of these issues. We have looked at the three areas of problem solving, critical thinking and creative thinking separately. However, as Nickerson et al. suggested when they too examined these areas separately, "partitioning is primarily [a] matter of convenience" (264, p. 87). We have cited many ways that they have been interrelated, both theoretically and as they are implemented in school programs. Two questions arise from the conflicting positions here. First, can we reach a definite conclusion as to how they are related? Second, does it matter?

At this point in the development of theory and research, we probably cannot reach a definite conclusion about how they are related, although there certainly is consensus that they are related. We propose the following. Decision making is the umbrella. Decision making implies that there will be an outcome, a product, a result. We concur and thus place this at the top because we agree with those who hold that thinking results in a product. In order to make a decision you must engage in problem solving, since decisions of necessity involve the resolution of one or more problems. Part of problem solving is creating alternatives, expanding the possibilities. Another part is evaluating, judging, critiquing the alternatives and possibilities as you go through the process. We concur with those who see creative and critical thinking as two closely entwined, although different processes, and place them on an equal level with problem solving under the decision making umbrella.

The implication of this model for theory is that thinking is a global process, supported by skills, strategies and knowledge. Young children can think creatively and critically, solve problems and make decisions. The implication of this model for practice is that we need to expect complex thought from thinkers of all ages and abilities. We need to provide opportunities, situations and materials where complex thought is possible. We also need to isolate and stress specific skills and strategies as appropriate within the context of complex thought.

Now that we have thrown our model into the ring, can we assert that this is the final, definitive one? No, no more than any of the other ones are final, definitive models. It makes sense to us, based on our review of the research, on our teaching of all ages, from young children through graduate students, and on our analysis of our own thinking and of our experiences while engaged in thinking. The model we propose reflects input from these sources.

Finally, does it matter whether we have a definitive model of how these areas are related in the act of thinking? It may be that right now the final definitive model matters less than the fact that the program developer and the teacher have some workable model to use as a framework. The model needs to take into account the major areas of thinking, the skills and strategies involved, the role of content in thinking, and the variety of products that are possible as a result of thinking. If these are an integral part of the model and are consistently and continuously involved in the instructional procedures used, then the exact relationship of the kinds of thinking may be of secondary importance. This is in no way denying the importance of continuing the quest to research and conceptualize a model of thinking.

Perhaps of more importance is how instruction is provided. We began this book believing that thinking instruction should take place within the content areas (and within the basic skill areas). The arguments, however, for providing some initial instruction in thinking outside the content areas, for highlighting and isolating the process being taught and then incorporating the procedures into all aspects of the curriculum seem convincing. This procedure focuses attention on the importance of thinking and allows for transfer of generic skills to be made and adopted or adapted to meet the demands of the various academic areas as well as of real life situations.

Whether you agree with us or not, no matter where instruction takes place, the teacher has to make decisions about when to use direct instruction, inquiry learning or a combination of both. The literature is certainly not clear on this issue. Three elements must be considered in the decision: the teacher, the student and the task. Part of the decision has to rest with the teacher's level of comfort in teaching, with the degree of knowledge of the topic, and with the teacher's confidence in the students. In discussing this we disagree ourselves about how comfortable we are in allowing inquiry learning in our own classrooms. One reason for this is our own disposition to take a risk, to let students assume control. Another reason may be related to the level of knowledge and confidence we have in our understanding of the topic we are teaching. If we know the topic well we feel comfortable allowing students to engage in inquiry learning. The first time we teach a topic, skill or strategy we might use direct instruction. When we feel comfortable and competent about our own knowledge of the topic we can set up the inquiry situation and intervene if needed. In addition, if we know the students well we may be willing to let them assume the responsibility for inquiry learning.

Part of the decision as to which kind of instruction to use also rests on the students' motivation, level of competence and their willingness and ability to take risks. The interaction between the teacher and the students is one of the factors that affects these dispositions and abilities. The more that interaction enhances motivation, competence and risk taking, the more choices the teacher has in selecting direct instruction, inquiry learning, or a combination of the two, depending on what is appropriate. For example, the teacher who says "I never want you to make a mistake" never has the option of choosing inquiry learning.

The third element to be considered is the thinking task. To get students involved in and understanding thinking as a whole, for example, to get them to experience problem solving and decision making, and to reflect on these processes, inquiry learning may be useful. If we want to teach them specific explicit facts, strategies or skills, we may choose direct instruction. Beyer (36) suggests that all three are possible: direct instruction, inquiry learning or a combination of the two. We concur with Beyer's model of instruction in which inquiry learning involves the students, motivates them and creates cognitive dissonance, which direct instruction then clarifies and reinforces.

How do we decide what we are going to teach and how we are going to teach it? In examining thinking skills we have identified a number of major areas in which decisions have to be made and have suggested some questions to be explored. We can't answer all these questions nor can we resolve all the issues. We might be paralyzed by the current lack of strong research support for one methodology or program over all the rest. However, as Sternberg and Bhana suggest we can take what we do know and begin to "reach what we believe are informed conclusions" (373, p. 62). We can also begin, as teachers and school administrators, to become part of the solution to the lack of research. The "teacher as researcher" movement is gaining momentum in many areas of education. Certainly there is a need here for careful record keeping, for formulating and testing hypotheses, for routinely assessing performance, observing students as they engage in tasks, and maintaining files of student work. Teachers have the opportunity to engage in the process of model building.

We might also be paralyzed by the number of variables to be considered and decisions to be made. However, this book can be used to provide a framework for the decisions to be made, the questions to be answered, and the sources to be checked for more information. Probably the most important element in these decisions is the teacher. "Incorporation of thinking strategies into the curriculum depends almost entirely on the teachers' willingness and ability to plan their lessons that way" (348, p. 241). In addition to having commitment and ability, the teacher must also engage in thinking activities, not in routine and rote sequences of instructional steps. "In short, learning how to teach thinking effectively is a major challenge to teachers, but an even greater challenge and one that logically precedes it is learning to think well oneself" (263, p. 39).

Thinking: A Final Definition

We have already suggested a possible definition of thinking.

Thinking is the orchestration of skills, strategies, and content knowledge, in a planful way, to enable the thinker to generate his own new product.

Now we are ready to flesh out the definition and provide an example that will describe it.

What are the skills of thinking? We think they are micro and macrolevel skills with the microlevel skills supporting, enhancing and enabling thinking in the areas of problem solving and decision making, critical thinking and creative thinking. These macrolevel skills are interrelated, with the thinker moving from one to the other, emphasizing one or the other macroskill depending on the thinking task. Strategies enable the thinker to engage in these tasks through organizing information (cognitive strategy), questioning and summarizing (active study strategies), and monitoring success or failure (metacognitive strategy). The willingness to engage in thinking is the bottom line in all this (support strategy). In addition to skills and strategies, a sufficient and appropriate amount of knowledge of the content is critical; knowledge of the structure of the content is fundamental; knowledge of what is unknown moves the thinker into new areas of thought. Finally, we know that thinking results in a new idea for the individual.

Let's apply our definition of thinking to real life examples: painting and cooking. Painting is the orchestration of skills, strategies and content knowledge, in a planful way, to enable the painter to generate his own new picture. Cooking is the orchestration of skills, strategies and content knowledge, in a planful way, to enable the cook to generate his own new dish. Our emerging definition may include these two examples but does not fully explain them. These are examples of thinking only if we include the element of cognition. Thinking is cognition. We need to revise our definition:

> Thinking is cognition: the orchestration of skills, strategies, and content knowledge, in a planful way, to enable the thinker to generate his own new product.

The journey we have taken in writing this book has certainly been a prolonged experience in thinking and will illustrate our definition.

We were constantly engaged in using both micro and macrolevel skills. The initial decision to write the book started the process and became the umbrella under which the various kinds of thinking occurred. We were intimately, and sometimes urgently, involved in the problem solving process right from the beginning. Defining the problem was translated into identifying the issues and topics that needed to be addressed and determining how best to research them and present them. Here we were using generic skills and content specific skills. Knowing how to conduct an ERIC search is definitely a content specific skill! All along the way, microlevel skills were important. With the mountains of articles and books we collected, we certainly had to be able to develop categories and put the information into appropriate categories. We employed critical thinking skills in deciding when we needed more information and what sources were suitable. The pile of unused articles on one study floor was a testimony to critical thinking. The height of the pile changed as we engaged in critical thinking. Articles were taken out of the pile when we decided they were too old, too vague, inappropriate, not on the topic, etc., etc. Creative thinking came to the fore when we created an outline, recreated an outline, and created it again. (The microskill of word processing certainly enabled us to be creative!)

Our strategies enabled us to use these skills. We were able to take the vast amounts of complex information and organize and reorganize it in usable ways. We were engaged in a cognitive strategy. We asked questions. We asked questions of ourselves, of each other, of the authors. We asked questions of our readers. We summarized as we read the works of others. We summarized our own writing. We were engaged in active strategies. We certainly were flexible. There were many changes to our original outline. We were risk takers. We put our ideas in writing for all to see. Motivation was sometimes high and sometimes low but always needed. We wouldn't have written this book without support strategies. We monitored our text and our progress as we went along. We discussed, clarified, controlled, questioned. We combined metacognitive with cognitive strategies. We wished we had heuristic for writing this book but we didn't.

We knew content. We knew theory, research and practice. We also knew when we didn't know. We knew we were dissatisfied with that others concluded. We knew when we had to go back to the books. We knew when we couldn't write because our knowledge of content and of the structure of content was insufficient. We knew when we had to stop and "think." We knew when we learned something new that changed our minds, for example, our view of where instruction should take place.

The form of our final product was never in doubt. Because of the recursive nature of thinking, the content and format changed over time. Our final product was the orchestration of our skills, strategies and content knowledge. It was the planful compilation of the ideas of others and the generation of our own unique idea. It was a cognitive act.

PART C
Annotated Bibliography

XIV
Bibliography

1. Adams, Marilyn Jager. "Thinking Skills Curricula: Their Promise and Progress." *Educational Psychologist 24* (Winter 1989): 25–77.

In this article, Adams reviews six thinking skills programs in terms of their transferability, accommodation of individual differences, and ease of use by teachers. She reviews three microlevel, generic programs: Feuerstein's Instrumental Enrichment, Think, and Intuitive Math. She also reviews three macrolevel, content-tied programs: CoRT Thinking Materials, Philosophy for Children, and The Productive Thinking Program: A Course in Learning to Think.

Several important issues are discussed in the article: the organization of thinking skills programs, generic versus content-bound programs, and their benefits to low achievers. She reviews recent related research and theory and asserts that thinking skills should be taught generically, with practice in content to facilitate transfer. This is the only way, according to Adams, that a single, well integrated thinking schema can be developed, and only through such a schema can transfer take place. This is particularly important for low achieving students because teaching skills in content depends on amount of prior knowledge of the content and prior knowledge differs widely and is often deficient in low achievers.

Adams reviews the Odyssey program, which is a self-contained program teaching abstract generic skills, with practice in a variety of domains. Odyssey, according to Adams, is effective for a wide range of students, requires little teacher training and is inexpensive to implement. Assuming that thinking generates more thinking, she cites the need for longitudinal investigation of these programs.

2. Alexander, Patricia A., and Judith E. Judy. "The Interaction of Domain-Specific and Strategic Knowledge in Academic Performance." *Review of Educational Research 58* (Winter 1988): 375–404.

This article explores the relationship between domain knowledge and strategy use and the interactive effects of both on academic performance. The authors first present a comprehensive literature review with a discussion of their limitations. For example, young subjects (below 7th grade) are not usually studied; samples are especially small; criteria used to define experts versus novices are not consistent; baseline data on subjects are too general; content areas in which strategy use is investigated are not always clearly specified; and content used is not always directly related to classroom content. Additional concerns reflected by the authors include the lack of specificity and consistency within the strategies examined, conflicting interpretations and definitions of domain-specific and strategic knowledge, and methodological weaknesses such as poor design, invalid sampling procedures, and problems inherent in the use of verbal report data. In the last section of the article Alexander and Judy make several suggestions for future research on the domain knowledge-strategy use interaction.

3. Anderson, John R., James G. Greeno, Paul J. Kline, and David M. Neves. "Acquisition of Problem-Solving Skill." *Cognitive Skills and Their Acquisition.* Edited by John R. Anderson. Hillsdale, New Jersey: Lawrence Erlbaum Associates, Pub., 1981, pp. 191–229.

The authors investigate general principles of learning and the specific nature of problem solving skill in geometry proofs. They include discussion of how a student plans and searches for a proof, how he learns from text by examples and definitions, how he uses what he knows to encode new information, transfers new knowledge into more useful, procedural form, and finally, uses new, procedural knowledge most efficiently. The authors provide a chart which gives a good overview of the learning processes involved in geometry problem solving.

4. Anderson, Thomas H., and Bonnie B. Armbruster. "Studying." *Handbook of Reading Research*. Edited by P. David Pearson. New York: Longman, 1984, pp. 657–679.

The authors review the research on studying and relate it to other areas of educational and psychological theories and research. They discuss "state variables," those aspects of studying related to the students and the materials such as knowledge of the criterion task and knowledge of the content itself. They also discuss processing variables or those aspects of studying related to the skills and strategies used to learn and remember the materials, such as focusing attention and encoding and retrieval strategies. They introduce the concept of "transfer appropriateness," the ability to use the study strategy which requires the same or similar processing activities as those which are required in the criterion task.

5. Anderson, Valerie, and Suzanne Hidi. "Teaching Students to Summarize." *Educational Leadership* 46 (December 1988/ January 1989): 26–28.

Anderson and Hidi review the different purposes for developing a summary, depending whether the summary is writer based or reader based. Both types require a selection and a reduction process. They provide specific suggestions for instruction beginning with the first purpose and moving to the second one. They stress the need to begin instruction in summarizing "from the earliest years of literacy" (p. 28).

6. Annis, Linda Ferrill. "Student-Generated Paragraph Summaries and the Information-Processing Theory of Prose Learning." *Journal of Experimental Education* 54 (Fall 1985): 4–10.

Annis reviews a study conducted to determine the effects of reading only, traditional notetaking, and paragraph summaries on Bloom's six levels of cognitive learning. The three strategies produced the same results for the two lowest levels: knowledge and comprehension. The use of paragraph summaries was the most effective of the three at the application and analysis levels, perhaps because students had to stop frequently and put the text into their own words. The use of paragraph summaries was the least effective for the synthesis and evaluation levels. Annis suggests that because of the time constraint and because of the requirement that the students write an original response, they did not have the time or motivation to relate and evaluate information. She speculates that if the instructions given had emphasized the need to include these last two levels in the summaries, they might have been included. "This needs to be tested by further research" (p. 9).

7. Applebee, Arthur N. "Writing and Reasoning." *Review of Educational Research* 54 (Winter 1984): 577–596.

Applebee argues that writing affects the ability to reason and think in general but that we have not yet developed a convincing research base to say so. He reviews recent literature on the process of writing and concludes that writing is a recursive process, that use of the process differs among individuals, and that the writing task affects the process itself. Applebee explores the relationship between writing and thinking and the ways in which current practice in writing instruction affects thinking. He concludes that we really know very little about the nature of the understanding that develops about a topic when we write about it. He suggests three areas for future research: the cultural effects of literacy, individual effects of writing on thinking and, finally, the interaction between classroom writing activities and instructional goals.

8.   Arnold, Genevieve H., Alice Hart, and Karen Campbell. "Introducing the Wednesday Revolution." *Educational Leadership* 45 (April 1988): 48.

Because of a need to develop children's critical thinking skills, one school district initiated a program based on the ideas presented by Mortimer Adler in *The Paideia Proposal*. Every child in the district participates in a Socratic seminar for two and a half hours each week, using quality literature as the basis for discussion. Parents are invited to participate.

9.   Arrendondo, Daisy E., and Robert J. Marzano. "One District's Approach to Implementing a Comprehensive K-12 Thinking Skills Program." *Educational Leadership* 43 (May 1986): 28–30.

Arrendondo and Marzano describe the process of adapting Marzano's thinking skills model to the needs and realities of one school district. The roll of local teachers and administrators is central in the process of decision-making, training and implementation. Learning-to-learn skills, content thinking skills, and reasoning skills are introduced in particular content areas and at particular grade levels but are "used, reviewed, and retaught as necessary throughout the curriculum" (p. 30).

10.   Arter, Judith A., and Jennifer R. Salmon. *Assessing Higher Order Thinking Skills. A Consumer's Guide*. Portland,

Oregon: Northwest Regional Educational Laboratory, 1987.

Arter and Salmon review a number of tests designed to measure critical thinking, problem solving/decision making, creativity, achievement, and ability. In addition, they identify issues related to the assessment of higher order thinking and explore possibilities for assessment in the future. Finally, they provide detailed guidelines for choosing tests.

11.   Baer, John. "Let's Not Handicap Able Thinkers." *Educational Leadership* 45 (April 1988): 66–72.

Baer strikes a note of caution concerning the rush to include thinking skills in the school curriculum since we still have unanswered questions in this field. Two such questions are addressed: Is thinking unconscious? Is thinking hard-wired in our brains? According to Baer, thinking may be unconscious and occur without learning. He is particularly concerned with the possible negative effects of direct instruction in thinking skills and of self-reports of thinking processes on students who are already able thinkers. He suggests assessing students before instruction in a thinking skill and allowing for alternate thinking styles. In addition, he is concerned that we put too much emphasis on the thinking process with students who are effective thinkers even though they cannot articulate how they think. Baer proposes that thinking skill instruction take place in a separate course with skillful trained teachers with "infusion" by regular classroom teachers. (See entry 298.)

12.   Baird, John R. and Richard T. White. "Improving Learning Through Enhanced Metacognition: A Classroom Study." Paper presented at the Annual Meeting of the American Educational Research Association, New Orleans, April 23–27, 1984. 40 pp. (ED 249 250)

This is a report of a metacognitive training study in 9th and 11th grade science classes which attempted to increase students' knowledge of learning, awareness of their own learning, control over their learning through decision making, and improvement of attitudes toward learning. The training program demonstrated improvement in both learning and attitudes toward learning. Instructional implications are discussed.

13. Baker, John D. "Building Thinking Skills." *Developing Minds: A Resource Book for Teaching Thinking.* Edited by Arthur L. Costa. Alexandria, Virginia: Association for Supervision and Curriculum Development, 1985, pp. 236–238.

Analytic and critical thinking skills are taught directly and sequentially in this program, using both words and graphics. The skills are presented with critical thinking building on the basic analytic skills of seeing similarities, sequencing, classifying and making analogies. The books in the series are intended to be used along with class discussion and verbalization of the thinking processes involved.

14. Baker, Paul J., and Louis E. Anderson. *Teaching Social Problems Through Critical Reasoning.* Washington, D.C.: American Sociological Association, 1983.

Baker and Anderson present a manual to be used in introductory courses in sociology and social problems. They identify three perspectives in social thinking: sociology, common sense and journalism. The course is designed to develop critical thinking that "transcends the three types of social knowledge" (p. ii). The application of critical reasoning to social problems includes: definition of the problem, assessment of evidence, determination of cause-effect relationships, clarification of value judgments, and assessment of logical consistency in stated solutions.

Activities and materials are included which can be used to develop a course, which might be adapted to high school students.

15. Baldwin, Dorothy. "The Thinking Strand in Social Studies." *Educational Leadership* 42 (September 1984): 79–80.

Using the taxonomies of Bloom and Sanders, teachers in a New Jersey school district are taught to incorporate all levels of thinking in their instruction. Through inservice programs, social studies teachers develop their own materials and approaches for including critical thinking, memorization and problem solving strategies in their courses. An example of the Thinking Strand from an eighth grade class is included.

16. Barbieri, Edmund L. "Talents Unlimited: One School's Success Story." *Educational Leadership* 45 (April 1988): 35.

Barbieri describes one lesson that illustrates the critical and creative thinking that is the focus of Talents Unlimited. The children are active agents in developing productive thinking, communication, forecasting, decision making, and planning. The lessons are developed by the teachers in this elementary school and are incorporated into the content areas.

17. Barbour, Nita H. "Can We Prepackage THINKING?" *Childhood Education* 65 (Winter 1988): 67–68.

Barbour expresses a number of concerns about using prepackaged programs to teach thinking. Teachers may not analyze the reasons for the lessons. Thus, in routinely following someone else's plan, they will not provide a model of thinking themselves. The focus may be on steps and outcomes rather than on process. In order to teach thinking, teachers must view themselves as thinkers, and this may not happen with prepackaged programs. The author advocates open discussions, interesting experiences and play as ways to develop thinking in young children.

18. Barell, John, Rosemarie Liebmann, and Irving Sigel. "Fostering Thoughtful Self-Direction In Students." *Educational Leadership* 45 (April 1988): 14–17.

Barell, Liebmann and Sigel highlight the importance of empowering students to become independent thinkers, able to set goals, identify their own problems, and find solutions, monitoring their progress as they go. The authors provide a number of practical suggestions drawn from classrooms on a variety of grade levels.

19. Baron, Joan Boykoff, and Bena Kallick. "What Are We Looking For and How Can We Find It?" *Developing Minds: A Resource Book for Teaching Thinking.* Edited by Arthur L. Costa. Alexandria, Virginia: Association for Supervision and Curriculum Development, 1985, pp. 281–287.

Baron and Kallick examine two approaches to assessing growth in thinking skills. The first is the use of standardized testing. They describe how the assessment of thinking skills has been incorporated into the Connecticut Assessment of Educational Progress and the Connecticut Mastery Test. In the second approach, classroom measures can provide much additional information. They suggest the use of student and teacher journals to record thinking, tape recordings of class sessions, interviews that focus on thinking, and the review of student work such as writings and drawings.

20. Baron, Jonathan. "What Kinds of Intelligence Components are Fundamental?" *Thinking and Learning*

Skills. Research and Open Questions. Volume 2. Edited by Susan F. Chipman, Judith W. Segal, and Robert Glaser. Hillsdale, New Jersey: Lawrence Erlbaum Associates, Pub., 1985, pp. 365–390.

Baron uses the label "component" instead of "skill" because of its broader scope and includes processing components, strategies and styles in the discussion. He reviews the history of the research and development of each of these elements. He concludes that processing skills are probably not teachable. We need to examine both strategies and styles more closely, since these seem to hold the most potential.

21. Barton, Judy A. "Problem-Solving Strategies in Learning Disabled and Normal Boys: Developmental and Instructional Effects." *Journal of Educational Psychology* 80 (1988): 184–191.

Barton's study demonstrated differences between LDs and non LDs in the ability to use specific problem solving strategies. She studied older learning disabled and non-disabled students, (11 to 13 years old) and younger learning disabled and non-disabled students (8 to 10 years old) to see which groups would select a more efficient strategy—asking constraining questions rather than hypothesis scanning questions to reduce alternatives—in a game to 20 questions. Older non-disabled students were consistently superior to all other groups; younger non-disabled and older disabled were similar; younger disabled consistently scored worst. Barton concluded that that there may be about a two year lag in problem solving strategy development in the learning disabled.

22. Batcheller, Michael F. "Implementing a Critical Thinking Skills Program in the Social Studies Curriculum K-12." *Social Education* 49 (April 1985): 308.

Batcheller reports on the integration of thinking skills in the social studies curriculum in the Greenwich, Connecticut schools. Sequence, teaching methodology and approach, teacher involvement in planning, process and change must all be considered. A vehicle or committee is necessary to drive the changes. Batcheller recommends a demonstration/observation model pilot program to initiate such a major curricular innovation in order to link change to teacher participation, provide a forum for teacher criticism and build a sense of ownership for the staff. Batcheller observes that it takes time and money to implement a critical thinking skills programs due to the necessity of involving staff in design, development and implementation.

23. Bean, Thomas W. "Classroom Questioning Strategies: Directions for Applied Research." *The Psychology of Questions.* Edited by Arthur C. Graesser and John B. Black. Hillsdale, New Jersey: Lawrence Erlbaum Associates, Pub., 1985, pp. 335–358.

Bean reviews his research and that of others in the field of classroom questioning. He explores and illustrates a pseudo-Socratic method, teacher-directed questioning, and student-generated questioning. A number of classroom strategies are discussed, including, for example, adjunct aids, group discussion, and the use of heuristics in developing questions.

24. Bean, Thomas W., Jack Sorter, Harry Singer, Charles Frazee. "Teaching Students How to Make Predictions about Events in History with a Graphic Organizer Plus Options Guide." *Journal of Reading* 29 (May 1986): 739–745.

The authors developed a program for high school history students in which they were taught to construct graphic organizers. Students read to a critical point in the text, constructed their organizer, and examined options provided by the teacher which might be possible in the historical situation. The students evaluated the options in groups, chose one, and then read the remainder of the text to find out what actually occurred. The option guide is useful as a means of extending students' understanding and of engaging students in critical thinking. "The graphic organizer plus options guide places students in the driver's seat as decision makers" (p. 744).

25. Beck, Isabel L. "Reading and Reasoning." *The Reading Teacher* 42 (May 1989): 676–682.

Beck cites the "often unconvincing" (p. 677) evidence that separate thinking programs actually teach reasoning and problem solving. The fact that they are content-free is a disadvantage, since thinking is so closely tied to content and prior knowledge. She advocates teaching thinking within content areas using a problem solving framework to foster reasoning and critical thinking. She suggests that we make all the higher order thinking skills the center of reading instruction.

26. Bellanca, James A. "A Call for Staff Development." *Developing Minds: A Resource Book for Teaching Thinking.* Edited by Arthur L. Costa. Alexandria, Virginia: Association for Supervision and Curriculum Development, 1985, pp. 13-19.

Bellanca advocates long term, well planned systematic staff development programs in thinking skills which are an integral part of the total curriculum, rather than "one-shot" inservice workshops. Committees should be formed to consider student, teacher and administrative outcomes as well as cost in time, resources and money. Students should be taught a small number of essential thinking skills formally, without content, and then taught to transfer to subject areas. Teachers must spend more time helping students apply new skills and less time covering material. They must be skilled at developing higher order, complex questions. The chapter gives examples of how to teach transfer to all level students and provides guidance for a well designed beginning inservice workshop.

27. Benderson, Albert (Editor). *Critical Thinking, Focus* 15. Princeton, New Jersey: Educational Testing Service, 1984.

Benderson takes a broad view of critical thinking, exploring a range of issues. Citing the lack of instruction in critical thinking and the "distressing results" of studies and reports on thinking skills, he reviews such topics as current philosophical and psychological approaches to critical thinking, the teacher's role in instruction, the status of testing, possible approaches to curriculum development, and which students to include in programs.

28. Bereiter, Carl. "How To Keep Thinking Skills from Going the Way of All Frills." *Educational Leadership* 42 (September 1984): 75–77.

Bereiter's message is explicit. Thinking skills must be integrated into already accepted educational objectives, a contingency strategy, and must permeate the entire instructional process and curriculum, a permeation strategy. He asserts that every page of material must reflect thinking instruction and all programs must give evidence of improving thinking skills. Examples from a mathematics curriculum are provided that illustrate this approach.

29. Beyer, Barry K. "Common Sense About Teaching Thinking Skills." *Educational Leadership* 41 (November 1983): 44–49.

Beyer identifies three essential components in the teaching of thinking skills. First, there is the need for a supportive learning environment which allows risk-taking and which provides lessons that go beyond content and require processing to obtain meaning. Second, there is the need for instruction which is "systematic, direct, integrated, and developmental" (p. 45). Finally, there is the need to develop thinking skills across the curriculum and to provide teachers with effective guidelines.

30. ———. "Improving Thinking Skills—Defining the Problem." *Phi Delta Kappan* 65 (March 1984): 485–490.

In this article, Beyer identifies the five significant obstacles to improving the teaching and learning of thinking skills. First, he identifies the lack of consensus regarding what constitutes thinking skills, and a vagueness in defining them. As a result "educators today continue to exhibit both haziness and great diversity" (p. 485) in what is taught. In addition, all thinking skills, regardless of complexity or significance, are given the same weight and time in the curriculum. Second, we have failed to identify the cognitive operations required by the various thinking skills.

The third obstacle, our failure to provide appropriate instruction, follows from these. Much of what is labeled as instruction is, in reality, testing. Questioning and teacher-led discussions are identified as instructional strategies, but since we fail to provide students with guidelines and direct instruction in how to think and how to answer questions, these strategies afford opportunities for practice or testing, not for teaching.

A fourth obstacle is the skill overload students experience, "too many skills in too little time" (p. 489). Students need time to develop and practice skills; schools need "developmental, sequential, or integrated curricula for teaching thinking skills" (p. 489). Finally, since testing frequently determines what is taught, the inappropriate tests for thinking skills are actually obstacles to teaching.

31. ———. "Improving Thinking Skills—Practical Approaches." *Phi Delta Kappan* 65 (April 1984): 556–560.

Beyer addresses the issues raised in his previous article and provides suggestions for the vast majority of educators as well as government and business leaders concerned with improving instruction in thinking skills. First, he suggests that thinking skills need to be viewed as differing in complexity: 1) the basic skills, or discrete operations, similar to those advocated by Bloom, and 2) the complex skills, broad, general processes, such as problem solving, decision making and conceptualizing, which involve those basic, discrete skills. He further identifies critical thinking as "a mix of the two" (p. 557) differing from them in that it is a "combination of analysis and evaluation" (p. 557).

Each type of thinking skill consists of a set of operations or procedures and rules that guide them. The thinker must know the operations and the rules and have criteria for judging the effectiveness of the skill. In addition, the individual needs knowledge of the subject and its related concepts.

Beyer advocates direct instruction in all the components of thinking skills, with the teacher modeling and providing models and with the student repeatedly applying the skill, reflecting on it, and discussing the process and the rules governing the use of the skill. Skills cannot be taught in isolation. They must be part of a planned curriculum which introduces only a few skills at each grade level, provides teachers with explicit descriptions of them, involves all content areas, uses a variety of media and contexts, and most importantly, develops the skills sequentially. For example, basic skills must be mastered before complex skills can be introduced.

32.   ———. "Critical Thinking Revisited." *Social Education* 49 (April 1985): 268–269.

In this introductory article for the April 1985 issue of *Social Education,* which is devoted exclusively to the teaching of critical thinking in the social studies curriculum, Beyer points out the lack of explicit teaching of critical thinking skills by social studies teachers. He discusses the report by the National Council for the Social Studies and those of other professional organizations which cite the inability of college students and adults to analyze data and think and judge critically. These organizations strongly advocate explicit instruction in these skills. Beyer introduces subsequent articles in the journal which include a research overview, a definition of the nature of critical thinking, elaborations on the definition, and instructional suggestions.

33.   ———. "Critical Thinking: What Is It?" *Social Education* 49 (April 1985): 270–276.

Beyer attempts to define critical thinking and notes the lack of agreement by educators on a definition. He suggests that it is the analysis of knowledge and the evaluation of its worth. He describes critical thinking in terms of its structure, which is a frame of mind inclined to consider all sides and to search for truth, and its function, the specific mental operations which, when combined, analyze and evaluate a given argument or bit of knowledge. He lists 10 mental operations which together constitute critical thinking, according to educational research and classroom experience. Beyer reviews the research and assessments of critical thinking, including tests developed by Ennis (1962) and Watson and Glaser (1980). A comprehensive inventory and elaboration on the major skills associated with critical thinking are included in the article.

34. ———. "Practical Strategies for the Direct Teaching of Thinking Skills." *Developing Minds: A Resource Book for Teaching Thinking.* Edited by Arthur L. Costa. Alexandria, Virginia: Association for Supervision and Curriculum Development, 1985, pp. 145–150.

Beyer advocates a direct instruction model for teaching thinking skills which includes selecting examples of a particular skill, introducing, presenting and demonstrating the components of the skills, providing guided practice and transfer, and allowing for application in new situations with appropriate feedback. Some skills will need to be introduced before others, thus requiring sequential skill instruction and practice in integrating skills into more complex thinking activities. In addition, students need knowledge about a subject in order to think about it. Thus, thinking must be taught in conjunction with content.

35. ———. "Teaching Critical Thinking: A Direct Approach." *Social Education* 49 (April 1985): 297–303.

Beyer asserts that critical thinking is not a skill acquired by students automatically. Direct systematic instruction is necessary. Students should be provided with specific examples of the skills before using them and should practice them often and regularly. Feedback should be provided; generalization and transfer opportunities should be available. Finally, skills should be taught within a specific content area rather than in isolation. The article describes in detail an inductive teaching strategy for teaching critical thinking. The author discusses the need for direct instruction in specific critical thinking skills within the social studies curriculum.

36. ———. *Practical Strategies for the Teaching of Thinking.* Boston: Allyn and Bacon, Inc., 1987.

Beyer defines thinking as "the search for meaning" (p. 16), either stated or implied. He explores the components of thinking, the cognitive and metacognitive operations, as well as the knowledge and attitudes or dispositions involved in thinking. Cognitive operations consist of complex strategies including problem solving, decision making, and conceptualizing, microthinking skills which are the building blocks for other operations, and critical thinking, an evaluative operation which can be used in conjunction with any of the thinking strategies.

Citing the benefits to students and to society that accrue from the teaching of thinking, Beyer points out that many of the strategies currently used by teachers do not provide instruction and assistance in the acquisition of thinking abilities. In order to instruct students, teachers must understand and include the attributes of thinking operations in their lessons. The attributes include the procedures, rules and knowledge needed to execute the operation or skill. Classroom environment, the subject matter which provides the context for thinking, and the instructional strategies are all critical to the teaching of thinking. Beyer provides detailed examples within content areas of an inductive strategy, a directive strategy and a developmental strategy. In all of these strategies, it is essential that modeling by the teacher, a competent student or the text occurs and that the students are aware the modeling is being done, the components are explicitly defined and that discussion is "extremely useful" (p. 127). The author explores ways of helping students develop metacognitive abilities as an integral part of instruction in thinking.

37. ———. "Practice Is Not Enough." *Thinking Skills Instruction: Concepts and Techniques.* Edited by Marcia Heiman and Joshua Slomianko. Washington, D.C.: National Education Association, 1987, pp. 77–86.

Beyer examines current practices that are commonly used by teachers to teach thinking, such as asking and answering questions, engaging in hypothesizing and validating, writing, discussing, debating, and researching. Beyer documents that, in spite of these activities, students are not able to engage in "skillful thinking" (p. 78). He suggests that the reason is that these activities constitute practice not instruction. Students need direct instruction, with overlearning in specific thinking skills. The author provides detailed descriptions of two introductory teaching strategies using direct instruction.

38. ———. "Developing a Scope and Sequence for Thinking Skills Instruction." *Educational Leadership* 45 (April 1988): 26–30.

Beyer provides specific guidance in choosing and sequencing thinking skills, drawing from the complex strategies of problem solving, decision-making and conceptualizing, the discrete mental operations comprising critical thinking, and the basic thinking operations of information processing. He relates the skills to grade level and to content areas. The proposal is based on the need to limit the number of skills and strategies taught in order to avoid overloading students, to insure mastery before adding new skills, and to build from simple skills to complex. In addition, Beyer suggests providing instruction in thinking in more than one content area. A final caution is added: "attention must also be given to the habits and values of skillful thinking" (p. 30).

39. Bippus, Stanley L. "Think Before You Ask." *Educational Leadership* 45 (April 1988): 50–51.

The focus of the program described by Bippus is on increasing and improving teacher and student questioning as well as on involving students in their own learning. Real problems provided by the local community as well as teachers and students form the content of the program.

40. Black, John B., Karen Swan, and Daniel L. Schwartz. "Developing Thinking Skills with Computers." *Teachers College Record* 89 (Spring 1988): 384–407.

Black, Swan and Schwartz examine problem solving and reasoning in some detail. They report on the results of an experiment in which fourth through eighth grade students were introduced to six problem solving strategies and provided structured opportunities to use the strategies to solve verbal problems with Logo. There was evidence that transfer from the computer to verbal problems did occur. Although the authors were not certain what "specific cognitive processes" (p. 393) accounted for the transfer, they suggest that we teach students problem solving strategies using a focused, forced approach, modeling metacognitive behaviors, and requiring that students work through the process, detailing the procedures. "There is some reason to believe that explicit modeling of metacognitive behaviors helps students isolate and assimilate them" (p. 390).

The authors also found evidence of a developmental sequence in readiness for specific strategies. Based on this and on the reasoning skills of mature thinkers, the authors review the possibilities of using Prolog to teach reasoning. In addition, they suggest possibilities for teaching students how to think in images using computers. They conclude that it is possible to teach students both rule-based and experience-based reasoning and to coordinate the two.

41. Blair, J. Anthony. "The Keegstra Affair. A Test Case for Critical Thinking." *History and Social Science Teacher* 21 (Spring 1986): 158–164.

Blair contends that since the goal in teaching critical thinking is to get students to use the skill spontaneously outside the classroom and not just in response to teacher-assigned tasks, they should be taught and evaluated on current controversial public issues. He uses the case against an Alberta social studies teacher to teach students to evaluate views as they relate to the teaching of history and social sciences, to question the teacher's theory as a historical theory, to examine flaws in his methodology of historical research, and in his attitude toward the study and teaching of history. He teaches students to identify prejudices, stereotypes, biases, flawed arguments and evidence.

42. Bland, Carol, and Irene Koppel. "Writing as a Thinking Tool." *Educational Leadership* 45 (April 1988): 58–60.

Motivated by the need to improve both student writing and thinking and encouraged by the connections between the two, high school teachers developed a program linking writing and thinking in all content areas. Bland and Koppel describe the teacher training component of the program and list suggestions for the three steps in the process: producing ideas, expressing ideas and refining expression.

43. Bondy, Elizabeth. "Thinking About Thinking." *Childhood Education* 60 (March/April 1984): 234–238.

Bondy advocates an emphasis on teaching students how to be in control of their thinking in order to make them lifelong learners. According to Bondy, we can no longer give students an adequate body of information to function in the world; we now need to focus on the process rather than the content of learning. She suggests ways to develop metacognitive ability in children: promote general metacognitive awareness by having students keep daily learning logs to direct their attention to their own learning process and by teacher modeling of thinking and learning tasks; facilitate comprehension monitoring by adequate feedback, instruction in self-questioning, summarizing and rating of comprehension; encourage a systematic approach to learning by following a specific learning model and studying model, and through ThinkAbout, a television series by the Agency for Instructional Television which focuses on systematic problem solving, which the author advocates.

44. Borkowski, John G., Martha Carr, Elizabeth Rellinger, and Michael Pressley. "Self-Regulated Cognition: Interdependence of Metacognition, Attributions, and Self-Esteem." *Dimensions of Thinking and Cognitive Instruction.* Edited by Beau Fly Jones and Lorna Idol. Hillsdale, New Jersey: Lawrence Erlbaum Associates, Pub., 1990, pp. 53–92.

The authors review the history of metacognitive research and confirm the links between children's view of themselves as competent, motivated learners and the development of metacognitive strategies. "The failure to develop a functional self-system, and corresponding metacognitive skills and knowledge, is likely to result in poor performance as well as the reinforcement of negative self-perceptions and beliefs" (p. 65). They relate this notion to giftedness, learning disabilities and learned helplessness. They report on two studies conducted in the area of underachievement, examining the roles of motivation, affect and metacognition. They concluded that direct instruction and the use of reciprocal teaching were effective in teaching strategy choice, use, and transfer, linking motivation, affect, and metacognitive and cognitive strategies. Students need to learn to "believe in themselves" (p. 84).

45. Brainin, Sema Sharon. "Mediating Learning: Pedagogic Issues in the Improvement of Cognitive Functioning." *Review of Research In Education.* Edited by Edmund W. Gordon. Washington, D.C.: American Educational Research Association, 1985.

Brainin reviews the research on a broad range of issues concerning instruction in cognitive functioning in general and in low-functioning adolescents in particular. She reviews existing programs and concludes that the lack of research available to evaluate them is a serious problem. In order to provide effective instruction, we must make objectives and strategies explicit to the student. We must help students construct a "bridge" between existing schemata and new content. Cognitive training must be generalized to academic areas. Students must feel competent, equipped to be "active generators of knowledge" (p. 137). The teacher's role as the mediator of learning cognitive skills and strategies is critical. In fact, the training of teachers is cited as the major challenge we face.

46. Brandt, Ronald S. "On Creativity and Thinking Skills: A Conversation with David Perkins." *Education Leadership* 43 (May 1986): 12–18.

Perkins and Brandt explore the dimensions of both creative and critical thinking, stating that the two are intertwined. In order to be creative, the thinker must also be critical, examining and evaluating in the process of creating. The products of thinking, primary products (such as poems and theories) as well as critical products (such as the reviews of the poems and theories) involve both creative and critical thinking. In fact, Perkins suggests that creativity is not an ability. It is "a way of deploying one's abilities" (p. 14). They further examine ways of teaching thinking in schools, although the point is made repeatedly that there is a serious shortage of useful research in the area of programs and program effectiveness. The discussion of whether we should offer separate thinking skills programs or integrate instruction into content areas addresses theoretical and practical issues such as the problem of transfer, the question of "power-generality trade-off" and the feasibility of the two approaches in schools. There is no easy answer to the question of how to structure instruction.

47. ———. "On Teaching Thinking: A Conversation with Art Costa." *Educational Leadership* 45 (April 1988): 10–13.

Costa responds to questions on a wide variety of issues related to teaching thinking. He sees more teaching of thinking skills in schools today than in the recent past. He considers one of the benefits of thinking programs to be the positive impact on teacher thinking. He admits the lack of hard data to support the effectiveness of including thinking skills in the curriculum but is encouraged by the results seen by teachers in the classroom. Costa asserts the need for new measurement and research techniques to assess thinking behaviors. He suggests two specific ways to improve teacher skills: include teaching thinking as part of the undergraduate teacher preparation and provide a model in how to think in the person of the school principal.

48. ———. "Overview: New Possibilities." *Educational Leadership* 45 (April 1988): 3.

Brandt, Executive Editor of *Educational Leadership*, introduces this issue devoted to teaching thinking throughout the curriculum. The general consensus among educational practitioners, according to Brandt, is that thinking should be taught within the regular curriculum. He cites research which supports his view and suggests that we approach this task in three ways: teaching for, of and about thinking. The issue provides examples of how schools are currently teaching thinking.

49. Bransford, John D., Ruth Arbitman-Smith, Barry S. Stein, and Nancy J. Vye. "Improving Thinking and Learning Skills: An Analysis of Three Approaches." *Thinking and Learning Skills*. Relating Instruction to Research. Volume

1. Edited by Judith W. Segal, Susan F. Chipman, and Robert Glaser. Hillsdale, New Jersey: Lawrence Erlbaum Associates, Pub., 1985, pp. 133–206.

Bransford et al. describe, review and compare three thinking programs: Instrumental Enrichment, Philosophy for Children and Problem Solving and Comprehension. The detailed discussion and numerous examples are useful in highlighting the theoretical rationale, the materials used, the instructional procedures recommended, the strategies used by students, and the effectiveness of the programs in relation to their stated goals.

50. ———, Robert Sherwood, Nancy Vye and John Reiser. "Teaching Thinking and Problem Solving." *American Psychologist* 41 (October 1986): 1078–1089.

This article on thinking skills reviews the research on two theoretical bases for development of thinking skills instruction: the role of domain-specific knowledge in thinking ability and the role of metacognitive or control processes in thinking First the authors examine the body of research on the role of knowledge in thinking and the implications of the major findings for teaching thinking and problem solving. They discuss the importance of the ability to access knowledge at appropriate times. The authors investigate ways in which we use knowledge to learn new information. They present their own problem solving model, "IDEAL" (Identify, Define, Explore, Act and Look and Learn) which considers the acquisition of new information as a problem to be solved. They compare an effective learner and a less effective learner in the execution of this model.

Next they examine research on the effectiveness of metacognitive training in improving thinking and problem solving, and they discuss the relationship between metacognition and domain-specific knowledge and the implications of this relationship for teaching thinking. The authors then discuss various programs that emphasize metacognitive processes and programs that teach thinking in context. They suggest that effective programs might focus more on the addition and organization of content knowledge with metacognitive training to facilitate access of the knowledge base.

The authors conclude with suggestions for future research: the conditions under which access to previous knowledge occurs, the effectiveness of a combined focus on metacognitive training and content knowledge, and the development of cognition.

51. ————, Nancy Vye, Charles Kinzer, and Victoria Risko. "Teaching Thinking and Content Knowledge: Toward an Integrated Approach." *Dimensions of Thinking and Cognitive Instruction.* Edited by Beau Fly Jones and Lorna Idol. Hillsdale, New Jersey: Lawrence Erlbaum Associates, Pub., 1990, pp. 381–413.

Bransford, Vye, Kinzer, and Risko examine the complex relationships between content knowledge and thinking, concluding that not only is the knowledge important but also the ability to access it when it is relevant. They report on a long term study, The Young Sherlock Project, in which students are provided with "anchored" instruction, in which they actively engage in a problem solving situation, examine it from multiple perspectives, and transfer knowledge, skills and strategies to various academic areas. The approach is based on an integrated view of content instruction.

52. Bratton, Libby. "You Have to Think Real Hard When You Write." *Educational Leadership* 45 (April 1988): 62.

Bratton reports on a teacher developed program for all grade levels which emphasizes thinking clearly and precisely through writing in all content areas. She describes the use of visual organizers and the verbalization of the thinking process by students.

53. Bromley, Karen D'Angelo, and Laurie McKeveney. "Precis Writing: Suggestions for Instruction in Summarizing." *Journal of Reading* 29 (February 1986): 392–395.

The authors present theory and research which support the use of precis writing to develop vocabulary, promote critical reading, comprehension and learning in general. Precis writing is a summarizing technique which integrates reading and writing. Students benefit from reprocessing text by selecting main ideas, rejecting details, substituting synonyms and paraphrasing content material. Precis are study aids because they emphasize major points.

The authors offer some suggestions for instruction in precis writing. In the prewriting stage they discuss the importance of establishing a purpose, making a commitment to the strategy, demonstrating and simulating the skills involved, providing materials at appropriate levels, and providing for verbal practice. During the writing stage students should be permitted to work together and to adapt as they learn. Post-writing should include models of acceptable precis, use of precis folders for studying, ad ample study time.

54. Brooks, Martin. "A Constructivist Approach to Staff Development." *Educational Leadership* 42 (November 1984): 23–27.

Brooks examines two critical aspects of the Cognitive Levels Matching project as implemented in a Long Island, New York school district. First, he explores the theory and research behind the project. It is based on the Piagetian notion that individuals construct their own reality in order to organize and understand information and concepts. This process of construction is influenced by the development of the child as he/she matures and moves through the cognitive levels. In order to implement the program teachers need to be trained to understand and apply the notions in the classroom.

The second aspect of the project is its staff development program. Teachers were involved throughout the development of the curriculum and its implementation. Training occurred not just in a special, separate class but also in the teacher's own classroom through the use of peer and consultant coaching.

55. Brostoff, Anita. "Using Problem-Solving to Think and Write: Tagmemtics for High School Students." Paper presented at the Annual Meeting of the Conference on College Composition and Communication, Detroit, Michigan, March 17–19, 1983. 15 pp. (ED 234 383)

Brostoff advocates the use of tagmemtic heuristics in teaching writing. She defines this as providing "a problem solving procedure as an approach to rhetoric" (p. 3). The author discusses three heuristics and their steps which students can learn to develop writing as a thinking process. These include one for identifying the problem, exploring the problem through the use of a grid, and one for evaluating solutions. She provides detailed questions and checklists that can be used.

56. Brown, Ann L., Bonnie B. Armbruster, and Linda Baker. "The Role of Metacognition in Reading and Studying." *Reading Comprehension: From Research To Practice.* Edited by Judith Orasanu. Hillsdale, New Jersey: Lawrence Erlbaum Associates, Pub., 1986, pp. 49–75.

The authors give an overview of metacognition, discuss developmental differences, review recent training studies and their implications for instruction, propose curriculum and classroom applications, and finally, point out areas of research which should be pursued. Recent research has revealed the pervasiveness of metacognitive difficulties at all ages and for all levels of students but mostly for poorest students. According to the authors, the most important outcome of this research has been the development of remediation programs which work in classrooms as well as in laboratories.

Brown et al. distinguish between "blind" training studies, that is, training in the rules themselves, without explaining the importance of the rules, informed training, when students are given some information about the significance of the activity, and self-control training, when students are given explicit instruction in monitoring and regulating the strategies. The authors believe that a good cognitive skills training program should include all three types of training, and they suggest application of the following five criteria for deciding that a particular training program is successful: clear improvement on the target task, independent evidence of process change, effects which are reliable and durable, evidence of several different kinds of transfer, and training which is instructionally feasible. They describe two successful training programs that meet all five criteria, the Palincsar and Brown (1982) program, which is a laboratory to classroom process, and the Paris et al. (1982) program, a curriculum development approach.

57. ———, John D. Bransford, Roberta A. Ferrara, and Joseph C. Campione. "Learning, Remembering, and Understanding." *Carmichael's Manual of Child Psychology* Volume 1. Edited by John H. Flavell and Elaine M. Markman. New York: Wiley Press, 1983, pp. 77–166.

The authors explore the relationship between amounts of knowledge and development of the ability to solve problems, organize information, etc. These abilities, according to the authors, develop with age through the acquisition of new knowledge. At different levels of development, children have different short term memory capacities, strategy use and ability to spontaneously use and transfer strategy knowledge. The authors emphasize the importance of specific content knowledge in effective thinking and problem solving.

58. ——, Joseph C. Campione and Jeanne D. Day. "Learning to Learn: On Training Students to Learn from Texts." *Education Researcher.* 10 (1981): 14–21.

The authors review the literature on memory training and on training in the effectiveness of strategy use, particularly in study strategies, i.e., rote recall, summarization strategies, and other "learning to learn" studies. They present a tetrahedal model which can be used as a framework for further investigation in this area. The four components of the model are the learning activities, the characteristics of the learner, the nature of the materials and the criterion tasks. The authors point out that we need to make students aware of the basic strategies required for reading and remembering, the rules of text construction, the differences in task demands, and the importance of using prior knowledge in learning.

59. ——, and Jeanne D. Day. "Macrorules for Summarizing Texts: The Development of Expertise." *Journal of Verbal Learning and Verbal Behavior* 22 (1983): 1–14.

Brown and Day found that children are able to use increasingly more complex macrorules, or strategies for forming a global representation of a text, to form summaries as they get older. Children as young as fifth grade were able to use simple summarization rules, such as delete redundant information, and their ability to use more complex rules increased as they got older.

60. Brown, Jerry L. "On Teaching Thinking Skills in the Elementary and Middle School." *Phi Delta Kappan* 64 (June 1983): 709–714.

Brown describes a television series, ThinkAbout, designed to help students reason and solve problems effectively. The television program presents students with a real-life problem. Teachers use this problem to begin discussion and then to connect the problem and solution to real problems that exist for their students. The program provides direct instruction in problem solving, the use of a mnemonic, and practice in applying strategies and techniques. Skills and subject matter from language arts, math, science, and study skills have been included. In addition, instruction and practice is provided in twelve cognitive skills such as generating alternatives and estimating and approximating.

61. Brown, John Seely, Allan Collins, and Paul Duguid. "Situated Cognition and the Culture of Learning." *Educational Researcher* 32 (January/February 1989) 32–42.

The authors suggest that school activities and content knowledge learned in school are confined to within the culture or context of the school itself and are limited to use within the self-confirming culture of the school. Consequently, the authors suggest "contrary to the aim of schooling, success within this culture often has little bearing on performance elsewhere" (p. 34). They offer the example of learning vocabulary through dictionary exercises. Dictionaries are self-contained cultures, in and of themselves, and their definitions are irrelevant and impossible to understand without real world contact.

People who have acquired a knowledge base from real world experience approach comprehension and problem solving in a pragmatic, relevant, resourceful way that they could not do with a generic, abstract, "school-learned" domain-rigid sort of schema. Problem solving, the authors suggest, needs to be carried out in conjunction with the environment, distinct from the generic, abstract type of learning. Rather the problem solver should use the environment and envision a physical situation when possible.

62. Brown, Lisbeth J. "Developing Thinking and Problem-Solving Skills with Children's Books." *Childhood Education* 63 (December 1986): 102–107.

Brown notes the lack of thinking skills instruction in the classroom and suggests that this may be a result of the lack of agreement on what skills to teach. She suggests using Bloom's taxonomy of thinking skills as a basis to develop questions to encourage higher level thought, and she offers several practical suggestions for questioning techniques. The author also presents a problem solving guide, which is correlated with Bloom's thinking levels, for use in a literature program. She discusses other ways to infuse thinking skills into the literature curriculum. These include demonstrating how characters think and solve problems, using characters as models for role playing to think through and to solve problems and to learn how to apply these problem solving methods to their own lives.

63. Brown, Rexford. "Testing and Thoughtfulness." *Educational Leadership* 46 (April 1989): 31–33.

Brown describes a literacy of thoughtfulness, which calls for learners actively engaged in analyzing, thinking critically, evaluating, synthesizing, communicating, solving problems, and learning how to learn. Thoughtfulness means the construction and generation of meaning. This literacy of thoughtfulness requires tests that reflect what students are actually doing, not information they are passively acquiring.

He makes a number of suggestions, including having students create their own exams (generating and supporting both questions and answers), develop portfolios, prepare and give performances, and tie learning to testing by making questions the basis for learning.

64. Burns, Marilyn. "Teaching 'What to Do' in Arithmetic vs. Teaching 'What to Do and Why'." *Educational Leadership* 43 (April 1986): 34–38.

Burns urges teachers to include reasoning and thinking skills in computation instruction. She cites as evidence of the need for this the failure of students to reason effectively on the NAEP mathematics assessment. A transcript of the discussion of mathematics processes used and why they are used by three groups of elementary school students is enlightening. It demonstrates that children can arrive at a "correct" answer without understanding how and why they got there. She makes some suggestions for ways to develop understanding.

65. Cagle, Michael. "A General Abstract-Concrete Model of Creative Thinking." *Journal of Creative Behavior* 19 (Second Quarter 1985): 104–109.

Cagle provides an model for creative thinking which includes mental attitudes, types of thought, dimensions of stages and abstract and concrete domains. Creative thought begins with the abstract, understood only by the creator. It then moves to the concrete. It is suggested that the model be used to generate more hypotheses that can be tested to aid our understanding of the creative process.

66. Camplone, Joseph C., and Bonnie Armbruster. "Acquiring Information from Texts: An Analysis of Four Approaches." *Thinking and Learning Skills*. Relating Instruction to Research. Volume 1. Edited by Judith W.

Segal, Susan F. Chipman, and Robert Glaser. Hillsdale, New Jersey: Lawrence Erlbaum Associates, Pub., 1985, pp. 317–359.

Camplone and Armbruster review and compare a number of programs designed to develop the skills needed for students to learn from text by reading critically and thoughtfully. The comparison goes beyond looking at materials, target populations, etc., and focuses on theoretical and research differences. The authors present a model for learning and examine differences between expert and novice learners. They explore issues, such as the question of how to train students in the use of strategies and whether strategies are specific or general, concluding that strategies are probably both and need to be taught explicitly, particularly with younger students.

67.   Cannon, Dale, and Mark Weinstein. "Reasoning Skills: An Overview." *Thinking: The Journal of Philosophy for Children* 6 (1985): 29–33.

Cannon and Weinstein advocate Philosophy for Children because it develops and encourages the use and integration of the four dimensions of reasoning. They define and provide examples of the four dimensions: formal reasoning, using rules of logic and inference; informal reasoning, including critical inquiry, problem solving and evaluation; interpersonal reasoning, involving other people and their points of view; and philosophical reasoning reviewing thinking and the process of thinking. The program provides for an environment that allows for discussion and interaction.

68.   Carey, Susan. "Are Children Fundamentally Different Kinds of Thinkers and Learners than Adults?" *Thinking and Learning Skills*. Research and Open Questions. Volume 2. Edited by Susan F. Chipman, Judith W. Segal,

and Robert Glaser. Hillsdale, New Jersey: Lawrence Erlbaum Associates, Pub., 1985, pp. 485–517.

Carey examines five ways in which children's thinking might differ from that of adults. She concludes that "by far the most important source of variance is in domain-specific knowledge" (p. 514). Children can represent information and processes; they can think about what they are doing; they possess underlying concepts, such as causality; and they can acquire basic tools needed for thinking in content areas. The major difference between children and adults is that children generally do not know as much in any domain as adults do.

69. Carr, Eileen, and Donna Ogle. "K-W-L Plus: A Strategy for Comprehension and Summarization." *Journal of Reading* 30 (April 1987): 626–631.

Carr and Ogle describe K-W-L, a metacognitive strategy designed to elicit and confirm for students: what I Know, what I Want to know, and what I Learned about a topic. A three column guide is complete by students in groups and individually. They also describe "Plus," the use of mapping and summarizing to promote critical thinking as students organize and reorganize information as they think about the text. The map can serve as an outline for the summary.

70. Carr, John, Peter Eppig, and Peter Monether. "Learning by Solving Real Problems." *Middle School Journal XVII* (February 1986): 14–16.

Middle school students in the INTERFACE program engage in a total immersion program, which can range from a few days to two weeks in which a real problem of interest and importance to them is solved using a variety of "critical" skills. These include skills in problem solving, decision making, communicating, organizing, managing, learning independently, documenting, and cooperating. The process of solving a typical problem is described with both student's and teacher's role and function outlined. All curriculum areas are included in the problem. Students are motivated to engage in the process and are actively involved in the solution.

71. Chambers, John H. "Teaching Thinking Throughout the Curriculum—Where Else?" *Educational Leadership* 45 (April 1988): 4–6.

Chambers takes the position that thinking occurs within various contexts. Thus, it is essential that children be given the opportunity to think within the "particular forms of knowledge and their disciplines" (p. 5). We do not need special teachers of thinking but rather need teachers who are competent in their content area, understand the structure and demands of the content and can pass this on to their students.

72. Chance, Paul. *Thinking in the Classroom*: A Survey of Programs. New York: Teachers College Press, 1986.

Chance looks at the assumptions, goals, methods, materials, audience, teacher qualifications, benefits, problems, and evaluation available for seven major thinking programs. These include: CoRT, Productive Thinking, Philosophy for Children, Odyssey, Problem Solving and Comprehension, Instrumental Enrichment, and Techniques of Learning. After reviewing these approaches, he outlines one that he calls "thoughtful teaching" which incorporates thinking into the classroom and is developed by individual teachers using a variety of strategies.

73. Charlton, Ronald E. "The Direct Teaching of Analysis." *Thinking Skills Instruction: Concepts and Techniques.* Edited by Marcia Heiman and Joshua Slomianko.

Washington, D.C.: National Education Association, 1987, pp. 152–159.

We generally do not teach the skill of analysis; we only require practice of that skill. Because of this, Charlton recommends careful teaching of all three levels of analysis as defined by Bloom using the direct teaching strategies advocated by Beyer. The author provides explicit examples in a variety of content areas.

74. Chase, William G., and K. Anders Ericsson. "Skilled Memory." *Cognitive Skills and Their Acquisition.* Edited by John R. Anderson. Hillsdale, New Jersey: Lawrence Erlbaum Associates, Pub., 1981, pp. 141–189.

Skilled memory, according to Chase and Eriksson, is the ability to use memory in a particular domain rapidly and efficiently, i.e., at an expert level. The authors present a subject trained to have an expanded memory span capacity of 80 digits and offer theoretical principles which might underlie this trained ability.

They discuss the development of memory and how it is used by experts, how they are able to bypass the normal limits of STM in skilled performance in their particular area of expertise (such as math, chess). In a careful analysis of verbal reports and recall data, the authors concluded that two mechanisms operated which were important: use of mnemonics and the retrieval structure. With practice, the subject was able to speed up and improve the reliability of his encoding processes and strengthen the links between his mnemonic codes and retrieval structure, which resulted in more direct, faster and reliable retrieval. He was able to search systematically and efficiently through his knowledge base to retrieve large amounts of information.

75. Chi, Michelene T. H. "Interactive Role of Knowledge and Strategies in the Development of Organized Sorting and

Recall." *Thinking and Learning Skills*. Research and Open Questions. Volume 2. Edited by Susan F. Chipman, Judith W. Segal, and Robert Glaser. Hillsdale, New Jersey: Lawrence Erlbaum Associates, Pub., 1985, pp. 457–483.

Chi reports on a group of four studies conducted with individual children or a group of two children between the ages of 4.5 and 7.2, designed to examine the use of cognitive strategies in sorting and recalling information. She concludes that there is an interdependence between the possession and use of strategies and knowledge about the content. In this particular case, "the development of classification skill interacts strongly with knowledge about the stimulus domain" (p. 479). The suggestion is that subject or content knowledge is a key variable in the use of strategies in young children.

76.   ———, P. Feltovich, and Robert Glaser. "Categorization and Representation of Physics Problems by Experts and Novices." *Cognitive Science* 5 (1981): 121–152.

On a sorting task in mechanics, novices sorted on the basis of surface features, while experts sorted by higher level principles. The expert encodes facts about a skill and rehearses them. Knowledge is compiled, rehearsed and eventually converted to a set of procedures which then become automatic with more practice. The expert problem solver can represent a problem accurately and completely in terms of a schema containing both factual and procedural knowledge for solutions. The same problems may be represented at different levels of complexity according to the expertise of the solver.

77.   ———, Robert Glaser, and E. Rees. "Expertise in Problem Solving." *Advances in the Psychology of Human Intelligence*. Volume 1. Edited by Robert Sternberg.

Hillsdale, New Jersey: Laurence Erlbaum Associates, Pub., 1982.

This study demonstrated that experts not only know more than novices about their area of expertise, but that knowledge is organized in memory on a different, more abstract, conceptual level which represents their deeper, more thorough understanding of that area. Novices organize their knowledge of the area in a more literal, concrete way. An expert problem solver in a mechanics problem represents a set of formulas by a single concept or chunk.

78. Chipman, Susan F., and Judith W. Segal. "Higher Cognitive Goals for Education: An Introduction." *Thinking and Learning Skills*. Relating Instruction to Research. Volume 1. Edited by Judith W. Segal, Susan F. Chipman, and Robert Glaser. Hillsdale, New Jersey: Lawrence Erlbaum Associates, Pub., 1985. pp. 1–19.

Chipman and Segal provide an overview of the complex topic of thinking and learning skills as well as an overview to their two volumes that deal with the topic. They cite the failure to teach students effective ways to think and learn in schools in spite of a long held belief that this is the mission of education. They examine briefly the areas of knowledge acquisition, problem solving and metacognition. Finally, the authors identify three current issues: the generality of cognitive skills, the teachability of cognitive skills, and developmental differences between children and adults.

79. Clarke, John H., James Raths, and Gary L. Gilbert. "Inductive Towers: Letting Students See How They Think." *Journal of Reading* 33 (November 1989): 86–95.

Clarke, Raths, and Gilbert advocate the use of inductive towers to aid students in viewing their own thinking and to enable them to manipulate and reorganize information in order to construct generalizations. The tower is constructed from the bottom up, starting with the concrete and moving to the theoretical. The article gives specific examples and guidance in evaluating the process.

80. Clements, Douglas H. "Logo and Cognition: A Theoretical Framework." *Computers in Human Behavior* 2 (1986): 95–110.

Clements proposes a theoretical foundation, based on Sternberg's componential theory of intelligence, to provide researchers with a framework for investigating the cognitive effects of training in LOGO programming. He reviews research in metacognition and knowledge acquisition to support his proposal. He concludes that there is reason to believe that LOGO does facilitate certain information processing abilities but doesn't guarantee the development of cognition in general. Further, he advocates future investigations of LOGO effects based on specific conponents of Sternberg's theory.

81. Cole, Nancy S. "Conceptions of Educational Achievement." *Educational Researcher* 19 (April 1990): 2–7.

Cole explores two notions of educational achievement and their impact on instruction and on educational research. The achievement of basic skills and facts has dominated much of our thinking about education and has resulted in separate, isolated skill instruction and criterion-referenced testing. The "achievement of higher order skills (using such terms as critical thinking or problem solving) and of advanced knowledge of subjects (using words such as understanding or expertise)" (p. 3) is a very different and more complex concept. The author examines a wide range of instructional possibilities related to this view of achievement, including reciprocal teaching, coaching, and integrating thinking and content.

82. Collins, Allan. "Teaching Reasoning Skills." *Thinking and Learning Skills: Research and Open Questions.* Volume 2. Edited by Susan F. Chipman, Judith W. Segal, and Robert Glaser. Hillsdale, New Jersey: Lawrence Erlbaum Associates, Pub., 1985, pp. 579–586.

Collins suggests that inquiry learning using teacher questioning and modeling may be the most effective way to teach thinking skills needed for science and mathematics. He provides examples of cases that can be used in inquiry learning and of the role of questioning.

83. Commeyras, Michelle. "Using Literature to Teach Critical Thinking." *Journal of Reading* 32 (May 1989): 703–707.

Commeyras proposes using literature to teach critical thinking because it reflects the everyday decisions and problems that thinkers must face. She includes a sample grid for use in inductive reasoning about a narrative text. The grid illustrates how the dispositions and abilities of a critical thinker can be developed.

84. Common, Dianne L. "Conversations in the Social Studies Classroom: A Setting for Inquiry." *The History and Social Studies Teacher* 20 (Spring 1985): 69–74.

While the inquiry method of instruction has been widely advocated for social studies, it has not generally been adopted. Common identifies teachers' lack of confidence in their own abilities as a major reason for this situation. She describes and develops the notion of "conversations" as a means for enabling inquiry and the development of critical thinking. Critical thinking is equated with rational thinking, with the critical thinker engaging in theorizing while examining personal presuppositions. In this process, a critical attitude, "a willingness to entertain dispute" (p. 72), is essential. Within this framework, Common defines the teacher's role, explores the relevance of information, and suggests how conversations for critical inquiry might proceed.

85. "Conversation with Arthur Whimbey." *Thinking Skills Instruction: Concepts and Techniques.* Edited by Marcia Heiman and Joshua Slomianko. Washington, D.C.: National Education Association, 1987, pp. 160–166.

Whimbey traces the development of his approach to teaching thinking skills from an early study by Bloom and Broder (1950) in which differences in thinking between low-aptitude and high-aptitude college students were identified. As a result, the author developed a program in which teachers and students think aloud as they are solving problems in which they have all the needed information. Pairs of students engage in this process, with one student thinking aloud and the other student listening and probing.

86. Cook, Ruth E., and Brent D. Slife. "Developing Problem-Solving Skills." *Academic Therapy* 21 (September 1985): 5–13.

Cook and Slife explore issues identified with the poor problem solving abilities often exhibited by handicapped students. They suggest that one reason for this situation may be that teachers and parents protect these students from problems. Thus, they don't learn to identify problems and engage in solving them. Frequently students acquire an attitude of "learned helplessness" and won't risk engaging in the process. Because of the time pressure of many special education curriculums, teachers will give students solutions rather than take the time to allow the student to solve the problem. The authors review the problem solving process, identify difficult areas, and suggest remedial strategies. One example is the inability of many learning disabled students to recognize that a problem exists. They suggest the need to "make the task relevant or important to the child" (p. 8). Other strategies include using mnemonics, thinking aloud, and engaging in solving a variety of problems separately from classroom activities in order to avoid the notion that there is a right or wrong solution.

87. Copeland, A.P., and C.S. Weissbrod. "Cognitive Strategies Used by Learning Disabled Children: Does Hyperactivity Always Make Things Worse?" *Journal of Learning Disabilities* 16 (1983): 473–477.

The authors studied hyperactive and non-hyperactive learning disabled subjects and compared them with non-disabled subjects on a variety of problem solving tasks, including the "Twenty Questions Test," to investigate the effects of hyperactivity on learning disability. They found that the non-disabled subjects performed better than all LDs, and the hyperactive and non hyperactive LD subjects performed at the same levels. The authors conclude that having a learning disability effects strategy use, but, in general, hyperactivity doesn't account for this detriment or lag in performance. LD children demonstrate a lag, a lack of mature strategy use, whether hyperactive or not.

88. Copeland, Willis D. "Teaching Students to 'Do' History: The Teacher and the Computer in Partnership." *The History Teacher* 18 (February 1985): 189–197.

The vision of students actively engaged in "doing" history through the inquiry method has not been realized. This has not been because we have failed to train teachers. A great deal of time, effort and money has been devoted to this end. The problem is that we failed to appreciate the difficulties of engaging in inquiry and problem solving in the classroom. Classroom management of the many activities, materials, questions, and far-reaching discussions place a burden on the teacher. The unpredictable nature of inquiry learning requires a substantial number of initiating and response behaviors on the part of the teacher. Copeland suggests that the microcomputer can be useful in structuring inquiry activities and in providing responses. The computer can serve as a data base and a model of the process of historical inquiry. He describes a program developed at the University of California, Santa Barbara, which simulates the problem solving process in historical situations. The intention is not to replace the teacher, but rather to provide a tool to be "used by the teacher to shape the students' learning experience" (p. 195).

89. Cortes, Carlos E., and Elinor Richardson. "'Why In The World': Using Television to Develop Critical Thinking Skills." *Phi Delta Kappan* 64 (June 1983): 715–716.

The authors describe a television series designed "as an example of critical thinking in action and as a tool for developing those skills in young people" (p. 716). The programs use current events as the basis for a discussion between a public figure and a group of high school students. Cortes and Richardson describe seven teaching strategies that can be used immediately after a program and subsequently to develop critical thinking abilities in high school students.

90. Costa, Arthur L. "Teaching for Intelligent Behavior." *Educational Leadership* 39 (October 1981): 29–32.

Costa proposes eleven criteria for identifying classroom conditions that promote intelligent behavior. Students must accept the ultimate responsibility for engaging in thinking behaviors. Teachers, however, can structure the classroom to enable this to happen through, for example, the sequencing of activities to encourage higher levels of thinking, the phrasing of questions to stimulate problem solving, and the use of verbal and nonverbal feedback to foster risk taking rather than conformity.

91. ———. "Teaching Toward Intelligent Behavior." *Thinking: An Expanding Frontier.* Edited by William Maxwell. Philadelphia, Pennsylvania: The Franklin Press, 1983, pp. 211–222.

Costa provides fourteen questions to guide the development of curriculum and instruction in teaching students to engage in intelligent behavior. They range from an examination of the value placed on thinking by the school and the community and whether intellectual behavior can be developed through teaching to questions related to the capacities included in intelligent behavior and how to structure teacher time and behavior to develop it. While these questions are not intended as a check list and while the answers provided may not be acceptable to all, the questions do help focus our thinking on areas to consider.

92. ———. "Mediating the Metacognitive." *Educational Leadership* 42 (November 1984): 57–62.

Costa defines metacognition as the "ability to know what we know and what we don't know . . . . to plan a strategy for producing what information is needed, to be conscious of our own steps and strategies during the act of problem solving and to reflect on and evaluate the productivity of our own thinking" (p. 57). He discusses twelve strategies teachers can use to enhance metacognition: involving students in planning, choosing, evaluating, clarifying, and reflecting as part of the process of actively monitoring their own learning. The instructional technique that seems the most promising, according to Costa, is that of teacher modeling.

93. ———. "Teaching For, Of, and About Thinking." *Developing Minds: A Resource Book for Teaching*

Thinking. Edited by Arthur L. Costa. Alexandria, Virginia: Association for Supervision and Curriculum Development, 1985, pp. 20–23.

Costa discusses three levels of teaching thinking. Teaching *for* thinking means creating a classroom climate that is conducive to thinking, i.e., through questions, problems, materials, modeling and response behaviors. Teaching *of* thinking is the direct instruction of skills and strategies. Finally, teaching *about* thinking means making students aware of their own thinking processes and their applications to real life situations. Costa includes in this category teaching about how the brain functions, about metacognition and about epistemology. He proposes a set of teacher competencies required for teaching thinking at each of these levels and organizes these into a matrix which may be used as a basis for staff development in thinking skills instruction.

94.   ———. "Toward a Model of Human Intellectual Functioning." *Developing Minds: A Resource Book for Teaching Thinking.* Edited by Arthur L. Costa. Alexandria, Virginia: Association for Supervision and Curriculum Development, 1985, pp. 62–65.

Costa compares thinking models in terms of input, processing and output constructs and presents a simplified model of intellectual functioning useful as a guide to curriculum and instructional development, material selection and staff development programming.

95.   ———. "The Behaviors of Intelligence." *Developing Minds: A Resource Book for Teaching Thinking.* Edited by Arthur L. Costa. Alexandria, Virginia: Association for Supervision and Curriculum Development, 1985, pp. 66–68.

Costa presents a list of intelligent behaviors which are characteristic of intelligent action: taking in information through all senses; deriving meaning from information and acting on it; communicating, applying and constantly evaluating meaning; and monitoring intelligent behaviors and their effects on environment. He presents a classification of behaviors useful for teaching and selecting programs and for adopting and developing instructional materials at levels of discrete skills, strategies, creativity and attitudes, which he refers to as the "cognitive spirit" (p. 68).

96. ———. "How Scientists Think When They Are Doing Science." *Developing Minds: A Resource Book for Teaching Thinking.* Edited by Arthur L. Costa. Alexandria, Virginia: Association for Supervision and Curriculum Development, 1985, pp. 114–117.

This is a scientist's description of what he did and how he felt as he solved a problem, including notes identifying the cognitive processes used to solve a simple scientific problem.

97. ———. "Teacher Behaviors That Enable Student Thinking." *Developing Minds: A Resource Book for Teaching Thinking.* Edited by Arthur L. Costa. Alexandria, Virginia: Association for Supervision and Curriculum Development, 1985, pp. 125–137.

The foundation for effective teacher behavior, according to Costa, is discussion. This interaction is essential for the development of thinking skills and of self-confidence in using them, yet it occurs in only 4 to 8 percent of classroom time. The behaviors suggested in the areas of teacher questioning, structuring of the classroom and activities, responding to students, and modeling thinking behaviors all involve discussion. Detailed examples are provided on wording questions to aid students in gathering and recalling information, making sense of it, and applying and evaluating information, concepts and principles in new situations.

Since student achievement appears to be higher in well structured classrooms, Costa provides suggestions in the areas of giving clear instructions which focus on the thinking aspects of the task and which place the responsibility for thinking on the student. Structure also includes insuring that sufficient time, probably over the course of two years, is provided and that time is spent "throughout the school day, across the content areas" (p. 129) on active engagement of the student in thinking tasks in order to insure that transfer of thinking skills and strategies takes place. Essential to student growth is student responsibility for making critical decisions concerned with thinking, such as choosing and evaluating problem-solving strategies and setting goals and assessing achievement of those goals. The kind of response the teacher makes is critical in fostering the development of thinking and a valuing of thinking. Open responses, such as accepting, clarifying and facilitating student responses, are effective because they require that teachers listen to students. Finally, modeling of thinking behavior is one of the most effective strategies teachers can use.

98.   ———. "How Can We Recognize Improved Student Thinking?" *Developing Minds: A Resource Book for Teaching Thinking.* Edited by Arthur L. Costa. Alexandria, Virginia: Association for Supervision and Curriculum Development, 1985, pp. 288–290.

Costa provides a list of indicators of intellectual growth which teachers can use to identify improved thinking. The list includes student perseverance, decreased impulsiveness, flexible thinking, metacognition, careful review, problem posing, use of prior knowledge and experiences, transference to real life, and the use of precise language and enjoyment of problem solving.

99. ———. "Thinking Skills: Neither an Add-on Nor a Quick Fix." *Thinking Skills Instruction: Concepts and Techniques*. Edited by Marcia Heiman and Joshua Slomianko. Washington, D.C.: National Education Association, 1987, pp. 16-23.

Costa suggests that, although the research is not definitive yet, when thinking skills are integrated into the total curriculum achievement in content areas increases. Thinking skills need to be viewed from a broad perspective and should include generic intelligent behavior such as risk taking, persistence and flexibility. All students can benefit from thinking skills instruction. "Teachers CAN grow intelligence" (p. 17). One way to do this is to increase the quantity and quality of verbal interaction in the classroom, especially in light of the questionable amount and complexity of linguistic and cognitive interaction that takes place in many homes. Another way to infuse thinking into the curriculum and into learning is to put teachers in control of the classroom and in touch with other teachers and current ideas and strategies.

100. Covington, Martin V. "Strategic Thinking and the Fear of Failure." *Thinking and Learning Skills*. Relating Instruction to Research. Volume 1. Edited by Judith W. Segal, Susan F. Chipman, and Robert Glaser. Hillsdale, New Jersey: Lawrence Erlbaum Associates., Pub., 1985, pp. 389-416.

Covington links cognitive and affective variables in educational situations by examining ways to motivate students. The most effective way is to "help students develop more effective thinking skills so that they can take advantage of. . .opportunities for classroom achievement" (p. 390). The Productive Thinking Program provides teachers with a way of rewarding students appropriately and teaching them strategic thinking. Strategic thinking aids in problem solving by enabling students to formulate a problem, select strategies for solving it, and monitor progress in reaching a solution. The author discusses some of the research conducted on the program, highlighting its effectiveness.

101. Crabbe, Anne B. "Future Problem Solving." *Developing Minds: A Resource Book for Teaching Thinking.* Edited by Arthur L Costa. Alexandria, Virginia: Association for Supervision and Curriculum Development, 1985, pp. 217–219.

Crabbe describes the program developed by E. Paul Torrance which fosters creative thinking about predicted problems in the future. In addition, the program develops skills in the areas of communication, interpersonal relations, daily problem solving, and critical thinking. The approach has been used primarily with gifted students, although it is appropriate for all students. Students, working in teams, define, research, and solve problems, establishing their own criteria for the solutions. Written responses by the teams are submitted to state and national competitions. Teams are chosen to solve real business and governmental problems.

102. ———. "The Future Problem Solving Program." *Educational Leadership* 47 (September 1989): 27–29.

Crabbe describes the history of the Future Problem Solving Program and the process students are taught. They explore and research topics, identify a major problem from a number of problem areas, brainstorm solutions, develop criteria for evaluation, and select the best solution. Emphasis is placed on problems related to real life and on students competing with each other in solving them.

103. Cradler, John. "CompuTHINK and Criteria for Selecting Software." *Developing Minds: A Resource Book for Teaching Thinking.* Edited by Arthur L. Costa.

Alexandria, Virginia: Association for Supervision and Curriculum Development, 1985, pp. 256–265.

CompuTHINK connects thinking and technology by identifying 33 specific thinking skills based on Bloom's Taxonomy and on Project IMPACT's Universe of Critical Thinking Skills. Computer programs are analyzed and matched to the skills, and materials and training are provided for using computers to develop the skills. The skills included are the enabling skills associated with perceiving, conceiving and sequencing, the processes associated with analyzing and inferring, and the operations associated with logical reasoning, creative thinking and problem solving. Detailed suggestions and forms are provided for selecting and evaluating software.

104. Cuban, Larry. "Policy and Research Dilemmas in the Teaching of Reasoning: Unplanned Designs," *Review of Educational Research* 54 Winter 1984): 655–681.

Cuban discusses the teaching of thinking from a historical perspective and as a problem of our existing educational structure. Organization, staffing and governance of classrooms, mandated by school, district, state and federal policies and goals as well as by parental expectations, constrains the classroom teacher and interferes with the teaching of thinking and reasoning. Moreover, Cuban traces earlier attempts to develop good thinkers, and notes that these same policies, goals and expectations have not changed and have been detrimental to the development of reasoning since the beginning of this century.

Among current problems Cuban suggests the following: there is no clear-cut body of knowledge generated by research on the subject; the inclination toward whole class teaching prohibits individual instruction, application and assessment so necessary to develop reasoning; the secondary school system of chopping content into separate discrete courses with equal allocations of time and resources does the same; and current practice focuses on assessment of product, rather than process.

He advocates that we first acknowledge the fact that current school organization and governance impedes the teaching of reasoning, and the fact that current university research is of little benefit in developing policy; that we focus research on elementary rather than secondary schools, on the school as a unit rather than the individual classroom as the unit of change, that cognitive psychologists direct research to the thinking processes of teachers and learners, and finally, that schools must provide opportunities for teachers as well as students to learn and grow professionally.

105. Dansereau, Donald F. "Learning Strategy Research." *Thinking and Learning Skills.* Relating Instruction to Research. Volume 1. Edited by Judith W. Segal, Susan F. Chipman, and Robert Glaser. Hillsdale, New Jersey: Lawrence Erlbaum Associates, Pub., 1985, pp. 209–239.

Dansereau provides an overview of learning strategy research and relates it to learning from science textbooks. A series of essential decisions are outlined in which the teacher determines what strategies to include and how to sequence them, what instructional techniques to use, how to individualize instruction, and how to evaluate effectiveness of instruction. General research is included, with specific suggestions based on the author's experience. For example, modeling by the teacher is recommended as "one of the most potent methods" (p. 215), but the author also includes three specific strategies with which he has had substantial success. He also details content-independent strategies such as networking, mapping, and summarizing and content-dependent strategies such as knowledge schema for science and the use of headings in science textbooks.

106.   de Bono, Edward. "The Cognitive Research Trust (CoRT) Thinking Program." *Thinking: The Expanding Frontier.* Edited by William Maxwell. Philadelphia, Pennsylvania: The Franklin Institute Press, 1983, pp. 115–127.

De Bono asserts that thinking processes are essentially the same for all ages and abilities. Thinking is defined as "the operating skill with which intelligence acts upon experience" (p. 117). He describes his program which has been taught by both trained and untrained teachers throughout the world to a wide range of students of all ages. The lessons are nonhierarchical, with skills designed to be easily transferred to new situations. The program is concerned with the perceptual area of thinking. Perception is defined as "the process of using our experience to find our way around the present situation" (p. 117). The focus here is on process, not on content. Thus, the lessons deal directly with thinking. Students work in small groups. The author outlines the six aspects of thinking included in the program and reviews some of the evaluation that has been conducted on CoRT programs.

107.   ———. "The Direct Teaching of Thinking as a Skill." *Phi Delta Kappan* 64 (June 1983): 703–708.

De Bono provides a rationale for teaching thinking skills, an overview of critical aspects of thinking and a description of his widely used program, CoRT. The program focuses on perception which is "the way our minds make sense of the world around us" (p. 704) It provides tools to enable the student to accomplish this goal. The sections of the program include breadth, organization, interaction, creativity, information and feeling, and action. De Bono suggests that although it can be used with any age, it is most effective with students 9 to 11 years old. He also recommends that it be taught as a separate course, later integrated into content areas. The most common outcome of the program is

probably the increase in self-confidence experienced by the
students. They think of themselves as thinkers.

108.   ———. "The CoRT Thinking Program." *Thinking and
        Learning Skills.* Relating Instruction to Research. Volume
        1. Edited by Judith W. Segal, Susan F. Chipman, and
        Robert Glaser. Hillsdale, New Jersey: Lawrence Erlbaum
        Associates, Pub. 1985, pp. 363–388.

De Bono describes the objectives of the CoRT Program,
the materials used, the tools for thinking which are
developed, a sample lesson, and field testing of the program.

109.   ———. "Beyond Critical Thinking." *Educational
        Leadership* 25 (January/February 1986): 13–16.

De Bono agrees that critical thinking is a necessary
thinking skill, but he asserts that it is not the only, or even
the major, thinking skill. We must go beyond evaluating and
must solve problems and generate new ideas. "Our society
strongly needs thinking that is constructive, generative, and
organizing. Just being critical is not nearly enough" (p. 13).
The CoRT program is based on the premise that it is possible
to teach thinking directly and to provide the thinker with
tools that he/she can use independently in many situations.
Direct instruction is provided outside of content areas in
order to promote concentration on thinking and to develop
within the student the concept of himself as a thinker.

110.   Delclos, Victor R., John D. Bransford, and H. Carl
        Haywood. "Instrumental Enrichment: A Program for
        Teaching Thinking." *Childhood Education* 60
        (March/April 1989): 256–259.

The authors summarize and review Feuerstein's
Instrumental Enrichment program. They present a sampling
of the paper and pencil tasks that are found in the program
and an overview of a typical day's lesson, which includes a

discussion of the work done that day and the strategies students used to work their way through problems. Finally, an attempt is made to extract a principle learned through the work which can be applied to various other tasks. The authors discuss the success of the program in terms of gains in the development of thinking and general problem solving ability. Improvement in academic performance is a complex issue, not easily or immediately measured. The authors suggest that the IE program, combined and integrated with a strong content curriculum, should lead to improved academic achievement.

111.   Derrico, Patricia J. "Learning to Think with Philosophy for Children." *Educational Leadership* 45 (April 1988): 34.

Derrico describes the adoption and adaptation of Philosophy for Children by middle school teachers in different content areas. The students demonstrate an ability to listen, to engage in dialogue, and to provide reasons for their views.

112.   Didsbury, Kendall. "Teaching Precise Processing Through Writing Instruction." *Thinking Skills Instruction: Concepts and Techniques.* Edited by Marcia Heiman and Joshua Slomianko. Washington, D.C.: National Education Association, 1987, pp. 167–173.

Didsbury relates how precise processing, advocated by Whimbey, is applied to a writing program. The author describes, in some detail, three innovative strategies for improving expository writing skills and thinking skills. The central innovation is the use of a series of problems in which the students need to classify, compare and contrast, analyze structure and character, and solve problems. Second, in order to provide feedback to the student on how he/she is processing information, teachers and students confer on a regular basis. Third, the editing process has been extended and structured.

113.   Dillon, J.T. "Research on Questioning and Discussion." *Educational Leadership* 42 (November 1984): 50–56.

Dillon asserts that "discussions are hard to conduct, and they are hard to learn how to conduct" (p. 53). The author reviews much of the available but limited research in this area, suggesting preconditions and kinds of discussions. A number of guidelines are included for teachers, such as insuring the classroom atmosphere allows for risk-taking and is open to ideas and opinion. Teachers need to allow for wait-time, use statements instead of questions, and encourage student elaboration and questioning.

114.   Duffy, Gerald G., and Laura R. Roehler. "The Subtleties of Instructional Mediation." *Educational Leadership* 43 (April 1986): 23–27.

Verbal mediation shapes the way students not only engage in a task but also the way they "restructure information" (p. 26). The teacher's role in mediating learning is subtle and occurs over a sustained period of time. This article provides an analysis of dialogue which illustrates how this may happen.

115.   Edwards, John, and Richard B. Baldauf, Jr. "Teaching Thinking in Secondary Science." *Thinking: The Expanding Frontier.* Edited by William Maxwell. Philadelphia, Pennsylvania: The Franklin Institute Press, 1983, pp. 129–137.

Edwards and Baldauf report on the results of teaching thinking to secondary school science students through the focused lessons of the CoRT program. The program was introduced because students did not appear to be acquiring thinking skills through the use of the scientific method.

Direct instruction by means of the CoRT program appeared to have a positive effect on student thinking which was "probably generalizable" (p. 136). Based on this pilot project the authors suggest some shortcomings to their research and possible avenues to explore, particularly in the evaluation of the CoRT program.

116. Ennis, Robert H. "Goals for a Critical Thinking Curriculum." *Developing Minds: A Resource Book for Teaching Thinking.* Edited by Arthur L. Costa. Alexandria, Virginia: Association for Supervision and Curriculum Development, 1985, pp. 54–57.

Ennis presents a comprehensive outline for teaching critical thinking in any subject matter. Topics are organized by dispositions and attributes of a good thinker, i.e. the ability to clarify, support and infer, and by strategies and tactics used in the attainment of these attributes.

117. ———. "A Logical Basis for Measuring Critical Thinking Skills." *Educational Leadership* 43 (October 1985): 44–48

Ennis defines critical thinking as "a reflective and reasonable thinking that is focused on deciding what to believe or do" (p. 45). This definition, which Ennis concedes is a somewhat narrow one, includes creative activities and implies that thinking is a practical activity. He compares the term critical thinking to "higher-order thinking," which he concludes is too vague to be useful. Bloom's taxonomy, while more specific, is also too vague, using general terms too widely applied with no criteria for judging outcomes. He suggests that the term critical thinking includes much of what is implied in higher-order thinking and is specific in terms of disposition and abilities. The four general sets of abilities include those related to developing clarity, making inferences, establishing a sound basis for the inferences and making decisions. The relationships between abilities and disposition are explored and examples provided. The four sets of abilities have been included in statewide tests developed by Connecticut and California.

118.   ————. "Critical Thinking and the Curriculum." *Thinking Skills Instruction: Concepts and Techniques.* Edited by Marcia Heiman and Joshua Slomianko. Washington, D.C.: National Education Association, 1987, pp. 40–48.

The current, widespread interest in developing students' critical thinking abilities is evident from the inclusion of critical thinking into required courses for college students, the development of graduate programs in critical thinking, and the surge of interest in including critical thinking in school curricula. Ennis examines the problems and issues related to teaching critical thinking. He suggests that although we need to have knowledge of a subject if we are to critically examine it, there are principles in critical thinking that cross subject lines. The issue is not whether there are general principles but the extent to which students can transfer them from one subject to another. After examining vaguenesses in terms and conditions, he concludes that transfer can and does occur if we allow students opportunities to engage in critical thinking practices and strategies. The need for additional research in all areas of critical thinking instruction is cited.

119.   ————. "Critical Thinking and Subject Specificity: Clarification and Needed Research." *Educational Researcher* 18 (April 1989): 4–10.

Ennis discusses critical thinking, the issue of subject specificity within critical thinking, the confusions which exist in the literature regarding aspects of subject specificity, and the implications of this issue for education. He presents four instructional approaches: critical thinking taught 1) free of content, 2) infused into content subjects, 3) content instruction with implicit thinking skills instruction, or 4) a mixed model—instruction in critical thinking and content specific critical thinking instruction. Ennis presents several areas of much needed research, including the need to study and develop instruments for the evaluation of critical thinking. (See also entries 120 and 230.)

120.   ———. "The Extent to Which Critical Thinking Is Subject-Specific: Further Clarification." *Educational Researcher* 19 (May 1990): 13–16.

Ennis responds to McPeck's critique of his April 1989 article, citing their differences of opinion. He clarifies his position that while there is an overlap between school and life problems, difficulties in transfer between the two may exist because of the fact that some life problems are not included in school subjects. Critical thinking in life must be the goal of schools. (See also entries 119 and 230.)

121.   Ericson, Bonnie, Mary Hubler, Thomas W. Bean, Christine C. Smith, and Joanna Vellone McKenzie. "Increasing Critical Reading in Junior High Classrooms." *Journal of Reading* 30 (February 1987): 430–439.

The authors identify the need for critical reading and critical thinking in junior high schools if students are to succeed in high school and beyond. They adopt Turner's definition of critical reading as involving "analytic thinking for the purpose of evaluation of what is read" (p. 431). What does analytic thinking require? It involves using prior knowledge, generating hypotheses, and testing and evaluating them. In order to accomplish this, Ericson et al. suggest using three reading strategies: anticipation-reaction guides, text previews and 3-level study guides. Underlying these strategies is the need for both students and teachers to understand and use the relationships between questions and answers in terms of whether answers come from the text or the reader's prior knowledge. Emphasis is placed on inquiry learning and on cooperative group learning.

122.   Falkof, Lucille, and Janet Moss. "When Teachers Tackle Thinking Skills." *Educational Leadership* 42 (November 1984): 4–9.

Falkof and Moss describe the evolution of a program of teaching thinking skills throughout a school curriculum. Questioning, based on a simplified version of Bloom's Taxonomy, is the key element in the program. Specific aspects of each thinking skill were identified and sequenced according to the developmental level of the children. Some detail is provided for how to teach making inferences and analogies. Teachers were involved in all stages of the development of the program.

123.   Feuerstein, Reuven, Mogens Reimer Jensen, Mildred B. Hoffman, and Yaacov Rand. "Instrumental Enrichment, An Intervention Program for Structural Cognitive Modifiability: Theory and Practice." *Thinking and Learning Skills*. Relating Instruction to Research. Volume 1. Edited by Judith W. Segal, Susan F. Chipman, and Robert Glaser. Hillsdale, New Jersey: Lawrence Erlbaum Associates, Pub. 1985, pp. 43–82.

The authors present a detailed analysis of the nature of "retarded performance" and the role of "mediated learning experiences" in modifying cognitive performance. The Instrumental Enrichment program was specifically developed to "enhance the capacity of the low functioning adolescent" (p. 59). The content-free program, using a series of instruments focusing on individual, specific skills, is described in detail. The results of studies conducted on the effectiveness of the program are included.

124. Fitzgerald, Jill. "Enhancing Two Related Though Processes: Revision in Writing and Critical Reading." *The Reading Teacher* 43 (October 1989): 42–48.

Citing the similarities underlying the process of reading and writing, Fitzgerald stresses the particular links between revision in writing and critical reading. They both are a "dissonance-resolution process" (pp. 43–44). In both instances the student compares the text to the writer's/reader's goals, intentions and beliefs. If dissonance occurs, the student must engage in decision making in order to resolve the differences. The author suggests group thinking conferences as one way to help student engage in these related tasks.

125. Flavell, John H., and Henry M. Wellman. "Metamemory." *Perspective on the Development of Memory and Cognition.* Edited by R.V. Kail, Jr. and J.W. Hagen. Hillsdale, New Jersey: Lawrence Erlbaum Associates, Pub., 1977, pp. 3–33.

The authors investigate the development of memory, its operations, processes, the unconscious and conscious behaviors that affect memory, and the knowledge and awareness of one's own memory processes. The article offers a survey of the literature on metamemory to that date and discusses the relationship between metamemory and memory itself. Flavell and Wellman conclude with some speculations as to how metamemory may develop.

126. Flemming, Paula K. "Questioning in a Writing Program to Develop Thinking." *Thinking Skills Instruction: Concepts and Techniques.* Edited by Marcia Heiman and Joshua Slomianko. Washington, D.C.: National Education Association, 1987, pp. 255–261.

Flemming provides numerous examples of teacher questioning to aid student thinking during writing. She also includes lists of questions that can be used for specific purposes such as clarifying the focus of the writing or strengthening a weak ending. The aim of all the questions is to force students to solve problems, make decisions and think critically.

127.   Flower, Linda. *Problem-Solving Strategies for Writing.* New York: Harcourt Brace Jovanovich, Inc., 1981.

Flower equates the process of writing with problem solving and suggests that in writing, as in problem solving in other areas, the writer must draw on his/her prior knowledge and on a "set of problem-solving strategies" (p. 3), or heuristics. The book guides the reader through nine strategies for effective, powerful and persuasive writing. In addition to providing a set of problem solving heuristics for writing, Flower explores the process of writing as a thinking activity. Much of the planning the writer does is similar to defining and exploring the problem in problem solving. Creative thinking is essential in the development of ideas, the generation of new ideas, and the connection or networking of ideas. These ideas may or may not be in a well-defined formal state. The writer needs to "turn such intuitions into clearly stated ideas and then organize and develop those ideas into a logical, well-supported argument." (p. 82). The act of organizing involves many aspects of critical thinking.

128.   ——, and John R. Hayes. "A Cognitive process Theory of Writing." *College Composition and Communication* 32 (December 1981): 365-387.

Flower and Hayes examine the stage model of writing and suggest that it does not explain the process of decision making that takes place during writing. They propose a cognitive process model in which there are elementary mental processes occurring at any stage during the writing process and which are hierarchical in structure. For example. planning which can involve such tasks as generating ideas and organizing them occurs not only before the act of translating thought into words but also during the translation. As we write we generate new ideas and organized them. The authors analyze protocols of students writing and develop a model based on the analysis.

129. Flynn, Linda L. "Developing Critical Reading Skills Through Cooperative Problem Solving." *The Reading Teacher* 42 (May 1989): 664-668.

Flynn advocates developing critical thinking skills through problem solving in cooperative learning groups. Using children's mystery stories, the steps in the IDEAL approach are followed. These include Identifying the problem, Defining (and representing) it, Exploring alternatives, Acting on ideas and Looking for effects. The cooperative learning, with its emphasis on "discussion, negotiation, clarification of ideas, and evaluation of others' ideas" (p. 666) promotes critical thinking.

130. Frager, Alan M., and Loren C. Thompson. "Conflict: The Key to Critical Reading Instruction." *Journal of Reading* 28 (May 1985): 676-683.

Frager and Thompson equate critical reading and critical thinking, identifying the need for the reader to establish a critical purpose, engage in ongoing evaluation, and test the critical view acquired from the text. One of the key elements in helping this happen is to motivate the student. The authors suggest providing examples of conflict around an issue or a topic, allowing students to examine issues and evidence, modeling critical thinking behaviors, and extending the experience through additional reading and discussions. The use of conflict engenders "cognitive dissonance" in the reader. The disharmony or dissonance "will motivate the person to try to reduce the dissonance and achieve consonance" (p. 677). The authors provide detailed examples of issues and two ways to structure the lesson, both involving inquiry on the part of the students.

131.   Frederikson, John R., and Allan Collins. "A Systems Approach to Educational Testing." *Educational Researcher* 18 (December 1989): 27–32.

Educational testing influences the direction of instruction and learning. Because of this Frederikson and Collins propose that we develop tests that focus on higher level processes, cognitive skills and problem solving abilities. They propose a system for assessment which includes the tasks needed, the traits to be assessed, examples of responses, and training for teachers in scoring. In each area a wide range of issues is addressed.

132.   Furlong, John, and William Carroll. "Teaching Reasoning with Computers." *Thinking: The Journal of Philosophy for Children* 5 (1985): 29–32.

Furlong and Carroll examine the notion of teaching reasoning skills and review Computer Assisted Instruction that has attempted it. They conclude that for the present time we are better off training expert teachers than developing expert software to accomplish improvement of reasoning. Part of their conclusion rests on the premise that reasoning, with the exception of metacognition, is context-bound. In order to insure transfer we should focus on metacognition. This can best be taught by a teacher who is expert in the Socratic method. The use of a computer for this is limited to particular contexts. For example, reasoning in BASIC probably will not transfer to reasoning in French.

133.   Fusco, Esther. "Cognitive Levels Matching and Curriculum Analysis." *Developing Minds: A Resource*

Book for Teaching Thinking. Edited by Arthur L. Costa. Alexandria, Virginia: Association for Supervision and Curriculum Development, 1985, pp. 81–86.

Fusco defines and describes concept levels associated with concrete and formal stages of cognitive development. Teachers must formally and informally assess students' cognitive abilities to analyze and modify the cognitive demands of the curriculum and to guide students' acquisition of knowledge and problem solving. Creation of a match between students' cognitive levels and curriculum is vital. Fusco describes the Cognitive Levels Matching (CLM) course at Brandels University. Teachers learn cognitive assessment of a curriculum. The article describes how to do this and gives several examples. It shows how to identify what specific processes students must use to comprehend particular concepts and provides examples in prereading, 7th grade language, social studies and science lessons. It also includes a sample lesson using the cognitive strategies identified in the assessment.

134. Gagne, Robert M. "Learnable Aspects of Problem Solving." *Educational Psychologist* 15 (Summer 1980): 84–92.

Gagne demonstrates that for many years the development of better thinkers and problem solvers has been a major goal of education. Unfortunately, even though we are committed to this, we have not succeeded in accomplishing the goal. As a way of trying to determine why we are not doing better, he looks at the intellectual skills (concepts and rules), verbal knowledge (organized subject knowledge) and cognitive strategies needed for problem solving. Finally, an executive strategy is probably needed which enables the problem solver to evaluate and choose from among the various strategies available. It is this last component that Gagne suggests has not been successfully learned by students.

135. Gall, Meredith. "Synthesis of Research on Teachers' Questioning." *Educational Leadership* 42 (November 1984): 40–47.

Gall reviews a substantial body of research dealing with the role of questioning as an instructional strategy. The author suggests that teachers need to develop their questioning strategies to include an emphasis on higher level cognitive questions instead of factual questions and need to develop other strategies such as the use of silence and perplexity. In addition, the process of answering questions is explored and the suggestion made that students be taught how to answer questions.

136. Gallo, Delores. "Educating for Creativity: A Holistic Approach." *Thinking: The Expanding Frontier.* Edited by William Maxwell. Philadelphia, Pennsylvania: The Franklin Institute Press, 1983, pp. 149–158.

According to Gallo the single most important influence on the development of creativity in students is the teacher. The task for teachers is difficult because of the complex nature of creativity. It involves cognitive abilities in both divergent and convergent thinking. It also involves a variety of personality dispositions including, for example, dominance, openness and creative motivation. The author describes a graduate program for teachers which is designed to prepare them to develop and encourage creativity in their students. In an attempt to overcome the problem of transferring learning to new situations, the program uses content based on real-life problems.

137. ———. "Think Metric." *Thinking Skills Instruction: Concepts and Techniques.* Edited by Marcia Heiman and

Joshua Slomianko. Washington, D.C.: National Education Association, 1987, pp. 284–303.

Gallo identifies the lack of problem solving, critical thinking and creative thinking abilities in students as a serious educational problem. She suggests integrating instruction in these skills into the content areas and provides guidelines and a detailed unit plan for implementing her suggestions. The guidelines include teachers and students relating new information to prior knowledge, working toward an explicit goal, organizing and integrating knowledge, building images, using critical evaluation procedures, learning and using metacognitive strategies, accommodating learning styles, developing and using questions to research and discuss, and transferring learning to new situations. A detailed unit on the metric system which illustrates the guidelines is included.

138. Garner, Ruth. "Rules for Summarizing Texts: Is Classroom Instruction Being Provided?" *Journal of Educational Research* 77 (June 1984): 304–308.

Garner discusses the importance of direct instruction in distinguishing important from unimportant information and in text condensation and summarization. She reviews the summarization rules of Kintsch and Van Dyke (1978) and Brown and Day (1983). Her study investigates whether or not explicit instruction in these rules is being given. Twelve teachers were monitored as they gave what they considered instruction in text summarization. Garner found that of the twelve, only three actually explicitly taught the rules themselves. The rest merely assisted students in the actual summaries. Garner concludes that teachers will need summarization instruction assistance in pre-service and in-service programs, must be made aware of the necessity of these techniques, and be given detailed procedural information as well. She cites the Palincsar and Brown (1983) study as a possible model for staff development.

139.   ———. *Metacognition and Reading Comprehension.* Norwood, New Jersey: Ablex Publishing Corporation, 1987.

Garner provides a comprehensive overview of theoretical issues and research findings in the area of metacognition. She explores developmental differences in strategy use and provides guidelines for training students to use strategies. Specific strategies discussed include summarization, text reinspection, studying, drawing inferences, and monitoring and resolving text comprehension obstacles.

140.   ———, and Victoria Chou Hare. "Efficacy of Text Lookback Training for Poor Comprehenders at Two Age Levels." *Journal of Educational Research* 77 (August 1984): 376–381.

The authors trained middle school and high school subjects to use a text "lookback" strategy to answer questions. They define text lookbacks as "intentional reaccessing of portions of text to locate relevant text-explicit information once read but not now remembered" (p. 376). Only the middle school subjects tested significantly better than untrained peers. The authors conclude that it is important to teach effective reading and studying strategies early, in the elementary grades, before ineffective strategies become entrenched.

141.   Gavelik, James R., and Taffy E. Raphael. "Instructing Metacognitive Awareness of Question-Answer Relationships: Implications for the Learning Disabled." *Topics In Learning and Learning Disabilities* 2 (April 1982): 69–77.

Gavelik and Raphael suggest that the learning disabled have difficulty in understanding their own cognitive activities and cognitive states, thus making either the goals of a task or the means to achieve those goals difficult to identify. "These children fail to understand the basic relationship between means and ends" (p. 71). Therefore teachers of the learning disabled need to make learning strategies such as identifying sources of information in answering questions more overt and subject to feedback and verification.

The authors review the early training studies in Question-Answer Relationships (QARs). In these studies Raphael and her colleagues were able to increase the ability of reading delayed and average students to locate sources of information and thereby improve their ability to answer questions. They suggest that learners must be aware that 1) there are questions for which there are no answers; 2) some sources of response to questions are one's own prior knowledge; 3) some sources of response to questions are one's partial knowledge; 4) sometimes we must search the external environment for answers, e.g. a reference book; 5) sometimes we must integrate information from different sources to answer a question. They suggest that research is needed to investigate the difficulties that the learning disabled have in identifying sources of information.

142. Gelman, Rochel. "The Developmental Perspective on the Problem of Knowledge Acquisition: A Discussion." *Thinking and Learning Skills.* Research and Open Questions. Volume 2. Edited by Susan F. Chipman, Judith W. Segal, and Robert Glaser. Hillsdale, New Jersey: Lawrence Erlbaum Associates, Pub., 1985. pp. 537–544.

Gelman documents that "research over the last decade has revealed some remarkable abilities in young children" (p. 543). He explores issues of children's mental structure in classifying, organizing and reasoning. Preschool age children are able to demonstrate competence at cognitive tasks often considered beyond them. The author suggests the possibility that the way the task is designed has an impact on the child's ability to demonstrate cognitive competence. The younger child may be able to demonstrate it on one carefully designed task while the older child can do so on a variety of tasks. It may be this ability to generalize and transfer that develops with age and experience. In addition, young children are motivated to learn and monitor their learning on their own. Gelman suggests that we need "to consider the role of early cognitive abilities vis-à-vis school curricula" (p. 543).

143.   Ghatala, Elizabeth S. "Strategy-Monitoring Training Enables Young Learners to Select Effective Strategies." *Educational Psychologist* 21 (Winter & Spring 1986): 43–54.

Ghatala investigates the theory that strategy use depends on the learner's metacognitive understanding of the strategy itself. She discusses research on the relationship between metamemory knowledge and memory strategy use. Although research demonstrates a definite link between the two, she suggests it is inconclusive. She reports on a study by Ghatala, Levin, Pressley and Goodwin (1986) which demonstrated that training young children in strategy utilization as well as strategy instruction is effective in increasing use of the strategy. She suggests that teaching young children to monitor their learning strategies enables children to acquire a metacognitive understanding of the strategies which are transferrable to other strategies.

144.   ——, Joel R. Levin, Michael Pressley and Diane Goodwin. "A Componential Analysis of the Effects of Derived and Supplied Strategy-Utility Information on Children's Strategy Selections." *Journal of Experimental Child Psychology* 41 (February 1986): 76–92.

The authors discuss the effectiveness of supplying subjects with a maximum amount of strategy-utility information. Second grade subjects were given information on the relative effectiveness of one, two, or all three memory strategies: 1) assess changes in performance which results from using a strategy; 2) attribute the change to the strategy used; and 3) use the assessment and attribution information to select the best strategy for a particular task. Those subjects who were trained in all three components of information selected the more effective strategy and had better metacognitive awareness than those who were given fewer components, particularly when they were cued to recall the training condition.

145. ———, Joel R. Levin, Michael Pressley, and Marguerite G. Lodico. "Training Cognitive-Strategy Monitoring in Children." *American Educational Research Journal* 22 (1985): 199–215.

This is a report on a study in which the authors trained second graders about the usefulness of particular strategies and the efficacy of strategy use decisions. Metamemory knowledge was also affected by the training. Children in the strategy-utility training condition noticed the change in their performance and the relation between use of the strategy and subsequent performance, better than children in the no-strategy monitoring or strategy-affect (use of strategy was more fun) conditions. The authors point out the importance of including instruction in strategy monitoring in training programs.

146. Gick, Mary. "Problem-Solving Strategies." *Educational Psychologist* 21 (Winter & Spring 1986): 99–120.

Gick investigates problem solving strategies and their relationship to the process of problem solving. She makes a distinction between schema-driven and search-based strategies. Schema-driven strategies are invoked when an appropriate schema is activated by the solver. Schema-driven problem solving leads more directly to implementation of strategies and solution procedures whereas search-based problem solving requires a search before a solution procedure can be implemented. Gick discusses educational implications such as training in schema-driven domain-specific and general strategies. She suggests that we need research on whether training in general problem solving strategies and domain-specific strategy use is possible. She also advocates research on how experts use search-based strategies to solve unfamiliar problems. This article served as a catalyst for much of the recent research in strategy training.

147.   ——, and Keith J. Holyoak. "Schema Induction and Analogical Transfer." *Cognitive Psychology* 15 (1983): 1–38.

The authors investigated whether induction of a general schema from concrete analogies would facilitate transfer to other analogies. They measured subjects' ability to abstract a problem schema from a story when a single story was given when they received one of the following: summarization instructions, a verbal statement of the underlying principle, or diagrammatic representation of the problem. They found that subjects could derive a problem schema with any of the above aids, which they could then transfer to an analogous problem when they were provided with two analogous problems to solve. They suggest that, in complex domains, much of the detailed procedural knowledge which experts possess may not be easy to verbalize explicitly. However, presenting several analogies may convey that information implicitly.

148.   Girle, Roderic A. "A Top-Down Approach to the Teaching of Reasoning Skills." *Thinking: The Expanding Frontier.*

Edited by William Maxwell. Philadelphia, Pennsylvania: The Franklin Institute Press, 1983, pp. 139–147.

Most textbooks and courses in reasoning reflect a "bottom-up" approach in which the focus is on small units and on details, gradually moving toward the complex. This is both negative and impractical. It is negative because the reasoner tends to look for fallacies and not to evaluation and the creation of concepts. It is impractical because arguments and discussion occur in context not in isolation. Girle outlines a course in reasoning based on questions related to an eight point analysis of dialogues.

149. Glade, John J., and Howard Citron. "Strategic Reasoning." *Developing Minds: A Resource Book for Teaching Thinking.* Edited by Arthur L. Costa. Alexandria, Virginia: Association for Supervision and Curriculum Development, 1985, pp. 196–202.

This program provides instruction and practice for students from fourth grade up in six fundamental thinking skills (thing-making, qualification, classification, structure analysis, operation analysis, and seeing analogies), reasoning and problem solving. The student is introduced to each skill, encouraged to verbalize the thinking process, taught to monitor success or failure, and given opportunities to transfer it to academic areas and real-life problem solving. Glade and Citron provide examples from the materials, describe the support provided by the teacher's manual, and offer evidence of the program's effectiveness.

150. Glaser, Robert. "Education and Thinking: The Role of Knowledge." *American Psychologist* 39 (February 1984): 93–104.

Glaser points out the current trend in education to teach the basics at the expense of thinking and "mindfulness." He reviews psychological theories and empirical research which have influenced different approaches to the teaching of thinking: associationism, Gestalt, problem solving, information processing, and, recently, effects of acquired knowledge. Glaser's view is that thinking and reasoning ability are best taught by explicit teaching of specific knowledge and skills, not as "subsequent add-ons to what we have learned" (p. 93). He reviews recent thinking skills programs and materials, including Problem Solving, Instrumental Enrichment, CoRT, and Philosophy for Children.

151.   Glatthorn, Allan A. "How Do You Improve Critical Thinking (or Some Other Set of Skills) Across the Curriculum?" *Curriculum Renewal.* Alexandria, Virginia: Association for Supervision and Curriculum Development, 1987, pp. 63–85.

Glatthorn identifies the components of a plan for improving the fundamental skills of critical thinking, writing, studying, and reading in the content areas. He provides some specific examples in the area of critical thinking, outlining complex thinking processes and specific thinking skills and relating these to content areas.

152.   ———, and Jonathan Baron. "The Good Thinker." *Developing Minds: A Resource Book for Teaching Thinking.* Edited by Arthur L. Costa. Alexanderia, Virginia: Association for Supervision and Curriculum Development, 1985, pp. 49–53.

The authors present a model of a good thinker. They describe the attributes of good thinker, what processes are involved and how he/she is distinguished from a poor thinker, particularly in the approach taken to thinking, differences in goals, consideration of possibilities, and use of evidence in problem solving. The model describes a classroom climate which fosters good thinking, i.e., a spirit of inquiry with emphasis on problem finding and a more deliberative pace.

The authors discuss particularly effective instructional methods which foster good thinking, i.e., teach thinking in all subjects where appropriate; present students with case studies of good thinkers and with problems which require them to use good thinking processes; focus on the relationships between the processes used and the particular subjects; and, finally, provide appropriate opportunities for applying the model to personal decision making. The authors suggest that this is a good model to use as guide for assessing different types of thinking programs.

153. Green, Bert F., Michael McCloskey, and Alfonso Caramazza. "The Relation of Knowledge to Problem Solving, with Examples from Kinematics." *Thinking and Learning Skills*. Research and Open Questions. Volume 2. Edited by Susan F. Chipman, Judith W. Segal, and Robert Glaser. Hillsdale, New Jersey: Lawrence Erlbaum Associates, Pub., 1985, pp. 127–139.

In examining issues of problem solving in science, Green, McCloskey and Caramazza find there is an urgent need to address issues raised by inappropriate prior knowledge. Teachers must address the misconceptions directly and provide appropriate experiences.

154. Grice, George L., and M. Anway Jones. "Teaching Thinking Skills: State Mandates and the K-12 Curriculum." *The Clearinghouse* 62 (April 1989): 337–341.

Grice and Jones provide a broad overview of a complex topic. They examine the wide range of skills included in thinking, the various instructional frameworks, and guidelines for teacher training. In spite of a demonstrated need for instruction in thinking, the authors found that "thinking skills programs have received low priority" (p. 339) in the various states.

155. Guysenir, Maurice G. "Motivate Your Students by Presenting a Problem to be Solved." *Illinois Schools Journal* 63 (1983):18–23.

Guysenir suggests that teachers present their classes with a problem to be solved instead of asking a series of questions to which there is a "correct" answer. The problem becomes the focus of the lesson or of a group of lessons and can be phrased in the form of a question. However, this kind of question is provocative, leading the student to engage in problem solving. He provides numerous examples of the traditional classroom approach and of the problem solving approach to instruction in social studies.

156. Hall, Vernon, and Marie Esposito. "What Does Research on Metacognition Have to Offer Educators?" Paper presented at the Annual Meeting of the Northeastern Educational Research Association, Ellenville, New York, October 24–26, 1984. 48 pp. (ED 254 552)

This paper discusses recent research in development of metacognitive strategies and reviews several well known training studies. The authors advocate identification of strategies of experts to use for teaching novices. They review the Bransford et al. (1982) work in this area and point out the importance of developing instruction based on findings of recent metacognitive research.

157. Haller, Eileen P., David A. Child, and Herbert J. Wallberg. "Can Comprehension Be Taught? A Quantitative Synthesis of 'Metacognitive' Studies." *Educational Researcher* 17 (December 1988): 5–8.

These authors analyzed the accumulation of research on the effectiveness of metacognitive training. Characteristics such as size, time, location, student ability level and type of strategy trained were all considered. According to the analysis, largest effects were shown by seventh and eighth grades, smallest by fourth, fifth and sixth. Metacognitive strategies most "trainable" were inconsistency awareness and self-questioning. The authors conclude that metacognitive skills can, indeed, be trained.

158. Halpern, Diane F. "Thinking Across the Disciplines: Methods and Strategies to Promote Higher-Order Thinking in Every Classroom." *Thinking Skills Instruction: Concepts and Techniques.* Edited by Marcia Heiman and Joshua Slomianko. Washington, D.C.: National Education Association, 1987, pp. 69–86.

Halpern presents a wealth of practical strategies in various content classrooms which teachers can use to promote both thinking and a positive attitude toward thinking in students. Her suggestions range from the teacher using a think-aloud procedure to students engaging in peer teaching. Her final suggestion that we "add some humor to everything" (p. 75) in unique and certainly welcome.

159. ———. *Thought and Knowledge*: An Introduction to Critical Thinking. Hillsdale, New Jersey: Lawrence Erlbaum Associates, Pub., 1989.

Halpern combines a review of theory and research with numerous practical, detailed examples of a critical thinking. She defines it as an evaluative kind of thinking which is involved in solving problems and making decisions as well as formulating inferences. Because of this perspective the book also deals with these other aspects of thinking. The author examines components of thinking such as memory, language and knowledge. In all of this, the thinker is urged to be an active participant in the process of thinking and, in fact, the book has been written so that the reader can participate as an active thinker. Strategies for thinking are detailed and reported in many contexts. The use of graphic representation, for example, is suggested for critical thinking, problem solving and decision making and is illustrated in a number of content areas. There are some suggestions for application in the classroom and in real life.

160.   Hare, Victoria Chou, and Kathleen M. Borchardt. "Direct Instruction of Summarization Skills." *Reading Research Quarterly* XX (Fall 1984): 62–78.

Hare and Borchardt used the summarization rules developed by Brown and Day as the basis for a study with high school students, using direct instruction in summarization with one group and indirect instruction with another group. Both groups showed gains in ability to summarize over a control group with little difference between the two instructional approaches.

161.   Hayes, David A. "Helping Students GRASP the Knack of Writing Summaries." *Journal of Reading* 33 (November 1989): 96–106:

Hayes presents a classroom procedure for teaching students to compose summaries. The Guided Reading and Summarizing Procedure (GRASP) is a series of steps in which the teacher guides students through reading, understanding, organizing and summarizing of text. Hayes states that the procedure makes the summarizing process clear to students, and, because it is used in the classroom, students are more likely to use it independently.

162.   Hayes, John R. "Three Problems in Teaching General Skills." *Thinking and Learning Skills.* Research and Open Questions. Volume 2. Edited by Susan F. Chipman, Judith W. Segal, and Robert Glaser. Hillsdale, New Jersey: Lawrence Erlbaum Associates, Pub., 1985, pp. 391–405.

According to Hayes, three problems need to be addressed in teaching general thinking skills. These include: the substantial amount of content knowledge needed, the large number of possible strategies that can be used, and the difficulties encountered in transferring and applying strategies to new situations. He offers some general directions to be explored in meeting these problems.

163. Heiman, Marcia. "Learning to Learn: Improving Thinking Skills Across the Curriculum." *Thinking Skills Instruction: Concepts and Techniques.* Edited by Marcia Heiman and Joshua Slomianko. Washington, D.C.: National Education Association, 1987, pp. 87–98.

Heiman describes a program that developed from a project at the University of Michigan which was designed to improve students' ability to learn. Learning to Learn is built on specific learning strategies that good learners use, such as breaking tasks and ideas down into manageable units, asking questions and predicting, monitoring progress, and establishing goals and focusing behavior. A complete program has been developed for secondary schools and colleges which is suitable for either content classrooms or for a separate course in thinking. Positive results from using the program include improvement in basic skills, content-area skills and thinking skills. Student motivation and teacher morale also improve.

164. Heller, Mary F. "How Do You Know What You Know? Metacognitive Modeling in the Content Areas." *Journal of Reading* 29 (February 1986): 415–422.

Heller describes the use of a "What I Know" sheet designed to help students identify what they already know, what they know after reading, and what they don't know. She emphasizes the use of teacher modeling as an instructional

strategy to engage students in this metacognitive activity.
Specific directions and examples are included.

165.   Helu, I. Futa. "Thinking in Tongan Society." *Thinking:
       The Expanding Frontier.* Edited by William Maxwell.
       Philadelphia, Pennsylvania: The Franklin Press, 1983, pp.
       43–56.

       Helu, writing within a philosophical framework, makes a
distinction between the scope of thinking and the nature of
thinking. The latter encompasses a variety of skills and is
universal, applying to all situations and all cultures. The
former develops from the particular society and
environment and includes the "subjects, areas, topics and
ideas" (p. 47) relevant to the situation. The author concludes
that "society determines the *focus* or scope of thinking but
not its nature, *i.e.*, it determines *what we think* but not *how
we think*" (p. 43).

166.   Herrnstein, Richard J., Raymond S. Nickerson, Margarita
       de Sanchez, and John A. Swets. "Teaching Thinking
       Skills." *American Psychologist* 41 (November 1986):
       1279–1289.

       This is a report on a large scale instructional program in
thinking skills conducted in the Venezuela schools in 1982–
1983. The authors provided a brief description of the course
itself, which consisted of approximately 100 lessons
organized into 20 units of instruction, primarily in generic
skills, using curriculum-free materials. The authors
acknowledge the difficulties inherent in evaluating such a
project but do describe in some detail their evaluation.
Results indicated a substantial, beneficial effect on subjects.
The authors suggest that, although they believe the effects of
the course will be sustained, long term evaluation is
necessary.

167. Hobbs, Nicholas. "Feuerstein's Instrumental Enrichment: Teaching Intelligence to Adolescents." *Educational Leadership* 37 (April 1980): 566–568.

Hobbs provides background information on the rationale and history of Feuerstein's Instrumental Enrichment. It was developed in order to identify and foster the intelligence and thinking abilities of adolescents from diverse backgrounds, disrupted lives and limited opportunities to learn. The focus is on identifying the student's learning potential and on providing opportunities to overcome learning deficiencies. The author describes two situations in which he observed students engaging in the program.

168. Hoelzel, Norma J. "Basics in Bloom." *Thinking Skills Instruction: Concepts and Techniques.* Edited by Marcia Heiman and Joshua Slomianko Washington, D.C.: National Education Association, 1987, pp. 128–133.

Hoelzel suggests that Bloom's Taxonomy of Educational Objectives be used to develop student-generated questions at all grade levels. She provides a list of verbs appropriate to each level and examples developed by students.

169. Hopper, Robert B., and Daniel S. Kirschenbaum. "Social Problem Solving and Social Competence in Preadolescents: Is Inconsistency the Hobgoblin of Little Minds?" *Cognitive Therapy and Research* 9 (1985): 685–701.

Hopper and Kirschenbaum investigated the relationship between social problem solving and social competence and found that middle school children who were inconsistent in their attempts to solve social problems were also viewed as socially less competent by their teachers and peers. The authors suggest five interrelated skills used to solve social problems: 1) problem recognition, 2) alternative thinking,

3) means-end thinking, 4) consequential thinking, and (5) evaluative thinking. Their study suggest that the ability to generate a large quantity of alternatives (the quantity breeds quality principle) may not be related to competent problem solving ability. In their study, measures of quantity and quality were not significantly correlated and unrelated to social competence. This study suggests that quality of problem solving may be more important than quantity of solutions generated.

170.   Howard, V.A., and J.H. Barton. *Thinking on Paper.* New York: Quill/William Morrow, 1986.

The authors treat thinking and writing as one process and suggest that thinking and shaping thoughts for writing is a form of understanding and that writing and language are instruments of thought. They offer three propositions to explain the complex relations among writing, thinking and communicating: writing is a symbolic activity of meaning making; writing for others is a staged performance; and writing is a tool of understanding as well as of communication. The thinker uses writing to find his own meaning. They suggest that many of our thoughts are first generated when they are put to paper.

The first part of the book is concerned with writing—what it is, how to generate, collect and organize ideas, how to compose. The second part relates reasoning and writing—how to structure arguments; how to write rationally; how to be persuasive.

171.   Hudgins, Bryce B., and Sybil Edelman. "Teaching Critical Thinking Skills to Fourth and Fifth Graders Through Teacher-Led Small-Group Discussions." *Journal of Educational Research* 79 (July/August 1986): 333–342.

This article describes a study in which teachers were trained to encourage critical thinking by leading small groups of children in discussions. They learned how to loosen teacher control, to encourage the children to assume more responsibility for group learning, in order to alleviate the pressure that speaking in front of large groups generates, and thereby encouraging children's participation. Results of the study indicate that teachers talked significantly less, children spoke significantly more, and when they did speak they gave more evidence than unsubstantiated conclusions. Authors suggest that in-service training programs should provide demonstrations of behavior to be altered, in this case, leading discussion groups. Teachers should be given the opportunity to play out the same kind of situations their students will be subjected to.

172. Hudson-Ross, Sally. "Student Questions: Moving Naturally into the Student-Centered Classroom." *The Social Studies* 80 (May/June 1989): 110–113.

Student-generated questions enable the empowerment of students. Hudson-Ross details ways of doing this in discussion before reading, as part of a journal activity, during discussion after reading, as the basis for research projects, and as part of the writing process.

173. Hull, Glynda, and David Bartholomae. "Teaching Writing as Learning and Process." *Educational Leadership* 43 (April 1986): 44–53.

It is only within the past decade, according to Hull and Bartholomae, that we have begun to look at and be concerned with the process of composing. They examine it as complex behavior in which the writer moves back and forward in the processes of planning, translating and reviewing. It is also a means of learning, "of taking intellectual control of a subject, of discovering what it is that one wants or is able to say about something" (p. 49). Because writing can help students learn about a topic, writing across the curriculum has become an important development in schools. This also provides a way to teach students the conventions of writing in particular fields.

174.   Hyde, Arthur A., and Marilyn Bizar. *Thinking In Context.* New York: Longman, 1989.

Hyde and Bizar take a strong stand on the question of instruction in cognitive processes in elementary schools. The focus must be on meaning, on learning in context, and on learning as a cognitive activity. The message is that schools must emphasize thinking in context. They explore basic and complex thinking (critical thinking, problem solving and decision making), providing useful examples in which the reader can participate in the thinking processes. They outline the requirements for successful thinking instruction, including developing prior knowledge, involving students in cooperative/collaborative learning, and emphasizing metacognition. Specific, detailed suggestions are given for developing thinking in context in reading, mathematics, the sciences, and social studies. The suggestions require active student participation and discussion. A wide range of strategies are included, for example, K-W-L, mapping, grids, and student-generated questions. Illustrations are provided for useful learning strategies such as direct instruction, inquiry learning, and the use of heuristics.

175.   Isaksen, Scott G., and Sidney J. Parnes. "Curriculum Planning for Creative Thinking and Problem Solving." *The Journal of Creative Behavior* 19 (1st Quarter 1985): 1–29.

The authors review a considerable body of research documenting the rationale for training for creativity, its effectiveness, and implications for creative learning. Isaksen and Parnes conducted a survey of planners in business, industry and education to determine planning strategies to develop creative thinking and problem solving. The results are useful for those involved in curriculum development and are detailed enough to be helpful. The range of topics discussed includes getting started in planning a creative problem solving curriculum, using the Creative Problem Solving model, identifying instructional strategies, and encouraging program development. Some general conclusions emerge from the review. Inservice education for teachers is critical to the success of any program as are the personal attributes of the teachers. The establishment of networks for communication about programs is very useful. Finally, integration of instruction into all content areas is viewed as essential.

176. Jackson, Roberta M. "Thumbs Up for Direct Teaching of Thinking Skills." *Educational Leadership* 43 (May 1986): 32–36.

Jackson advocates the direct teaching of thinking skills as a way of reaching all students and as a way of insuring that instruction takes place in all content classrooms. She supplies a complete example and description from a language arts class illustrating the introduction of a skill, the explanation, demonstration, application of the skill and reflection on it. Direct instructions is predicated on the premise that we must "select a skill, identify its main attributes, introduce it at a time in the curriculum when the skill is needed and therefore meaningful, develop guided and independent practice lessons, and intersperse these practices throughout the year" (p. 33).

177. Johnson, David W., and Roger T. Johnson. "Toward a Cooperative Effort: A Response to Slavin." *Educational Leadership* 46 (April 1989): 80–82.

Johnson and Johnson outline the five critical elements to their approach to cooperative learning. These are: positive interdependence, face-to-face promotive interdependence, individual accountability, social skills, and group processing. They briefly review their research and take issue with Slavin's summary. Finally, however, they suggest the need for cooperation among researchers with room in the field for a variety of approaches. (See also 359.)

178. ———, Linda Skon, and Roger Johnson. "Effects of Cooperative, Competitive, and Individualistic Conditions on Children's Problem-solving Performance." *American Educational Research Journal* 17 (Spring 1980): 83–93.

Johnson, Skon and Johnson examined the effects of cooperative, competitive and individualistic conditions on first graders' performance in three problem-solving tasks: categorization and retrieval, spatial reasoning, and verbal problem solving. Students in the cooperative condition achieved higher performance levels than those in the individualistic condition in all tasks and higher than those in the cooperative condition in two out of three. The competitive condition also fostered the use of higher quality strategies than did the other two conditions. The authors suggest that the discussion process inherent in cooperation is in large measure responsible for the significant results obtained in that condition.

179. Johnson, Linda Lee. "Learning Across the Curriculum with Creative Graphing." *Journal of Reading* 32 (March 1989): 509–519.

Creative graphing, like writing, promises "the use of analytical thought and organizational abilities instead of rote learning" (p. 513). Johnson defines creative graphing as the process of rearranging text information in a visual, spatial form. The article provides a theoretical and research base as well as numerous examples of different kinds of graphs and the situations in which they might be used.

180. Johnson, Tony W. *Philosophy for Children: An Approach To Critical Thinking.* Fastback 206. Bloomington, Indiana: Phi Delta Kappa Educational Foundation, 1984.

Johnson provides examples from the program Philosophy for Children which illustrate how it develops children's abilities to think and to think about their thinking. It is a program designed to involve the learner actively in the process of discovering the rules of reasoning and applying them to the situations in the program's novels and in their own lives. The author examines the philosophical foundations of the program and the critical importance of dialogue and discussion in the learning process. Successful implementations of the program are discussed, as is the need for extensive teacher training.

181. Jones, Beau Fly. "Reading and Thinking." *Developing Minds: A Resource Book for Teaching Thinking.* Edited by Arthur L. Costa. Alexandria, Virginia: Association for Supervision and Curriculum Development, 1985, pp. 108–113.

Jones notes that reading involves the interaction of the reader, the text and the content. The reader's prior knowledge of content, his learning strategies, and his metacognitive abilities are important aspects of comprehension. Other variables in the comprehension process are text structure and teacher management. She discusses the need for good text design in order to promote high level thinking processes. A well written text should include advanced organizers, statistics, graphics, and summaries.

Jones describes different thinking activities employed at different stages of reading: before, during and after reading and in response to questions. She presents a detailed model of the interaction between the teacher, reader and text at each stage of the student's cognitive processing. Jones concludes that the teacher is vital in helping students process information from text, that constructing meaning from text is itself a high level thinking skill, and that, since most instruction is text based, it is critical to understand the textual materials and the interaction of the reader, the teacher and the text.

182.   ———. "Response Instruction." *Reading, Thinking, and Concept Development.* Edited by Theodore L. Harris and Eric J. Cooper. New York: College Entrance Examination Board, 1985, pp. 105–130.

Jones introduces the idea of teaching students how to answer questions, specifically, how to structure answers so that they cover required content, use the correct text structure and level of response appropriate for the question asked. Jones analyzes various types of questions and explores the nature of the relationship between the questions and the text: for example, are the answers to the questions asked stated explicitly in the text, are they implied in the text or is the prior knowledge of the reader needed to answer the question? She presents strategies for teaching students to organize answers, such as use of frames and nonlinear outlines, by providing general guidelines followed by particular examples, by explicit examples followed by general rules and by modeling response formulation. Sample response instruction lessons and scoring guides are provided in history and literature.

183.   ———. "Quality and Equality Through Cognitive Instruction." *Educational Leadership* 43 (April 1986): 4–11.

Jones examines the low test scores of students, potential teachers and practicing teachers and identifies that "what is needed in addition to greater rigor and increased time is cognitive instruction" (p. 7). This is defined as instruction designed to increase the meaningful processing of information and the ability of students to learn independently. The author reviews in some depth the implications of cognitive instruction for students. The goal is meaning, with students actively engaging in higher order thinking skills and monitoring their own success in choosing and using appropriate strategies at various stages in the process. She calls for tests that test this, direct instruction with the teacher mediating the process, and materials that are "'considerate,' in that features such as headings and the prose itself are designed to make explicit what is to be learned" (p. 9). Research is cited to support the conclusion that cognitive instruction benefits the low-achiever and reduces the differences found between younger and older students.

184. ———, Annemarie Sullivan Palincsar, Donna Sederburg Ogle, and Eileen Glynn Carr (Editors). *Strategic Teaching and Learning: Cognitive Instruction in the Content Areas.* Alexandria, Virginia: Association for Supervision and Curriculum Development in cooperation with the North Central Regional Educational Laboratory, 1987.

The editors define cognitive instruction as "instruction in the various dimensions of thinking such as comprehending and composing, problem solving and decision making, critical and creative thinking, and metacognition" (p. ix). It is based on a "new" definition of learning which is active and constructive, relates new information to old, and relies on the development of strategies. Strategic teaching requires making decisions on how, what and when to teach using these dimensions of thinking as the basis for instruction within the content areas.

The teacher bases these decisions on a thorough knowledge of: the content to be learned, strategies that may be useful to the students, and appropriate instructional strategies. The book examines theoretical issues, reviews current research, and provides detailed suggestions and examples for content area teachers.

185.   ———, Jean Pierce, and Barbara Hunter. "Teaching Students to Construct Graphic Representations." *Educational Leadership* 46 (December 1988/January 1989): 20–25.

Jones, Pierce and Hunter present a detailed description of how students should proceed when constructing a graphic organizer. The organizer needs to reflect the structure of the information and the text. The student surveys the text using a list of questions provided. Next, the student relates the information to prior knowledge about the topic and hypothesizes a form for an organizer. After reading the text, the student asks metacognitive questions to affirm the mental model being constructed. Then, a graphic representation is chosen and completed. (Samples are included). Finally, the information is summarized orally or in writing. Instructional strategies suggested include, for example, cooperative learning, modeling and coaching.

186.   Joyce, Bruce. "Models for Teaching Thinking." *Educational Leadership* 42 (May 1985): 4–7.

Joyce identifies and examines some of the crucial issues related to teaching thinking including whether thinking should be taught as enrichment, as a separate subject, or as part and parcel of content area instruction; whether and how we should choose one instructional model over all others; and how we should implement the needed changes in schools. On the first issue, he aligns himself clearly and forcefully in the camp of those who advocate thinking instruction as an integral part of content area instruction. On the second, he advocates combining models depending on the goals of the instruction. Finally, on the third, he identifies the need for "very strong staff development programs" (p. 7) of at least 10 days' duration in order to insure that the required changes in instruction take place.

187. ———, Beverly Showers, and Carol Rolhelser-Bennett. "Staff Development and Student Learning: A Synthesis of Research on Models of Teaching." *Educational Leadership* 45 (October 1987): 11–23.

The authors review a number of models of teaching, including social, information processing, personal, and behavioral systems. They link teaching strategies and staff development to these models. Of particular interest is the suggestion that models can be combined. For example, they combine cooperative learning and information processing with divergent thinking.

188. Kagan, Spencer. "The Structural Approach to Cooperative Learning." *Educational Leadership* 47 (December 1989/January 1990): 12–15.

The focus in this discussion is on the development of a variety of ways of structuring cooperative learning which can be used in any content area. Kagan provides specifics on a number of structures, detailing differences in purpose and participation. He makes suggestions for choosing appropriate structures and for providing staff development.

189. Kamil, Constance. "Encouraging Thinking in Mathematics." *Phi Delta Kappan* 64 (December 1982): 247–251.

Kamil states her position clearly. "The objective of arithmetic education should be thinking, not the writing of correct answers" (p. 248). Kamil draws on the concepts proposed by Piaget regarding the different kinds of knowledge and the differences between abstraction (thinking) and representation (writing). Writing is seen as a tool for thinking. Instead of merely giving feedback on written answers, she suggests that teachers allow children to defend their answers rather than tell them whether the answer they give is correct or not.

190.   Karmos, Joseph S., and Ann H. Karmos. "Strategies for Active Involvement in Problem Solving." *Thinking Skills Instruction: Concepts and Techniques.* Edited by Marcia Heiman and Joshua Slomianko. Washington, D.C.: National Education Association, 1987, pp. 99–110.

Karmos and Karmos identify the active involvement of the thinker as a key element in effective problem solving. They provide specific examples of academic activities at a variety of grade levels that can be used to teach active, effective problem solving strategies. They recommend that, in addition, students identify real problems and solve those.

191.   Katz, Lillian G., and Sylvia C. Chard. *Engaging Children's Minds.* Norwood, New Jersey: Ablex Publishing Corporation, 1989.

Katz and Chard present detailed and informative descriptions of projects that can be planned and developed for young children which actively engage their minds and involve them in the act of learning and thinking. The authors make clear that while learning should be enjoyable, enjoyment is not the goal of education. The projects are based on the notion that interaction will encourage learning and thinking.

192.   King, Lean, and Rita King. "Tactics for Thinking in Action." *Educational Leadership* 45 (April 1988): 42–44.

King and King discuss the reasons for the adoption of Tactics for Thinking. "The program integrates thinking into the content areas, develops reasoning skills, and places all of these aspects within the classroom teacher's control" (p. 42). They also describe the process of adoption and implementation, stressing the need to involve teachers, identify and discuss their apprehensions, and provide appropriate and sufficient training. A list of learning-to-learn skills, content thinking skills, and reasoning skills is also provided.

193. Kinney, James J. "Why Brother? The Importance of Critical Thinking." *New Directions for Teaching and Learning: Fostering Critical Thinking.* Edited by Robert E. Young. San Francisco: Jossey-Bass Inc., Pub., No. 3, 1980, pp. 1–9.

Kinney identifies a critical need for critical thinking in our technological, technical society coupled with a lack of interest in it on the part of students. He concludes that "maybe we should save education in critical thinking for those who value it enough to seek it out, or at least for those who have satiated their need for job training" (pp. 8-9). Kinney envisions instruction in critical thinking taking place within concentric circles with the student in the center and the context becoming increasingly abstract and distant from the student but always meaningful.

194. Kneedler, Peter. "California Assesses Critical Thinking." *Developing Minds: A Resource Book for Teaching Thinking.* Edited by Arthur L. Costa. Alexandria, Virginia: Association for Supervision and Curriculum Development, 1985, pp. 276–280.

Kneedler describes and analyzes the assessment of critical thinking skills that is part of the statewide history-social studies test for eighth graders in California. Critical thinking is define as "those behaviors associated with deciding what to believe and do" (p. 276). Twelve critical thinking skills were identified as appropriate for this population in defining and clarifying the problem, judging information related to the problem and solving problems/drawing conclusions. The assessment was done through objective questions, student essays, and critical thinking skills vocabulary. Examples from the categories are provided. The author stresses that other forms of assessment are very important such as teacher observation and student class performance.

195.   Kownslar, Alan O. "What's Worth Having Students Think Critically About?" *Social Education* 49 (April 1985): 304–307.

Kownslar discusses the importance of teaching students to think critically using content which is socially and personally relevant to them, to promote generalization and transfer. He presents ten key questions to get students analyzing and evaluating what they read and hear. The questions concern issues such as bias, value claims, relevancy, unstated assumptions, logical inconsistencies, ambiguities, and other interesting and significant areas.

196.   Kuhrt, Bonnie L., and Pamela J. Farris. "Empowering Students Through Reading, Writing, and Reasoning." *Journal of Reading* 33 (March 1990): 436–441.

Kuhrt and Farris link empowerment for students with metacognition, placing both squarely in the realm of reading and writing instruction. They provide a decision making chart which students can use to identify the problem presented in a text, develop alternatives, establish criteria and evaluate the alternatives. Group discussion plays as important part in the process. The success of this approach depends on empowering teachers, enabling them to make decisions rather than rely on teacher-proof materials.

197. Kurtz, Beth E., and John G. Borkowski. "Metacognition and the Development of Strategic Skills in Impulsive and Reflective Children." Paper presented at the Biennial Meeting of the Society for Research in Child Development, Toronto, 1985. 41 pp. (ED 257 572)

This paper is a detailed description of a longitudinal study which examined differences in metamemory and strategy use between impulsive and reflective children. The results lead to the conclusion that metacognitive ability in early years leads to later ability in strategy use and that metacognitive skills control lower-level strategies. The study demonstrates the causal relationships between meta-memory and strategy acquisition and the importance of metacognitive instruction along with explicit strategy training. It also supports the idea that early metamemory ability about low level strategies leads to later ability to transfer to a newer, more complex strategy, such as summarization. The authors conclude that there is a link between metamemory and memory which is developmental and related to affective areas such as impulsivity. They point out that training programs should account for differences in early metamemory ability when planning and using complex training packages.

198. Laney, James D. "Composition in the Intermediate Grades: How to Promote Thinking and Creativity." Paper presented at the Annual Meeting of the California Educational Research Association. Los Angeles, California, November 17–18, 1983. 33 pp. (ED 241 938)

Laney's message is clear. Thinking and creativity can be taught. It is the school's responsibility to do this. Writing provides an "ideal" way to accomplish these most important goals of education. The author uses metacognitive strategies, creative problem solving and creative thinking techniques as part of the process of writing to encourage thinking and creativity. He provides detailed lists, instructions and suggestions for the classroom.

199.   Langer, Judith A., and Arthur N. Applebee. "Learning to Write: Learning to Think." *Educational Horizons* 64 (Fall 1985): 36–38.

Langer and Applebee establish a clear relationship between writing and thinking. "To improve the teaching of writing, particularly in the context of academic tasks, is to improve also the quality of thinking required of school-aged children" (p. 36). They propose a system-wide change in writing instruction from teaching writing to report on learning to teaching writing to think. Writing takes place in all content areas with all teachers committed to using writing as a tool for thinking. They suggest a procedure for developing this approach and for encouraging different purposes for writing. Finally, student writings in science and social studies are reviewed to illustrate how writing can support thinking.

200.   ———, and Victoria Purcell-Gates. "Knowledge and Comprehension: Helping Students Use What They Know." *Reading, Thinking, and Concept Development.* Edited by Theodore L. Harris and Eric J. Cooper. New York: College Entrance Examination Board, 1985, pp. 53–70.

Langer and Purcell-Gates offer a three-step method to help students become aware of what they know about a topic and to reflect and build on that knowledge before they begin to read. The method also enables teachers to assess how much students already know about a particular topic. It involves a structured classroom discussion focused on free associations of what the student knows about a topic, reflections on that knowledge, and reformulation of ideas, based on classroom discussion. Students' responses enable the teacher to identify the amount and complexity of their knowledge about a concept.

201. Larkin, Jill H. "Enriching Formal Knowledge: A Model for Learning to Solve Textbook Physics Problems." *Cognitive Skills and Their Acquisition.* Edited by John R. Anderson. Hillsdale, New Jersey: Lawrence Erlbaum Associates, Pub., 1981, pp. 311–335.

Larkin discusses acquisition of problem solving skills in physics and how learners become experts in this domain. She describes ABLE, a computer-implemented model for applying acquired knowledge of principles of physics to problem solving.

202. ———. "Understanding, Problem Representations, and Skill in Physics." *Thinking and Learning Skills:* Research and Open Questions. Volume 2. Edited by Susan F. Chipman, Judith W. Segal, and Robert Glaser. Hillsdale, New Jersey: Lawrence Erlbaum Associates, Pub., 1985, pp. 141–159.

Larkin examines differences between experts and novices in understanding and representing physics problems. The possession of appropriate prior knowledge of content and scientific principles is essential in both areas. The author suggests that we should teach students to construct graphic representations or to invent notations for representing the problem.

203. Lasser-Cohen, Hadara. "A Program for Fostering of Reading and Thinking of Disadvantaged Adolescents in Israel." *Journal of Reading* 28 (March 1985): 542–547.

The program described by Lasser-Cohen is based on two premises: there is a "strong link existing between understanding of text and thinking" (p. 543) and "weakness in abstract thinking is a substantial factor in the failure of disadvantaged pupils at school" (p. 542). The Program for Fostering of Reading and Thinking includes both verbal and nonverbal exercises in which one cognitive operation is emphasized in each exercise. Workbooks, worksheets, case studies, and games using questions and group discussion form the basis of the program.

204. Levin, Joel R. "Four Cognitive Principles of Learning-Strategy Instruction." *Educational Psychologist* 21 (Winter & Spring 1986): 3–17.

Levin proposes four principles of learning strategy instruction which should be observed by research and practitioners. First, different learning strategies serve different cognitive purposes. Strategies must suit the type of text to be learned as well as the learning outcomes anticipated. Levin presents a model, URA (Understanding, Remembering, Applying), processes with which students select and use an appropriate learning strategy. Levin's second principle is that all individual components of an effective learning strategy need to be identified and analyzed. *How* and *why* a given strategy works needs to be specified in terms of cognitive processing principles. Levin explains, for example, that "concrete organizers facilitate students' comprehension of unfamiliar complex concepts through connections made with familiar concrete ones" (p. 11).

Third, he holds that learning strategies must match the learners' characteristics, must account for developmental differences, learning disabilities and differences, and the amount of domain-specific knowledge available to the learner. Finally, Levin suggests that the efficacy of learning strategies needs to be studied empirically. Too often their value is determined by intuition rather than by actual practice. According to Levin, learning strategies consist of cognitive and metacognitive processes. Educators need to design strategy instruction which coordinates both.

205. Levitsky, Ronald. "Simulation and Thinking." *Thinking Skills Instruction: Concepts and Techniques.* Edited by Marcia Heiman and Joshua Slomianko. Washington, D.C.: National Education Association, 1987, pp. 262–271.

Simulations are an appropriate activity to develop critical thinking skills in adolescents who are in Piaget's formal operation stage. Levitsky describes a simulation used with eighth graders to explore the question of whether the Civil War was inevitable. The activity involves historical research, role playing using historical information, and application of general concepts to present day situations.

206. Lewis, Clayton. "Skill in Algebra." *Cognitive Skills and Their Acquisition.* Edited by John R. Anderson. Hillsdale, New Jersey: Lawrence Erlbaum Associates, Pub., 1981, pp. 85–110.

Lewis analyzes the differences in algebraic skills between expert mathematicians and novices at various levels. He concludes that there is little or no difference in problem solving between skilled and unskilled mathematicians. Procedures are the same for all when using good, streamlined skills. Math experience, practice and insight have little effect. Lewis suggests that skills in algebra are really skills in use of basic procedures, supporting Thorndike's theory that we don't get better by practice.

207. Lindquist, Mary Montgomery. "The Elementary School Mathematics Curriculum: Issues for Today." *The Elementary School Journal* 84 (May 1984): 595–609.

Lindquist identifies problem solving as the top priority item in mathematics curriculum. She defines problem solving broadly, moving it from the realm of solving word problems to the larger context of nontextbook mathematical problems. She elaborates the definition by suggesting that problem solving includes not only the problem but also how the problem is presented. It must be included in all aspects of instruction, and instruction itself should be provided in a problem solving manner in which students are actively involved in the process of thinking. Other topics to be included in the curriculum are understanding, computation, and measurement, for example. However, in all those other elements of the curriculum, problem solving remains central. The author concludes with the statement "let me emphasize that problem solving should be integrated with other mathematics topics. . .in all lessons, except those that are straightforward practice of skill" (p. 603).

208. Link, Frances R. "Instrumental Enrichment." *Developing Minds: A Resource Book for Teaching Thinking.* Edited by Arthur L. Costa. Alexandria, Virginia: Association for Supervision and Curriculum Development, 1985, pp. 193–195.

Instrumental Enrichment is a content-free program which "focuses not on any specific skills or subject, but rather on the process of learning itself" (p. 193). The program is designed for upper elementary through secondary students and takes between two to three years to complete. Transfer to other content areas and to real life is accomplished through discussion.

209. ———. "New Insights into Cognitive Development and Academic Learning." *Educational Horizons* 64 (Summer 1986): 204–207.

Link identifies failures in the process of learning as the root of many learning and academic problems. For example, a student may not be able to classify successfully because of a failure in the subtasks of gathering information, dealing with multiple sources of information, and comparing items. Instrumental Enrichment focuses on mental processes in a content-free program designed to promote effective, independent thinking through altering cognitive development. The author points out the positive implications of this approach for special education students. The program is intended as a two to three year addition to content courses, as a means of "learning to learn" (p. 205). The teacher, in order to be effective, must receive extensive training. Link cites a growing body of research that demonstrates the effectiveness of Instrumental Enrichment in increasing "self-image, motivation, and intellectual growth across various populations of students and improvement in teaching skills" (p. 207).

210. Linn, Marcia C. "The Cognitive Consequences of Programming Instruction in Classrooms." *Educational Researcher* 14 (May 1985): 14–16, 25–29.

Linn contrasts Papert's vision of the child learning programming and at the same time advancing in problem solving with the disappointing results obtained from programming courses. Computer programming by its very nature requires the use of sophisticated and complex problem solving skills. Unfortunately Linn points out that "recently, cognitive scientists have shown that learning is much more discipline-specific than had been thought" (p. 15) with little transfer from computer problem solving to problem solving in general. She examines the "chain of cognitive accomplishments" (p. 15) students engage in to determine where along the chain it might be possible to teach students to transfer what is learned to another context.

Typical middle school classrooms were studied to determine how far along the chain students got in programming courses. Most only learned the language and did not learn how to design programs or solve problems. Exemplary classrooms were also examined. These were characterized by having experienced teachers and students who had somewhat higher ability. In these classes students learned language and also how to design programs. These teachers explicitly taught procedures and encouraged students to discover the source of difficulties in programs they designed. In order to progress to solving problems, students will need instruction and suitable software. One of the critical elements appears to be that of organization of information and procedures. With "experienced teachers and an effective curriculum" (p. 29) students of all levels can be brought to the design stage and possibly learn to generalize strategies and procedures to other problem solving situations.

211.   Lipman, Matthew. "The Cultivation of Reasoning Through Philosophy." *Educational Leadership* 42 (September 1984): 51–56.

Lipman advocates the use of philosophy as an area of learning that has traditionally been concerned with thinking and reasoning. In fact, "one of the traditional definitions of philosophy has been that it is thinking that devotes itself to the improvement of thinking" (p. 51). It is possible to do this, even in elementary classrooms, through the use of short novels in which the characters deal with issues such as fairness, friendship and truth and through class discussion of the episodes. Teachers must be adept at leading discussions and sensitive to what the children are actually saying. Teachers receive weekly training while providing three sessions weekly for the children. Reasoning is not a "fourth R" but rather is fundamental to the others.

212. ———. "Philosophy for Children." *Developing Minds: A Resource Book for Teaching Thinking.* Edited by Arthur L. Costa. Alexandria, Virginia: Association for Supervision and Curriculum Development, 1985, pp. 212–214.

Lipman describes the program Philosophy for Children, providing examples of how the novels written for the program develop concepts and reasoning through discussion and inquiry. He highlights the need for openness on the part of the teacher, suggesting that not all teachers are suited to this approach.

213. ———. "Thinking Skills Fostered by Philosophy for Children." *Thinking and Learning Skills.* Relating Instruction to Research. Volume 1. Edited by Judith W. Segal, Susan F. Chipman, and Robert Glaser. Hillsdale, New Jersey: Lawrence Erlbaum Associates, Pub., 1985, pp. 83–108.

Lipman provides a detailed overview of the 30 skills and dispositions taught in Philosophy for Children and gives a flavor of the program through numerous examples of the materials and the discussion engendered by them. The role of the teacher as a model and a discussion leader is critical. The author also reports on studies conducted on the effectiveness of the program.

214. Lochhead, Jack. "Teaching Analytic Reasoning Skills Through Pair Problem Solving." *Thinking and Learning Skills.* Relating Instruction to Research. Volume 1. Edited by Judith W. Segal, Susan F. Chipman, and Robert Glaser. Hillsdale, New Jersey: Lawrence Erlbaum Associates, Pub., 1985, pp. 109–131.

Lochhead describes a program designed to overcome obstacles to developing the most important characteristic of successful problem solvers: "the degree to which their approach to the problem might be characterized as active or passive" (p. 110). Students work in pairs to solve problems, with one student solving and explaining and the other student listening, probing and questioning. The teacher is a coach, helping students discover the process and assume a leadership role in understanding problem solving. The article also includes a discussion of the theoretical rationale for the program and evaluation issues as well as specific examples of problems and solutions.

215. ———. "Thinking About Learning: An Anarchistic Approach to Teaching Problem Solving." *Thinking Skills Instruction: Concepts and Techniques*. Edited by Marcia Heiman and Joshua Slomianko. Washington, D.C.: National Education Association, 1987, pp. 174–182.

Lochhead takes issue with those who advocate that students of science engage in one, absolute "scientific method." Rather, he suggests that in solving scientific problems students must be free to explore those methods that work best for them and for the particular problem. The key issue is not the choice of a single method but the development of students' metacognitive awareness and control of the strategies invented and used. This process is advanced through discussion and persistence.

216. Lodico, Marguerite G., Elizabeth S. Ghatala, Joel R. Levin, Michael Pressley, and John A. Bell. "The Effects of Strategy Monitoring Training on Children's Selection of Effective Memory Strategies." *Journal of Experimental Child Psychology* 35 (April 1983): 263–277.

This study investigated the relationship between metacognitive knowledge of strategies and strategy use. Second graders were taught general principles of strategy monitoring and how to monitor their own strategy use. Trained subjects performed better than untrained subjects on a recall task, could attribute their success to the strategy they used, and they then were able to select the more effective strategy for a subsequent task. Lodico et al. state that this study provides experimental support for the notion that there is a relationship between metamemory and strategy use. They suggest that future research should investigate long term effects on strategy maintenance and memory monitoring.

217. Long, James D., and Elizabeth W. Long. "Enhancing Student Achievement Through Metacomprehension Training." *Journal of Developmental Education* 11 (September 1987): 2–5.

Long and Long review some of the current research dealing with two important questions: the differences in metacomprehension efforts in successful and less successful students and the effects of teaching strategies to the less successful students. Successful students are more likely to go beyond the information provided and look for connections, interrelationships, and inferences. In other words, they are actively involved in making the information their own and using it to generate meaning for themselves using a variety of strategies. The authors identify a number of strategies, such as self-generating questions and summarizing, that can be taught to college students. They provide some specific examples that can be used to increase metacomprehension.

218. Lowery, Lawrence F. "The Biological Basis for Thinking." *Developing Minds: A Resource Book for Teaching Thinking.* Edited by Arthur L. Costa. Alexandria, Virginia: Association for Supervision and Curriculum Development, 1985, pp. 71–80.

The brain is the biological basis of behavior, thought is the process involved; thinking depends on the biological development of the brain and the psychological development of the thinker. Lowery describes the sequence of development of the thinking process in terms of biological and psychological development and application to classroom instruction. He traces the Piagetian sequence of intellectual development and describes how particular processes evolve, i.e., classification, categorization, hierarchical relationships, and deductive and inductive reasoning at each stage from perception to metacognition. He gives examples of classroom competencies at each stage.

In the section on educational implications he correlates Piagetian development with curriculum and instructional implications. Lowery advocates a "horizontal curriculum" which challenges students to use a particular stage of thinking with different materials at various levels of abstraction without the progressive requirement of having to be at a more and more advanced developmental stage. This allows students at a particular stage other experiences around that stage, enabling them to perform progressively challenging tasks without inviting failure. Thus teachers can teach and not just manage material which is dictated by a sequence of instruction. Lowery's point is that the understanding of biology leads to a better, more responsive curriculum.

219. Markman, Elaine M. "Realizing That You Don't Understand: A Preliminary Investigation." *Child Development* 46 (1977): 986–992.

Markman invested the ability of first and third graders to evaluate their own understanding of oral information. She gave students directions to play a card game, omitting some critical details. Third graders were more aware than first graders that instructions were incomplete. First graders often had to attempt to play the game before they realized that they did not understand completely. However, when warned that there would be something wrong with the message, and given practice examples, both groups were able to detect the problems and give an accurate account of their understanding.

220. Martin, David S. "Infusing Cognitive Strategies Into Teacher Preparation Programs." *Educational Leadership* 42 (November 1984): 68–72.

Martin highlights the need for preservice teachers to experience instruction in cognitive skills, an area that has not received attention. He describes a program based on Feuerstein's Instrumental Enrichment program in which students were instructed in the 14 cognitive skills identified by Feuerstein in all of their education courses. Each session included a discussion of how the skill could transfer to the problems and situations experienced by teachers. A model for implementing this approach in preservice programs is included along with suggestions for integrating it into existing programs and courses, not adding additional courses.

221. Marzano, Robert J. *The Theoretical Framework for An Instructional Model of Higher Order Thinking Skills.* Denver, Colorado: Mid-Continent Regional Educational Lab, Inc., February 1984. 51 pp. (ED 248 045)

Marzano cites the growing recognition that we need to develop thinking skills in schools and that our present models for doing this are not sufficient or instructionally explicit. He proposes a nonhierarchical model of ten skills, including recognition of concepts, relationship and patterns; reconstruction, evaluation and extrapolation of information; problem solving; and knowledge of basic input/output processes, content-specific tasks and self as learner. He advocates that teachers identify and instruct students in the processes involved and the use of algorithms to guide them through these processes. Each skill is defined, related research examined and instructional strategies suggested.

222.   ———, and Daisy E. Arrendondo. "Restructuring Schools Through the Teaching of Thinking Skills." *Educational Leadership* 43 (May 1986): 20–26.

Marzano and Arrendondo describe the thinking skills model developed by Marzano and the educational implications suggested by the model. The model includes learning-to-learn strategies which provide the learner with metacognitive control over learning; content thinking skills which enable him to learn both information and procedure relevant to a particular content area; and basic reasoning skills which apply to all cognitive activity but which can be useful in content areas. The description of the model makes clear the role of the learner as an active participant in the learning process and, in fact, as the center of responsibility for learning. Instruction must involve nonverbal as well as verbal strategies, a focus on basic concepts, an emphasis on patterns of organization and a stress on process, not product.

223.   ———, Ronald S. Brandt, Carolyn Sue Hughes, Beau Fly Jones, Barbara Z. Presseisen, Stuart C. Rankin, and Charles Suhor. *Dimensions of Thinking: A Framework for Curriculum and Instruction*. Alexandria, Virginia: Association for Supervision and Curriculum Development, 1988.

The authors of this book cite the development of independent thinkers as the central goal of education and, at the same time, recognize that we are not accomplishing this goal. They suggest the need to examine five dimensions of thinking and to integrate them into the total curriculum, not teach them as isolated skills. The five dimensions include metacognition (the awareness and control of our own thinking), critical and creative thinking, thinking processes (macrolevel operations composed of a sequence of generic skills), core thinking skills (microlevel, basic skills), and the relationship of knowledge to thinking. Each dimension is examined in some depth. With appropriate instruction, content, and materials, it is suggested that even young children can think abstractly and in a variety of dimensions.

224. Matsumoto, Carolee. "The Potential of Computers for Teaching Thinking." *Developing Minds: A Resource Book for Teaching Thinking.* Edited by Arthur L. Costa. Alexandria, Virginia: Association for Supervision and Curriculum Development, 1985, pp. 249–254.

Matsumoto presents a set of questions to be answered and issues to be defined if schools are to take advantage of the potential for enhancing thinking through the use of computer software whether by aiding the student in thinking or by teaching thinking. A list of companies, software and skill areas is included.

225. Maxwell, William. "Games Children Play: Powerful Tools That Teach Some Thinking Skills." *Thinking: The Expanding Frontier.* Edited by William Maxwell. Philadelphia, Pennsylvania: The Franklin Institute Press, 1983, pp. 101–113.

Maxwell suggests that we use fun as a natural, motivating way of teaching thinking skills. All children are potential geniuses; the secret is for us to encourage the development of the intellect, or problem-solving abilities possibly through games. He identifies games from various cultures and periods of history which may be useful for this purpose.

226. Mays, Wolfe. "Thinking Skills Programmes: An Analysis." *New Ideas In Philosophy* 3 (1985): 149–163.

Mays reviews de Bono's CoRT, Feuerstein's Instrumental Enrichment, and Lipman's Philosophy for Children, describing each and comparing and contrasting them. All three programs are based on the premise that thinking skills in children can be improved, although different materials and procedures may be used in different programs.

227. McCormack, Alan J. "Teaching Inventiveness." *Childhood Education* 60 (March/April 1984): 249–255.

McCormack suggests that students tend to think creatively at an early age. Social pressures to conform eventually repress their creative urges, according to the author. He describes his "Invention Workshops" designed to stimulate children's creativity. Workshops focus on the history of inventions, the inventors themselves and the invention process. The author presents evaluative data on his program which suggest that participating in Invention Workshops may lead to greater flexibility and originality of thinking, as well as more positive feelings toward science, school, and one's own problem solving abilities.

228. McFarland, Mary A. "Critical Thinking in Elementary School Social Studies." *Social Education* 49 (April 1985): 277–280.

McFarland contends that teaching analysis and evaluation in the context of the social studies curriculum is important and should begin early in elementary school. She offers two strategies for teaching which are aimed at developing and improving the ability to distinguish relevant from irrelevant material. The first, Word Associates, teaches students to evaluate a list of five words and decide on its relevancy to a given social studies topic. The second, Defending a Point of View, teaches children to develop relevant arguments to support a particular point of view. McFarland describes the procedures, criteria and rules involved in learning and practicing both of these strategies.

229. McPeck, John E. "A Second Look at de Bono's Heuristics for Thinking." *Thinking: The Expanding Frontier.* Edited by William Maxwell. Philadelphia, Pennsylvania: The Franklin Institute Press, 1983, pp. 163–175.

McPeck, citing the widespread use of the CoRT program developed by de Bono, examines the vagueness of de Bono's definitions of thinking and his confusion in equating divergent thinking with thinking in general. The author reviews the program in some detail and concludes that the many areas of confusion results in "operations [which], when abstracted from subject-content, are empty and superficial in the context of discovery and would be absolutely useless as methods of justification" (p. 172).

230. ———. "Critical Thinking and Subject Specificity: A Reply to Ennis." *Educational Researcher* 19 (May 1990): 10–12.

McPeck replies to and critiques the 1989 article by Ennis which discusses subject specificity and critical thinking. He calls for a closer examination of "the precise scope and limits of the putative skills that various critical thinking programs are alleged to promote" (p. 10). (See entries 119 and 120.)

231. McTighe, James J. "Teaching for Thinking, of Thinking, and about Thinking." *Thinking Skills Instruction: Concepts and Techniques.* Edited by Marcia Heiman and Joshua Slomianko. Washington, D.C.: National Education Association, 1987, pp. 24–30.

McTighe, recognizing the need to develop thinking skills as basic to other skills and to knowledge acquisition, identifies three approaches to instruction. First, teaching for thinking involves students in the act of thinking, often by teacher-generated questions. The emphasis is on gaining knowledge of the content with no instruction in thinking. The author questions whether this approach is sufficient to improve thinking since it involves mainly practice of thinking. The second approach is teaching of thinking. Direct instruction is used to teach skills and processes that are part of thinking. Content material is used for instruction but it is not the focus of the lesson. Teaching about thinking constitutes a third approach. This approach emphasizes awareness of the thinking process and monitoring its success. All three approaches have their place in school curriculum.

232. McTighe, Jay, and Glen Cutlip. "The State's Role in Improving Student Thinking." *Educational Horizons* 64 (Summer 1986): 186–189.

McTighe and Cutlip outline the activities of one state department of education which were designed to improve student thinking and discuss the assumptions that guided the decision-making process. The assumptions include, for example, the notion that all children would benefit from explicit instruction in becoming better thinkers. This instruction should be provided over an extended period of time as part of a comprehensive model of organization, curriculum and instruction, reaching into all grade levels and content areas. The state department of education provided support in a variety of ways. It sponsored conferences, provided incentive grants for pilot projects, and reviewed programs and assumptions as an integral part of the process.

233. ———, and Frank T. Lyman, Jr. "Cueing Thinking in the Classroom: The Promise of Theory-Embedded Tools." *Educational Leadership* 45 (April 1988): 18–24.

Tools are defined by the authors as "tangible teaching/learning devices" (p. 19) that are based on educational theory. McTighe and Lyman provide useful details on six such tools. Think/pair/share is based on the need to insure wait time after a question is asked and a response given. The questioning/discussion strategies bookmark provides the teacher with a list of cues to develop questions and strategies to extend thinking. The thinking matrix is designed to aid students in developing their own questions, organizing thoughts, and monitoring comprehension. The Ready Reading Reference bookmark provides a concise list of strategies used by good readers before, during and after reading. Teachers can post a Problem-Solving Strategies Wheel which lists 12 useful strategies. Finally, a number of cognitive maps provide ways for students to organize and extend thought. Tools such as these are effective, according to the authors, because they aid memory, provide teachers and students with a common frame of reference, are easily available and ready for use, and are permanent.

234.   ———, and Jan Schollenberger. "Why Teach Thinking: A Statement of Rationale." *Developing Minds: A Resource Book for Teaching Thinking.* Edited by Arthur L. Costa. Alexandria, Virginia: Association for Supervision and Curriculum Development, 1985, pp. 3–6.

This article contains a rationale for devoting resources to thinking skills programs which is useful for support and program justification for school boards, parents and supervisors. While the rapid increase in available knowledge requires more efficient thinking skills, critical thinking and problem solving skills are actually declining rapidly. Little direct teaching of thinking skills is occurring although national organizations and the demands of a democratic society press for more.

235.   Meeker, Mary N. "SOI." *Developing Minds: A Resource Book for Teaching Thinking.* Edited by Arthur L. Costa. Alexandria, Virginia: Association for Supervision and Curriculum Development, 1985, pp. 187–192.

Meeker briefly describes the application of Guilford's Structure of the Intellect (SOI) to the assessment of intellectual abilities and its validation in research. SOI is also used to develop curriculum to teach higher-level thinking abilities. The approach is based on basic and higher level thinking abilities and their application in reading and mathematics, as well as developmental differences in students. Basic abilities must be developed first, with critical thinking considered a final stage. The abilities differ in reading and in mathematics because of the nature of the content. In fact, it is important to teach the thinking abilities separately in verbal and quantitative areas. This approach requires teacher preparation in both diagnosis and instruction.

236. Meeks, Lynn Langer. "Developing Metacognition in Composition with Peer Response Groups." *Thinking Skills Instruction: Concepts and Techniques.* Edited by Marcia Heiman and Joshua Slomianko. Washington, D.C.: National Education Association, 1987, pp. 119–127.

Meeks provides a rationale for peer response groups in revising student writing. She suggests that this procedure will improve both the product and the process of writing. The process becomes student centered with the teacher modeling the "messy" aspects of writing: rewriting, moving, adding, deleting. Peer interaction and response confirms that writing needs to be viewed from the perspective of a reader. Metacognition is developed through questions and knowledge of strategies and process.

237. Melchior, Timothy M., Robert E. Kaufold, and Ellen Edwards. "Using CoRT Thinking in Schools." *Educational Leadership* 45 (April 1988): 32–33.

The authors describe the application of the CoRT program for students in a variety of content areas and for teachers in the decision-making process in one school district. All teachers have been trained in using the program, but the decision to do so is left up to each individual teacher.

238. Meyer, Bonnie, J. F., David M. Brandt, and George J. Bluth. "Use of Top-level Structure in Text: Key for Reading Comprehension of Ninth-Grade Students." *Reading Research Quarterly* 16 (1980): 72–101.

The authors investigated whether following the organization of a text, i.e., its top level structure, to determine what is important is related to how well ninth grade students read. They found that good comprehenders used this strategy, but poor comprehenders did not, and use of the strategy aided recall. The authors concluded that there is a close relationship between comprehension ability and use of top level structure.

239. Miccinati, Jeannette L. "Mapping the Terrain: Connecting Reading with Academic Writing." *Journal of Reading* 31 (March 1988): 542–552.

"Creating a map requires students to think about what they read" (p. 542). This is the basis for Miccinati's proposals for developing graphic organizers to aid in reading comprehension and to organize information and ideas for writing. Underlying these activities is active critical thinking. The author provides an overview of the theory and research supporting mapping as a thinking strategy as well as detailed descriptions of a variety of simple and advanced maps.

240. Miles, Curtis. "The Fourth R: A Consumer's Guide to Thinking Skills Programs." *Journal of Developmental Education* 9 (1985): 26–27.

Miles presents a series of questions "to help you measure the degree and type of fit between a particular approach and your own personality, students, situation, and energy level"

(p. 26). The questions cover a range of areas from theoretical to practical and are supplemented with the author's personal comments.

241.   ——. "Making Choices: It Ought To Be Carefully Taught." *Thinking and Learning Skills.* Relating Instruction to Research. Volume 1. Edited by Judith W. Segal, Susan F. Chipman, and Robert Glaser. Hillsdale, New Jersey: Lawrence Erlbaum Associates, Pub., 1985, pp. 473–497.

Miles uses the term "choice making" to encompass all of the overlapping thinking skills including problem solving, decision making, critical thinking, creative thinking, cognition and logic. He holds that all college students in some way can benefit from instruction and experience in making choices and presents numerous examples from research and practice demonstrating the links between choice making and academic competence. Unfortunately, few colleges prepare students to make choices in either academic disciplines or in real life situations. Although there is uncertainty about exactly what skills and strategies to teach and how to teach them, Miles presents an overview of basic reasoning tools and choice making skills, heuristics and attitudes that should be included in a program. He presents a substantial list of research questions which need to be addressed.

242.   Mirga, Tom. "Emerging Interest in Reasoning Skills Marks Meeting on 'Critical Thinking'." *Education Week III* (August 29, 1984): 1, 10.

Mirga reports on a conference at the Harvard Graduate School of Education which focused on examining the many theoretical aspects of critical thinking, approaches being developed and issues unresolved.

243. Mirman, Jill, and Shari Tishman. "Infusing Thinking Through 'Connections'." *Educational Leadership* 45 (April 1988): 64–65.

Based on the conviction that thinking skills should be integrated into the curriculum, not taught as a separate subject, a set of thinking strategies have been developed to enable the student to engage in fundamental thinking skills such as decision making, problem solving, communicating and understanding. An example is provided of a three-step strategy for decision making as well as one for Understanding through Design which links purpose and structure. The strategies are simple, can be easily integrated into the classroom and can be used in any content area.

244. Mochamer, Randi Ward. *Teaching Writing As Thinking Across The Secondary Curriculum: An Annotated Bibliography.* June 1985. 46 pp. (ED 259 401)

The author cites some of the literature on writing and defines writing as a process of thinking, revising as a backward process of thinking, and reading comprehension and composition as part of the same process. Writing as thinking is a positive teaching strategy stretching into all areas of the curriculum. Research agrees that the student-teacher relationship is especially important in the process of learning and teaching writing.

Mochamer suggests that specific skill instruction be removed as soon as skills are internalized, that emphasis should be placed on content and not form, that English department faculty consult across the curriculum to reinforce thinking skills and provide in-service training for non-English faculty. In addition she recommends that writing experiences be positive, peer centered, and content oriented; and finally that interdepartmental writing assignments be given through a concerted faculty effort.

245. Moely, Barbara E., Silvia S. Hart, Kevin Santulli, Linda Leal, Terry Johnson, Nirmala Rao, and Libbi Burney. "How Do Teachers Teach Memory Skills?" *Educational Psychologist* 21 (Winter & Spring 1986): 55–71.

The authors review theory and current practice in memory training in elementary schools, suggesting that more instruction focus on cognitive processes and that teacher training include the development of memory and metacognition. They cite recent studies which demonstrate that memory strategy use can be successfully trained and note that little research has been done on how teachers use theories of memory development and strategy use in their classrooms. They also note that little attention is given in educational psychology texts to information processing, memory and metamemory. How then, ask the authors, can teachers create lessons which influence the development of memory in children?

The authors suggest that greater emphasis be given to teaching metacognitive strategies at all levels. They report on an observational study which investigated the cognitive instruction focus of elementary school teachers which demonstrated a correlation between teachers who frequently instructed in cognitive processes and children's ability to profit from memory instruction.

246. Montague, Marjorie, and Candace Bos. "The Effect of Cognitive Strategy Training on Verbal Math Problem Solving Performance of Learning Disabled Adolescents." *Journal of Learning Disabilities* (January 1986): pp. 26–33.

The authors cite studies which indicate that learning disabled students may have a deficit in verbal math problem solving related not only to reading and computational difficulties but to the level or stages of reasoning. They attempted an eight-step cognitive strategy training program on six learning disabled adolescents to teach them to understand and solve verbal math problems. They describe and give examples for the eight steps: 1) read the problem aloud, 2) paraphrase the problem aloud, 3) visualize and 4) state the problem, 5) hypothesize, 6) estimate, 7) calculate, 8) self check. Positive results indicate that a cognitive strategy training may be valuable in improving problem solving abilities for LDs.

247.   Morales, Romelia V., Valerie J. Shute, and James W. Pelligrino. "Developmental Differences in Understanding and Solving Simple Mathematics Word Problems." *Cognition and Instruction* 2 (1985): 41–57.

In math word problem solution and sorting tasks, using third and sixth graders of low socioeconomic status, the authors demonstrated that problem sorting patterns for older children were different from those for younger children. Older children had a more refined conceptual schema, and sorted problems in a manner consistent with their schema. Younger children sorted using a surface structure strategy and were less accurate and consistent. Their errors were almost totally attributable to a conceptual error (as opposed to a calculation error). For example, not knowing which operation to use may have been due to a failure in problem representation or selection of schema.

248.   Morante, Edward A., and Anita Ulesky. "Assessment of Reasoning Abilities." *Educational Leadership* 42 (September 1984): 71–74.

Morante and Ulesky provide an overview of the list of thinking competencies that was used to review tests of thinking suitable for college students. These tests, Cornell Critical Thinking, Whimbey Analytical Skills Inventory, and New Jersey Test of Reasoning, were administered to college students to determine if there was a relationship between these tests and basic skills scores in reading, writing and math. Preliminary results indicate that many students are operating below the level of formal reasoning; tests contain items that are not "productive. Some items are ambiguous; some do not relate to the total score; some do not discriminate well between those who reason well and those who do not (as measured by the total score); some appear to be more related to mathematics or vocabulary than to reasoning" (p. 74). In addition, correlations appear to exist between all sections of the basic skills tests and the thinking tests.

249.   Moses, Monte C., and Jan Thomas. "Teaching Students to Think—What Can Principals Do?" *Nassp Bulletin* 70 (February 1986); 16–20.

Moses and Thomas, citing the volume of research supporting the leadership role of the principal in the education of children, propose a number of steps the principal can take to insure that effective instruction in thinking takes place. Thinking instruction should be made a building priority, supported by staff development that creates "cognitive dissonance in the minds of the teachers" (p. 17), encouraging them to review their current instructional procedures and to adopt "specific strategies that facilitate learning and thinking beyond rote memory" (p. 18). In addition, curriculum revision may be needed to emphasize thinking as a means of understanding content.

250.   Moss, Pamela, and Anthony R. Petrosky. *A Proposal for Measuring Critical Thinking.* Pittsburgh, Pennsylvania: Pittsburgh Board of Public Education; Richard King Mellon Foundation, September 1983. 23 pp. (ED 237 399)

The assessment of critical thinking is part of a larger project developed by the Pittsburgh Board of Public Education which also includes instruction and staff development. The authors recognize the lack of agreement on a definition of critical thinking because of the varied cognitive processes, knowledge structures and effective orientations that are included in the definitions. They believe that critical thinking is not a series of discrete skills but rather is "a dynamic process of questioning and reasoning" (p. 2). It is active, not passive. Present tests do not adequately reflect the view of critical thinking as a generative act, as a way of making or creating meaning, involving a process that is more than the sum of individual skills.

There are few "correct" answers in critical thinking. The answers that students present must be explained and supported, with the process made clear, in ways not possible in short answer or multiple choice format. Therefore, students are asked to read social studies passages and respond in essays which evaluate the text or draw inferences from it. In order to insure that teachers look at the student's critical thinking, not his/her writing skills, an analytic scoring guide was developed. An example from the test, scoring standards and sample responses are included.

251. Munro, George, and Allen Slater. "The Know-How of Teaching Critical Thinking." *Social Education* 49 (April 1985): 284–292.

The authors introduce a framework for teaching critical thinking skills developed by the Halton, Ontario, school system. They describe the planning and teaching program using the skill of distinguishing fact from opinion as an example. A chart is used to divide learning components into cognitive and affective learning. Teaching steps for developing critical thinking are included and specific steps in teaching identification and classification of facts and opinion are discussed in detail. The authors report increased teacher satisfaction and improved student performance in higher mental operations, including critical thinking, as a result of their program.

252. Muth, K. Denise. "Teachers' Connection Questions: Promoting Students to Organize Ideas." *Journal of Reading* 31 (December 1987): 254–259.

Muth briefly reviews the research on the relevance of text structure to comprehension and suggests that teachers engage in two kinds of questioning which will help students utilize this in organizing information and ideas. One line of questioning builds connections within the text and the other line builds connections between text ideas and those the students already possess. Guidelines and examples are included.

253. "NAEP Results Show Little Change in Reading Skills." *Reading Today* 7 (February/March 1990): 1, 8.

This brief summary of the results of the NAEP (National Assessment of Educational Progress) study conducted in 1988 showed little change since 1984. The results demonstrated a serious problem in higher level reading which requires reasoning and making inferences.

254. Nardi, Anne H., and Charles E. Wales. "Teaching Decision Making with Guided Design." *Developing Minds: A Resource Book for Teaching Thinking.* Edited by Arthur L. Costa. Alexandria, Virginia: Association for Supervision and Curriculum Development, 1985, pp. 220–223.

Nardi and Wales view decision making as the heart of any educational program. The other thinking skills, such as creative thinking and critical thinking, are viewed as needed in order to support the development of decision making. The process can be taught to any school age child as long as adaptations are made in light of the prior experience and the developmental level of the child. Students learn four operations: state the goal, consider the options, prepare a plan, and take actions. These four operations can be used with three processes: find the cause of the problem, solve the problem, and anticipate potential problems. It is essential to teach decision making within the content areas, as an integrated part of the curriculum. Students, working in teams, identify the problem and follow suggested steps and procedures in order to take action. In the process they "learn how to think critically, draw inferences, devise analogies, explore alternatives, and make value judgments" (p. 223).

255. Nessel, Denise D., Margaret B. Jones, and Carol N. Dixon. *Thinking Through The Language Arts.* New York: Macmillan Publishing Company, 1989.

Nessel, Jones, and Dixon come out firmly on the side of those who believe that instruction in thinking skills should be part of content instruction. They assert that special programs are not needed, in fact they may be a waste of time. Transfer to the language arts areas from self-contained programs with special kits and books "cannot be assumed" (p. 21). The book details ways to do this within all of the language arts areas, integrating instruction in content and strategies.

256. Neves, David M., and John R. Anderson. "Knowledge Compilation: Mechanisms for the Automatization of Cognitive Skills." *Cognitive Skills and Their Acquisition.* Edited by John R. Anderson. Hillsdale, New Jersey: Lawrence Erlbaum Associates, Pub., 1981, pp. 57–84.

The authors trace the development of a geometry skill-utilization of postulates in proofs—from memorizing and initial application to automaticity through practice. They describe how postulates are initially encoded, how particular procedures are created and then accelerated through practice.

257. Newell, Allen, and Paul S. Rosenbloom. "Mechanisms of Skill Acquisition and the Law of Practice." *Cognitive Skills and Their Acquisition.* Edited by John R. Anderson. Hillsdale, New Jersey: Lawrence Erlbaum Associates, Pub., 1981, pp. 1–55.

This article investigates the "power law," i.e., the direct relationship between amount of time taken to perform a task and amount of practice. It provides a variety of examples of the law and offers possible theories which might explain it; for example it may occur as a result of chunking and variabilities in the environment.

258. Nezu, Arthur M. "Cognitive Appraisal of Problem Solving Effectiveness: Relation to Depression and Depressive Symptoms." *Journal of Clinical Psychology* 42 (January 1986): 42–48.

Nezu investigated the relationship between college students' perceptions of their problem solving abilities and their levels of depression. He found that depressed students perceived themselves to be less effective at problem solving. In other words, if they thought they couldn't cope with social problems well, they became depressed. Further, Nezu suggests that self-appraisal of problem solving ability is probably a good predictor of actual problem solving ability, therefore, truly poor problem solvers will get less positive reinforcement from their social environment.

259. ——, Christine M. Nezu, Lisa Saraydarian, Kathleen Kalmar, and George F. Ronan. "Social Problem Solving as a Moderating Variable Between Negative Life Stress and Depressive Symptoms." *Cognitive Therapy and Research* 10 (1986): 480–498.

The authors studied the effects of problem solving ability on the ability to cope with negative life stress. They concluded that effective problem solvers are better able to cope with negative life stress and, therefore, are less prone to depression during high stress circumstances.

260. Nickerson, Raymond S. "Thoughts on Teaching Thinking." *Educational Leadership* 39 (October 1981): 21–24.

Nickerson suggests a broad approach "to improve student ability to perform intellectually demanding tasks" (p. 21). Programs need to focus on four areas: abilities, methods, knowledge and attitudes. Abilities are seen as specific competencies that may be developed and measured and may or may not contribute to thinking abilities.

Methods may include both general strategies or heuristics that can apply to a range of situations and step-by-step prescriptions for specific tasks. Knowledge of the particular content is essential for thinking. Finally, attitudes should be fostered that encourage curiosity, pride and a respect for the opinions of others.

261. ———. *Reflections on Reasoning.* Hillsdale, New Jersey: Lawrence Erlbaum Associates, Pub., 1986.

Nickerson provides a "collection of thoughts' (p. xi) on reasoning rather than a textbook or a review of scholarly research and literature. This book is a guide through the related concepts of language, logic, inventiveness, knowledge and truth, the components of reasoning including beliefs, assertions and arguments, the strategies used to persuade and common fallacies in reasoning. Reasoning involves more than the rules of logic; it is "a matter of both attitude and knowledge: one is unlikely to reason well about any subject unless one is deeply desirous of doing so, and one has some knowledge of the subject about which the reasoning is to be done" (p. 1). Within this framework, Nickerson provides numerous clear examples illustrating the components involved in beliefs, assertions and arguments.

262.   ———. "New Directors in Educational Assessment." *Educational Researcher* 18 (December 1989): 3–7.

Nickerson cites the wide range of uses for educational tests for teachers, school districts, and students and the limitations of most current instruments. They test recall, not high level thinking. Since tests frequently drive instruction, it is critical that we examine test construction and validity. The author raises a number of questions, reviews current research and provides some cautions. He concludes that there are a number of possibilities, including, for example, the use of computers. However, no matter what direction is taken, teacher training in the construction and use of tests is critical.

263.   ———. "On Improving Thinking Through Instruction." *Review of Research In Education* 15. Edited by E. Z. Rothkopf. Washington, D.C.: American Educational Research Association, 1989, pp. 3–57.

This is a comprehensive review of the research and historical perspective on thinking instruction. Nickerson provides a cogent argument for the need for and feasibility of thinking instruction and reviews specifically what, when and how instruction has been provided in the past. He suggests that attitudes, values and beliefs fostered in the classroom have a particularly important influence on the development of thinking ability and that "the idea that any teacher, if given the right material, can teach thinking effectively is not tenable" (p. 37).

Nickerson notes the lack of conclusive information about the effectiveness of various approaches to the teaching of thinking, the lack of understanding of what kinds of information we need to know in order to select an approach, and, most importantly, the lack of a good model of thinking to use as a framework in making such a decision. He concludes that the production of effective problem solvers, reflective, inquisitive, metacognitive, open-minded thinkers, who are eager to understand the world and highly skilled in formal and informal tools of thought, should be the fundamental goal of education.

264. ———, David N. Perkins, and Edward E. Smith, *The Teaching of Thinking*. Hillsdale, New Jersey: Lawrence Erlbaum Associates, Pub., 1985.

In this ambitious work, Nickerson, Perkins, and Smith provide a detailed review and analysis of the theory and research in the areas of intelligence, thinking in general, problem solving, creativity, metacognition and reasoning. They identify and address a substantial number of serious issues, exploring their background, relevant research and potential implications as well as stating their own viewpoint. One example will illustrate this. The most serious issue they identify is whether there are general thinking skills or whether thinking skills are context bound. After examining both sides of the issue, they conclude that "skilled thinking is often more context bound than one might suppose" (p. 58). The implications are that thinking should be encouraged in terms of models rather than rules; we should provide explicit guidance; thinking should be linked closely to the requirements of specific content areas.

The authors review, in detail, many thinking programs, categorized into five broad groups; cognitive operations approaches, heuristic oriented approaches, formal thinking approaches, symbolic facility approaches and thinking-about-thinking approaches. The review is extremely helpful in sorting out the emphasis, similarities, differences, specifics, etc., for a wide range of approaches and programs. Issues related to evaluation are identified and examined, and recommendations are made where appropriate. Questions related to program adoption are also explored, with the caution that in order to be effective any program must have strong teacher support.

265. Norris, Stephen P. "Synthesis of Research on Critical Thinking." *Educational Leadership* 42 (May 1985): 40–45.

Norris reviews selected research on the meaning of critical thinking, on the ability to transfer critical thinking skills to other subject areas, and on a variety of teaching methods. He covers empirical, philosophical and policy research and concludes that being able to think critically is a necessary condition for being educated, that high school and college students do not perform well on tasks that demonstrate critical thinking competence, that critical thinking is strongly related to students' personal experiences and background knowledge, and that critical thinking tests themselves should be evaluated. He reminds us that research in critical thinking has yet to explain specifically how or why students do or do not achieve this ability. (See entry 287.)

266. ———. "Can We Test Validly for Critical Thinking?" *Educational Researcher* 18 (December 1989): 21–26.

In order to answer the question posed by the title of the article, Norris explores the lack of consensus as to whether critical thinking is generalizable from one subject to another and whether people actually apply critical thinking learned in one subject to another subject. Because of our lack of definitive knowledge here it is difficult to interpret scores on critical thinking tests. In addition, critical thinking dispositions are identified and illustrated. The author concludes that current critical thinking tests are unable to measure dispositions. He explores possibilities for assessment, including multiple choice tests used in conjunction with verbal reports.

267. ———, and Linda M. Phillips. "Explanations of Reading Comprehension: Schema Theory and Critical Thinking Theory." *Teachers College Record* 89 (Winter 1987): 281-306.

The authors discuss aspects and problems of a schema-based theory of reading comprehension and attempt to combine and supplement it with principles of critical thinking. They present protocols from two readers, one good and one poor, in a reading comprehension task; they explain their differences according to principles of schema theory; and finally, they point out weaknesses in the theory.

According to the authors, to use one's schema to understand and interpret a piece of text, one must understand the piece of text, and to understand the piece of text, one must generate and use one's schema. Thus the explanation of the role of schema in comprehension is tautological. They offer an alternate explanation. Critical thinking theory provides a means of explaining the ability to work out ambiguous text by generating alternative interpretations, consider them in light of experience and world knowledge, and suspend decision until further information is available, accepting alternative explanations. In the example they give, the better reader was a better critical thinker rather than a better schema user. He was able to use good critical thinking skills to proceed through the text, gradually clarifying and refining his understanding through a series of planned, high level critical thinking procedures.

According to Norris and Phillips, the difference between schema theory and critical thinking theory is that schema theory concentrates on the product—the correctness of the understanding of the text—while the focus of critical thinking theory is the process the reader uses to understand. The authors conclude that schemas are necessary for comprehension, and that we need to critically evaluate the selection and construction of those schemas to read and understand.

268.   Ogle, Donna S. "K–W–L: A Teaching Model That Develops Active Reading of Expository Text." *The Reading Teacher* 39 (February 1986): 564–570.

Ogle describes this active strategy for students which accesses what they Know, determines what they Want to know and helps them recall what they Learn. The procedure is explained in depth and is illustrated by an example from a fourth grade classroom. It makes use of students' prior knowledge, develops their own reasons for reading and focuses on their own decision to learn something specific rather than whatever information the author has chosen to include in the text. Ogle suggests that the procedure can be used with nonfiction selections at any grade level and in any content area, whether in reading instruction or content learning. The article concludes with several specific suggestions for evaluating whether the procedure works.

269.   ———. "Implementing Strategic Teaching." *Educational Leadership* 46 (December 1988/January 1989): 47–48, 57–60.

Recognizing the critical importance of providing teachers with opportunities to engage in collaborative thinking, planning and decision making, Ogle describes in detail the implementation of a program designed to develops students' thinking and learning abilities. The strategies were linked directly to content with specific lessons and units developed by the teachers. A detailed example is provided for a 6th grade science unit, incorporating strategies such as activating and linking prior knowledge to new information and developing a graphic organizer.

270. Olson, Carol Booth. "Fostering Critical Thinking Skills Through Writing." *Educational Leadership* 42 (November 1984): 28–39.

Olson links thinking and writing, demonstrating how they are integrated in the University of California at Irvine Writing Project. The focus of the project is on using thinking to promote writing and writing to promote thinking. She examines the role of the teacher in enhancing development of thinking as the student moves through the stages of the growth of thought from the concrete to the abstract. Similarities between the writing process and Bloom's levels of educational thought form the foundation for the project. Olson points out that writing is a recursive process and that there is no neat linear progression from one level to the next. A detailed description is included of the progression of a sequence of lessons from the prewriting stage to the final stages of writing, moving from knowledge to evaluation.

271. ———. "The Thinking/Writing Connection." *Developing Minds: A Resource Book for Teaching Thinking.* Edited by Arthur L. Costa. Alexandria, Virginia: Association for Supervision and Curriculum Development, 1985, pp. 102–107.

Olson proposes that writing is a reflection of thinking, stating that "depth and clarity of thinking enhance the quality of writing, while at the same time, writing is a learning tool for heightening and refining thinking" (p. 102). She acknowledges the important role of teachers in providing children with activities which will encourage cognitive growth, since how people think may be determined by the quality of thinking experiences they have had. Writing involves using memory, reviewing prior knowledge, organizing ideas, constructing a framework of information, transforming this framework of thoughts into words and, finally, evaluating them as a whole.

Several lessons illustrate the stages of composition, moving the students through all levels of thinking. Stages include prewriting, precomposing, writing, sharing, revising, editing, evaluation and extension activities. Olson views the writing process as a way to develop thinking skills across content areas.

272.   Olson, David R. "Computers as Tools of the Intellect." *Educational Research* 14 (May 1985): 5–8.

Computers, according to Olson, can help children "learn to make their meanings fully explicit" (p. 5), distinguishing between what is said and what is interpreted or inferred. Computers do not tolerate ambiguity and through feedback will communicate the need for explicitness in expression.

273.   O'Reilly, Kevin. "Teaching Critical Thinking in High School U.S. History." *Social Education* 49 (April 1985): 281–284.

The author points out the fact that historians often disagree when reporting on people and events in history, and that this is an especially good context for teaching critical thinking. Students must first be taught to be skeptical, to learn to counter the "textbook truth" syndrome and to question what they read. He offers a case study which he uses in class to teach argument evaluation and suggests that teachers might want to rewrite lengthy historical viewpoints into shorter more easily understandable arguments for classroom use.

274.   O'Sullivan, J.T., and Michael Pressley. "Completeness of Instruction and Strategy Transfer." *Journal of Experimental Child Psychology* 38 (1984): 275–288.

Fifth and sixth graders were given comprehensive instruction in how to use a "keyword" strategy, i.e., they were taught the strategy, they were told how, when, why and where to use the strategy, and they were given practice with the strategy. As a result of the comprehensive instruction, they were able to transfer the strategy to other tasks. The authors also found that adults did not need the same amount of instruction to be able to transfer the strategy. They suggest that their finding supports the research which indicates that with explicit metacognitive training, young children can perform at higher, "adult" metacognitive levels.

275. Owen, Elizabeth, and John Sweller. "What Do Students Learn While Solving Mathematics Problems?" *Journal of Educational Psychology* 77 (June 1985): 272–284.

Owen and Sweller describe Newell and Simon's (1972) means-end analysis of problem solving and review the related research. The authors assert that use of means-end analysis by novices is ineffective because it requires great cognitive effort and therefore interferes with the ability to acquire the knowledge and schemas necessary to become an expert, to solve problems automatically. They performed a series of math experiments, reducing goal specificity, thereby eliminating the ability to use means-end analysis. This resulted in more rapid schema acquisition by novices. According to the authors, means-end strategy causes heavy cognitive load because the problem solver must perform a variety of activities simultaneously.

276. Palincsar, Annemarie Sullivan. "The Role of Dialogue in Providing Scaffolded Instruction." *Educational Psychologist* 21 (Winter & Spring 1986): 73–98.

The author describes ways in which dialogue in the classroom can provide scaffolded instruction to accomplish tasks which, without specifically structured instructional supports, the student would not be able to accomplish. Scaffolded instruction is, primarily, an interactive teaching-learning process. Dialogue plays a vital part in this interaction between teacher and student and between student and student.

Palincsar reviews the literature and concludes that lots of talk, but very little actual instructional dialogue goes on in the classroom. Her Reciprocal Teaching program, which uses dialogue as the main vehicle of instruction, is reviewed and a study of its extension to high risk first graders is presented. Transcripts from this study are provided to demonstrate how dialogue can be used to foster scaffolding in instruction. Important variables which affect how profitable dialogue can be in the classroom include: the extent to which teachers focused on ideas, not words, used students' contributions optimally, kept the dialogue focused and directed, made the point of instruction explicit and constructively evaluated students' contributions. Palincsar suggests that teachers and researchers collaborate more in advancing the use of scaffolding in instruction.

277. ———, and Ann L. Brown. "Reciprocal Teaching: Activities to Promote 'Reading with Your Mind'." *Reading, Thinking, and Concept Development.* Edited by Theodore L. Harris and Eric J. Cooper. New York: College Entrance Examination Board, 1985, pp. 147–158.

Palincsar and Brown present their Reciprocal Teaching Program, an instructional technique comprised of four comprehension and studying strategies: question-generating, summarizing, predicting and clarifying. In this procedure, first the teacher models the four strategies. Gradually, with the teacher's guidance, students assume responsibility for using the strategies independently. Palincsar and Brown report that research on this program indicates that the strategies are durable, i.e., trained students maintained effective use of the strategies over several months at least, and that they were able to generalize reading gains to classroom content areas. They provide a series of steps to follow to teach the strategies and to implement the program, including applications to content areas and to peer tutoring situations.

278. ——, Kathryn Ransom, and Sue Derber. "Collaborative Research and Development of Reciprocal Teaching." *Educational Leadership* 46 (December 1988/January 1989): 37–40.

Palincsar, Ransom and Derber describe Reciprocal Teaching, a dialogue in which students generate questions, summarize, clarify and predict. They present research results on the effectiveness and efficiency of the strategy and describe in some detail a project to test the feasibility of implementing it in a school system. An extensive program of initial staff development and ongoing networking is described.

279. Papert, Seymour. *Mindstorms Children: Computers and Powerful Ideas.* New York: Basic Books, Inc., 1980.

Papert introduces LOGO, a programming language which is intended to develop children's ability to think and learn. Papert states that LOGO strengthens metacognitive abilities and knowledge acquisition skills. By programming, children reflect on how they themselves think. They are encouraged to be explicitly aware of their own thinking and to analyze their own thought processes for errors frequently. LOGO teaches children to "debug," to find and correct their own errors, thereby learning from them. Papert relates the concept of LOGO to the Piagetian notion of the child as the "builder" of his own knowledge.

280. Paris, Scott G. "Using Classroom Dialogues and Guided Practice to Teach Comprehension Strategies." *Reading, Thinking, and Concept Development.* Edited by Theodore L. Harris and Eric J. Cooper. New York: College Entrance Examination Board, 1985, pp. 105–130.

Paris describes the basic comprehension strategies a skilled reader uses and the kinds of metacognitive knowledge needed to become an independent, strategic reader. According to Paris, a reader first needs declarative knowledge, or "knowing that" knowledge, i.e., the facts about reading, such as the fact that titles provide cues to meaning. They also need procedural knowledge, "knowing how knowledge," i.e., how to skim by reading high information words, for example. Finally, readers need conditional knowledge, or "knowing when and why" knowledge, such as knowing why a certain strategy is reasonable, worth the effort and functionally effective.

Paris discusses the need for guided instruction that is interactive, that shifts responsibility for learning to the student, that provides modeling, feedback and persuasion, so that students can internalize the way the teacher regulates his or her own comprehension. He suggests that teaching strategies which include classroom dialogues "make thinking public," and help students become metacognitive, motivated readers.

Paris offers a teaching method for direct instruction in comprehension strategies. Informed Strategies for Learning (ISL) is based on group discussion and direct instruction about the value of reading strategies. Students use metaphors to depict and discuss strategies. Metaphors make abstract cognitive strategies tangible and stimulate interest and motivation. For example, ISL illustrates how "rounding up your ideas" with a corral of horses is similar to summarizing the main points of a story. Paris discusses the success of the ISL project with third through fifth graders and offers a general description of the program as well as several sample lesson plans for grades 3, 7 and 11.

281.   ———, and Peter Winograd. "How Metacognition Can Promote Academic Learning and Instruction."

Dimensions of Thinking and Cognitive Instruction. Edited by Beau Fly Jones and Lorna Idol. Hillsdale, New Jersey: Lawrence Erlbaum Associates, Pub., 1990, pp. 15–51.

Paris and Winograd begin with the generally accepted view of metacognition as the monitoring of one's own thinking and add to it. They suggest that metacognition has two aspects: self-appraisal and self-management. Knowledge about these aspects can be shared with others. In addition, the concept of metacognition should be expanded to include affective and motivational variables. "Self-appraisal and self-management are personal assessments filled with affect" (p. 24). The links to classroom instruction are clearly drawn. They review and advocate the use of direct instruction, scaffolded instruction, cognitive coaching and cooperative learning.

282. Parker, Walter C. "Trends: Social Studies." *Educational Leadership* 43 (November 1985): 83–84.

Parker succinctly identifies a "serious and longstanding contradiction" (p. 83) in social studies instruction. The development of critical thinking is considered essential but is not included in social studies lessons. He identifies three reasons for this. First, critical thinking is much more than a set of discrete skills; it is a "disposition" to reflect and be sceptical. This cannot be taught by behavioral objectives. Second, state-run schools may be leery of promoting thinking that will bring political institutions and activities into question. Third, teachers and administrators themselves, because of their own lack of models, are seldom critical thinkers. He describes instructional activities that require discussion and critical inquiry on the part of both teacher and students.

283.   ———. "Trends: Social Studies." *Educational Leadership*
       47 (May 1990): 91–92.

Parker reviews a current program developed for high
school social studies classes which takes an issues approach
to studying history. The critical element is the emphasis on
the use of thinking as an integral part of the program.
Questions are raised about the issues which are designed to
develop critical thinking and problem solving. The issues are
real life issues, ones that students must ultimately address.
The knowledge gained and the thinking skills used and
developed are applied to both the academic areas of history
and social studies and to real life issues. Transfer is built into
the program.

284.   Parnes, Sidney J. "Creative Problem Solving." *Developing
       Minds: A Resource Book for Teaching Thinking*. Edited by
       Arthur L. Costa. Alexandria, Virginia: Association for
       Supervision and Curriculum Development, 1985, pp.
       230–232.

Creative Problem Solving is offered as a course for gifted
middle school students and all secondary students. It is
designed to develop curiosity, openness and creativity in
learning and problem solving.

285.   Paul, Richard W. "Critical Thinking: Fundamental to
       Education for a Free Society." *Educational Leadership* 42
       (September 1984): 4–14.

Paul presents a case for teaching critical thinking skills in
schools. However, his definition of critical thinking skills
goes beyond the "discrete micrological skills ultimately
extrinsic to the character of the person; skills that can be
tacked onto other learning" (p. 5) and includes "a set of
integrated macrological skills ultimately intrinsic to the
character of the person and to insight into one's own
cognitive and affective processes" (p. 5). He is concerned

with the individual's abilities to think critically in situations of conflict and of differing opinions, crossing "category or disciplinary lines" (p. 13) and requiring open-mindedness. He advocates teaching the traditional, technical, analytic thinking skills but also allowing for the development of dialectical reasoning through instruction and through dialogue.

286. ———. "Bloom's Taxonomy and Critical Thinking Instruction." *Educational Leadership* 42 (May 1985): 36–39.

The author discusses the influence of Bloom's taxonomy on critical thinking instruction and concludes that it attempts to be "neutral," to make no value judgments or favor no particular educational philosophy. This, says Paul, is impossible and contradictory to a commitment to critical thinking skills. The author concludes that Bloom's taxonomy gives us important insights into cognitive processes and their relationships but actually limits our insights into the nature of critical thinking. Teachers must realize that learning is process not product oriented, processes which should foster rational thought and learning. Critical thinking is not such a simple matter; teachers should take courses to learn how to analyze and nurture their own thinking skills.

287. ———. "Critical Thinking Research: A Response to Stephen Norris." *Educational Leadership* 42 (May 1985): 46.

Paul points out that Norris (1985) failed to cover a wide range of the literature on critical thinking which cuts across a variety of disciplines, including sociology, anthropology and psychology. He suggests that Norris also failed to emphasize the importance of teaching dialectical thinking. (See entry 265.)

288. ———. "Critical and Reflective Thinking: A Philosophical
      Perspective." *Dimensions of Thinking and Cognitive
      Instruction.* Edited by Beau Fly Jones and Lorna Idol.
      Hillsdale, New Jersey: Lawrence Erlbaum Associates,
      Pub., 1990, pp. 445–494.

      Paul contrasts a philosophy-based approach to teaching
      critical thinking to a psychology-based approach, examining
      philosophy as a framework for thinking and the need for
      philosophy. He relates this approach to the classroom,
      illustrating that it enables "students to begin to integrate
      their thinking across subject matter divisions" (p. 455). A
      detailed comparison of philosophy and cognitive psychology
      provides the basis for infusing philosophy throughout the
      curriculum. He provides a list of strategies, a sample lesson
      and a set of assumptions about knowledge, learning and
      literacy.

289. Pearson, P. David, and Taffy E. Raphael. "Reading
      Comprehension as a Dimension of Thinking."
      Dimensions of Thinking and Cognitive Instruction.
      Edited by Beau Fly Jones and Lorna Idol. Hillsdale, New
      Jersey: Lawrence Erlbaum Associates, Pub., 1990, pp.
      209–240.

      Pearson and Raphael review frameworks for
      comprehension, instruction and learning, relating the act of
      comprehension to thinking. Both comprehension and
      thinking are social processes in which meaning can be
      developed collaboratively and is influenced by a society and
      a culture. Both can be enhanced by "scaffolding" and both
      must deal with the instructional issue of whether to provide
      instruction separately or in a content area. Comprehension
      and thinking both include many of the same skills; the
      authors provide many examples of overlapping skills, such
      as categorizing, determining levels of importance, inductive
      reasoning, and critical thinking.

290. Pelligrini, David S. "Social Cognition and Competence in Middle Childhood." *Child Development* 56 (1985): 253–264.

Pelligrini looked at two aspects of social problem solving in middle school children, interpersonal understanding and means-end problem solving ability. He found that both contributed significantly to his measure of competence in children. Maturity in reasoning about the social world and resourcefulness in planning solutions to hypothetical social dilemmas were found to be salient characteristics of children who are competent in the school environment.

291. Perfetto, Greg A., John D. Bransford, and Jeffery J. Franks. "Constraints on Access in a Problem Solving Context." *Memory and Cognition* 11 (1983): 24–31.

The authors found that subjects do not use obvious cues or access relevant information to solve problems that are closely related, i.e., they use insight rather than domain related information to solve problems. Their ability to spontaneously access relevant information depends on their representation and quality of organization of the relevant knowledge.

292. Perkins, D.N. "Creativity by Design." *Educational Leadership* 42 (September 1984): 18–25.

Perkins holds that "creative thinking is thinking patterned in a way that tends to lead to creative results" (p. 18). It is the output that identifies the thinking as creative but the output is not limited to a grand effort in the arts or in writing. Creative output can be modest and can appear in all areas of human endeavor. Six principles of creative thinking are proposed including: 1) both aesthetic and practical standards, 2) attention to purpose as well as results, 3) mobility and competence more than flexibility, 4) willingness to take risks, experience failure and extend the limits of competence, 5) objectivity as well as subjectivity, and 6) reliance on intrinsic rather than extrinsic motivation.

Schools generally are not structured to encourage creative thinking primarily because of their emphasis on knowledge as a given and on tasks that do not encourage or even allow creative thinking. Perkins suggests ways of encouraging the development of creative thinking in all classes by examining knowledge in terms of design questions and by requiring that students generate products as a result of those questions.

293.   ———. "The Fingertip Effect: How Information-Processing Technology Shapes Thinking." *Educational Researcher* 14 (August/September 1985): 11–17.

Perkins identifies two levels of fingertip effects of information-processing technology on thinking. The first level deals with "the difference an innovation straightforwardly makes" (p. 11). This effect, enabling flexibility and active participation, seems widely accepted. The second level, and the one that is the major concern of this article, deals with the "deeper and more wide-ranging repercussions on society, personality, and thought" (p. 11). Since this effect is not as widely accepted the author suggests we need to attempt to forecast the effects we might have on this second level.

Perkins cites the numerous opportunities for thinking and learning available to the student in using Logo, word processing programs and data base programs. Unfortunately the opportunities to learn "a general lesson naturally" (p. 13), according to research in Logo and word processing, are not taken by students. The opportunities are there. Perkins suggests that without explicit instruction students do not perceive opportunities to learn, think and transfer what they have learned. Finally, students may not be motivated to pursue the task of uncovering these opportunities if they are not readily apparent. With the gradual infusion into society of technologies which enable information-processing, students will be able to learn and practice more frequently and with more ease. This, along with instruction, should provide more chances to develop second level effects.

294. ——. "General Cognitive Skills: Why Not?" *Thinking and Learning Skills*. Research and Open Questions. Volume 2. Edited by Susan F. Chipman, Judith W. Segal, and Robert Glaser. Hillsdale, New Jersey: Lawrence Erlbaum Associates, Pub., 1985, pp. 339–363.

Perkins addresses the issue of whether there are general cognitive skills or whether cognitive skills are related and linked to content by examining the assumptions underlying the statement "intellectual competence consists largely of a few cognitive-control strategies that can be taught by informing learners of them and providing some practice" (p. 340). He concludes that although there are many reservations associated with this statement, there are some general cognitive-control strategies. However, they are linked closely to content. Instruction needs to recognize this. Perkins provides suggestions for instruction such as teaching a general skill through a product approach which will cut across content lines.

295. ——. "Postprimary Education Has Little Impact on Informal Reasoning." *Journal of Educational Psychology* 77 (1985): 562–571.

Perkins studied high school, college and graduate students to see how much, if any, effect schooling had on their ability to think informally, to construct an argument in a way that is different from formal reasoning. He found that the amount of education had only a marginal effect on this ability. Perkins suggests that the educational process does little to prepare students for generating lines of arguments, examining both sides of a case, and elaborating and testing a particular line of argument against the student's own general knowledge. We need to redesign education to provide explicit instruction and practice in these skills.

296.   ———. "What Creative Thinking Is." *Developing Minds: A Resource Book for Teaching Thinking.* Edited by Arthur L. Costa. Alexandria, Virginia: Association for Supervision and Curriculum Development, 1985, pp 58–61.

Perkins discusses common myths about what creative thinking is and how a creative person functions. Creative thinking involves aesthetic as much as practical standards, depends on attention to purpose as much as to results, and mobility more than fluency. The creative person works at the edge more than the center of competence, is as objective as subjective and is intrinsically, more than extrinsically, motivated. The creative thinker mixes strategies, skills and attitude in a particular way. The author discourages the use of brief, special purpose instruction in teaching creativity and chides current educational practices which he says may "work against the creative pattern of thinking" (p. 60), since schools generally present knowledge as a given rather than as the product of a creative effort to accomplish something and give students tasks that do not exercise or allow creative effort.

297.   ———. *Knowledge As Design.* Englewood Cliffs, New Jersey: Laurence Erlbaum Associates, Pub., 1986.

This book is about the transmission of knowledge. It explores more effective ways to give and receive knowledge in various settings such as the school, the home and the workplace. Design, according to Perkins, means shaping objects to purposes. In terms of education, it means viewing bits of knowledge as structures adapted to a purpose for a particular use. Perkins advocates focusing education on the purpose of teaching and learning, as opposed to knowing "important facts," which is a passive kind of knowledge. He discusses the differences between knowledge "in storage" rather than knowledge as implements of action.

He suggests four questions to structure aspects of the transmission of knowledge: 1) what is its purpose? 2) what is its structure? 3) what are model cases of it? and (4) what are the arguments that explain and evaluate it? Perkins advocates using the four questions as a structure to investigate thinking processes involved in gaining knowledge (reading and writing) and in giving knowledge (modeling and arguing). Focusing on teaching knowledge as information concentrates on the teacher's role—the teacher has information and imparts it. Rather, teaching knowledge as design focuses the problem of instruction on teaching, how to use a particular bit of knowledge, what it is good for. Perkins discusses the importance of teaching the integration of various subjects and their transfer from context to context.

298. ———. "Teaching Thinking Needn't Put Able Thinkers at Risk: A Response to John Baer." *Educational Leadership* 45 (April 1988): 76–77.

Perkins, in responding to Baer's concerns about teaching thinking to able thinkers, addresses the major issues. His response is calming, reminding the reader that students able to engage in one kind of thinking may be less able in another kind. Generally even able students can benefit from learning about new strategies and if they don't prove useful the students will drop them from their repertoire. (See entry 11.)

299. ———. "The Nature and Nurture of Creativity." *Dimensions of Thinking and Cognitive Instruction.* Edited by Beau Fly Jones and Lorna Idol. Hillsdale, New Jersey: Lawrence Erlbaum Associates, Pub., 1990, pp. 415–443.

Perkins associates novelty and appropriateness with creativity and the creative product. In examining how individuals develop these creative products, he refutes the notion that ideational fluency and ideational flexibility, both indicators of the power to "generate original appropriate ideas" (p. 418) are indicators of the potential for creativity. There is some evidence that the ability to engage in patterns of thinking may have an impact on creativity but even more evidence that valuing and enjoying originality and tolerating uncertainty are even more important. In addition, he explores the complex relationships between creative thinking, critical thinking, metacognition and content area knowledge. These are all interrelated, with creative and critical thinking seen both as opposites and as interacting and working together "in the richest and more far-reaching episodes of thinking" (p. 428).

It is certainly possible to teach creative thinking based on what we know about it; unfortunately we have little concrete data showing that it has been done. In addition, "conventional schooling does not serve the needs of creative thinking very well" (p. 435). We need more emphasis on the development of values for creative thinking and on patterns of thinking that will encourage it. Knowledge as Design is suggested as a program that can develop creative and critical thinking in various subject areas.

300. ———, Richard Allen, and James Hafner. "Difficulties in Everyday Reasoning." *Thinking: The Expanding Frontier.* Edited by William Maxwell. Philadelphia, Pennsylvania: The Franklin Press, 1983, pp. 177–189.

Perkins, Allen and Hafner examine both formal, traditional reasoning and everyday reasoning. In the former, the premises from which reasoning proceeds are "sacrosanct" (p. 179). Proper reasoning requires the ability to make inferences from those premises. In everyday, nonformal reasoning, the premises "must be generated by the reasoner" (p. 179), their adequacy examined, and conclusions reached. As the result of a study conducted with subjects from fourth grade to graduate level, the authors conclude that nonformal reasoning requires model-retrieving and model-building. They stress that a large knowledge repertoire and the ability to evoke particular knowledge when needed are requirements for reasoning as well as all cognitive endeavors. In addition, sources of information must be integrated in order to develop a critical approach to building a model of reasoning.

Perkins et al. contrast the critical skills of a skilled reasoner with a "make-sense" approach in which the thinker, in order to reduce cognitive load, determines that an argument appears to "make sense." A skilled reasoner, on the other hand, asks questions, refusing "to accept at face value what seems to be an adequate account" (p. 188). The "Why Not?" question examines premises and conclusions. The authors conclude that this process can be taught.

301. ———, and Gavriel Salomon. "Are Cognitive Skills Context-Bound?" *Educational Researcher* 18 (January-February 1989): 16–25.

Perkins and Salomon review the history of the controversy about whether thinking is generic or tied to the context in which it was taught. The authors lead us through a detailed historical review of this issue. The cognitive theories and empirical research underlying each position are reviewed and analyzed. The authors pose the question of whether a master chess player can transfer his abilities to politics or military theory. Is he a master because he has mastered the rules and content of chess or because he is an expert problem solver?

According to the authors, the pendulum has swung from supporting the notion that general thinking skills and heuristics, not content or context, were critical to supporting "the view that cognitive skills in the main were context bound" (p. 23). The authors conclude that there is a synthesis between the two: which "acknowledges the importance of domain specific adjustments. . .while maintaining the reality and power of general cognitive skills" (p. 23). Generic thinking is a flexible tool that adjusts to fit each domain in which it is used. Accumulation of a rich content knowledge base is a necessary component of the process. Generic cognitive skills do not take the place of domain specific knowledge; they differ from domain to domain.

The implications for education are clearly identified: the general and the content-specific must be woven together. The authors advocate a course separate from academics, and "the intimate intermingling of generality and context-specificity in instruction" (p. 25).

302. Peters, William H. "Developing Reasoning Skills Through an Integrated Curriculum Approach." Paper presented at the Annual Meeting of the National Council of Teachers of English Spring Conference. 1985. 9 pp. (ED 257 102)

The author suggests ways to use an integrated curriculum approach to study English in order to develop reasoning skills for secondary education, as opposed to the traditional methods, i.e., studying language, literature and composition independently. An English curriculum should include aspects of reasoning skills such as argument, deductive reasoning, persuasion, interaction of thought and language, symbolism in language, and the ability to draw inferences and to understand connotations in literature. The unit he suggests offers the opportunity to inquire, reflect, relate and generalize information in an integrated framework.

303. Phipps, Rita. "Critical Thinking and Community College Students." Paper presented at the Annual National Conference of the National Association for

Developmental Education, Philadelphia, Pennsylvania. 1984. 29 pp. (ED 253 264)

Phipps discusses principles of learning and suggests that a learner needs enough concrete knowledge about a given topic in order to be able to think on an abstract level about that topic. Students must be given the opportunity to learn low level, factual, concrete knowledge before they are presented with lectures, readings and other assignments which require abstract critical thinking. A lecture is included to be given to students at the beginning of a course which helps to make them aware of the processes by which they learn. They are given six specific steps to use when learning new materials. A sample lesson is included which demonstrates a sequence of teaching one topic or skill from concrete to abstract levels. Some examples of a student's progression in a developmental writing course are provided.

304. Pickering, Debra, and Karen Harvey. "Toward an Integrating Framework for Teaching Thinking." *Educational Leadership* 45 (April 1988): 46.

Pickering and Harvey report on a school district which includes thinking skills as part of the curriculum but allows each teacher to determine how this mandate will be implemented. The result is that a number of different programs are used: Philosophy for Children, Tactics for Thinking and Instrumental Enrichment. In order to make this approach work, the district has provided staff development and coaching within the classroom.

305. Picus, Larry, Thomas P. Sachse, and Ronald M. Smith. *Teaching Problem Solving: A Research Synthesis.* Portland, Oregon: Northwest Regional Educational Laboratory, June 1983. 35 pp. (ED 238 875)

This paper reviews the research on problem solving concerned with classroom applications and cites statements on the poor performance of students on such tests as the National Assessment of Educational Progress in the area of problem solving and evaluative thinking. Although there are a number of different definitions of problem solving and variations in the steps to take in solving problems, the authors conclude that Polya's steps were the most widely used and applicable. These include understanding the problem, devising a plan for solving it, carrying out the plan and evaluating the solution.

Problem solving can be taught using focused instruction and direct teaching of strategies. Growth in problem solving can be measured if we are clear about what skills are taught and measured. Instruction in problem solving should be integrated into the content areas, and all content areas are appropriate. The literature reviewed left unanswered the question of whether it was better to teach problem solving and then integrate it into the content areas or to have students solve content area problems and then determine the problem solving techniques which were used. The questions of what to teach and how to teach are addressed in some detail.

306. Pogrow, Stanley. "HOTS: A Computer-Based Approach." *Developing Minds: A Resource Book for Teaching Thinking.* Edited by Arthur L. Costa. Alexandria, Virginia: Association for Supervision and Curriculum Development, 1985, pp. 239–240.

The Higher Order Thinking Skills (HOTS) program is based on the premise that students do not need to master basic skills before engaging in higher order thinking. Computer software is used in conjunction with high quality classroom teaching.

307. ———. "Teaching Thinking to At-Risk Elementary Students." *Educational Leadership* 45 (April 1988): 79–85.

Pogrow discusses the conditions required for teaching thinking skills to at-risk students based on the successful experience of a large city school district. Instruction in thinking skills should be isolated in the beginning, later becoming integrated into the content areas. Emphasis should be placed on "understanding conversations" in which students explore ideas and issues in order to understand and generalize. Students are not allowed to "con" the teacher into accepting simple answers. They are required to participate and to think and are encouraged to by motivating activities. Because of the complexity of the teaching task, Pogrow recommends the use of specialists teaching isolated intensive courses in thinking, with other teachers concentrating on content.

308. ———. "Challenging At-Risk Students: Findings from the HOTS Program." *Phi Delta Kappan* 71 (January 1990): 389–397.

Pogrow describes, in some detail, the HOTS program in which Chapter 1 students engage in thinking activities, using four general thinking techniques: metacognition, inference from context, decontextualization and synthesis of information. The program is conducted outside of the regular classroom, with transfer made after a substantial period of time in analyzing literature and solving math word problems. He advocates the "35-minute principle of school improvement" in which schools spend 35 minutes a day with at-risk students teaching them how to understand. Numerous examples from sites throughout the country illustrate the discussion.

309. ———, and Barbara Buchanan. "Higher-Order Thinking for Compensatory Students." *Educational Leadership* 43 (September 1985): 40–43.

Using the computer Chapter 1 students in grade 3–6 receive systematic instruction in higher-order thinking skills to solve problems as the basis for developing basic skills. The emphasis is on students taking responsibility for their own learning, solving their own problems while at the same time helping other students.

310. Polson, Peter G., and Robin Jeffries. "Instruction in General Problem-Solving Skills: An Analysis of Four Approaches." *Thinking and Learning Skills.* Relating Instruction to Research. Volume 1. Edited by Judith W. Segal, Susan F. Chipman, and Robert Glaser. Hillsdale, New Jersey: Lawrence Erlbaum Associates, Pub., 1985, pp. 417–455.

Polson and Jeffries provide a theoretical background for problem solving, looking at it from an information processing approach, such as means-ends analysis, and from a divergent thinking perspective. The latter has had direct applications to educational settings through programs such as CoRT, Productive Thinking and lateral thinking. The authors compare these two approaches and look at specific programs. The review raises a series of unanswered questions including, for example, how to link instruction and specific content and tasks. They conclude that there is a need for further research and make specific suggestions here.

311. Pradl, Gordon M., and John S. Mayher. "Reinvigorating Learning Through Writing." *Educational Leadership* 42 (February 1985): 4–8.

Pradl and Mayher advocate using writing in content classes as a means of ensuring students are active participants in the learning process and as a way to connect new learning to students' experiences. Questions that can be addressed in a learning log and examples of learning logs are provided. Students are encouraged to react to learning experiences by identifying what they learned, what puzzled them, what they enjoyed, hated, accomplished and what their performance in class was like.

312. Prawat, Richard S. "Promoting Access to Knowledge, Strategy, and Disposition in Students: A Research Synthesis." *Review of Educational Research* 59 (Spring 1989): 1–41.

Prawat identifies the transfer of knowledge and skills as the ultimate goal of education. In order for this to happen students need to be able and willing to access and use their knowledge and strategies in new situations. The author reviews a considerable body of research in examining the knowledge base, strategies and dispositions needed to accomplish this and in proposing ways that teachers can foster the development of these areas. Prawat examines such topics as organization of information and ideas, the role of discussion in developing awareness, the representation of problems, the role of heuristics in thinking and the relationships between motivation and strategic thinking.

313. Presseisen, Barbara Z. *Thinking Skills: Meanings, Models, and Materials*, Research for Better Schools, Inc., Philadelphia, Pennsylvania, November 1984. 24pp. (ED 257 858)

The article presents several definitions of thinking skills which reflect different levels of thought. A three-level model includes cognition, metacognition and epistemic cognition. This model enables a more accurate and meaningful examination of the role of subject matter in thinking instruction, teachers' understanding of thinking skills training, and the valid assessment of students' achievement in thinking ability.

314.   ———. "Thinking Skills: Meanings, Models, Materials."
        Developing Minds: A Resource Book for Teaching
        Thinking. Edited by Arthur L. Costa. Alexandria, Virginia:
        Association for Supervision and Curriculum
        Development, 1985, pp. 43–48.

"Thinking is a cognitive process, a mental act by which knowledge is acquired. . . [it] is a complex and reflective endeavor, as well as a creative experience" (p. 43). Presseisen moves from this definition to an exploration of what is involved in thinking and how to encourage and develop it. Thinking requires active involvement and produces products such as thoughts, knowledge, higher processes and complex relationships. Bloom's taxonomy of thinking skills and Guilford's Structure of the Intellect are reviewed and compared. A brief review of Piagetian intellectual development is also included.

Her three-stage model of thinking skills is presented (basic, complex and metacognitive stages) with a discussion of the processes involved at each level of development. For example, basic processes are causation, transformations, relationships classification, qualification, while complex processes include problem solving, decision making, critical thinking and creative thinking.

Presseisen agrees with Beyer's suggestion "that an effective thinking skills curriculum will introduce only a limited number of skills at a particular grade level, will teach these across all appropriate content areas, and will vary the media and content of presentation" (p. 45). In the discussion of metacognitive stages, it is suggested that thinking skills should be taught directly, in context-free situations, at least initially, since learners can apply them more readily if they understand them better.

315.   ———. "Thinking and Curriculum: Critical Crossroads
        for Educational Change." *Thinking Skills Instruction:*
        Concepts and Techniques. Edited by Marcia Heiman and

Joshua Slomianko. Washington, D.C.: National Educational Association, 1987, pp. 31–39.

Presseisen examines some of the issues related to thinking skills instruction and concludes that all children can benefit from it and that intelligence is not "immutable." In determining what to include in a school curriculum, educators need to look at the subjects being taught, the student body and appropriate models of learning. If teachers are to integrate thinking instruction into their classrooms in the various content areas, they must receive quality staff development and become thinkers themselves.

316. ——. *Thinking Skills Throughout The Curriculum: A Conceptual Design.* Bloomington, Indiana: Pi Lambda Theta, Inc., 1987.

Presseisen reviews current literature on thinking skills and related instruction, presents a three-level model of thinking skills, and makes suggestions for instruction and curriculum development. She cites Sternberg and Whimbey as support for the notion that intelligence can be taught using those processes and skills used by good thinkers. Instruction must conform to the developmental sequences experienced by the student and must reflect the learning process. Here, the work of Campione and Armbruster is cited in a discussion of the dimensions of learning which include the characteristics of the learner, critical tasks, learning activities and the nature of materials.

Thinking skills have been organized into three levels. The first consists of those skills which are basic and those which are complex, including for example problem solving and critical thinking. In addition, she identifies a second level which is composed of metacognitive skills and a third level which is concerned with the relationship between content knowledge and cognition. Presseisen recommends that curriculum be developed sequentially with young students working on basic skills, older students working on complex skills and all students working on metacognitive skills. Various content areas are identified as appropriate for specific thinking skills, with the caveat that thinking skills must be integrated into the entire K-12 curriculum and not "added on." The author recommends direct instruction, following the Beyer model. Numerous suggestions and examples are provided.

317. ———. "Avoiding Battle at Curriculum Gulch: Teaching Thinking AND Content." *Educational Leadership* 45 (April 1988): 7–8.

Presseisen squarely addresses the issue of process vs. content in teaching thinking skills and comes up on the side of process and content. She holds that the critical question is not whether to focus on one or the other but rather on how to relate them "for the creation of meaningful learning" (p. 7). Content includes both the knowledge and the specific methodology of a particular discipline. These can become the tools of thinking, aiding thinking and understanding.

318. Pressley, Michael. "The Relevance of the Good Strategy User Model to the Teaching of Mathematics." *Educational Psychologist* 21 (Winter & Spring 1986): 139–161.

Pressley describes a good strategy user (GSU) in terms of strategy use, metacognition and knowledge. He suggests five principles: teach strategies, knowledge of when, where and how to use them, knowledge about factors that promote strategy functioning, and relevant nonstrategic knowledge as well as provide practice in good strategy coordination and use.

319. ———, J.G. Borkowski, and J.T. O'Sullivan. "Children's Metamemory and the Teaching of Memory Strategies."

Metacognition, Cognition, and Human Performance. Edited by D.L. Forrest-Pressley, G.E. MacKinnon, and T.G. Waller. New York: Academic Press, 1985, pp. 111–153.

The authors trained subjects in memory strategy use. They taught children to monitor the quality of their memory performance and regulate their own memory activities. They conclude that knowledge about a strategy itself, explicit instruction about how, when and where to use the strategy, and extended practice in a variety of settings positively affect strategy selection and use. According to the authors, subjects use "metacognitive acquisition procedures"; they test their use of a strategy and reflect on its effects, thereby acquiring specific knowledge about the strategy.

320. Quellmalz, Edys S. "Needed: Better Methods for Testing Higher-Order Thinking Skills." *Educational Leadership* 43 (October 1985): 29–35.

Testing procedures have the potential to direct instruction in the future. We have the theory and research now that is needed to develop tests of fundamental thinking skills that can apply to any content area. Because we are not now teaching these skills, the tests can serve as a way of focusing instruction. Quellmalz reviews higher order thinking skills from the perspective of philosophy, psychology and curriculum theory and presents a clear overview of the relationships between the three. Problem solving strategies from the field of psychology include and require critical thinking skills from the field of philosophy. From this framework she identifies cognitive processes (the ability to analyze, compare, infer/interpret, and evaluate) and metacognitive processes (the ability to plan, monitor, review/revise) that are applicable in the various content areas. Examples in the fields of science, social science and literature are provided.

Based on this theoretical framework, Quellmalz makes recommendations for designing tests of higher-order thinking skills. She suggests identifying important recurring issues in subject domains, requiring integration of skills, allowing for alternative solutions, including student explanation of reasoning, testing for generalization and transfer and assessing metacognition. She provides examples for each recommendation.

321.   ———, and Janita Hoskyn, "Making Difference in Arkansas: The Multicultural Reading and Thinking Project." *Educational Leadership* 45 (April 1988): 52–55.

A program designed to develop critical thinking abilities and cultural awareness has been developed by the teachers in grades 4, 5, and 6 in seven school districts. Four categories of reasoning skills have been identified that can be used in content areas and in real life. These include analysis, comparison, inference/interpretation and evaluation. These form the basis for inquiry, problem solving and critical thinking. Generic lessons and questions have been developed using direct instruction in thinking skills and strategies.

322.   Quinby, Nelson. "On Testing and Teaching Intelligence: A Conversation with Robert Sternberg." *Educational Leadership* 43 (October 1985): 50–53.

In this board ranging discussion, Strenberg examines instruction and assessment from the perspective of his triarchic model of intelligence. For example, students need to apply thinking skills in social, practical situations. The best way to insure this will happen is to provide a separate course with direct instruction in thinking skills and have all teachers include thinking skills applications in their content courses. He cautions that we must be careful not to neglect creative thinking while we emphasize critical thinking.

323. Rankin, Stuart C. "Evaluating Efforts to Teach Thinking." *Developing Minds: A Resource Book for Teaching Thinking.* Edited by Arthur L. Costa. Alexandria, Virginia: Association for Supervision and Curriculum Development, 1985, pp. 272–275.

Rankin outlines, in some detail, the steps to be taken in designing the evaluation, collecting data and analyzing the results for both the formative and summative evaluation of thinking skills programs. He provides a useful list of both quantitative and qualitative indicators of growth in thinking.

324. Raphael, Taffy E. "Teaching Question Answer Relationships, Revisited. " *The Reading Teacher* 39 (February 1986): 516–522.

Raphael reviews the original QAR program, with its emphasis on finding answers to questions about text from three sources, text explicit (right there), text implicit (think and search) and script implicit (on your own). She elaborates on modifications and extensions of the program, including simplifying it for younger children and adding another category for older children (author and you), and using the approach as a basis for comprehension instruction.

325. Raths, Louis E., Selma Wassermann, Arthur Jonas, and Arnold Rothstein. *Teaching for Thinking: Theory, Strategies, & Activities for the Classroom.* New York: Teachers College Press, 1986.

This text identifies and describes fifteen thinking operations and provides examples for elementary and secondary school students. In addition, the authors address issues related to the role of the teacher and provide numerous examples and lists.

326. Reahm, Douglas E. "Developing Thinking Skills in Music Rehearsal Class." *Thinking Skills Instruction: Concepts*

and Techniques. Edited by Marcia Heiman and Joshua Slomianko. Washington, D.C.: National Education Association, 1987, pp. 236–240.

Reahm suggests that a critical task for music students is that of making decisions regarding the performance of the music written by a composer. In fact, it is the decisions about what is not written on the paper that make a difference in the performance. The role of the teacher is not that of conductor but rather that of educator/conductor, exploring with students the possible decisions and modeling the processes involved.

327. Reder, Lynn, and John A. Anderson. "A Comparison of Texts and Their Summaries: Memorial Consequences." *Journal of Verbal Learning and Verbal Behavior* 19 (1980): 121–134.

Using college textbooks, the authors investigated whether it was more effective to study chapters in a text than a summary of the chapters. They found that studying just the summary helped students remember the main points of a chapter better than the chapter itself.

328. Rembert, Ron B. "Philosophy for Children Exercises and a Social Studies Text." *Thinking: The Journal of Philosophy for Children* 5 (1983): 14–18.

Rembert illustrates how Philosophy for Children can be adapted to address issues raised in a content textbook and can be used as the basis for the creation of thinking activities to supplement the text. Specific examples are included.

329. Resnick, Lauren B. *Education and Learning To Think.* Washington, D.C.: National Academy Press, 1987.

Resnick traces the history of teaching higher-order thinking skills and concludes that we have always done this, but now we are concerned with providing instruction for all students not just the elite. The term "higher order" may be misleading because the thinking skills included should be part of all instruction, not saved until some basic skills have been learned. She examines reading and mathematics as higher order processes and concludes that they both involve constructing meaning, monitoring understanding and asking questions. The question of general thinking skills that can be transferred from one domain to another is examined. Research is not conclusive on how and under what conditions these general skills can be transferred.

A wide variety of programs are presented and examined. One group includes programs which teach problem solving in the disciplines, such as Guided Design. There has been relatively little consistent evaluation done on these programs, so the results while encouraging are not convincing. General problem solving has been taught in programs such as CoRT and Productive Thinking. While there is some evidence that children learn the skills taught, there is little evidence for the wider effects on school learning in general and problem solving in real life. Reading and study strategies, patterned after those seen in strong readers and good students, have been widely taught and studied.

It has been difficult to evaluate the component strategies over a long period of time. Self-monitoring strategies, particularly "reciprocal teaching," have been taught and evaluated. The results for reciprocal teaching have been extremely encouraging for both retention and transfer of strategies. While there have been promising steps taken in terms of question asking and summarizing, we still do not know exactly what the "essential components" are of self-monitoring skills and strategies. Programs designed to improve general intelligence such as the Analytical Reasoning Program of Whimbey and Lochhead, Instrumental Enrichment, and the Venezuela Project Intelligence Course have provided little evidence that performance in school tasks or real life improves. The last category, programs designed to improve informal logic and critical thinking, is exemplified by Philosophy for Children. This program has been evaluated and "can produce rather general gains on tests, including improvement on reading comprehension and IQ scores" (p. 32).

Resnick concludes with a sense of "cautious optimism" (p. 35). She advocates linking instruction in cognitive skills to school disciplines, particularly concentrating on those disciplines such as reading, writing and mathematics which enable thinking in other areas. Social settings for instruction allow for modeling, thinking aloud, scaffolding, motivating, and teaching dispositions or habits of thinking.

330. ———, and Wendy W. Ford. *The Psychology of Mathematics for Instruction.* Hillsdale, New Jersey: Lawrence Erlbaum Associates, Pub., 1981.

Resnick and Ford examine three definitions of mathematics: computational, conceptual and problem solving and reasoning. They are all placed within a historical context and are reviewed from the dual perspective of psychology and mathematics. In developing mathematical abilities in problem solving and thinking, both computational skills and conceptual knowledge are needed as part of the student's prior knowledge. In addition, the student needs an understanding of the context of the problem and a repertoire of problem solving strategies.

The authors review the influence of psychological theorists, examine the role of insight and discovery learning and suggest instructional procedures. Resnick and Ford compare and contrast rote learning and meaningful learning, concluding that "by viewing mathematics as thinking, one is led to focus on problem solving and discovery not just as a means of teaching mathematical concepts but as a major goal of mathematics education" (p. 7). Unfortunately, they find that the definition of mathematics "as a body of computational rules and procedures. . .pervades most of mathematics instruction in our elementary schools. . .despite efforts to reform the mathematics curriculum in the 1960s" (p. 9).

331. Riley, Mary S., James G. Greeno, and Joan I. Heller. "Development of Children's Problem-Solving Ability in Arithmetic." *The Development of Mathematical Thinking*. Edited by Herbert Ginsberg. New York: Academic Press, 1983.

This chapter looks at the factors that enable older children to perform better in arithmetic word problems than younger ones. Riley et al. suggest that this might be due to an increase in the complexity of conceptual knowledge about the problem domain or the sophistication of the problem solving procedures. They cite studies which indicate that development in problem solving ability is related to an increase in the complexity of conceptual knowledge required to understand the situations described in the problems. For example, problems with the same arithmetic structure but different conceptual structures, such problems having different semantics but requiring the same operation for solution, differ substantially in their difficulty for students.

The authors propose a theory of problem understanding and solution finding in which they distinguish between three main kinds of knowledge during problem solving. The first is a problem schema for understanding various semantic relations. For example, language schemas organize given information and expand the representation to include components not explicitly stated. The second kind of knowledge required for problem solving is an action schema for representing knowledge about actions involved in problem solutions. The third kind of knowledge is strategic knowledge for planning solutions to problems. According to their model, to solve a word problem, knowledge of problem schemas enables representation of the particular problem situation being described. Planning procedures use action schemas to generate a solution to the problem. Conceptual knowledge influences which actions are selected. The solver's schemas are used to monitor the effects of selected actions on a problem situation.

Thus, in their analysis, the main factor in children's development of problem solving ability is the acquisition of schemas for understanding the problem in a way that relates to already available action schemas.

332.   Rinehart, Steven D., Steven A. Stahl, and Lawrence G. Erikson. "Some Effects of Summarization Training on Reading." *Reading Research Quarterly* 21 (Fall 1986): 422–438.

The authors trained sixth grade students to summarize text through direct explicit instruction and through training in self-control, i.e., monitoring, checking and evaluating their use of the summarization procedures. Classroom teachers provided the instruction, after a brief orientation. Results indicated that the training program improved both reading and studying behaviors of these students. A brief description of the training program is provided.

333.   Roeber, Ed, and Peggy Dutcher. "Michigan's Innovative Assessment of Reading." *Educational Leadership* 46 (April 1989): 64–69.

Roeber and Dutcher describe the rationale for and the process of developing a reading test which reflects current thinking on learning and the assessment of learning and thinking. The test includes items for Constructing Meaning, Knowledge about Reading, Attitudes and Self-Perceptions and Topic Familiarity. Sample items are included.

334. Roller, Cathy M. "Using Passage Structure as an Aid to Summarizing Social Studies Texts." *The Social Studies* 75 (November/December 1984): 268–272.

Roller reports on a study conducted with junior high school students in which they read a selection from an expository text, summarized it, answered questions and paraphrased the selection. The "most striking feature of the summaries is, that on the whole, they are so poor" (p. 270). The author concludes that readers fail to use the text structure as an aid in identifying important elements of the text. She provides instructional suggestions for overcoming this problem.

335. Roth, Joyce. "Literature as a Springboard to Critical Thinking." In "Curriculum Connection: Literature." Virginia Kalb (Column Ed.). *School Library Media Quarterly* 17 (Spring 1989): 143–144.

The author suggests that good literature is often based on a situation or problem which can lead to development of critical thinking skills, i.e., planning, decision making, reflecting and evaluating. A reader can become involved in a range of thinking activities. Roth lists a range of literary selections from kindergarten through high school. She suggests ways in which they might be used to pose problems and promote critical and creative thinking.

336. Rubin, Ronald Lee. "Developing Students' Thinking Skills Through Multiple Perspectives." *Thinking Skills Instruction: Concepts and Techniques.* Edited by Marcia Heiman and Joshua Slomianko. Washington, D.C.: National Education Association, 1987, pp. 230–235.

Rubin presents a group of learning activities using divergent thinking which are designed to develop "an appreciation and understanding of multiple perspectives" (p. 230). The activities are appropriate for grades six through twelve but might be adapted for younger students. They all require active involvement on the part of the students in developing criteria, making choices and supporting decisions. In the activities, students must examine the situation presented from a variety of perspectives.

337.   Ruggiero, Vincent Ryan. *Teaching Thinking Across The Curriculum.* New York: Harper & Row, 1988.

Ruggiero proposes a holistic model for teaching thinking which includes both creative and critical thinking, which engages in both problem solving and issues analysis and is taught within the various curriculum areas. He presents a detailed discussion and comparison of creative and critical thinking and a problem solving/issue analysis heuristic as well as many specific suggestions for teacher and student. Finally, many specific, helpful ideas about developing new materials and adapting current resources are included.

338.   Rumelhart, David E., and Donald A. Norman. "Analogical Processes in Learning." *Cognitive Skills and Their Acquisition.* Edited by John R. Anderson. Hillsdale, New Jersey: Lawrence Erlbaum Associates, Pub., 1981, pp. 335–359.

The authors of this chapter discuss the importance of making analogies in instruction. They describe the process a learner goes through in forming a new schema by making an analogy to an old schema. Important instructional implications include providing the student with new information that is rooted in familiar information and has a minimal number of differences from old to new schema.

339.   Sadler, William A., Jr., "Holistic Thinking Skills Instruction: An Interdisciplinary Approach to Improving Intellectual Performance." *Thinking Skills Instruction: Concepts and Techniques.* Edited by Marcia Heiman and

Joshua Slomianko. Washington, D.C.: National Education Association, 1987, pp. 183–188.

Sadler describes a program in teaching cognitive skills to middle and senior high school as well as college students. The aim is to improve analytic thinking and communication skills. This is accomplished through precise definition of the goals of the program. Students work on their own, asking questions and verbalizing their thinking processes. Teachers serve as coaches while monitoring student mastery of the skills needed to move to more advanced levels. Faculty involvement, training and commitment are essential ingredients in this program.

340. ──────, and Arthur Whimbey. "A Holistic Approach to Improving Thinking Skills." *Phi Delta Kappan* 67 (November 1985): 199–203.

Sadler and Whimbey cite the increased interest in teaching thinking skills in schools worldwide. They suggest that we should continue and in fact expand our efforts in this direction using a holistic approach rather than an approach stressing instruction in and use of discrete skills. Any instruction in thinking should include active learning, the articulation of thinking, intuitive understanding, developmental sequences, motivation and a positive social climate. Examples are provided from a high school program and a college program illustrating these principles.

341. Sanders, Arlette. "Learning Logs: A Communication Strategy for All Subject Areas." *Educational Leadership* 42 (February 1985): 7.

Sanders provides some practical suggestions for helping students "learn *from* writing rather than writing what they have learned" (p. 7). Suggestions include a set of generic questions students can use to ponder learning events and experiences, activities for younger children, questions for older students to guide exploration of their feelings about their own learning, and possible dialogues about critical points in lessons.

342. Savell, Joel M., Paul T. Twohig, and Douglas L. Rachford. "Empirical Status of Feuerstein's 'Instrumental Enrichment' (FIE) Technique as a Method of Teaching Thinking Skills." *Review of Educational Research* 56 (Winter 1986): 381–409.

The authors cite the growing interest in teaching thinking skills, the development of techniques and programs to accomplish this, and the paucity of research documenting the effectiveness of these interventions. There have, however, been a number of studies of the effectiveness of Instrumental Enrichment. Savell, Twohig and Rachford describe the technique, the theory behind it, the conditions needed for its implementation and review, in some detail, the relevant studies from Israel, Venezuela, Canada and the United States. Many of the studies were difficult to interpret and did not yield clear effects. However, there were indications that there were positive effects, particularly in nonverbal areas, for elementary and secondary students, both normal and culturally or educationally disadvantaged and in hearing-impaired groups. Suggestions are made for further research.

343. Schlichter, Carol L. "Talents Unlimited: An Inservice Educational Model for Teaching Thinking Skills." *Gifted Child Quarterly* 30 (Summer 1986): 119–123.

Schlichter describes an inservice program designed to enable teachers to develop students' creative and critical thinking skills. The staff development program is based on components identified by Joyce and Showers which include presentation of theory, modeling or demonstration, practice, feedback, and coaching for transfer to the classroom. Each component is described and illustrated.

344. ———, and James A. Cross. "Odyssey of the Mind: Creative Thinking in the Classroom. *Early Years: K–8* 16 (April 1986): 35–39.

Schlichter and Cross describe an international program for the development of creative thinking in solving problems. Generally, classes or schools develop teams to work on the problems which are provided by Odyssey of the Mind Association. The solutions are frequently entered into a competition. The authors provide an overview of sample activities and a list of benefits to students and teachers. Emphasis is placed on involving the community in the solutions.

345. ———, Deborah Hobbs, and W. Donald Crump. "Extending Talents Unlimited to Secondary Schools." *Educational Leadership* 45 (April 1988): 36–40.

Schlichter, Hobbs and Crump describe and illustrate the five talent areas of productive thinking, decision making, planning, forecasting and communication. The emphasis in instruction and practice is on integration into the content areas. Not only will students improve in thinking abilities but also in their academic achievement.

346. Schrag, Francis. *Thinking In School and Society.* New York: Routledge, Chapman and Hall, Inc., 1988.

Schrag discusses the implications of theories of cognitive psychology on instruction. Current views of cognitive development lead us to conclude that even very young children are capable of complex learning and thinking and, therefore, active problem solving should be encouraged in schools. He discusses settings which promote thoughtfulness and suggests that the school environment, with its need for order and control, may not be the best setting for encouraging thinking. The physical environment, the focus on grades, which tends to preclude open ended tasks, and the lack of opportunity and time to think do little to encourage thoughtfulness.

Schrag sees the school as a reflection of society and its values and discusses society in terms of its economy, its polity, television and its schools. He suggests that society rarely recognizes those who think, that the economy does not demand or provide jobs which elicit or reward thoughtfulness. While capitalism rewards exploration of opportunity and problem solving with financial gain, the majority of workers do little high level thinking on their jobs.

The author suggests that rather than think about issues and information, citizens allow the media to make their decisions and that television, by its economic structure, is prevented from promoting thoughtfulness. Schrag concludes by suggesting that, rather than perpetuating a repressive educational system which instills subordination, we need to develop educational systems which require only the minimum of adherence to institutional norms, to encourage, rather than suppress future innovators.

347. Segal, Judith W. "Introduction to Volume 1: Approaches to Instruction." *Thinking and Learning Skills.* Relating Instruction to Research. Volume 1. Edited by Judith W. Segal, Susan F. Chipman, and Robert Glaser. Hillsdale, New Jersey: Lawrence Erlbaum Associates, Pub., 1985, pp. 43–82.

Segal describes and compares a wide variety of programs and approaches toward teaching thinking skills. The programs discussed vary in the skills included and the instructional methods suggested. Segal provides a useful overview of both this volume and of critical issues in thinking instruction and programs.

348. Seiger-Ehrenberg, Sydelle. "BASICS." *Developing Minds: A Resource Book for Teaching Thinking*. Edited by Arthur L. Costa. Alexandria, Virginia: Association for Supervision and Curriculum Development, 1985, pp. 241–243.

BASICS is an approach to developing students' abilities to engage in appropriate thinking for tasks in the school curriculum. Thinking cannot be separated from content. Therefore, the program includes two models: a curriculum model in which thinking strategies are included in content areas, and a staff development model in which teachers are trained to include these strategies. Objectives are developed to include thinking strategies as part of the overall curriculum.

349. ———."Educational Outcomes for a K-12 Curriculum." *Developing Minds: A Resource Book for Teaching Thinking*. Edited by Arthur L. Costa. Alexander, Virginia: Association for Supervision and Curriculum Development, 1985, pp. 7–10.

Seiger-Ehrenberg describes the Institute for Curriculum and Instruction (ICI) Curriculum model, which categorizes tasks into those which are expected of every member of society and those which are necessary to establish personal goals. She advocates the use of ICI model outcomes to select specific content and instructional methods. The ultimate goal for students, according to the model, is to develop certain behavioral characteristics, accomplished by focusing the curriculum around them.

350. Shenkman, Harriet. "A Description and Field Test of a Decision-Making Framework for Reading and Studying." *Reading Improvement* 23 (Spring 1986): 72–77.

The approach described by Shenkman links comprehension-fostering, comprehension-monitoring and executive-monitoring strategies with reading and studying in content areas. Students are provided with training and practice in LETME, a series of decision-making activities which relate to thinking strategies. Students Link the expository text to be studied to their prior knowledge and purpose for reading, Extract information and ideas, Transform by organizing and reorganizing using outlining, summarizing and mapping, Monitor comprehension and progress and Extend through critical thinking. In order to aid students in making decisions as they progress through the LETME Framework, a LETME study plan using a grid and a series of questions is utilized.

351. Siegler, Robert S. "Encoding and the Development of Problem Solving." *Thinking and Learning Skills.* Research and Open Questions. Volume 2. Edited by Susan F. Chipman, Judith W. Segal, and Robert Glaser. Hillsdale, New Jersey: Lawrence Erlbaum Association, Pub., 1985, pp. 161–185.

Siegler describes a series of experiments conducted to examine the role and development of encoding in children and adolescents. He concludes that "inadequate encoding is frequently associated with difficulty in solving problems" (p. 182). Inadequate encoding may involve including inappropriate dimensions of the problem, providing inappropriate detail or representing the problem inappropriately.

352. ———. "Strategy Diversity and Cognitive Assessment." *Educational Researcher* 18 (December 1989): 15–20.

Siegler is concerned with the assessment of strategy use in thinking and reasoning. Even young children can use a variety of strategies in solving complex problems. Current assessment strategies fall to identify the use of strategies in thinking at all levels. Siegler reviews a variety of possible methods, including verbal self-reporting and video-taping of sessions. The benefits of this approach to assessment are illustrated from the author's research on "good students," "not-so-good students" and "perfectionists."

353. Sigel, Irving E. "A Constructivist Perspective for Teaching Thinking." *Educational Leadership* 42 (November 1984): 18–21.

Sigel places the responsibility for teaching thinking squarely on the schools and the responsibility for becoming a more effective thinker squarely on the learner. Citing the dissatisfaction with children's thinking skills, declining test scores and a current emphasis on cognitive growth, he stresses the need to develop challenging, effective programs designed to encourage thinking competency in children. The author provides guidelines for the development of these programs based on a consideration of developmental stages of cognitive growth, the processes that occur at all stages and the personal, social and cultural influences on thinking. Specific examples and suggestions are made, particularly for teaching strategies.

354. ———, and Ruth A. Saunders. "On Becoming a Thinker: An Educational Preschool Program." *Early Child Development and Care* 12 (NO. 1, 1983): 39–65.

Sigel and Saunders preface a discussion of the principles underlying preschool programs and of relevant instructional strategies with an overview of five curriculum areas requiring decisions: what to teach, when to teach it, how to develop teaching strategies, who to involve, and where to place the program. Over-riding all of these and applicable to each is the question of why. Sigel and Saunders base their instructional suggestions firmly on a developmental, Piagetian view of the child and on a view of thinking as including increasing representational competence in using mental symbols and pictures or words to stand for objects and experience. The child is encouraged and enabled by the teacher by questioning, presenting choices, observing, waiting and responding, while arranging the physical environment to allow for connections and integration.

355. Silver, Edward A., and Sandra P. Marshall. "Mathematical and Scientific Problem Solving: Findings, Issues, and Instructional Implications. " *Dimensions of Thinking and Cognitive Instruction.* Edited by Beau Fly Jones and Lorna Idol. Hillsdale, New Jersey: Lawrence Erlbaum Associates, Pub. 1990, pp. 265–290.

Silver and Marshall examine critical areas of research on problem solving in mathematics and science. The first area, content knowledge, is a given. "It hardly needs to be said that an important component of successful problem solving is an adequate store of domain-relevant knowledge" (p. 266). Knowledge is broadly defined to include both formal and informal as well as explicit and implicit knowledge. It is important to address students' misconceptions and organization of knowledge as well as what they know and understand appropriately. In the area of problem solving processes, "problem representations are viewed as central" (p. 274), and heuristics have been found to be useful in both mathematics and science. In addition, in problem solving metacognitive processes seem important. Finally, students need repeated experiences over a period of time, experiences that occur in a setting where discussion and cooperative problem solving can take place.

356. Simon, Herbert A. "Problem Solving and Education: Issues in Teaching and Research." *Problem Solving and Education: Issues In Teaching and Research.* Edited by D.T. Tama and F. Relif. Hillsdale, New Jersey: Lawrence Erlbaum Associates, Pub., 1980, pp. 81–96.

Simon discusses issues in problem solving instruction as well as society's need to cope with constant and continuous change which demands thinkers who can solve new and different problems. He investigates the role of knowledge in problem solving and suggests that even though we may have the relevant knowledge useful to solve a problem in a given situation, this doesn't guarantee that that knowledge will be accessed and applied when needed. Failure to use knowledge may be the result of a lack of conditional knowledge, that is, understanding of the conditions under which certain knowledge should be used. Simon suggests that the ability to access appropriate knowledge when needed can be trained, but we need to teach the conditions under which the strategies that are being learned are to be applied.

357. Simon, Martin A. "The Teacher's Role in Increasing Student Understanding of Mathematics." *Educational Leadership* 43 (April 1986): 40–43.

Simon suggests two instructional strategies that address students' lack of understanding of mathematics. The first strategy, an exploration/discovery approach, requires that students actively discover for themselves math concepts, linking them to their prior knowledge. The second strategy, pair and group problem solving, enables the discovery process to proceed effectively, exposes students to a variety of thinking approaches and develops metacognitive skills. The teacher's role is critical and involves organizing content and concepts as well as using questions to develop students' awareness of their own thought processes.

358. Singer, Harry, and Dan Donlan. "Active Comprehension: Problem-solving Schema With Question Generation for Comprehension of Complex Short Stories." *Reading Research Quarterly* 2 (1982): 166–185.

The authors taught eleventh grade students to transform a set of general questions based on story structure components, using a problem solving framework, into questions specific to the narrative being read. Story components included character, goal, obstacle, outcome and theme. As a result of their training, students' comprehension was significantly improved.

359. Slavin, Robert E. "Research on Cooperative Learning: Consensus and Controversy." *Educational Leadership* 47 (December 1989/January 1990): 52–54.

Slavin identifies some areas, such as improvement in academic achievement, higher order thinking, and intergroup relations, in which there is consensus about the effects of cooperative learning. He also suggests areas where there is not consensus, such as why and how cooperative learning works. Here, according to Slavin, we need more research. (See also 177.)

360. Slife, Brent D., Jane Weiss, and Thomas Bell. "Separability of Metacognition and Cognition: Problem Solving in Learning Disabled and Regular Students." *Journal of Educational Psychology* 77 (1985): 437–445.

The authors suggest that studies in metacognition have been confused in the literature with cognition itself and attempt to separate the two by measuring metacognitive factors in learning disabled and normal mathematics problem solving, apart from cognitive processes. Their results indicated that the two are distinct, independent constructs. Normals were more aware of their cognitive (problem solving) skills than LDs and were better able to monitor and regulate their problem solving performance.

361. Snow, Richard E. "Toward Assessment of Cognitive and Conative Structures in Learning." *Educational Researcher* 18 (December 1989): 8–14.

Snow provides an indepth review of cognitive knowledge, skills and strategy and conative strategy, regulation and motivation as the basis for examining assessment issues and models. Assessment needs to relate to instruction and be diagnostic for learning. He provides an overview of a number of approaches, including teacher-computer collaboration and a teach-back procedure in which the student teaches a novice.

362. Spiegel, Dixie Lee. "Critical Reading Materials: A Review of Three Criteria." *The Reading Teacher* 43 (February 1990): 410–412.

The three criteria Spiegel advocates for judging materials designed to promote critical reading and thinking include content validity, transfer potential and amount of reinforcement. In reviewing materials, she considers the need to teach thinking strategies, the importance of metacognitive awareness, the relevance of group discussion and cooperative learning and the necessity of providing multiple, diverse opportunities for transfer.

363. Staab, Claire. "What Happened to the Sixth Graders: Are Elementary Students Losing Their Need to Forecast and to Reason?" *Reading Psychology* 7 (1986): 289–296.

Staab compared the use of oral language to forecast and to reason by kindergarteners, third graders and sixth graders. She found that sixth graders were "markedly below" (p. 292) the other two groups. She suggests that this finding is contradictory to what a developmental view of thinking would indicate. The performance of children should increase, not decrease, as they go through school. One possible explanation is that schooling inhibits the development of these thinking skills. Insufficient time is allowed in the school day for group discussion which will foster these skills. The emphasis is on finishing workbooks and taking tests, not on developing creative thinking and reasoning abilities. Staab places the responsibility for change on the school administration. The support and rewards for redirecting schools must begin there.

364. Staton, Jana. *Thinking Together: Language interaction In Children's Reasoning. The Talking and Writing Series, K-12: Successful Classroom Practices.* Washington, D.C.: Dingle Associates, Inc. 1983. 51 pp. (ED 233 379).

Staton suggests that "direct student-teacher language interaction is a primary—and powerful—force for learning" (p. 25). It is through this process of language interaction that students become independent, active thinkers. During language interaction, the teacher models the thinking process, keeps the discussion focused, and builds an interactional scaffold which allows the student to assume the teacher's strategies. The author provides examples of dialogue between students and teachers and reviews current research supporting these notions. Ideas are included for analyzing the present level and kinds of interactions in a classroom and for restructuring where needed. How to organize and respond to "dialogue journals" between student and teacher is explained in some detail.

365. Steen, Lynn Arthur. "Teaching Mathematics for Tomorrow's World." *Educational Leadership* 47 (September 1989): 18–22.

Steen explores the demands in the field of mathematics that are being and will be made on students. She concludes that the need to value math, reason mathematically, communicate mathematics, solve problems and develop confidence will necessitate curricular and instructional changes. Students will learn to solve problems and reason in math holistically, emphasizing process as well as product.

366. Sternberg, Robert J. "Intelligence as Thinking and Learning Skills." *Educational Leadership* 39 (October 1981): 18-20.

Sternberg holds that "intelligence consists of a set of developed thinking and learning skills used in academic and everyday problem solving" (p. 18) and that these skills "potentially at least, can be separately diagnosed and taught" (p. 20). He outlines the steps involved in problem solving including: problem identification, process selection, representation selection, strategy selection, processing allocation, solution monitoring, sensitively to feedback, translation of feedback into an action plan and implementation of the plan. At the present time we do not have adequate means of measuring performance in these skills. It is possible to teach them effectively but the author cites the need for more research if we are to bring this "from the realm of hypothesis to the realm of practical reality" (p. 20).

367. ———. "Criteria for Intellectual Skills Training. *Educational Researcher* 12 (February 1983): 6–12, 26.

Sternberg stresses the need for criteria or prerequisites for intellectual skills training programs in order to plan effectively and to evaluate the programs once established. Not only do we need to be sure they are "good," we must also be sure they are not doing "harm." The prerequisites he suggests are spelled out in some detail and include such items as a clear theoretical base, social relevance to the individual, training in both executive and nonexecutive information processing, responsiveness to motivational and intellectual needs, awareness of individual differences, tie-in to real life behavior, empirical evaluation and, finally, modest claims for program outcomes.

368.   ———. "Teaching Critical Thinking, Part 1: Are We Making Mistakes?" *Phi Delta Kappan* 67 (November 1985): 194–198.

Sternberg links critical thinking and problem solving, suggesting that in teaching critical thinking "we are preparing students to deal with problems that are in many respects unlike those that they will face as adults" (p. 194). He identifies ten characteristics of everyday problems, ranging from identifying the existence of a problem and defining it to exploring solutions and their consequences. Everyday problems are often characterized by a lack of structure and a messiness that defies a single or best solution. These problems pervade our lives and frequently reoccur in the same or somewhat different form. He reviews current school efforts at teaching critical thinking, showing that there is a "lack of correspondence between what is required for critical thinking in adulthood and what is being taught in school programs intended to develop critical thinking" (p. 194).

369.   ———. "Teaching Critical Thinking, Part 2: Possible Solutions." *Phi Delta Kappan* 67 (December 1985): 277–280.

Sternberg relates the "critical mistakes" identified in critical thinking courses to a program he developed which includes instruction in metacomponents, performance components and knowledge components in solving academic, novel and everyday problems using critical thinking skills. He stresses that "programs need to sample a variety of contents domains and a variety of thinking skills — and to sample them in ways that are true to the way problems appear in our everyday lives" (p. 278).

370. ——. "Inside Intelligence." *American Scientist* 74 (March-April 1986): 137–143.

Sternberg reviews a body of research relating to intelligence and to the ability of individuals to solve problems effectively. He examines cognitive processes related to performance, the use people make of what they know. He concludes that these processes of encoding, inferencing, mapping, application and response are basic to intelligent functioning. The cognitive processes of selective encoding, selective combination, and selective comparison are related to learning, how people acquire the information they have. Finally, the metacognitive processes of planning, monitoring and evaluating direct the cognitive processes and are redirected by them. Developmental differences are suggested and elaborated.

371. ——. "Questions and Answers about the Nature and Teaching of Thinking Skills." *Teaching Thinking Skills: Theory and Practice.* Edited by Joan Boykoff Baron and Robert J. Sternberg. New York: W.H. Freeman, 1986, pp. 251–259.

Sternberg integrates 12 essays on teaching thinking skills which comprise this book by asking and answering questions generated from issues raised in these essays. He divides thinking skills into three kinds: executive processes—those used to plan, monitor and evaluate one's thinking, performance processes—those used to carry out the thinking, and learning processes—those used to learn how to think. He says that, in addition to having the right thought processes, to be a good thinker one must also know how to combine those processes into workable problem solving strategies, know how to form adequate mental representations of information, possess a strong knowledge base and be motivated to use thinking skills.

Sternberg advocates teaching thinking skills as a separate course and, at the same time, infusing and reinforcing them throughout the entire curriculum. He also advocates using a preexisting program only if the school system can afford it, if it fits in the school's schedule, if there are adequate time and funds for staff development and if the program can be tailored to fit the school's needs. Sternberg stresses the need for expert, carefully planned evaluations of thinking skills programs for which a school system may have spent a great deal of time and money. He also notes that there is no one perfect program; a program must be selected considering its suitability for students, teachers, time and cost factors. He suggests that a good thinking skills program should last at least one year and ideally continue throughout a student's schooling.

The author also stresses the importance of transfer and suggests several ways to maximize transfer: 1) include development of executive skills; 2) present thinking rules and principles in a variety of academic disciplines, in abstract and concrete and academic and practical contexts; 3) use multiple forms of media; and 4) individualize programs according to student need. Sternberg talks about the need to gain administrative support for thinking skills programs and suggests that their ultimate goals should be to have students who are better thinkers in general and in specific disciplines, who can capitalize on their strengths, remedy deficiencies and be aware of their potential.

372.   ———, and Joan B. Baron. "A Statewide Approach to Measuring Critical Thinking Skills," *Educational Leadership* 43 (October 1985): 40–43.

Sternberg and Baron assert that it is possible to relate widespread assessment instruments that can measure thinking skills to the "fairly elaborate theories of thinking processes" (p. 40). They describe the process and product of one such effort using the collaborative efforts of educators from the Connecticut State Department of Education and cognitive psychologists, which resulted in the Connecticut Statewide Mastery Test—Grade 4.

The test reflects more than one theory of thinking skills, resulting in a broad approach to assessment. Ennis' thinking skills, including the abilities to define and clarify, judge information, infer, solve problems, and draw reasonable conclusions, are measured directly through multiple choice items. His 13 dispositions of critical thinkers are not measured directly. However, the authors assert that it may be possible to measure them only incompletely through standardized tests.

The test also reflects Sternberg's triarchic theory of intelligence. The three basic kinds of mental processes, including metacomponents, performance components and knowledge-acquisition components, have been considered in developing the test framework and items. In addition, the developers also considered the other two components of the triarchic model, the degree of familiarity with the tasks and situations in which the components are applied and the real world contexts in which they are used. Finally, the authors caution against testing without follow up intervention. Examples of test items are included.

373. ———, and Kastoor Bhana. "Synthesis of Research on the Effectiveness of Intellectual Skills Programs: Snake-Oil Remedies or Miracle Cures?" *Educational Leadership* 44 (October 1986): 60–67.

Sternberg and Bhana present a critical review of studies documenting the effectiveness of five thinking skills programs: Instrumental Enrichment, Philosophy for Children, SOI, Problem Solving and Comprehension: A Short Course in Analytical Reasoning, and Odyssey. They express concern over the lack of outside, objective evaluations, utilizing adequate control groups and published in refereed journals. The five programs are described and some results discussed. Instrumental Enrichment seems most appropriate for average or below average junior high school students, with gains most likely in abstract reasoning and spatial abilities. Philosophy for Children seems to produce gains in verbal tests of critical thinking, with transfer possible to real life. The studies for SOI are "poorly reported and appear to have many design problems" (p. 65). The authors express doubt about the transfer of skills to real life. Problem Solving and Comprehension is suitable for high school and college students, but has little basis in psychological theory, and is not supported by a broad range of empirical studies. Odyssey, while documented by only one major study, appears to be a "promising program for future development and evaluation" (p. 67).

374.   ———, and Marie Martin. "When Teaching Thinking Does Not Work, What Goes Wrong?" *Teachers College Record* 89 (Summer 1988): 555–578.

The authors offer a comprehensive explanation of potential problems which may cause failure in the attempt to teach thinking skills. They present four models of what may go wrong, from the teacher, the materials and the student's perspective. In the first model, the teaching method may be to blame. A combination of teaching styles, which mainly focuses on interaction, questioning and dialogue, appears to be most effective. The match between the teacher's style and the intellectual preference of the student must also be considered.

In the second model, thinking skills instruction is weakened by the way the materials presented. They may be isolated from, rather than integrated with, the curriculum, the rest of the text, and even from other thinking skills.

Model three blames the failure on inadequate instruction and suggests instruction which includes direct instruction in initial presentation as well as intra-, intergroup and individual problem solving. Model four suggests that students may not use the thinking skills they have learned because they don't know how to use them; their thinking skills knowledge is "inert." The problem here, according to the authors, is that the problems we are using to teach are not well connected to the real world; thus transfer to real world problems is not easy.

375. Sternglass, Marilyn. "How Commitment to a Task Stimulates Critical Thinking Processes." Paper presented at the Annual Meeting of the Conference on College Composition and Communication. New York, N.Y., 1984. 12 pp. (ED 208 387)

Sternglass traces the development of the writing ability of a college freshman from a very concrete level of writing, full of direct quotations in which the student showed little personal interaction, to a somewhat more abstract style, with much paraphrasing, and, finally to a more abstract level of writing in which the student interacted deeply and personally with the material, using her own words, giving original examples. The author points out the fact that as the student's writing became more abstract and demonstrated a higher cognitive level of thinking, the more personally meaningful it became to her and that it is important to use many different kinds of samples to accurately evaluate a student's writing ability.

376. Stonewater, Jerry K. "Strategies for Problem Solving." *New Directions for Teaching and Learning: Fostering Critical Thinking*. Edited by Robert E. Young. San Francisco: Jossey-Bass Inc., Pub., No. 3, 1980, pp. 33–57.

Stonewater views problem solving as an "important aspect of critical thinking" (p. 34). He examines four strategies for teaching problem solving, chooses the most effective aspects of each and suggests five components for successful problem solving instruction on the college level.

He reviews the Guided Design strategy, ADAPT, Rubinstein's Patterns of Problem Solving and remedial and developmental education. From this discussion, he concludes that problem solving instruction should be based on Piaget's developmental stages and require mastery of content or process as a result of self-paced learning. Instruction must reflect a systematic design that leads students through the process to improved performance, includes feedback to students on details as well as on major successes and, finally, uses group learning "because a group can bring more strategies to bear on the solution, remember more information, propose more alternative solutions, and verify solutions more readily" (p. 55).

377.   Strahan, David B. "Guided Thinking: A Strategy for Encouraging Excellence at the Middle Level." *Nassp Bulletin* 70 (February 1986): 75-80.

Strahan describes the process of guided thinking as an instructional strategy designed to overcome passive learning with its emphasis on seatwork. Guided thinking incorporates student discussion and involvement with the development of reasoning and thinking abilities. He recommends its use in content areas. Guided thinking includes "assessing thinking, analyzing curricular requirements, observing interactions, and extending thinking" (p. 77). These elements are described and ways of implementing the approach in the classroom are suggested. The author stresses the need for effective inservice education and for the principal to play a critical role in the entire process.

378.   Strong, Richard W., Harvey F. Silver, and Robert Hanson. "Integrating Teaching Strategies and Thinking Styles with the Elements of Effective Instruction." *Educational Leadership* 42 (May 1985): 9–15.

Strong, Silver and Hanson have identified five principal goals of education: mastery (of basic skills); understanding (concept formation and critical thinking); synthesis (the creation of something new and the application of skills in new contexts); involvement (leading to academic maturity and sound decisions); and cultural literacy (knowledge of the information important to a culture). Each of these goals involves a set of teaching strategies which can be incorporated into the elements of an effective lesson. These elements include developing an anticipatory set, providing or modeling information, checking for understanding, providing guided practice and requiring independent practice. The elements and the strategies together allow for the development of the various thinking styles.

379. Svinicki, Marilla D., and Richard H. Kraemer, "Critical Thinking: Some Views from the Front Line.: *New Directions for Teaching and Learning*: Fostering Critical Thinking. Edited by Robert E. Young. San Francisco: Jossey-Bass Inc., Pub. No. 3, 1980, pp. 59–75.

Svinicki and Kraemer describe the ups and downs of a required course in the American Experience which focuses on the development of critical thinking for decision-making through an examination of controversial issues and topics. The emphasis is not on facts and on content but rather on process. This emphasis seems to provide both the ups and the downs of the course. The stress on critical thinking requires that students become active participants in their own learning and that they use critical thinking in ways that make them grow but that may also cause tension and frustration.

The emphasis of the course also requires that the instructor and the teaching assistants do more than impart knowledge; they must interact with the students in the process of thinking critically. Again, this may shake complacency. Student concern over the difficulty of receiving fair and understandable grades and of covering basic content required for subsequent courses seems balanced by increased confidence in ability to take charge of learning and thinking.

380. Swartz, Alma M. "Critical Thinking Attitudes and the Transfer Questions." *Thinking Skills Instruction: Concepts and Techniques.* Edited by Marcia Heiman and Joshua Slomianko. Washington, D.C.: National Education Association, 1987, pp. 58–68.

A major problem in the teaching of thinking is that of insuring that transfer of critical thinking takes place both to academic areas and to everyday situations. Swartz reviews current research documenting the differences of opinions in this area and concludes that more is required than application and practice in various settings. Rather, we must develop critical attitudes in students. The focus is not, in fact, on teaching critical thinking which is an "innate, species-specific trait " (p. 60) that cannot be taught but must be developed. Lessons should include not only specific skills but also groups of critical and creative skills. The author analyzes an interview protocol according to Ennis' list of dispositions in critical thinking and also includes an inventory of critical and creative dispositions and attitudes to be used with students.

381. Swartz, Robert J. "Restructuring Curriculum for Critical Thinking." *Educational Leadership* 43 (May 1986): 43–44.

Swartz advocates integrating teaching for critical thinking in all content areas and at all grade levels rather than using a pre-packaged program or curriculum. This calls for a restructuring of the content curriculum, incorporating skills, strategies and instruction relating to critical thinking into the traditional course content. The author provides examples for a variety of grade levels and content areas, as well as real life situations, illustrating his proposal. Total district commitment is essential for the success of this approach. Swartz suggest that "the same skill can be taught, reinforced, and elaborated in many other contexts, subject areas, and at other grade levels" (p. 43).

382. Tabor, Marilyn. "Better Student Thinking Through Changing Teacher Behaviors." *Educational Leadership* 45 (April 1988): 49.

A positive change in the flexibility, level and quality of students' thinking is attributed to "a specific set of teacher verbal behaviors" (p. 49) rather than to direct instruction in thinking skills. The stress in this locally developed program is on teacher questioning and responding skills that encourage and develop thinking in all content areas.

383. Tama, M. Carrol. "Critical Thinking Has a Place in Every Classroom." *Journal of Reading* 33 (October 1989): 64–65.

Critical thinking, the umbrella which includes logical inquiry and problem solving, involves three principles: active learning, articulation about thinking and thinking about thinking. Tama suggests ways this can be accomplished in several curriculum areas.

384. Tant, Judy L., and V.I. Douglas. "Problem Solving in Hyperactive, Normal, and Reading Disabled Boys." *Journal of Abnormal Child Psychology* 10 (1982): 285–306.

The authors investigated differences in hyperactive, normal and reading disabled boys in their ability to use problem solving strategies. They found that hyperactive subjects used less efficient strategies than normal or reading disabled subjects, and reading disabled and normal subjects performed at the same levels. The authors concluded that attentional problems of the hyperactive retard the development of strategies for complex problem solving The nonhyperactive reading disabled were not as affected, because they do not have attentional problems.

385.   Thistlethwaite, Linda L. "Critical Reading for At-Risk Students." *Journal of Reading* 33 (May 1990): 586–593.

Thistlethwaite, equating critical thinking and critical reading, cites those who advocate providing holistic instruction, not focusing on isolated skills. She provides detailed examples of strategies and activities that link critical thinking, critical reading and metacognition in content classrooms. In addition three checklists or heuristics are provided which can be used with any text. They are a critical reading checklist, a guide to critical reading of editorials, and a comparison of descriptions of two historical events, persons or ideas.

386.   Thomas, John W., and William D. Rohwer, Jr. "Academic Studying: The Role of Learning Strategies." *Educational Psychologist* 21 (Winter & Spring 1986): 19–41.

Thomas and Rohwer investigate how students use learning strategies to study academic content. They review theory and research on studying and describe the characteristics of studying. According to the authors studying is effortful, isolated, an individual activity, requires content and volition or disposition, is context-dependent and is ill-defined, i.e., criteria for effectiveness are not clear. They proposed the autonomous learning model which includes components—factors that affect studying—and processes—stages of studying. The model includes outcomes, study activities, course characteristics (lecture, grading, instructional support, criterion knowledge, assignments, review activities), student characteristics (developmental and academic levels, amount of prior knowledge of the particular strategy being used, domain knowledge in the content, metacognitive ability, volition and perceived self-efficacy).

Four factors which determine study effectiveness, according to the authors, are: 1) knowledge of the criteria to be met, i.e., what information is to be learned, how it is to be organized, how it is to be presented; 2) a congruence between what was learned and what will actually be tested; 3) the availability of instructional support; and 4) maintenance and use of the specific strategies.

Thomas and Rohwer suggest that to be effective in studying, learning strategies must be specific, i.e., there must be a match between strategies selected, course and learners' characteristics; they must be generative, i.e., the more they elaborate on the content the more effective they will be; they must be monitored by the studier, i.e., the studier must be in charge, must planfully select, use and evaluate the strategy in use; and must lead to an attitude of personal efficacy, that is the student must believe he or she is in charge of use of the strategy. The authors suggest a comprehensive list of areas for further research.

387.   Thomas, Louise. "Readers' Metacognition and Comprehension: Are They Related?" July 1984. (ED 252 815)

Thomas used 100 sixth graders to study the relationship between reading ability and attitudes and awareness of reading performance. She found that good readers perceive reading differently than poor readers. Poor readers were unaware that they were using reading to search for meaning or of the need to apply particular strategies.

388.   Thurmond, Vera B. "Analytical Reading: A Course That Stresses Thinking Aloud." *Journal of Reading* 29 (May 1986): 729–732.

Thurmond describes a reading course for minority high school students which was based on the approach suggested by Whimbey, analytic reasoning, using a think-aloud procedure. Significant improvement was noted on a reading comprehension text.

389.   Tierney, Robert J., Anna Soter, John F. O'Flahavan, and William McGinley. "The Effects of Reading and Writing Upon Thinking Critically." *Reading Research Quarterly* *XXIV* (Spring 1989): pp. 134–173.

The authors investigated differences in the effects of reading and writing, separately and in combination, activation of background knowledge and questioning on students' ability to think critically. Critical thinking was equated with a willingness to change one's mind and subsequently revise text. College students were assigned to 12 different combinations of reading, writing, background knowledge activation and questioning activities. Data were examined in a variety of interesting ways, particularly the analysis of students' revisions. The combination of the reading and writing appeared to extend original thinking and provide different perspectives on a topic. Students were able to compare new ideas to ideas originally held and critically evaluate them. The change was evident from the revisions and from debriefing interviews.

Several significant limitations to the study were noted. For example it would be very difficult to generalize the results of this study widely: task conditions were artificial, long term results and transferability were not measured, topics for materials used were somewhat controversial and may have elicited varying amounts of prior knowledge. However, with these limitations acknowledged the authors make the following conclusions: reading and writing, when taught in combination "have the power to contribute in powerful ways to thinking" (p. 166). "Writing appeared to serve as a mode through which the learner allowed ideas to come to fruition and resolved disputes. Reading served as a resource for opposing views or for further elaborations upon an idea" (p. 166). Students who were trained in reading and writing made more revisions in their work and, the authors propose, in their thinking.

Finally, the authors suggest several implications for research, including the examination of reasoning and thinking within the context of task involvement. The results of the study suggest that reading and writing afford more opportunity to think critically about a topic and to acquire multiple perspectives on it.

390.   Treffinger, Donald J. "Research on Creativity," *Gifted Child Quarterly* 30 (Winter 1986): 15–19.

Treffinger reviews and synthesizes a substantial body of research in the field of creativity. He reaches a number of conclusions. First, there is not and probably won't be one single theory of creativity. Similarly, there is no one instrument that can be used to identify and measure creativity. In fact, "it is unrealistic to expect that there will ever be (or that there should be) a single, easily administered simply scored test booklet that educators can use to decide who is at least one standard deviation above other students in creativity" (p. 16).

The author reviews in some detail a model of creative learning on three levels. In the first level, students learn basic thinking tools for generating (divergent or creative thinking) and analyzing (convergent or critical thinking). Both of these processes are important and are related to the development of effective thinking. In the second level, the tools are used in complex situations involving problem solving and creative problem solving such as Odyssey of the Mind or Future Problem Solving programs. In the third level, students use what they have learned in real life situations. It is important to include this level in a program for creative learning because transfer to new situations will not occur automatically.

Treffinger makes the point that much of this creative learning should be going on in all classrooms, not just gifted classrooms. Teachers also need hands-on training in order to implement this approach. In the first level, students need direct instruction in the tools. In the second and third level, students begin to assume more responsibility for using the tools in complex situations. Finally, Treffinger proposes a variety of areas in which research is needed.

391.   Valencia, Sheila W., P. David Pearson, Charles W. Peters, and Karen K. Wixson. "Theory and Practice in Statewide Assessment: Closing the Gap." *Educational Leadership* 46 (April 1989): 57–63.

The authors highlight the discrepancy between current reading theory which emphasizes the integration of prior and new knowledge and the construction of meaning and assessment instruments which examine individual skills. The assessments developed for Illinois and Michigan are presented in some detail with examples. Both formats have the construction of meaning as the central feature, with topic familiarity, metacognitive knowledge and strategies, and attitudes and self-perceptions as important supporting components.

392.   Vockell, Edward, and Robert M. van Deusen. *The Computer and Higher Order Thinking Skills.* Watsonville, California: Mitchell Publishing, Inc., 1989.

This handbook offers a variety of suggestions on ways to use the computer to teach higher order thinking skills. The authors provide a brief review and description of these skills. They include metacognition, critical, and creative thinking as well as thinking processes or global strategies that involve several thinking skills. They present a table of instructional strategies and guidelines for using the computer and a discussion of various computer "tools" for teaching thinking, i.e., word processing, data base management, spreadsheets and programming. They discuss use of the computer in specific content areas including English, science, social studies and math and review a number of popular software programs.

393. Vye, Nancy J., and John D. Bransford. "Programs for Teaching Thinking." *Educational Leadership* 39 (October 1981): 26–28.

Vye and Bransford compare and contrast three thinking skills programs: Instrumental Enrichment, Philosophy for Children and Analytical Reasoning. The common element in all programs is that they stress the need to make the thinking process clear and involve the student in identifying and understanding the process. They differ in how they do this, in the age of the student the program is designed for, in the level of thinking skill taught and in the reading level and background knowledge required and in the time required to complete the program. The authors conclude that "each program helps students develop more confidence in their own abilities" (p. 28). The question of transfer of skills learned is raised with the classroom teacher identified as the key to insuring that transfer takes place.

394. Wade, Suzanne E., and Ralph E. Reynolds. "Developing Metacognitive Awareness." *Journal of Reading* 33 (October 1989): 6–14.

Wade and Reynolds define metacognition as "the ability to think about and control one's own learning" (p. 6). In order to do this students need task awareness, strategy awareness, and performance awareness. In each area, the authors examine findings from research and provide suggestions for teachers and students. For example, students are taught to identify strategies that can be used, record strategies actually used, and analyze the success of the strategies. This is a metacognitive approach linking cognitive strategies and academic tasks. Appropriate worksheets for this technique are included.

395. Wales, Charles E., Anne H. Nardi, and Robert A. Stager. "Decision Making: New Paradigm for Education." *Educational Leadership* 43 (May 1986): 38–41.

The new paradigm for education as outlined by the authors is "schooling focused on decision making, the thinking skills that serve it, and the knowledge base that supports it" (p. 38). Decision making involves a series of stages: selecting a goal, generating ideas, preparing a plan and taking action. In each stage, the decision maker must identify the problem through analysis, generate ideas through synthesis and select an outcome through evaluation. Decision making is viewed as the umbrella requiring "many enabling skills" (p. 41) such as critical thinking and problem solving. The goal is not only to develop students' thinking abilities but also "their heritage as human beings" (p. 41).

396. Walsh, Debbie, and Richard W. Paul. *The Goal of Critical Thinking: From Educational Ideal to Educational Reality.* Washington, D.C.: American Federation of Teachers, 1986.

Critical thinking is viewed by Walsh and Paul in terms of dispositions and skills needed. They examine instructional possibilities, focusing on inquiry learning using coaching, discussion and guided practice. A number of examples of curriculum and lessons for different grade levels and content areas are included. Teacher training must be provided if critical thinking is to be stressed in the classroom.

397. Ware, Herbert W. "Thinking Skills: The Effort of One Public School System." *Thinking and Learning Skills.*

Relating Instruction to Research. Volume 1. Edited by Judith W. Segal, Susan F. Chipman, and Robert Glaser. Hillsdale, New Jersey: Lawrence Erlbaum Associates, Pub., 1985, pp. 515–527.

Ware compares the efforts of one school system in implementing a thinking skills program and also an expository writing program. The latter was successful; the former was not. He cites the inadequacy of resources, staff development and involvement of teachers in planning and managing as partly responsible for the failure of the thinking program. However, he also cites the basic "lack of a theory of higher cognitive skill instruction" (p. 527) with its resulting lack of clear definitions, objectives, strategies, procedures and hierarchies for sequencing instruction.

398. Wassermann, Selma. "Promoting Thinking in Your Classroom II." *Childhood Education* 60 (March/April 1984): 229–233.

Wasserman suggests that, despite our emphasis and purported interest in improving our students' thinking skills, little substantial change has occurred in recent years in our schools. Materials still emphasize correct answers, and teachers still ask information recall questions only. The author identifies four "means-ends" discrepancies, i.e., inconsistencies in the way we teach and our goal to teach higher level thinking. These are classroom materials which require low level thinking skills to master; classrooms dominated by teacher talk or restricted teacher-student interaction; suppression of independent thinking by our students; and professionals who are inadequately trained or otherwise unable to bring innovation into their classrooms.

399. Watts, Nancy A. "Developing Higher-Order Thinking Skills in Home Economics: A Lesson Plan." *Thinking Skills Instruction: Concepts and Techniques.* Edited by

Marcia Heiman and Joshua Slomianko. Washington, D.C.: National Education Association, 1987, pp. 241–245.

Critical thinking and problem solving are essential elements in consumer economics and, in fact, in life. This is the realm of Home Economics. Watts provides a lesson plan in which students identify characteristics of fabric and categorize samples in order to determine fabric construction.

400. Wearne, Diane, and James Hiebert. "Teaching for Thinking Mathematics." *Childhood Education* (March/April 1984): 239–245.

Although students begin school with a general ability to solve math problems based on their prior experience and everyday world knowledge, by the time they get through elementary school they have completely separated school type math problems from the use of mathematical problem solving in the real world.

The authors suggest three places where we can encourage students to make math more meaningful to students' lives and where we can teach them thinking skills. First, the symbols inherent in math problems (numbers, fractions, operations) need to be made more meaningful, i.e., related to real world aspects such as specific sets, joining actions, models and other physical referents. Second, the procedures and symbols used in mathematical problem solving need to be linked to concrete materials and to the actions on these concrete objects. Finally, the answers need to be evaluated for reasonableness by higher level thinking and monitoring of thinking. These three connections between formal math and real world math can greatly enhance students' ability to learn math in a more meaningful manner.

401. Weed, Keri, Ellen B. Ryan and Jeanne Day. "Motivational and Metacognitive Aspects of Strategy Use and Transfer." April 1984. (ED 246 113).

The authors report on a study in which 40 third and fourth graders were trained to use two different effective strategies. One group was also trained in monitoring their use of the particular strategy. Results indicated that those children who were aware of the influence of their strategy use on their success maintained and continued to use that strategy.

402. Weedle, Perry. "Critical Thinking in California: The Department of Education Testing Program in Social Studies." *History and Social Science Teacher* 21 (Spring 1986): 147–157.

This is a report on the California Assessment Program (CAP), which included critical thinking test items in its statewide social studies tests. A survey by CAP revealed that, although teachers recognized the importance of critical thinking ability in social studies learning, most statewide test items were purely recall of facts. CAP developed a bank of 720 questions, divided into 36 forms, to allow for flexibility within class groups. Fifteen critical thinking skills were identified and categorized as either 1) defining and clarifying a problem; 2) judging information related to the problem; or 3) solving problems/drawing conclusions. CAP defined critical thinking as "those skills involved in (reasonably) deciding what to believe and do" (p. 148).

403. Weinstein, Claire. "Fostering Learning Autonomy Through the Use of Learning Strategies." *Journal of Reading* 30 (April 1987): 590–595.

Weinstein identifies the components needed for effective learning, problem solving and decision making. These include prior knowledge of content in terms of both amount and organization as well as the ability to monitor these thinking tasks. The author focuses on the cognitive and strategic processes students can use in order to become independent. She reviews strategies in the categories of rehearsal, elaboration, organization, comprehension monitoring, and affect. The value of using heuristics is noted as is the difficulty of transferring to new situations.

404. ———, D. Scott Ridley, Tove Dahl, and E. Sue Weber. "Helping Students Develop Strategies for Effective Learning." *Educational Leadership* 46 (December 1988/January 1989): 17–19.

The authors focus on elaboration strategies, those strategies which link new information to prior knowledge and give personal meaning to the new. However, they stress that the strategies discussed here are applicable to other cognitive strategies. Students need a repertoire of strategies. Student generated questions are discussed in some detail with a list of possible questions that can aid students in accessing various strategies.

405. ———, and Vicki L. Underwood. "Learning Strategies: The How of Learning." *Thinking and Learning Skills.* Relating Instruction to Research. Volume 1. Edited by Judith W. Segal, Susan F. Chipman, and Robert Glaser. Hillsdale, New Jersey: Lawrence Erlbaum Associates, Pub., 1985, pp. 241–258.

Weinstein and Underwood review the history of learning strategies research, including cognitive information processing strategies such as organizing and elaborating; active study strategies, such as note-taking and test preparation; and support strategies, such as time management, attending to a task and reducing anxiety. They also review research on assessment and training programs.

They describe training studies conducted by the Cognitive Learning Strategies Project at the University of Texas which is concerned with developing programs and teaching practices to foster effective learning. They describe the LASSI, The Learning and Study Strategies Inventory, which they have developed to help educators and trainers diagnose strengths and weaknesses in students' learning and study strategies for use in planning individualized remedial training. They describe a course developed for college students in which a variety of content areas were used to teach students these strategies.

They note the limited time and resources for thinking and learning programs in schools and indicate that the data they are collecting from the LASSI are helping them to identify the skills and strategies most critical for inclusion in learning strategies instructional programs. Examples of the kinds of strategies they have identified as important include elaboration, selecting main idea, and self-testing and monitoring activities.

406. Whimbey, Arthur. "The Key to Higher Order Thinking Is Precise Processing." *Educational Leadership* 42 (September 1984): 66–70.

Whimbey examines the basic question of whether we can isolate and teach separate reasoning skills to students. After reviewing the process of analytic reasoning and available research, he concludes that it is not possible to isolate skills. The key here is not instruction in separate skills but rather an emphasis on the precise processing of the operations involved in analytic reasoning. He describes an approach of thinking aloud using content materials that is designed to develop and refine reasoning.

407. ———. "Reading, Writing, Reasoning Linked in Testing and Training." *Journal of Reading* 29 (November 1985): 118–123.

Whimbey provides examples of students' work which illustrate failures in analytic reasoning. He also demonstrates that the Whimbey Analytic Skills Inventory can identify these problem areas. He describes a program, Stress On Analytic Reasoning (SOAR), which uses a small group, inductive, problem solving, think-aloud procedure to develop these skills.

408. ———. "Test Results from Teaching Thinking." *Developing Minds: A Resource Book for Teaching Thinking.* Edited by Arthur L. Costa. Alexandria, Virginia: Association for Supervision and Curriculum Development, 1985, pp. 269–271.

Whimbey reviews a number of studies that demonstrate the positive effect instruction in thinking skills has had on academic performance. The bulk of the studies examined the Whimbey and Lochhead approach to teaching problem solving. Evidence is presented from standardized test scores, academic performance, and self-reported successes in real life.

409. ———. "You Don't Need a Special 'Reasoning' Test to Implement and Evaluate Reasoning Training." *Educational Leadership* 43 (October 1985): 37–39.

Whimbey, after examining the correlations between tests designed to measure reasoning and the New Jersey College Basic Skills Placement Test (NJCBSPT) concluded that the reasoning abilities measured by the special tests were also measured by the NJCBSPT. Thus, no special reasoning test is needed. In addition, he examined results obtained by a verbal reasoning program, a nonverbal reasoning program, and one that combined both. He found that growth in all three approaches could be measured by reading comprehension tests. Again, he concluded that no special reasoning tests are needed.

410. ——, and Jack Lochhead. *Beyond Problem Solving and Comprehension: An Exploration of Quantitative Reasoning.* Philadelphia: The Franklin Institute Press, 1984.

This book is intended to train technical students to improve their quantitative reasoning skills. Instructional methods are based on research in cognitive psychology and education. The authors point out the increasing importance of good analytic reasoning skills in an advanced technological society. The book advocates pair problem solving, a method by which two people work together to solve a problem, discussing their thought processes aloud as they work through a problem. The benefit of pair problem solving is that it forces the student to think slowly and more accurately as he or she discusses thought processes, and it forces the listener to reflect on the partner's reasoning skills at the same time.

The book contains many opportunities for practice in analytical reasoning with word problems, graph interpretation and introductory probability, skills which are important in technical and scientific occupations and in admissions tests such as SATs, GREs, and LSATs. Many exercises are also included which use computer programming problems as content.

411. Wiggins, Grant. "Teaching to the (Authentic) Test." *Educational Leadership* 46 (April 1989): 41–47.

Wiggins accepts that teachers teach for tests. He proposes that we develop tests that test what we really want students to be able to do, then use these tests for instruction. The tests then become sets of standards for students and schools. He offers some suggestions, including a final public exhibition of what was taught and learned with performances along the route to graduation. These are "authentic" tests, which demonstrate what the student is thinking. The author includes a set of characteristics for these authentic tests.

412. Williams, Belinda. "Implementing Thinking Skills Instruction in an Urban District: An Effort to Close the Gap." *Educational Leadership* 44 (March 1987): 50–53.

The Cognitive Instruction Project was developed in an urban setting with a high minority population in order to improve academic achievement. The program began in kindergarten and a grade was added each year. Instruction was separate from the other classroom activities and later integrated into content areas. Parent involvement and staff training were both high priorities.

413. Winocur, S. Lee. "Developing Lesson Plans with Cognitive Objectives." *Developing Minds: A Resource Book for Teaching Thinking.* Edited by Arthur L. Costa. Alexandria, Virginia: Association for Supervision and Curriculum Development. 1985, pp. 87–94.

The author describes Project IMPACT (Improve Minimal Proficiencies by Activating Critical Thinking), a professional training program with 120 model lessons. The program applies thinking skills in all content areas using a critical thinking skills taxonomy. It uses graphic organizers and diagrams to systematically map the organization of ideas in a given area. It encourages systematic planning for retrieving information and for interpreting and recreating it coherently, and makes students consciously aware of the need to search for, compare and evaluate ideas and concepts.

Winocur gives three examples of graphic organizers in remedial language arts lessons for 7th and 9th grades, to teach the concepts compare/contrast, cause/effect and concept formation. The program can be used at all stages of learning in a given area from orientation through transfer.

According to the author, the IMPACT program applies principles of information processing theory to instructional development.

414. ———. "Project IMPACT." *Developing Minds: A Resource Book for Teaching Thinking.* Edited by Arthur L. Costa. Alexandria, Virginia: Association for Supervision and Curriculum Development, 1985, pp. 210–211.

Winocur briefly describes Project IMPACT (Improving Minimal Proficiencies by Activating Critical Thinking), which has been replicated in a number of settings. The program assumes that critical thinking skills are developed in a hierarchical sequence and are best learned in a social context and as part of the content curriculum.

415. Winograd, Peter N. "Strategic Difficulties in Summarizing Texts." *Reading Research Quarterly XIX* (Summer 1984): 404–425.

Winograd investigated the differences in the ways eighth grade good and poor comprehenders use strategies to summarize text. He concluded that poor comprehenders may have difficulty using specific strategies. For example, poor readers weren't as sensitive as good readers to what the author considered important information in the text; they weren't as able as good readers to include what they considered important in their summaries; and they weren't able to use important information in the text to help them comprehend. Winograd suggests that teachers might want to informally assess children's sensitivity to what is important in a text when comprehension difficulties are evident and provide explicit training in this and other higher order comprehension strategies rather than training in decoding skills.

416. ———, and Scott Paris. "A Cognitive and Motivational Agenda for Reading Instruction." *Educational Leadership* 46 (December 1988/January 1989): 30–36.

The authors examine past practices in reading instruction which keep children from becoming thoughtful, independent readers and learners. They then present innovations in reading instruction which have been developed through recent research. They cite the mechanical, "management mentality" fostered by basal readers, methods of assessment which drive the reading curriculum and the emphasis on academic competition as major forces which constrain reading instruction. New research on strategic reading, prior knowledge, metacognition and text structure have led to a "cognitive agenda" for reading instruction which focuses on students' selective and thoughtful use of comprehension and metacognitive strategies.

The authors also discuss the importance of motivation and the need for focusing on reading for pleasure, for intrinsic goals rather than for superfluous extrinsic rewards. They describe four methods of helping children become thoughtful readers which can be adapted to any grade level with any reading program. These are modeling thoughtful reading, direct explanation of cognitive strategies, scaffolded instruction, or instructional dialogues, and cooperative learning. The authors suggest that we rethink the goals of reading instruction to include cognitive and motivational components to develop independent, motivated, lifelong readers.

417. Wirtz, Robert. "Some Thoughts About Mathematics and Problem Solving." *Developing Minds: A Resource Book for Teaching Thinking.* Edited by Arthur L. Costa. Alexandria, Virginia: Association for Supervision and Curriculum Development, 1985, pp. 97–101.

Wirtz notes that math instruction must combine rote memory with understanding and describes the difference between the "I get its," who understand and use language to make relationships and form full units of memory, and the "I don't get its," who cannot use language to form connections and relationships. Language, according to Wirtz, moves us from the unknown to the known.

He contrasts Piagetian theory, which says that children learn naturally, without adult intervention, with that of Bruner, which states that children need intervention to maximize their development at higher cognitive levels. He traces the slow transition from concrete to abstract thinking. He presents a diagram of the sequence of cognitive development going from the concrete to the abstract and from basic to higher cognitive levels, and he describes student intellectual development through these stages.

He suggests that a math curriculum must provide a variety of opportunities at the higher cognitive levels and always contribute to the continuous development of abstract thought. "The ultimate goal of education" according to Wirtz, " . . . (is) helping to provide all children with opportunities to enjoy making independent investigations at the abstract level" (p. 101).

418. Wolf, Dennie Palmer. "Portfolio Assessment: Sampling Student Work." *Educational Leadership* 46 (April 1989): 35–39.

PROPEL is a project designed to "assess the thinking processes characteristic of the arts and humanities in rigorous, but undistorted ways" (p. 36). To do this, students develop portfolios of their work often with written commentaries about how the work progressed and was completed. This can accomplish two purposes. First, students self-assess performance and progress. They can stand aside and become critics of the content and the process, while viewing the development of their thinking.

Second, student portfolios allow teachers an opportunity to become self-critics of their own teaching as they view their student's work over a period of time.

419. Wong, Bernice L. "Self-Questioning Instructional Research: A Review." *Review of Educational Research* 55 (Summer 1985): 227–268.

Wong provides a detailed review and analysis of 27 studies of self-questioning instruction. The studies viewed the role of questioning from the three different theoretical perspectives of questioning for increasing active processing, metacognitive awareness or activation of prior knowledge. She concludes that "the effects of self-uestioning training on students' prose processing are successful" (p. 227). In all of these approaches, it was evident that sufficient training, explicit instruction and adequate processing time were needed to enable students to generate questions appropriately and effectively.

420. Wood, Karen D. "Fostering Cooperative Learning in Middle and Secondary Level Classrooms." *Journal of Reading* 31 (October 1987): 10–18.

Wood documents the positive results of using cooperative learning as a catalyst for thinking. Positive results range from academic achievement to social interaction and self-esteem. She provides detailed descriptions of many ways of grouping students for cooperative learning, pulling together the suggestions of different people in the field.

421. Woodman, Richard W., and Lyle F. Schoenfeldt. "An Interactionist Model of Creative Behavior." *The Journal of Creative Behavior* 24 (First Quarter 1990): 10–20.

Woodman and Schoenfeldt assert that creativity is an imprecise kind of behavior. In order to understand it better they look at it from the perspective of personality, cognitive style and social interaction, reviewing relevant theory and research in these areas. They suggest the usefulness of an interactionist model in which all of these areas are linked.

422. Worsham, Antoinette. "A 'Grow as You Go' Thinking Skills Model." *Educational Leadership* 45 (April 1988): 56–57.

In comparison to a traditional teacher-centered approach to teaching thinking, Worsham describes the implementation and ongoing progress of the student-centered "Inclusion Process." This approach provides explicit instruction in thinking skills carried out throughout the curriculum.

423. ———, and Gilbert R. Austin. "Effects of Teaching Thinking Skills on SAT Scores." *Educational Leadership* 41 (November 1983): 50–51.

Worsham and Austin report on the favorable results obtained in raising SAT scores in the three verbal measures of vocabulary, reading comprehension and total score by providing systematic instruction in thinking skills. A commercially developed program was used for two of the weekly periods of English instruction. The emphasis on discussion and analysis in the program was cited as a possible reason for its success.

424. ———, and Anita J. Stockton. *A Model for Teaching Thinking Skills: The Inclusion Process.* Bloomington, Indiana: Phi Delta Kappa Educational Foundation, 1986.

Worsham and Stockton examine the discouraging evidence regarding students' abilities to think in a complex fashion, concluding that we can and must include instruction in thinking skills in school curriculum. The two broad categories of thinking, critical and creative, include problem solving and decision making as well as basic thinking skills "common to most curriculum tasks" (p. 11). They review the alternatives available for instruction, including infusing thinking skills throughout the curriculum, teaching them as a separate course and linking them to the existing curriculum. They reject these alternatives in favor of teaching the skills explicitly and including them "as part of the curriculum based on course requirements and student needs" (p. 13). The suggestions offered for lessons and sequence of skills are based on a developmental view of thinking skills, linking the skills taught not only to the curriculum but to the developmental level of the student.

425. Wright, Elena. "Odyssey: a Curriculum for Thinking." *Developing Minds: A Resource Book for Teaching Thinking.* Edited by Arthur L. Costa. Alexandria, Virginia: Association for Supervision and Curriculum Development, 1985, pp. 224–226.

A series of six student books is used from fourth grade up to teach foundations of reasoning, understanding language, verbal reasoning, problem solving, decision making, and inventive thinking. A variety of instructional techniques are used, including direct instruction, Socratic inquiry, and exploration and discovery. The program was originally developed for use in Venezuela.

426. Yeager, Natalie C. "Teaching Thinking to Teach Literature While Teaching Literature to Teach Thinking." *Thinking Skills Instruction: Concepts and Techniques.* Edited by Marcia Heiman and Joshua Slomianko. Washington, D.C.: National Education Association, 1987, pp. 134–144.

Yeager holds that teaching thinking aids in the comprehension of literature while, at the same time, the use of literature as a vehicle for teaching thinking is motivating to students. She bases her suggestions on Sanders' taxonomy of critical thinking which includes translation, interpretation, application, analysis, synthesis and evaluation. Her suggestions are specific and are illustrated with references to numerous pieces of literature.

427. Yinger, Robert J. "Can We Really Teach Them to Think?" *New Directions for Teaching and Learning*: Fostering Critical Thinking. Edited by Robert E. Young. San Francisco: Jossey-Bass Inc., Pub., 1980, pp. 11–31.

In examining the question posed in the title of the selection, Yinger links critical and creative thinking to the general body of intellectual activities. All thinking, including problem solving and decision making, requires creative/productive thinking as well as critical/evaluative thinking. He explores the factors affecting thinking: knowledge of both content and of rules and procedures; comprehension and integration of ideas and concepts, and attitudes and dispositions. He stresses the need to move beyond theoretical, academic problems to practical, uncertain problems.

428. Young, Robert E. "Testing for Critical Thinking: Issues and Resources." *New Directions for Teaching and Learning: Fostering Critical Thinking*. Edited by Robert E. Young. San Francisco: Jossey-Bass Inc., Pub., 1980, pp. 77–89.

Young recognizes that testing for critical thinking is not easy but then neither is teaching for critical thinking. He provides suggestions for a variety of sources of use in relating objectives in critical thinking to course content. He identifies published tests suitable for use with students or to use as examples for teacher-designed tests. Tests are also seen broadly as measures which can include papers, projects, exercises and self-assessments. Asking questions and posing problems are the two critical aspects of testing for critical thinking. The author provides a variety of resources for the former. The results of any testing must be used to further enhance students' critical thinking abilities. In order to accomplish this, the tests should reveal not just the answers to questions or the solutions to problems but also the process the students used to reach the end result.

429. ———. "The Next Agenda: Practical Reasoning and Action." *New Directions for Teaching and Learning: Fostering Critical Thinking*. Edited by Robert E. Young. San Francisco: Jossey-Bass Inc., Pub., 1980. pp. 91–97.

In summarizing the role of critical thinking in higher education, Young presents a persuasive case for grounding critical thinking instruction in "practical problems, practical problems of the discipline as well as of the society" (p. 93). This emphasis on the practical also requires action on the part of the thinker both in terms of participation in the thinking process and in terms of implementing an outcome. Young highlights the implications of this focus on the need to develop support structures that will allow students to take the risks involved.

430. Youngblood, Ed. "Reading, Thinking, and Writing." *English Journal* 74 (September 1985): 44–48.

Youngblood suggests that the act of writing about reading in a personal reading journal helps students comprehend textbook material as well as literature. He provides guidance for the teacher and suggestions for the student in how to engage in this activitiy.

431. Zenke, Larry, and Larry Alexander. "Teaching Thinking in Tulsa." *Educational Leadership* 42 (September 1984): 81–84.

Because of low achievement levels and low levels of student and teacher morale, a thinking skills program, the Think program also called Strategic Reasoning, was introduced to selected schools in Tulsa. Six generic analytic thinking skills were taught in separate courses to junior high school students. At the end of the first year, the authors saw a dramatic improvement in student achievement.

Author Index

P. = Page Number(s), E. = Entry Number(s)

Subject Index

P. = Page Number(s), E. = Entry Number(s)